"Kenneth Pearce and Graham Oppy are first-rate philosophers of religion. This book offers an engaging and fruitful dialogue between a theist and an atheist, addressing all key concepts and arguments in the contemporary debate on the existence of God. I recommend the book to all readers who are interested in studying both sides of the debate."

Yujin Nagasawa, *H. G. Wood Professor of the Philosophy of Religion, University of Birmingham, UK*

"This exchange between Oppy and Pearce represents the finest in philosophical inquiry. Together they create a new chandelier with structure and detail as they systematically discuss questions of worldview along the cutting edge of philosophical inquiry. Their exchange is professional, productive, and elegant."

Joshua Rasmussen, *Department of Philosophy, Azusa Pacific University, USA*

Is There a God?

Bertrand Russell famously quipped that he didn't believe in God for the same reason that he didn't believe in a teapot in orbit between the earth and Mars: it is a bizarre assertion for which no evidence can be provided. Is belief in God really like belief in Russell's teapot? Kenneth L. Pearce argues that God is no teapot. God is a real answer to the deepest question of all: why is there something rather than nothing? Graham Oppy argues that we should believe that there are none but natural causal entities with none but natural causal properties—and hence should believe that there are no gods. Beginning from this basic disagreement, the authors proceed to discuss and debate a wide range of philosophical questions, including questions about explanation, necessity, rationality, religious experience, mathematical objects, the foundations of ethics, and the methodology of philosophy. Each author first presents his own side, and then they interact through two rounds of objections and replies.

Pedagogical features include standard form arguments, section summaries, bolded key terms and principles, a glossary, and annotated reading lists. In the volume foreword, Helen De Cruz calls the debate "both edifying and a joy," and sums up what's at stake: "Here you have two carefully formulated positive proposals for worldviews that explain all that is: classical theism, or naturalistic atheism. You can follow along with the authors and deliberate: which one do you find more plausible?"

Though written with beginning students in mind, this debate will be of interest to philosophers at all levels and to anyone who values careful, rational thought about the nature of reality and our place in it.

Graham Oppy, FAHA, is Professor of Philosophy at Monash University in Australia. His authored books include *Arguing About*

Gods (2006), *Philosophical Perspectives on Infinity* (2006), *The Best Argument Against God* (2013), *Describing Gods* (2014), *Reinventing Philosophy of Religion* (2014), *Naturalism and Religion* (2018), *Atheism and Agnosticism* (2018), and *Atheism: The Basics* (2019).

Kenneth L. Pearce is Ussher Assistant Professor in Berkeley Studies at Trinity College Dublin. He has published extensively on philosophy of religion and the history of early modern philosophy, and was the winner of the 2016 Sanders Prize in Philosophy of Religion. He is the author of *Language and the Structure of Berkeley's World* (2017) and co-editor (with Tyron Goldschmidt) of *Idealism: New Essays in Metaphysics* (2017).

Helen De Cruz is Professor of Philosophy and the Danforth Chair in the Humanities at Saint Louis University, USA.

Little Debates About Big Questions

About the series:

Philosophy asks questions about the fundamental nature of reality, our place in the world, and what we should do. Some of these questions are perennial: for example, *Do we have free will? What is morality?* Some are much newer: for example, *How far should free speech on campus extend? Are race, sex and gender social constructs?* But all of these are among the big questions in philosophy and they remain controversial.

Each book in the *Little Debates About Big Questions* series features two professors on opposite sides of a big question. Each author presents their own side, and the authors then exchange objections and replies. Short, lively, and accessible, these debates showcase diverse and deep answers. Pedagogical features include standard form arguments, section summaries, bolded key terms and principles, glossaries, and annotated reading lists.

The debate format is an ideal way to learn about controversial topics. Whereas the usual essay or book risks overlooking objections against its own proposition or misrepresenting the opposite side, in a debate each side can make their case at equal length, and then present objections the other side must consider. Debates have a more conversational and fun style too, and we selected particularly talented philosophers—in substance and style—for these kinds of encounters.

Debates can be combative—sometimes even descending into anger and animosity. But debates can also be cooperative. While our authors disagree strongly, they work together to help each other and the reader get clearer on the ideas, arguments, and objections. This is intellectual progress, and a much-needed model for civil and constructive disagreement.

The substance and style of the debates will captivate interested readers new to the questions. But there's enough to interest experts too. The debates will be especially useful for courses in philosophy and related subjects—whether as primary or secondary readings—and a few debates can be combined to make up the reading for an entire course.

We thank the authors for their help in constructing this series. We are honored to showcase their work. They are all preeminent scholars or rising-stars in their fields, and through these debates they share what's been discovered with a wider audience. This is a paradigm for public philosophy, and will impress upon students, scholars, and other interested readers the enduring importance of debating the big questions.

Tyron Goldschmidt, Fellow of the Rutgers Center for Philosophy of Religion, USA
Dustin Crummett, Ludwig Maximilian University of Munich, Germany

Published Titles:

Do We Have Free Will?: A Debate
By Robert Kane and Carolina Sartorio

Is There a God?: A Debate
by Kenneth L. Pearce and Graham Oppy

Is Political Authority an Illusion?: A Debate
By Michael Huemer and Daniel Layman

Selected Forthcoming Titles:

Should We Want to Live Forever?: A Debate
by Stephen Cave and John Martin Fischer

Do Numbers Exist?: A Debate
by William Lane Craig and Peter van Inwagen

What Do We Owe Other Animals?: A Debate
by Bob Fischer and Anja Jauernig

For more information about this series, please visit:
https://www.routledge.com/Little-Debates-about-Big-Questions/book-series/LDABQ

Is There a God?

A Debate

Graham Oppy and
Kenneth L. Pearce

NEW YORK AND LONDON

First published 2022
by Routledge
605 Third Avenue, New York, NY 10158

and by Routledge
2 Park Square, Milton Park, Abingdon, Oxon, OX14 4RN

Routledge is an imprint of the Taylor & Francis Group, an informa business

© 2022 Taylor & Francis

The right of Graham Oppy and Kenneth L. Pearce to be identified as authors of this work has been asserted by them in accordance with sections 77 and 78 of the Copyright, Designs and Patents Act 1988.

All rights reserved. No part of this book may be reprinted or reproduced or utilised in any form or by any electronic, mechanical, or other means, now known or hereafter invented, including photocopying and recording, or in any information storage or retrieval system, without permission in writing from the publishers.

Trademark notice: Product or corporate names may be trademarks or registered trademarks, and are used only for identification and explanation without intent to infringe.

Library of Congress Cataloging-in-Publication Data
A catalog record for this book has been requested

ISBN: 978-0-367-24393-7 (hbk)
ISBN: 978-0-367-24394-4 (pbk)
ISBN: 978-1-003-21679-7 (ebk)

DOI: 10.4324/9781003216797

Typeset in Sabon
by Apex CoVantage, LLC

Contents

Foreword: Worldview Comparison and
Religious Commitment   1
HELEN DE CRUZ

Opening Statements   9

1   Classical Theism: An Exposition and Defense   11
KENNY PEARCE

2   Are There Any Gods?   92
GRAHAM OPPY

First Round of Replies   173

3   Reply to Graham Oppy   175
KENNY PEARCE

4   Reply to Kenny Pearce   218
GRAHAM OPPY

Second Round of Replies   239

5   Reply to Graham's Reply   241
KENNY PEARCE

6	Further Reply to Kenny Pearce GRAHAM OPPY	259

Further Readings	302
Glossary	305
Bibliography	337
Index	358

Foreword
Worldview Comparison and Religious Commitment

Helen De Cruz

Worldwide, more than 8 in 10 people identify with a religious group.[1] A significant proportion of these are Christians, Muslims, and Jews. These are the major monotheistic traditions that form the focus of a lot of philosophy of religion. In addition, the global religious landscape also has large numbers of Hindus, Buddhists, and a multitude of other religious beliefs.

What are our grounds of belief? For example, why be a Christian rather than a Muslim or atheist? Sociologically, we see that humans often belong to religious traditions mainly because they inherited these from their parents and elders. Some people are attracted to religion because it gives them a sense of belonging and meaning; others enjoy the rituals associated with the beliefs. There is also growing evidence that religion offers benefits in this world that are independent of the truth of those beliefs. So, for example, religions offer strategies for emotion management that help us to deal with the inevitable curveballs life throws at us (Asma 2018), and they provide us with unexpected sources of joy (Glucklich 2020). There is an increasing recognition in the philosophy of religion of these pragmatic benefits, and of the sometimes messy and clouded route through which people come to hold religious beliefs (e.g. De Cruz 2018).

Still, most work in philosophy of religion focuses on one specific aspect of religious life; namely, the soundness or plausibility of specific religious or areligious worldviews. At the basis of any religion lies a worldview, broadly construed, a big picture of the

---

1. https://assets.pewresearch.org/wp-content/uploads/sites/11/2017/04/07092755/FULL-REPORT-WITH-APPENDIXES-A-AND-B-APRIL-3.pdf

world that comes with certain commitments. These commitments are about what sorts of things exist in the world (ontological commitments) and what sort of concepts and axioms we need to accept to express these worldviews (ideological and theoretical commitments). Philosophers of religion such as Kenny Pearce and Graham Oppy excel at making the worldviews that underlie our religious beliefs and practices more explicit, and this Little Debate will significantly advance discussion on the relative plausibility of classical theism and of naturalism, the two worldviews under consideration.

It is worthwhile to ponder the importance of discussing the merits of worldviews, particularly in light of the broadening scope of philosophy of religion and the failure of classical foundationalism. Classical foundationalism is the idea that we can simply build up our picture of the world from self-evident, necessary truths and inferences and (for some foundationalists) sense perception. For example, René Descartes (the paradigm case for classical foundationalism) believed it was possible to scrutinize all one's inherited beliefs one by one, like testing apples in a basket to see if they are rotten, and only keeping the ones that survived scrutiny. While John Locke (unlike Descartes) also allowed for sense perception to play a fundamental role in the formation of our beliefs, he was (like Descartes) very much concerned with building up secure worldviews in the light of the crumbling medieval Christian consensus (Wolterstorff 1996). Both were desirous to not simply take the religious beliefs they inherited from their elders for granted, but rather to build up a worldview that could survive scrutiny.

In the second half of the twentieth century, classical foundationalism became increasingly untenable. We hold a wide range of beliefs that we can't derive in the way foundationalists think we ought to, yet that seem crucial for our everyday lives. A well-known example is the belief that other people have minds. As Plantinga (1967) argued, you can't perceive the minds of other people, the idea that other people have minds is not self-evidently true, and you can't simply derive it from other truths. Still, it would be hard to get around in one's life without this belief and we seem to be warranted in holding this belief. This and other examples (e.g. belief in the past, belief that one is not the only person in existence) indicate that we cannot build a worldview from scratch and proof it against all objections.

The failure of classical foundationalism in the second half of the twentieth century led some philosophers of religion, such as

Alvin Plantinga and William Alston, to look for different ways to evaluate the commitments that come with religious worldviews. If it is impossible to reason all the way from more basic premises into a worldview, what justification, or warrant (or other positive epistemic state) do we have for favoring classical theism, or some form of naturalism, over the many other worldviews that can be formulated? Moreover, philosophy of religion as it is being done in Western philosophy departments has not engaged in depth with the many different religious ideas across the world such as, say, Buddhism. Moreover, our religious views are at an early stage of the possible history of intelligent life on our planet, and we haven't even begun to scratch the surface of the possible religious worldviews we might entertain (see e.g. Schellenberg 2013). So how can we say that, for example, naturalistic atheism or classical theism is the best worldview on offer? We cannot.

Fortunately, worldview comparison doesn't require that we catalogue all the different forms of religious and naturalistic worldviews and pick the best among them. Rather, we can just pick two or more worldviews and compare them in terms of their relative plausibility. This is the project in which Kenny and Graham engage in the present debate book. They assess whether the worldviews they defend are internally coherent or whether they might have contradictions or tensions. All things being equal, a more coherent worldview—one that doesn't contain blatant contradictions, few tensions, and where all the elements fit neatly together—is preferable to a less coherent worldview. Secondly, they assess whether one worldview makes better sense of the world than another. Kenny Pearce is an expert on early modern philosophy, and his worldview of choice is classical theism. He defends a version of this thesis that is largely inspired by Leibniz. Graham Oppy has expertise in atheism and debates on God's existence, and defends—also in line with his earlier work—the broad position that no gods exist.

Kenny Pearce distinguishes classical theism from traditional theism, the commitment among believers of the Abrahamic theisms in an omnipotent, omnibenevolent, and omniscient God. Classical theism is a metaphysical theory that, in addition to the commitments just outlined, also sees God as a necessary being, who is also immutable (God cannot possibly change), impassible (no one can do anything to God) and atemporal (God is outside of time). We can find classical theists among the three Abrahamic traditions, including Philo of Alexandria, Avicenna, Maimonides, Aquinas, and Leibniz. Kenny also mentions several Abrahamic theist philosophers and theologians who are not classical theists, including al-Ghazali, Martin Luther, and John Calvin.

Kenny's main argument for classical theism is twofold. First, he uses a version of the cosmological argument from contingency. The main starting point of this argument is the question: why is there something, rather than nothing? More specifically, the focus of this argument is History—the total sequence of events, past, present, and future. History stands in need of explanation, and Kenny argues that classical theism can explain History, whereas naturalism cannot. In his view, God provides us with an explanation of History. This is not a causal explanation, as in some forms of the cosmological argument that attribute the big bang to God's creative action, but a grounding explanation: God, a more fundamental thing, gives rise to History, a less fundamental thing. In line with the commitments of classical theism, Kenny envisages the universe as the outcome of God's free choice. History is like a dance: it's not so much that a dance is caused by the movements of a dancer; rather, it is grounded in the movements of the dancer, and will continue to exist as long as the dancer engages in the movement. By contrast, Kenny argues that naturalism (unlike classical theism) cannot explain History. Thus, in comparing the worldviews of atheism and classical theism, classical theism fares better. A second argument for classical theism is religious experience. In Kenny's view, we have various reports of (and some of us have ourselves experienced) a variety of religious experiences. Considering challenges such as the objection from hallucinations and the objections from cognitive science of religion, which see the origin of religious experiences as naturalistic, Kenny concludes that monotheists have an advantage over naturalists, in that the latter need to assume that religious experiences are unreliable, whereas a monotheist can conclude they are authentic (i.e. real experiences of the divine).

Graham Oppy defends the position that no gods (not the God of classical theism, nor indeed any other god) exist. His opening statement proceeds in the following way: rather than offering a direct argument for atheism, he looks at a variety of different situations and arguments where theists have earlier argued that it is necessary to bring God into the picture, and where Graham argues this is not needed. Just as there are many versions of theism, even of Abrahamic monotheism, there are many ways to deny the existence of any gods. In Graham's view, the universe exists necessarily and the universe is entirely naturalistic. Moreover, he also holds that it is necessary that natural reality exhausts causal reality, that conscious, intelligent minds (such as human minds) appear late and local in history, and that nothing is divine. In Graham's view, we can answer the question "Why does natural reality exist?" as follows: "(a) it was necessary that natural reality exist initially; and (b) nothing has subsequently caused natural reality to cease to exist." This claim, if compelling, would undermine one of Kenny's main arguments for God's existence; namely, that History stands in need of explanation. Graham surveys a range of different phenomena, including mathematics, science, evolution, religion, and freedom, and offers reasons for why naturalism fares no worse as a worldview than classical theism (or any other form of theism) in accounting for them.

Reading through these opening statements and the subsequent replies, I was struck once again by the fact that philosophy of religion, sometimes dismissed as fringe, is undoubtedly the most comprehensive of all the philosophical disciplines because of its focus on worldview comparison. Worldview comparison not only requires that we take a range of worldviews (religious and non-religious) seriously; it also has deep ramifications for pretty much all domains philosophers care about, including the status of ethical truths, the existence of abstract mathematical objects, how to explain love, and human freedom. It is clear that in this case both the theist and the atheist have considered carefully the ramifications of their views for many of these different domains. Gaining more clarity on how our religious worldviews relate to these different domains is important, and philosophers of religion are particularly well positioned to make such comparisons.

But one might still ask the further question: what do these worldview comparisons matter to the everyday believer, the believer with no extensive training in philosophy or theology who is at best only partially aware of the worldview commitments of her tradition, and who might even hold beliefs that contradict those worldviews (so-called theologically incorrect beliefs)?

Since these debates are aimed at a broader audience than specialists, it is worth considering this question. I will note one thing here, namely that people care about having worldviews and commitments that are coherent and that help them to make sense of the world. This concern for having plausible beliefs is not restricted to theologians and philosophers; it is something we all share, particularly if we are members of pluralistic societies that have a variety of live religious options on offer. Surveying indicates an increasing fluidity of religious beliefs and commitments on a global scale, especially among younger people. Deconversion is frequent, and in the United States, Christianity (still the main religious affiliation in terms of cultural influence and number of adherents) is declining at a rapid pace.[2] Moreover, empirical work on (de)conversion indicates that people are driven by a variety of different factors, for example when they become atheists. Tensions of worldviews, for instance with established science, are one reason why some young people in the United States choose to become atheists (e.g. Fazzino 2014).

If the reasons why we adhere to certain religions (or areligious pictures of the world) are intellectual—in addition to all the pragmatic considerations of belonging and the benefits of emotion management I outlined earlier—then it is important for everyone who holds a religious or non-religious worldview to think carefully about their commitments. Worldview comparisons offer one way to engage in dispassionate, cool, and careful discourse regarding matters of religious disagreement. If done well, there might be virtues exhibited in the discussion, including humility, respect, open-mindedness, and imaginative sympathy. Reading such a discussion might entice non-specialists to embody such virtues in their own discussions of these matters.

We can make worldview comparisons across religious traditions. We are not bound (though we are still influenced) by the peculiar situation that we were born in and our life's trajectory; anyone (insider or outsider to a tradition) can do it. As authors such as Rudolph Carnap speculated, being more precise about our concepts, axioms, and other worldview commitments also potentially holds societal benefits as it can improve public discourse and reasoning. In many non-philosophical domains, once you have identified the experts, it is pretty clear which claims you should embrace. In philosophical domains, this is usually not the case. However, identifying experts can still help people to identify attitudes they can take towards those who disagree with them.

Thus, to read this careful, charitably held discussion of two deeply disagreeing interlocutors who are also smart philosophers

---

2. www.pewforum.org/2019/10/17/in-u-s-decline-of-christianity-continues-at-rapid-pace/

is both edifying and a joy. Here you have two carefully formulated positive proposals for worldviews that explain all that is: classical theism and naturalistic atheism. You can follow along with the authors and deliberate: which one do you find more plausible?

References

Asma, Stephen. (2018) *Why We Need Religion*. Oxford: Oxford University Press.

De Cruz, Helen. (2018) "Religious Beliefs and Philosophical Views: A Qualitative Study." *Res Philosophica* 95 (3): 477–504.

Fazzino, Lori L. (2014) "Leaving the Church Behind: Applying a Deconversion Perspective to Evangelical Exit Narratives." *Journal of Contemporary Religion* 29 (2): 249–266.

Glucklich, Ariel. (2020) *The Joy of Religion: Exploring the Nature of Pleasure in Spiritual Life*. Cambridge: Cambridge University Press.

Plantinga, Alvin. (1967) *God and Other Minds*. Ithaca, NY: Cornell University Press.

Schellenberg, John L. (2013) *Evolutionary Religion*. Oxford: Oxford University Press.

Wolterstorff, N. (1996) *John Locke and the Ethics of Belief*. Cambridge: Cambridge University Press.

Opening Statements

Chapter 1

Classical Theism
An Exposition and Defense[*]

Kenny Pearce

Contents

1 Theism Versus Naturalism	13
2 Classical Theism	17
2.1 What Is Classical Theism?	17
2.2 Objections to Classical Theism From Other Theists	20
2.3 A Formulation of Classical Theism	23
3 An Argument for Classical Theism	29
3.1 The Argument	30
3.2 History Needs an Explanation (Defense of Premise 1)	35
3.3 Classical Theism Can Explain History (Defense of Premise 2)	40
3.3.1 A Grounding Explanation	41
3.3.2 A Non-necessitating Explanation	47
3.3.3 An Ultimate Explanation	51
3.3.4 Conclusion	58
3.4 Naturalism Can't Explain History (Defense of Premise 2n)	59
3.5 Conclusion	63
4 Classical Theism and Religious Belief	65
4.1 Religion, Religious Belief, and Religious Experience	66

---

[*] In addition to Graham, I thank Tyron Goldschmidt, Frederick Choo, Scott Hill, Tim Troutman, Jay Hoeflinger, and the students in my autumn 2019 philosophy of religion lecture at Trinity College Dublin (TCD) for helpful comments on previous drafts of this opening statement. My work on this debate was also supported by a spring 2020 sabbatical from TCD, during which I was an academic visitor at the University of Pittsburgh. I thank both universities for their support.

DOI: 10.4324/9781003216797-3

4.2 Reidian Religious Epistemology	70
4.3 The Problem of Hallucination	78
4.4 The Reliability of Religious Experience	82
4.5 Resolving Conflicts	87
5 Conclusion	90

Bertrand Russell ([1952] 1997, 547–548) famously remarked that he didn't believe in God for the same reason he didn't believe that there was a teapot in orbit between Earth and Mars. According to Russell, there's no need to disprove the existence of the teapot since there's no reason to take the teapot claim seriously in the first place. The same, Russell claims, goes for God.

In a similar vein, Graham Oppy (my opponent in the present debate) has compared belief in God with belief in fairies (Oppy 2018a, §3). It is surprisingly difficult to disprove the existence of fairies (see Clark 1987), and some arguments could even be given in their favor.[1] Nevertheless, according to Graham, there is no obligation to take fairy claims seriously. In the absence of powerful evidence—much more powerful than any that has been produced so far—it is rational to believe that there are no fairies. The same, Graham claims, goes for God.

I think that this perspective underestimates the strength of the case for theism. I do not claim that the existence of God can be *proven* so that every rational person *must* believe in God. I do claim that theism provides a better explanation of the world than certain competing views, including the view endorsed by Graham. This provides us with *a good reason* for believing in God. However, one good reason for believing in God certainly does not amount to a proof of God's existence. Deciding whether we should, in the end, believe in God requires a comprehensive 'weighing up' of the pros and cons of theism and its competitors. I hope that this debate will help the reader to begin this task.

The plan of this opening statement is as follows. After some preliminaries (§1), I introduce a way of thinking about God known as 'classical theism' (§2). Then, in §3, I show that classical theism provides a satisfying explanation of the universe as a whole, while many competing views (including Graham's) necessarily leave this unexplained. Finally, in §4, I discuss the relevance of this philosophical

---

1. Tiddy Smith (2020) discusses a philosophical argument for the existence of nature spirits. Perhaps fairies should be considered a species of nature spirits.

theory about God to ordinary religious belief. I argue that, although classical theism differs from ordinary religious belief in certain important ways, these two kinds of belief about God can be combined to form an intellectually satisfying picture of the world.

1 Theism Versus Naturalism

In a number of publications, Graham has argued that the correct approach to philosophy of religion is **worldview comparison** (Oppy 2013a, ch. 1; 2013b, §5; 2018a, §2). I agree. In this section, I explain this approach and its application to the present debate.

Theism is a broad family of views, including every view that holds that there is a God (or god) *of some sort or other*. Since the word 'God' (or 'god') is extremely flexible, the variety of theisms (beliefs in God/gods) is almost limitless. Atheism is just the view that every one of these many theisms is false. In other words, atheists think that there are no gods of any kind.

> **Theism:** the thesis that a God (or god) of some sort or other exists.
>
> **Atheism:** the thesis that there are no gods of any kind.

Philosophers support their positions with arguments.

Arguments and Validity

An **argument** is a collection of beliefs (the **premises**) that are meant to provide rational support for some other belief (the **conclusion**). The strongest kind of rational support is known as **validity**. A valid argument is one where, if the premises are true, then the conclusion *must necessarily* be true. In other words, it is impossible for the premises of a valid argument to be true when the conclusion is false.

It is hard to imagine an argument that supported the claim that *some form of theism is true* without supporting a claim that is at least a bit more specific than this. That is, philosophers might construct arguments for a creator of the universe, or for an infinitely perfect being, and so on, but it's hard to see how they could make arguments for God (or a god) without making some specific claims about what God is like. An argument for God will be an argument for some particular sort of God.

On the other side, if the atheist confines herself to arguing against the theist's claims without setting up some positive view of her own, then it is hard to see how the atheist could argue against all of the theisms at once (see Diller 2016). Objections to theism are always objections to some *particular form* of theism. For instance, those who argue that if there were a God then there wouldn't be so much suffering in the world are typically arguing against the existence of a God who is both all-powerful and perfectly good (see Hume [1779] 2002, pt. 10). If a particular theist doesn't hold that God is all-powerful or doesn't hold that God is perfectly good, then that theist doesn't have to worry about this problem.

A defense of theism, then, should be a defense of a particular 'big picture' of the world that somehow involves or implies the existence of some particular God or gods. Similarly, a defense of atheism should be a defense of some 'big picture' that implies that there are no gods of any kind. These 'big pictures' are known as **worldviews**.

The method of worldview comparison proceeds by elaborating particular theistic and atheistic worldviews and examining their relative plausibility. In the first stage, we examine each worldview for internal **coherence**. That is, we ask, does this view make sense on its own terms? We are particularly concerned, at this stage, with whether a worldview contains internal contradictions. Many of the standard objections to theism allege such contradictions in traditional Western monotheistic worldviews. For instance, the so-called 'logical problem of evil' (Mackie 1955) alleges that it is contradictory to suppose that an all-powerful and all-good God exists and also that evil exists. Both of these beliefs are part of traditional Western monotheistic worldviews, so this objection is claiming that these worldviews have an internal contradiction.[2] Similarly, the **Stone Paradox** alleges that a believer in an all-powerful God is unable to give a consistent answer to the question, *can God create a stone so heavy that God cannot lift it?*[3]

A variety of solutions has been proposed for each of these problems. I agree with Graham that, while it is very hard to be sure that a worldview is internally consistent (someone might always find a

---

2. For an influential theistic response to this problem, see Plantinga (1977).
3. For an overview of this problem and the various solutions that have been proposed, see Pearce (2011).

new problem!), it is very likely that there are at least some theistic worldviews *and* at least some atheistic worldviews that are internally consistent. At least, no one has come close to *proving* that all theistic worldviews or all atheistic worldviews are inconsistent.

While *consistency* is an all-or-nothing matter (a worldview either contains contradictions or it doesn't), *coherence* comes in degrees. It is difficult to give a precise definition of 'coherence', but intuitively we can say:

> A **coherent** worldview is one whose different pieces fit together neatly.

A **contradiction** is the very worst kind of lack of coherence, where the pieces of the view actually conflict. However, worldviews also have internal tensions that fall short of contradiction.

> A **tension** is a case where a person who holds a certain worldview is pulled in both directions on a certain question.

(Pay attention to the metaphor: it's like the tension on the rope in a tug-of-war.) The problem of **evil** is probably best understood in this way within most traditional theistic worldviews: on the one hand, if God is all-good and all-powerful, one might not expect evil to exist. On the other hand, our life experience (and perhaps also the teaching of our religion) gives us very strong reason to believe that there is evil in the world. So the believer is pulled in both directions here.[4] Good worldviews are entirely free from contradictions, but all worldviews have some tensions. The less tension, the better.

In the next stage of worldview comparison, we attempt to determine whether one worldview makes better sense of the world than another. There are two main criteria here: simplicity and explanatory comprehensiveness.

> One worldview is **simpler** than another to the extent that it posits fewer things, or fewer kinds of things, or is in other respects more elegant and less convoluted.

> One worldview has greater **explanatory comprehensiveness** than another to the extent that it explains more things and leaves fewer unexplained.

---

4. Arguments that use this kind of tension as a reason against theism are known as 'evidential arguments from evil'. See Howard-Snyder (1996).

As Graham has emphasized (Oppy 2018a, §2.3), a worldview that posits extra things should not get credit for explaining *those* things. In a comparison between two worldviews, each one gets credit only for explaining things that both worldviews agree exist.

Ideally, if we were trying to assess whether it is more reasonable to be theists or atheists, we would compare the *best* theistic worldview with the *best* atheistic worldview. The debate format of this book means that we will be comparing the theistic worldview *I* think is best against the atheistic worldview *Graham* thinks is best. Other philosophers will not agree with us about which version of each view is best. (The reason for this is simple: philosophers never agree about anything.)

Graham, like most atheist philosophers today, holds that the best atheistic worldview is a version of naturalism.

Naturalism

Different philosophers give different definitions of 'naturalism', but the core idea in all of them is that the natural sciences (physics, biology, etc.) provide the correct methods for knowing about the world, so that philosophers need to take their cues from scientists. For most of our purposes here, this general characterization of naturalism will suffice. However, I will also sometimes refer to Graham's own more precise definition: "*Naturalism* is the view that (a) there are none but natural entities with none but natural causal powers, and (b) well-established science is the touchstone for identifying causal entities and causal powers" (Oppy 2018a, 13).[5] Graham does not define 'natural' here. We may say, at least as a rough approximation, that natural entities and natural causal powers are entities and causal powers of the sort studied by science.

---

5. Graham has given other definitions of 'naturalism' in other works (e.g. Oppy 2013a, 6; 2013b, 50), but I think this one best captures our disagreement.

Naturalism, as a component of an atheistic worldview, does the work it needs to do. It is not just a denial of (some particular version of) theism, but a broader view of the world that *implies* the non-existence of God/gods: God is not among the entities studied by science, so anyone who believes in God is going beyond science in the way naturalism says we shouldn't.

My aim in this opening statement is to argue that a certain form of theism has very significant advantages over Graham's brand of naturalism. I turn now to the task of describing this version of theism.

> In this section, we've seen that in order to determine whether we ought to believe in God, we should proceed by comparing the best theistic worldviews against the best atheistic worldviews. The criteria of comparison include internal coherence, simplicity, and explanatory comprehensiveness. Most philosophers think the best atheistic worldviews will be versions of naturalism, the view that there are no entities or causal powers beyond those studied by science.

2 Classical Theism

2.1 *What Is Classical Theism?*

According to the **Abrahamic religious traditions** (Judaism, Christianity, and Islam), there is exactly one God who created the universe from nothing, and this God is all-powerful (**omnipotent**), all-knowing (**omniscient**), and perfectly good. Similar ideas about God can also be found in a variety of other traditions. I will call this view 'traditional theism'. Traditional theism is something that ordinary religious believers within these traditions believe.

Classical theism, as I use that term, is a **metaphysical** theory developed in a dialogue between philosophers and theologians across the Abrahamic traditions. These philosophers and theologians used ideas and arguments derived from ancient Greek philosophy to try to make rational sense of traditional theism. Among the first thinkers in this tradition was Philo of Alexandria, a Jewish philosopher who lived at the same time as Jesus. Influential historical proponents of classical theism include Avicenna, Maimonides, and Aquinas. The particular form of classical theism I will defend is especially influenced by Leibniz.

Although there is a lot of variation in the details, classical theists generally see God as a **necessary being** (a being that had to exist no matter what) existing completely outside the universe and utterly unlike anything in the universe. Classical theists also generally hold that God is immutable, impassible, and atemporal.

> To say that God is **immutable** means that God cannot possibly change in any way.
>
> To say that God is **impassible** means that God is always completely active and never in any way passive (no one can *do anything to* God).
>
> To say that God is **atemporal** means that God is entirely outside of time.

Because classical theists see God as completely different from anything in the universe in all of these ways, they generally think that human language—which was developed for talking about humans and rocks and stars and things—has to be *stretched* somehow in order to talk about God. According to classical theists, when we say (for instance) that God's knowledge is infinite, we don't just mean that God knows a lot more facts than I do. Rather, God's knowledge is of an entirely different, and greater, *kind* than mine.

Classical theism, then, goes beyond (what I'm calling) traditional theism. It makes claims about God that are not generally held by ordinary religious believers. These are philosophical claims that a person would be unlikely to arrive at *just* by reading the Bible or the Quran. Nevertheless, it's important to recognize that classical theism is not therefore 'untraditional'. Historically, classical theism has had enormous influence on Abrahamic religions. In fact, in some branches of the Abrahamic religious traditions (e.g. Roman Catholicism), classical theism is part of religious orthodoxy. Nevertheless, it is important to distinguish between the core of the *religious* concept of God (what I'm calling 'traditional theism') and the *philosophical* concept of God within (what I call) classical theism. Classical theism, as I understand it, is a metaphysical theory (a theory of the fundamental nature of reality) that explains how traditional theism might really be true.

Some Classical Theists

Philo of Alexandria (c. 20 BCE–c. 40 CE) belonged to the large community of Greek-speaking Jews in Alexandria, Egypt. Unlike later classical theists, Philo did not write a systematic treatise on the existence and nature of God. However, his commentaries on the Torah (the first five books in the Jewish and Christian Bibles) helped to initiate a tradition of using ideas and arguments from Greek philosophy in an effort to understand Abrahamic theology. This is particularly visible in his works *On the Creation* and *On the Unchangeableness of God*, which have been translated by Colson and Whitaker (1929a, 1929b).

Abu Ali al-Husayn ibn Sina (c. 970–1037; also known by the Latin name 'Avicenna') was a Muslim philosopher and physician from the region of Bukhara, in modern Uzbekistan. He wrote a huge number of books on a variety of philosophical, theological, and scientific topics, not all of which have been translated into English. The *Metaphysica*—part of a longer work known as *The Book of Scientific Knowledge*—summarizes Avicenna's theory of God and the created world. This text has been translated by Morewedge (1973).

Moses Maimonides (1138–1204) was a rabbi, philosopher, and physician born in Cordova, Spain, which was at that time ruled by the Muslim Almoravid dynasty. When Maimonides was ten years old, Cordova was conquered by a different Muslim group, the Almohads, who refused to tolerate non-Muslims in their territory. As a result, his family was forced to flee. After some time in Fez, Morocco, Maimonides moved to Cairo, Egypt, where he spent most of his adult life. In addition to his philosophical work, Maimonides' interpretations of Jewish law still have very significant influence in Judaism today. His most important philosophical work, *The Guide of the Perplexed*, was completed in 1190. An abridged English translation has been provided by Rabin (1995).

Thomas Aquinas (1225–1274) was a Dominican monk, philosopher, and theologian. He was born in Italy and spent most of his life in Naples and Rome. Aquinas is revered as a saint in several Christian traditions and is officially recognized by Roman Catholics as one of the great 'doctors' (teachers) of the Christian church. Aquinas' best-known work is *Summa Theologiae*. Davies and Leftow (2006) have provided a simplified English translation, suitable for beginners, of the portion of the book that discusses the existence and nature of God.

Gottfried Wilhelm Leibniz (1646–1716) was a German Lutheran polymath who made major contributions to such diverse fields as mathematics, physics, linguistics, and law. He was also one of the first Europeans to undertake serious study of East Asian languages and philosophies. Besides his philosophical work, Leibniz is best remembered for his highly contentious dispute with Isaac Newton over which of them had been the first to discover calculus. His essay "On the Ultimate Origination of Things" (Leibniz [1697] 1989) provides a brief summary of his philosophical theory of God, while his book *Theodicy* (Leibniz [1710] 2005) provides the full details.

2.2 Objections to Classical Theism From Other Theists

The claim that classical theism is the best version of theism is controversial. One of the most important historical critics of classical theism was al-Ghazali, who criticized classical theists for elevating human reason above the Quran (see al-Ghazali, *The Incoherence of the Philosophers* 106, 181–182, 226).

Abu Hamid Muhammad al-Ghazali (c. 1056–1111) was a Muslim philosopher-theologian born in Tabaran-Tus, in modern Iran. Al-Ghazali was the head of an elite school in Baghdad, close to the circles of power, when he had a kind of conversion experience and determined that a life of power and privilege was incompatible with a genuine commitment to Islam. He tells the story of his conversion in his book *Freedom and Fulfillment* (also known as *Deliverance From Error*), which has been translated by McCarthy (1980). Al-Ghazali famously attacked Muslim classical theists like Avicenna in his book *The Incoherence of the Philosophers*, which has been translated by Marmura (2000).

Similar objections to classical theism were later raised within Christianity by the Protestant reformers Martin Luther (1483–1546) and John Calvin (1509–1564). Luther and Calvin argued that it was arrogant and impious to suppose that we mere mortals could come up with theories about God using reason rather than appealing to God's **revelation** in the Bible (see Luther [1520] 2018, 62–65; Calvin [1536] 1845, §§1.5.11–14, 2.2.18).

Although Luther and Calvin were hostile to classical theism, many later Protestants have taken friendlier attitudes. Leibniz, for instance, was Lutheran. The Puritan pastor, theologian, and philosopher Jonathan Edwards (1703–1758) was another influential Protestant classical theist (see Edwards 1765). Classical theism—and, more generally, the relationship between philosophy and theology—continues to be a disputed issue within Protestant theology.

Another worry about classical theism is that, because of major theological disagreements, there might not really be a single concept of God shared by Jews, Christians, and Muslims. Even if believers in all three traditions can use the same concept (the objection continues), they certainly shouldn't allow their thinking about God to be shaped by these Greek philosophers who were outside the Abrahamic traditions entirely.

These two objections are closely related: if al-Ghazali, Luther, and Calvin are correct that our concept of God can be derived only from revelation, then it seems that the only way to have the same concept of God is to accept the same sources of revelation. Since al-Ghazali's concept of God comes from the Quran but Luther's comes from the Bible, someone might think they don't have the same concept of God at all. On the other hand, if there is a philosophical concept of God derived from reason, then everyone should be able to have the same concept, regardless of whether they believe in the Bible or the Quran or whatever.

Al-Ghazali, Luther, and Calvin disagree with classical theism's general approach to thinking about God. They say that our thinking about God should rely less on human reason and more on divine revelation. However, at the end of the day, they mostly agree with the classical theists' descriptions of God. For instance, they agree that God is necessary and immutable. Other religious thinkers have departed from classical theism in much more significant ways. Often, these more serious departures have been motivated by worries that classical theism might conflict with certain particular beliefs of their religious traditions. For instance, some have objected that according to classical theism, since God is immutable and already knows everything we will do before we do it, God doesn't really engage in the kind of *relationship* with humans depicted in the Bible (Pinnock et al. 1994). Since I am here concerned with defending theism against atheism, not with defending classical theism against other kinds of theism, I won't be able to address these objections in any detail.[6] However, the discussion of the relationship of classical theism to religion in §4 will, I hope, go some way toward answering these objections. Readers who are worried about these issues are encouraged to skip ahead and read that section, then come back and pick up from here.

Another kind of objection to classical theism alleges that it depicts God as having some kind of tyrannical domination over the created world and privileges divine power over divine love. This objection is often raised by theologians who are concerned about the ways religion has been used as a tool of oppression: if God is a tyrant, then human tyranny can be justified as imitation of God (see e.g. Hartshorne 1984).

Although it must be admitted that classical theists have sometimes portrayed God in this tyrannical way, I do not think this is any necessary part of classical theism. However, this is not the place to answer these objections in detail. At this point I can only say that it seems to me that the metaphysical theory of God provided by classical theism can be appropriately combined with the religious image or symbol of God as loving parent (and not tyrant), and §4 will give some indication of how this is so.[7]

---

6. Eleonore Stump (2016) has provided a response to these kinds of objections that is concise, thorough, and accessible.
7. Elizabeth Johnson (1992) argues that, although classical theism has often been used as a tool of oppression, a modified version of classical theism can be retrieved as a tool of liberation, especially (but not only) for women. Johnson might reject some parts of my summary of classical theism, but her account is compatible with the general approach I am defending.

2.3 A Formulation of Classical Theism

The particular version of classical theism I will defend can be stated as follows:

> (CT) Spacetime and all of its contents exist because of the free and rational choice of a necessary being.

This definition requires some unpacking. In the first place, as the use of the word 'because' indicates, (CT) is proposed as an *explanation*. The thing to be explained is the existence of 'spacetime and all of its contents'. Following the most natural interpretation of modern physics, I think of space and time as a single four-dimensional entity in which physical objects are located. Further, I assume that all natural entities and all natural causes are located within spacetime.

More on Spacetime

Brian Greene (2005) provides a very readable layperson's introduction to thinking about space and time in modern physics. Tim Maudlin (1993) provides a philosophical argument that spacetime in modern physics is best understood as a genuine *entity* (substance).

Some (controversial) theories in modern physics take spacetime to be emergent rather than fundamental. Some theories (famously including string theory) take spacetime to have more than four dimensions (see Greene 2005, 360–402, 482–491; Randall 2005). These sorts of complexities will not matter to my argument.

(CT) refers to the free and rational choice of a necessary being (God) to explain spacetime and all of its contents. In order to keep our explanation from going in a circle, God and God's choice must not be among the contents of spacetime. The definition therefore strongly suggests that God is atemporal, as classical theists have usually held.

God and Time

My thesis (CT) *strongly suggests* that God is atemporal. However, divine atemporality is not, strictly speaking, a logical

> consequence of (CT). There are cosmological models in physics in which the existence of *our* spacetime is caused by events in some other spacetime. Adapting this view, a theist might hold that God exists in God's own spacetime, separate from ours.[8] Alternatively, some theists, such as Richard Swinburne (1994, 137–144), have argued that God *would have been atemporal* if God had not created spacetime, but that by creating spacetime God placed Godself within time. These complexities won't matter to my argument, so I will ignore them from here on. Readers interested in God's relation to time should see Natalja Deng's (2019) excellent introduction to these debates.

According to (CT), God is a necessary being. A necessary being is a being that had to exist no matter what. There are lots of ways for me not to exist (e.g. if my parents had never met), but there is no way for God not to exist.

Philosophers have distinguished several kinds of necessity. The kind of necessity I (and most other theistic philosophers) attribute to God is metaphysical necessity. Metaphysical necessity is meant to be a stronger form of necessity than physical necessity.

> A claim is **physically necessary** if the laws of nature require it to be true.

For instance, it is physically necessary that nothing moves faster than the speed of light. When I say God is a necessary being, I don't just mean that the laws of nature require that God exist; I mean that no matter what laws of nature there were, God would still have to exist.

> A claim is **metaphysically necessary** if it would still have to be true no matter what the laws of nature were.

Some philosophers have thought that metaphysical necessity was the same thing as logical necessity.

> A **logically necessary** claim is a claim that you can't reject without contradicting yourself.

---

8. I thank Graham for this suggestion.

So, for instance, it is logically necessary that all humans are human, because if you say 'not all humans are human' you contradict yourself. Some contradictions are a bit less obvious than this. For instance, it is necessary that all mothers are parents; to say 'not all mothers are parents' is to contradict yourself. But in order to see that this is a contradiction, you need to understand what's meant by the words 'mother' and 'parent'.

Anselm famously argued that the claim 'God does not exist' was contradictory in just this way. According to Anselm, atheism must necessarily rely on some kind of misunderstanding of what's meant by the word 'God'.[9] I will have a bit more to say about Anselm's argument later on. For now, suffice it to say that I (like most theistic philosophers) think that it is not very plausible to suppose that God is necessary in this way.

> Anselm of Canterbury (1033–1109) was a Benedictine monk and philosopher born in the Burgundy region of France. From 1093 until his death in 1109, he served as archbishop of Canterbury, England. Anselm is revered as a saint in several Christian traditions and is officially recognized by Roman Catholics as one of the great 'doctors' (teachers) of the Christian church. Anselm's major philosophical writings have been collected and translated by Williams (2007).

Fortunately, there is good reason to believe that not all metaphysical necessities are logical necessities.[10] For instance, most philosophers today think that it is metaphysically necessary that water contains hydrogen. Of course, it's possible for there to be no water in the universe, but no matter what the laws of nature were, stuff that didn't contain hydrogen just wouldn't be water. This is not a fact about what the word 'water' means: lots of people understood the word 'water' before they knew what that stuff was made of.

---

9. As we will see below, Anselm's argument can be interpreted in several ways. However, there are certainly texts where Anselm appears to say that the atheist has not understood the meaning of the word 'God'. See Anselm, *Proslogion*, chapter 4.

10. For a rather technical mathematical argument for this claim (which I find convincing), see Pruss and Rasmussen (2018, §2.2).

Rather, it's a fact about *what kind of stuff water is*. That water contains hydrogen was discovered by people doing chemistry, not people writing dictionaries. It's a claim about the world, not just a claim about words. Nevertheless, this claim is necessary in a stronger sense than physical necessity.

My view, then, is that although the sentence 'God does not exist' is not a contradiction, nevertheless it does not describe a way the world really could be. God has to exist no matter what. (Remember, I haven't defended any of these claims yet. In this section, I'm explaining what (CT) *means*; in the following sections I'll give reasons for thinking it's true.)

> ### Varieties of Necessity (Summary)
>
> A logically necessary claim is one whose denial is a contradiction, like 'all humans are human'.
>
> A physically necessary claim is one that, according to the laws of nature, *must* be true, like 'nothing moves faster than light'.
>
> A metaphysically necessary claim is one that would still have to be true even if the laws of nature were different.
>
> Many philosophers think there are some claims that are metaphysically necessary but not logically necessary. 'Water contains hydrogen' might be an example. According to my version of classical theism, 'God exists' is also an example.

Finally, (CT) appeals to a necessary being to explain spacetime and its contents in a specific way: by means of a *free and rational choice*. By a rational choice, I just mean a choice based on reasons. By a free choice, I mean a choice among multiple options.

Strictly speaking, this is all that (CT) contains. Again, my purpose here is to defend theism against atheism, not to defend one version of theism against others. It seems to me that (CT), all by itself, counts as a form of theism, even if we don't draw any further consequences from it. After all, (CT) implies the existence of a free and rational creator of the whole physical universe. That sounds like God to me. Nevertheless, let me briefly gesture at some reasons for thinking that the necessary being mentioned in (CT) should be regarded as having some of the other features attributed to God in traditional theism.

First, if the necessary being's choice explains spacetime and its contents, it should presumably also explain why other possible alternatives are not actual. For instance (and this will be important to my argument in §3.3), physics tells us that spacetime could have had a very different structure from the structure it in fact has. The necessary being's choice should explain why spacetime has this structure rather than some other structure. The simplest supposition here would be that all of the possibilities for spacetime and its contents were among the necessary being's options. Perhaps there are also other options, possibilities in which there is no spacetime at all. If every possibility is among the necessary being's options in its (free and rational) choice, then the necessary being presumably counts as omnipotent. If the necessary being chooses freely on the basis of reasons, then it needs to know all of its options and what's good and bad about each of them. If its options include all the possibilities, and the necessary being knows all of them, then presumably the necessary being counts as omniscient. Finally, if the necessary being decides on the basis of the *actual* reasons for and against each option, then it seems that this being should count as morally perfect, since it will make the best choice (the choice with the strongest reasons in its favor).

This is no more than a sketch of an argument. (That's why I kept saying 'presumably', 'it seems', and 'perhaps'!) When we try to spell out the details, we face very serious difficulties. The argument-sketch is inspired by Leibniz ([1710] 2005, §7),[11] and if the argument works, then it appears to lead directly to Leibniz's most (in)famous conclusions in philosophical theology: theological determinism and optimism.

> **Theological determinism** is the view that God chooses *every detail* of history, including all of our choices.
>
> **Optimism** is the view that God chooses the best among all possible worlds, which implies that *this* world is in fact the best of all possible worlds.

---

11. In citing *Theodicy*, I refer to the section numbers in the main body of the work, which should not be confused with the section numbers in the 'Preliminary Dissertation' or the various appendices.

Theological determinism is not very popular among theistic philosophers today, and optimism is simply not credible in light of the large quantities of evil and suffering we observe. As Voltaire ([1759] 2016, 15) famously quipped, "If this is the best of all possible worlds, what are the others like?"

I myself think that theological determinism might not be so bad (which is not to say that I'm prepared to endorse it), but I agree that Leibniz's optimism is simply not believable.

> ### More About Theological Determinism
>
> Although theological determinism is not very popular among theistic philosophers today, if we take a broader historical perspective we find that philosophers and theologians in the Abrahamic traditions are deeply divided on this question. Theological determinism would be considered the standard or orthodox view in most versions of Islam, as well as in the Reformed (Calvinist) traditions of Christianity, such as Presbyterianism. On the other side, the Arminian and Wesleyan traditions of Christianity, such as Methodism, have usually been opposed to theological determinism. In most other traditions there is no consensus.
>
> Theological determinism comes in two flavors: *theological compatibilism*, which holds that humans may have free will even if God determines their choices, and *theological fatalism*, which denies that humans have free will. Hugh McCann (2012) has recently defended theological compatibilism, while Derk Pereboom (2017) has defended theological fatalism. I think theological determinism might not be so bad because I think theological compatibilism might be true. For my most recent and most detailed thoughts on this issue, see Pearce (2020). For a general overview of debates about the relevance of God for human freedom, see Vicens and Kittle (2019).

The good news and the bad news about the path from (CT) to traditional theism is that the reasoning I've given is no more than a sketch, or a gesture in the direction of an argument. The details remain to be worked out. (Indeed, many of the classic works in Western philosophical theology can be seen, in large part, as attempts to work out the details of an argument along these general lines.) This is good news for the traditional theist because those who have tried to work out the complex details have come up with a variety of strategies for avoiding the blunt Leibnizian conclusions.[12] It's bad news for the traditional theist because it means that a lot more work needs to be done to show that something like traditional theism really does follow from (CT). However, even if (CT) turns out not to imply traditional theism, (CT) is still *some* kind of theism. My present aim is to argue that *some form of theism or other* is likely true. I therefore leave aside (for the moment) the question of traditional theism, and turn to my defense of (CT).

> Classical theism is a metaphysical theory about God and God's relation to creation that was developed in dialogue between Jewish, Christian, and Muslim thinkers, drawing on the methods and ideas of the Greek philosophical tradition. Although not all theists are happy with this theory, it has been accepted by many philosophers and theologians across the Abrahamic traditions. I'll be defending a particular version of classical theism, (CT), which states that spacetime and all of its contents exist because of the free and rational choice of a necessary being.

3 An Argument for Classical Theism

Traditionally, argument for the existence of God have been divided into three main categories:[13]

> **Ontological arguments**, like Anselm's argument mentioned earlier, try to make the case that just by sitting and thinking about the concept of God you can somehow see that God must exist.

---

12. Accounts of divine omnipotence, freedom, and moral perfection that attempt to avoid Leibniz's optimism include Adams (1972), Plantinga (1977, 34–53), Howard-Snyder and Howard-Snyder (1994), and Pruss (2016).
13. This classification is derived from Kant ([1781] 1998, A590/B618—A591/B619).

Cosmological arguments try to argue for the existence of a creator from the fact that the universe (cosmos) exists at all.

Teleological arguments rely on specific observed features of the world (for instance, the functioning of organs in animal bodies) to argue that the world must be the product of design.

Like most classical theists, I think that a cosmological argument provides the strongest reason for belief in classical theism. In this section, I present and defend such an argument.[14]

3.1 The Argument

Why is there anything at all? That is, why is there something rather than nothing? Out of all the somethings there could be, why is there *this* something in particular? Cosmological arguments claim that believing in God allows us to give good answers to these questions.

Cosmological arguments begin from the assumption that these are deep questions that require deep answers. Some philosophers have thought that these were shallow questions. Why is there something rather than nothing? Because there are prime numbers, and prime numbers are something and not nothing. Why are there prime numbers? A mathematical proof shows that there *have* to be prime numbers (infinitely many of them, in fact). Case closed.

This response misses the point. Our question was not about why there are prime numbers, but rather about why there are rocks and stars and penguins and things.

Let's begin again. Why are there rocks and stars and penguins and things? Well, it depends on what kind of things you are talking about. Presumably any explanation of why there are *rocks and penguins* is going to have to proceed by explaining why there are rocks and why there are penguins. There won't be one explanation that explains both the rocks *and* the penguins, because they don't have much to do with each other. Nevertheless, scientists do know, in quite a lot of detail, why there are rocks and why there are penguins. So why is there something rather than nothing? Stephen Maitzen (2013) answers: because there are penguins, and penguins are something and not nothing. 'Yes', one might respond, 'but why are there penguins?' That is, of course, an interesting question, but

---

14. I have defended a very similar argument in Pearce (2017b).

it's a question whose answer is found in evolutionary biology, not metaphysics. So, according to Maitzen, there is no deep metaphysical question here.

If any cosmological argument is to get off the ground, we need an interpretation of these questions on which they do in fact point to some kind of deep metaphysical puzzle.

Let's think for a moment about **explanation**. An explanation is an answer to a 'why?' question. A very common type of explanation—both in science and in everyday life—is **causal explanation**. For instance, if your parents want to know why there is a new dent in the car (after you borrowed it), they want to find out what caused the dent. That is, they want to know what happened that resulted in the dent.

Not all explanations are causal. For instance, it is possible to explain mathematical facts, although mathematical facts don't have causes.[15] There are also statistical explanations. You might try this one on your parents with the car: most cars that have been driven more than 50,000 miles have at least one dent, and this car has been driven more than 50,000 miles. That's why it has a dent. (This is just an example, not a real statistic.) This doesn't actually tell us where the dent came from, but by showing that it's normal for cars to have dents, it does make the dent less mysterious, and therefore may be seen as a kind of explanation. (Your parents probably won't like it.)

Although causal explanations aren't the only explanations, they are one very important class of explanations. Indeed, the fact that the physical universe has this kind of structure, in which one event causes others, seems to be part of why it's possible to explain events within it at all.

Recall that Graham defined 'naturalism' in part as the view that "there are none but natural entities with none but natural causal powers" (Oppy 2018a, 13). Recall further that the project of worldview comparison requires us to ask which worldview does the better job explaining the things that both worldviews agree exist. Graham and I agree that there is a sequence of causes and effects in the natural world. Graham thinks that this is all there is, while I think there is more to reality than this. What I'm trying to show

---

15. There are many philosophical puzzles about mathematical explanation. See Mancosu (2018) and D'Alessandro (2019).

here is that belief in God—who is not part of the natural world—is motivated because it allows for a more comprehensive explanation of the natural world.

To see why, consider the total sequence of causes and effects, past, present, and future. Call this sequence 'History' (with a capital 'H'). One way of interpreting the question, 'why is there anything at all?' is, 'why is History happening?' That is, why is there this long sequence of causes and effects? I claim that (CT) can explain History, and that no version of naturalism can explain History. My positive argument in favor of (CT) can thus be expressed as follows:

> **The Positive Argument**
> 1. History stands in need of explanation.
> 2. (CT) provides a good explanation of History.
> 3. If a theory provides a good explanation of something that stands in need of explanation, this is a good reason for endorsing that theory.
> 4. Therefore, there is a good reason for endorsing (CT).

The Positive Argument is valid. Premise 3 provides a general rule, and premises 1 and 2 show how this rule applies to (CT). So if the rule expressed by 3 is a good rule and the facts are as premises 1 and 2 claim they are, then the conclusion *must* be true.

Faced with a valid argument, there are two possible responses: either you can accept the conclusion, or you can reject (at least) one of the premises. So what should Graham do? He can't reject premise 3. That premise is a central element of the method of worldview comparison, a method Graham endorses. He could try to reject premise 1 and say that it is somehow a mistake to ask why History is occurring, or he could reject premise 2 and say that my (purported) explanation isn't any good. Note, however, that Graham also could just endorse the conclusion. All the conclusion says is that there is *one good reason* for endorsing (CT). Graham could accept that this is one good reason in favor of (CT) and try to argue that the reasons against (CT) are stronger.

Could we make a more ambitious argument? Historically, many classical theists thought they could use an argument along these lines to *prove* that theism is true. However, if we just change the conclusion to '(CT) is true', the argument will no longer be valid. To get a stronger conclusion, we would need stronger premises. Here is a valid argument for the claim that (CT) is true:

> **The Ambitious Argument**
>
> 1. History stands in need of explanation.
> 2* (CT) is the only possible explanation of History.
> 3* Everything that stands in need of explanation has an explanation (and explanations must be true).[16]
> 4* Therefore, (CT) is true.

Unfortunately, I think premise 2* is probably false. Premise 3* is a version of what's known as the '**Principle of Sufficient Reason**', a principle that Leibniz said was the core of his philosophy. I do think (some version of) this principle is true, but it's very controversial.[17] Premise 3 doesn't need any defense at all, because Graham already endorses it. Defending 3*, on the other hand, would be an uphill battle, and without 2* (or something similar) it wouldn't do us any good anyway. So I won't try to defend the Ambitious Argument.

We could construct a medium-strength version of the argument, in between the Positive Argument and the Ambitious Argument, like this:

> **The Medium-Strength Argument**
>
> 1. History stands in need of explanation.
> 2** Every possible explanation of History involves the existence of some kind of God/gods.
> 3* Everything that stands in need of explanation has an explanation (and explanations must be true).
> 4** Therefore, some kind of God/gods exist(s).

---

16. The reason for the phrase in parentheses is that in order for the argument to be valid, we need to assume that (CT) cannot explain History unless (CT) is true. This may seem obvious, but—like most things that seem obvious—it has been questioned by philosophers. See Cartwright (1980).
17. Alexander Pruss (2006) has provided a detailed defense of the Principle of Sufficient Reason.

Premise 2** of the Medium-Strength Argument is considerably more plausible than 2* of the Ambitious Argument. However, defending this argument would require us to figure out exactly what it takes for something to count as 'God' or 'a god' and to rule out every possible explanation that doesn't include one of those. Also, we would again have to defend 3*. It's better to have an argument with a more modest conclusion and be able to defend all of the premises than to have an argument for an ambitious conclusion with dubious premises. With this in mind, I'll stick to the Positive Argument and not aim for anything more ambitious.

Should Graham accept the conclusion of the Positive Argument? I would certainly be scoring points in this debate if I convinced Graham that the issue of the explanation of History provides a reason for favoring (CT) *over naturalism*. However, the Positive Argument is even more modest than that: it only says there's a reason in favor of (CT). Graham might try to claim that *the very same reason* favors (his version of) naturalism.[18] For comparison: if taking the bus will get you to class on time, that's a reason for taking the bus. However, if walking will also get you to class on time, then the fact that the bus will get you there on time doesn't help you decide *between* walking and taking the bus: the same reason supports them both. If naturalism also provides a good explanation of History, then looking at explanations of History won't help us decide between (CT) and naturalism.[19]

I do want to defend the stronger claim that these considerations give us reason to favor (CT) over naturalism, so I need to argue that naturalism can't explain History. Accordingly, in addition to my positive argument in favor of (CT), I will be defending a negative argument against naturalism:

---

18. In fact, Graham has made just this claim about some other versions of the cosmological argument, and I have already admitted that he's right about those other versions. See Oppy (2013b; 2013a, 23–37) and Pearce (2017b, 247).
19. It might be that one provides a better explanation than the other, even if both explanations are good. I'll be arguing that this is not the situation. Instead, (CT) provides a good explanation, while naturalism provides no explanation at all.

> **The Negative Argument**
> 1. History stands in need of explanation.
> 2n Naturalism cannot explain History.
> 3n If a worldview cannot explain something that stands in need of explanation, this is a good reason for rejecting that worldview.
> 4n Therefore, there is a good reason for rejecting naturalism.

I've added an 'n' (for 'negative') to these premises so we don't get overloaded with asterisks. The argument is valid, for the same reason as before. Premise 1 is still the same; I'll defend it in a moment. Premise 3n, though stated in negative form, is still a core part of the method of worldview comparison. Graham can't reject it. That leaves 2n as the additional controversial premise. If, therefore, I can defend premises 1 and 2 of the Positive Argument and premise 2n of the Negative Argument, I will have shown that there is a good reason for favoring (CT) over naturalism. In terms of the broader debate over the existence of God, this isn't the end of the game, but it's putting some points on the board.

3.2 History Needs an Explanation (Defense of Premise 1)

The same premise 1 is used in both the Positive Argument and the Negative Argument. This premise states that History (the total sequence of causes and effects) stands in need of explanation. In saying that History stands in need of explanation, I just mean that it makes sense to ask why History is occurring. Remember that we decided not to rely on premise 3* (the Principle of Sufficient Reason), so we are *not* assuming that everything that stands in need of explanation actually has an explanation. It may be that if we keep asking 'why?' we eventually come to a point where all we can say is 'it just is!'

> Facts that stand in need of explanation but don't have explanations are called **brute facts**.

Many philosophers think the fundamental laws of nature and the initial conditions of the universe might be brute facts. According to this kind of view, the goal of fundamental physics is to reduce the unexplained facts of the universe to a really small number of facts—a few basic laws, plus the initial conditions—and then use these few facts to explain everything else. It would still make sense to ask why the universe has these laws or why the universe started out the way it did, but there wouldn't be answers to these questions. Still, even philosophers who believe in brute facts (that is, philosophers who reject the Principle of Sufficient Reason) usually think that theories with fewer brute facts are better than those with more. After all, if brute facts didn't bother us at all, we would never start doing science or philosophy in the first place since we wouldn't feel any need to explain anything.

Does *everything* stand in need of explanation? Perhaps not. According to Shamik Dasgupta (2016, 383–387), there are some facts for which it is a mistake to ask 'why?' at all. He calls these 'autonomous facts'. He suggests that definitions may be examples of autonomous facts.

> An **autonomous fact** is a fact that needs no explanation.

Philosophers distinguish between two types of definitions: *real definitions* and *nominal definitions*.

> A **nominal definition** expresses the meaning of a word.

> A **real definition** tells us what a thing (or kind of thing) *really is*.

Not all philosophers believe in real definitions, but there is good reason to think that we need real definitions not only for philosophy but also for science. For instance, physicists know what the words 'dark matter' mean, but (as of 2020) no one knows what dark matter is. The physicists have a nominal definition, but not a real definition. Similarly, 'water is H_2O' looks like an example of a real definition from science.

Real definitions and nominal definitions both look like good candidates for autonomous facts. It seems to be a mistake to ask 'why is water H_2O?' or 'why are all mothers parents?' That's just what water is, and that's just (part of) what the word 'mother' means.

Someone might try to claim that our question 'why is History happening?' is making this kind of mistake. I defined 'History' as the total sequence of *actually occurring* causes and effects, so of course History is happening!

This points to an ambiguity in the definition of 'History'. 'History' is a name we're giving to the exact, particular sequence of causes and effects that is actually happening. It's not just a generic term for whatever sequence might occur.[20] Our question is: why is this particular causal sequence happening rather than some other causal sequence or none at all? That's not asking about a definition. The fact that History is happening is not autonomous in the way definitions are autonomous. Might there be some other way in which it doesn't stand in need of explanation?

One suggestion is that History might be *self*-explanatory. That is, even if there's some sense in which History can be explained, it might not need anything *outside itself* to explain it.

Why might someone think this? Responding to a similar cosmological argument, David Hume ([1779] 2002, pt. 9) wrote:

> Did I show you the particular causes of each individual in a collection of twenty particles of matter, I should think it very unreasonable, should you afterwards ask me, what was the cause of the whole twenty. This is sufficiently explained in explaining the cause of the parts.

Hume's suggestion, then, is that History stands in no need of any external explanation because each of the particular items within it is adequately explained by another item within History.

How could Hume's "twenty particles of matter" each have an explanation *within* the collection of twenty? Since there are only twenty of them, it seems that the explanations would have to go in a circle. Perhaps particle 1 causes particle 2, which causes particle 3, and so on, until particle 20 causes particle 1. In a case like this, though, it *does* seem appropriate to ask why the twenty particles exist. This is like one of those time-travel stories (e.g. Del Rey 1951) where the protagonist travels back in time to give the time machine to his or her younger self. Stories of this sort leave questions: why is there a time machine *at all*? Who invented it? How did it get built? In the story, the time machine was never invented or built. The time machine exists in the future because it existed in the past, and it existed in the past because it was going to exist in the future. Philosophers have debated whether this kind of case is metaphysically

---

20. In philosophy jargon: 'History' is a rigid designator. See Kripke (1972, 47–48).

possible (see Lewis 1976; Fernandes, forthcoming), but it seems clear that in a case like this there is a 'why' question left unanswered.

Some philosophers have thought that an infinite sequence of explanations would be better than a circle of explanations, so that an eternal universe would not require any explanation outside itself. Those who think this way have sometimes thought that the rise of the Big Bang Theory in modern physics provided some support for the cosmological argument. According to this theory, our universe is not infinitely old but rather has an age of about 14 billion years. This, some have thought, implies that there is some *first event* in History that can only be explained by something *outside* History. That would obviously be good for our argument.

Theism and the Big Bang

The cosmological model that came to be known as the Big Bang Theory was first proposed by the Belgian Catholic priest Georges Lemaître. Lemaître himself, despite his religious convictions, was opposed to the idea that his physical theory could be used to prove the existence of God. Nevertheless, the perceived connection between the Big Bang and theism appears to have been partly responsible for early resistance to the theory. For the history of this debate, see Singh (2004). Adolf Grünbaum (1989) provides an insightful philosophical analysis of the issues.

This line of thought, I am sorry to report, is mistaken on two counts. In the first place, although the Big Bang Theory implies that *our* universe is finite in age, physicists are divided on the question of whether our universe is all of physical reality. Physicists are currently investigating and debating theories that might allow our Big Bang to have a prior physical cause.

Multiverse Theories

Physicists have proposed a variety of *multiverse theories*, or theories according to which there is more to physical reality

> than just our universe. Some of these theories would allow our universe to have a prior physical cause elsewhere in the multiverse. Some kinds of multiverse theory are taken very seriously by physicists, while others are wildly speculative. Brian Greene (2011) provides an accessible survey of the different kinds of multiverse theories and the varying levels of support they enjoy.

In the second place, even if all of physical reality is 14 billion years old, this does not necessarily imply that there was a first event with no physical explanation. It could be, for instance, that the event that happened when the universe was one second old was caused by an event that happened at 1/2 second, which was caused by an event that happened at 1/4 second, caused by an event at 1/8 second, and so on. Since this sequence continues forever without reaching zero, this structure would allow every event to have an earlier cause even if the universe was finite in age. Indeed, some have argued that standard Big Bang models *must* be interpreted this way and are inconsistent with the idea of there being a first event (see Earman 1995, §7.4).

Physics is not going to come to the rescue of our argument.[21] For all we know, the sequence of causes and effects might extend infinitely into the past.

If each element in an infinite sequence is explained by another member of the sequence, does the sequence as a whole stand in need of explanation? In explaining why the answer is 'yes', Leibniz gave an illuminating example. Consider, he said, the book *The Elements of Geometry* by Euclid. Leibniz himself would have learned geometry from this book as a child. By the time Leibniz was learning geometry, students had already been using this same textbook for nearly 2,000 years. So Leibniz's copy of the *Elements* must have been copied from an earlier book, which must have been copied from an earlier book, which must have been copied from an earlier book, and so on through who knows how many copies, back to Euclid

---

21. For a broader critique of attempts to use modern physics to bolster theism, see Carroll (2012).

himself around 300 BCE. Now suppose Euclid didn't really write the book at all. Suppose he copied it from another book that already existed. Imagine that that book too was copied from another copy, which was copied from another copy, and so on *forever*. According to Leibniz ([1697] 1989, 149), in this kind of scenario, even though each copy of the book is explained, there are still major questions left unanswered: "no matter how many books back we go . . . we can always wonder why there have always been such books, why these books were written, and why they were written the way they were."

Part of what this shows is that the infinite case really isn't much different from the circular case: we can explain each individual thing, but when we 'zoom out' and look at the big picture, and we see that the sequence is circular or infinite, this is a new fact that calls out for explanation, and it's not something that can be explained from inside the sequence.

In the case of the infinite causal sequence in finite time, the situation is even worse. Alexander Pruss (2006, §3.1.4) asks us to consider the flight of a cannonball. Let $t = 0$ be the time at which the cannon is fired, and suppose we are trying to explain the cannonball's position at $t = 1$. Using projectile motion equations from basic physics, we could explain this in terms of the cannonball's position and momentum at $t = 1/2$. The cannonball's position and momentum at $t = 1/2$ could be explained by its position and momentum at $t = 1/4$, which could be explained by its position and momentum at $t = 1/8$, and so on. So we can explain the cannonball's position at every time $0 < t \leq 1$, *without ever talking about what happened at $t = 0$*. But it's absurd to suppose that a complete explanation of the cannonball's flight could be given without making reference to the cannon! So even if every item in the sequence is explained, the sequence still stands in need of explanation.

History—the total sequence of causes and effects—either has an uncaused beginning, or it stretches backward infinitely (in finite or infinite time), or it goes in a circle. In any of these cases, it makes sense to wonder why History is as it is. History stands in need of explanation.

3.3 Classical Theism Can Explain History (Defense of Premise 2)

Premise 2 states that (CT) provides a good explanation of History. The main thing we need to do to defend this premise is to spell out how this explanation is supposed to go. This is the task of the present section.

3.3.1 A Grounding Explanation

Many cosmological arguments try to explain the total sequence of *natural* causes and effects by introducing a *super*natural cause to kick things off at the beginning. This approach, however, is subject to three kinds of objections I want to avoid. In the first place, many philosophical theories of causation make use of concepts from physics like time, energy, momentum, or natural laws, and this creates serious difficulties in applying these concepts to God. In the second place, in previous work Graham has argued that, if the theist adopts this approach, then the naturalist can come up with her own naturalistic explanation for the universe by copying the theist's strategy (Oppy 2013b; 2013a, 23–27). For instance, if the theist says that the origination of the universe is caused by a supernatural necessary being (God), the naturalist can just say that the origination of the universe is caused by a natural necessary being—perhaps some kind of necessarily existing initial state. I have previously admitted that this criticism of Graham's is convincing (Pearce 2017b, 247). Third and finally, opponents of these arguments are likely to object that the argument just pushes the problem back a step because the total sequence of *all* causes and effects (what I'm calling 'History') still lacks an explanation: if God's act of creation is causal, then it's part of History and so can't provide a non-circular explanation of History.

Must Causes Be Physical?

Many philosophical theories about causation have the consequence that causation can only happen *within* the physical world. For instance, in his classic and still influential discussion of causation, David Hume ([1739–40] 2010, §§1.3.2 and 1.3.6) argued that a cause must be near its effect in space and prior to its effect in time and that all causes must follow natural regularities (that is, it must be that events of this type are *always* followed by events of that type, in the order of nature). This analysis would require all causes to be located within spacetime. More recently, Tim Maudlin (2007, ch. 5) has argued that causation is intimately connected with laws of nature, in such a way that there could not be causation outside natural laws. Hector-Neri Castañeda (1984) has argued

> that causation must necessarily involve the transfer of energy-momentum. Of course, not all philosophers agree that causes must be physical—indeed, most theistic philosophers do not agree—but versions of the cosmological argument that make God the cause of the origination of the universe become mired in these difficult debates about the nature of causation and its relation to physics.

I do not mean to say that these objections to other cosmological arguments are unanswerable. The proponents of these other arguments are, after all, my allies in the present debate. However, my approach will not be to answer these objections but rather to avoid them entirely. I assume, at least for the sake of argument, that all causes and effects are natural. In other words, I assume that all of History is contained within (physical) spacetime. Recall that, according to my thesis (CT), spacetime and everything it contains exists because of God's choice. History is part of the contents of spacetime, so History itself according to (CT) exists because of God's choice. God's choice itself must not be understood in a causal way, otherwise it would be part of History and our explanation would go in a circle.

We've already seen that not all explanations are causal. I suggest that the explanation involved in (CT) is best understood as a grounding explanation.

> **Grounding** occurs when more fundamental things give rise to less fundamental things.

> **Grounding—Big 'G' or Small 'g'?**
>
> Many theorists of grounding—such as Kit Fine (2001) and Jonathan Schaffer (2009a)—think there is *one* grounding relation that offers deep explanations of lots and lots of metaphysical problems. This has come to be known as 'big "G" Grounding'. Other theorists—such as Kathrin Koslicki (2012) and Jessica Wilson (2014)—are skeptical of this claim. According to these philosophers, there could not possibly be

one theory of grounding because grounding is not just one thing: there is a plethora of different grounding relations. These philosophers reject big 'G' Grounding but accept small 'g' grounding, or as they often prefer to call it, ontological dependence. My talk about grounding aims to be neutral between these two views. I understand grounding as the relation or family of relations whereby less fundamental things arise from more fundamental things.

A standard example of a grounding relation is the relation between a statue and the clay from which it is made. You might think that the statue *just is* the clay, but there's a serious problem with this idea: the clay existed before the statue was made, and if we smash it with a sledgehammer, the statue will be destroyed, but the clay won't. Since the clay existed before the statue did, and could exist after the statue is gone, the clay can't just be the same thing as the statue.

How should we understand the relation of the statue to the clay? On the one hand, we can't say that the statue just is the clay. But on the other hand, the statue is not a separate physical object from the clay. That is, there's no physical stuff in the statue besides the physical stuff that's in the clay. Still, the statue is certainly physical. So we need to say that the statue is *distinct* from the clay—that is, it's not the very same individual object—but it's also not *separate* from the clay. Philosophers often say that the statue is 'nothing over and above' the clay.[22]

I say that the statue is *grounded* in the clay, and that this provides a kind of non-causal explanation of the statue's existence. Why is there a statue? Because the arrangement of the clay corresponds to certain artistic intentions and the community regards the clay in light of these intentions. In other words, the statue exists because of certain physical, historical, and relational features of the clay.

The statue example is a standard one, but it actually touches on some quite complex issues in the philosophy of art. Simpler

---

22. Lynne Rudder Baker (2007) provides detailed analysis of the statue-clay case and other similar cases.

examples of grounding can be given. In response to the question 'why is there a sandwich?' one could give a causal explanation by saying who made the sandwich, but one could also give a grounding explanation by saying 'there's a sandwich because the meat is between the two slices of bread'. The sandwich is grounded in its parts. The arrangement of those parts provides a non-causal explanation of its existence.[23]

Some philosophers are skeptical of grounding (see e.g. Hofweber 2009, 268–273; Daly 2012). However, this is a hard line for a naturalist to take. Consider the existence of *debt*. In Aristophanes' play *The Clouds* (first performed in Athens in 423 BCE), the character Strepsiades hopes that by studying philosophy he can prove that he shouldn't have to pay his debts. This is obviously too good to be true. But debt isn't part of any theory in fundamental physics, nor can it be measured by any physics experiments. Must the naturalist deny the existence of debt unless and until there are debt-meters in physics labs? Certainly not. What the naturalist should say instead is that chemistry is built up from physics, and biology is built up from chemistry, and anthropology (the science of human beings) is built up from biology, and economics is built up from anthropology. Debt is one of the things studied by economics. (This story is, of course, oversimplified.) So the naturalist—taking her cues not just from fundamental physics but from science as a whole—has good reason to believe in debt. But what do we mean by 'built up from' in this story? It is most plausibly seen as something like grounding. The facts about debt (studied by economists) are grounded in facts about human beings (studied by anthropologists), which in turn are grounded in more general facts about living organisms (studied by biologists), and so on. Debt isn't some new thing *in addition to* (over and above) all the physical stuff, but on the other hand it's not identical to any particular physical thing. Economics is *grounded* in physics. Showing how less fundamental sciences are grounded in more fundamental sciences is a type of explanation the naturalist needs to recognize.

A certain kind of hard-nosed naturalist might still be skeptical. 'Of course we're going to keep *acting like* debt exists', this naturalist might say, 'but when we're doing serious metaphysics we have

---

23. I borrow the sandwich example from Fabrice Correia (2008, 1022).

to recognize that it's not a real thing'. Even this type of naturalist, though, will have to say something about biology and such, so there is still reason to endorse grounding. Further, grounding explanation looks like certain kinds of explanation we find within science, as when genes are shown to be grounded in the chemical properties of DNA (see Kitcher 1984b).

Again, a sufficiently hard-nosed naturalist might still be skeptical. Naturalists can't very well reject biology the way some might reject economics, but, they might think, there is no heavy-duty metaphysics involved here. Rather than the metaphysical notion of grounding, they might try to stick with the notion of **reduction**.

Philosophers and scientists use the term 'reduction' to mean a variety of different things, but really only one of these is metaphysically innocent in the way our imagined naturalistic opponent wants. This is the notion of reduction as a kind of *translation*. According to this view, chemistry can be seen as a kind of shorthand that allows us to say in a very short space things that would be very long and complicated to say in the language of physics. Similarly, biology is a shorthand for chemistry and so on.

The trouble with this view is that it's a lot of wishful thinking. No examples of this kind of reduction have been identified in actual science.[24] So the reductionist view (when 'reduction' is understood as translation) is not a view that's based on actually existing science, but a kind of *hope* or *guess* about what science might look like in the future.[25] The grounding view, on the other hand, gives a better account of the relationships between the actual sciences today. For instance, no mainstream biologist thinks there is any special biological stuff (like a 'life force' or something) over and above the physical stuff. All mainstream biologists would agree that the biological facts they study are as they are because of how the basic physical stuff is arranged. So physics can, in some sense, *explain* biology, and the biological stuff is nothing over and above the physical stuff. But that doesn't mean that biology is just shorthand for physics. Biology is its own science with its own subject-matter to study.

---

24. Proponents of the translation model of reduction often cite the reduction of thermodynamics to statistical mechanics as an example. In fact, however, the relation of thermodynamics to statistical mechanics is far more complex than the translation view supposes. See Batterman (2010).
25. For a classic naturalistic critique of the reductionist approach, see Fodor (1974).

Naturalists, who (by definition) think philosophy should take its cues from the best science available—the best *actually* available, and not some guess about future science—have very good reason to accept grounding, and in fact today many naturalistic philosophers do. Those who are skeptical of grounding are usually skeptical because grounding seems rather mysterious. Indeed it does: how can the statue be distinct from the clay if it's nothing over and above the clay? How does the arrangement of the clay explain the statue's existence? Philosophers have, in recent years, been working very hard to clarify these issues.[26] However, even if it is a bit mysterious, it seems like a mystery we're stuck with, since examples of grounding explanations can be found both in everyday life and in science.

My thesis (CT) states that spacetime and all of its contents exist because of the free and rational choice of a necessary being. I now suggest that the explanation indicated by the 'because' is best understood as a grounding explanation. The naturalist, I've argued, should accept grounding explanation as a legitimate variety of explanation. On the specific view I favor, spacetime and everything it contains are grounded in History (the sequence of causes and effects), and History is grounded in God's choice.

As with other instances of grounding, I say here that History is *distinct* from God's choice, and yet *nothing over and above* God's choice.[27] We shouldn't think that God's choosing is like kicking a ball. In this case, your action sets a chain of events going outside you, and once you've set it going you have no more to do but watch. Instead, God's choice is more like a dance. A waltz is grounded in (not caused by) the movements of the dancers, and it continues to exist as long as the dancers keep moving as the dance requires. God chooses that History occurs, and the fact that History does occur is nothing over and above God's choosing. It requires no cooperation from an external world, nor could it, like the ball, keep rolling along apart from God's choosing. It is for this reason that whatever God chooses must necessarily happen (see Pearce 2017a).

If the other examples of grounding I've given are examples of good explanations, it seems that this one is too. At least, an

---

26. For overviews of this discussion, see Correia (2008) and Bliss and Trogdon (2016).
27. For critical discussion of this aspect of my approach (and other similar approaches), see Segal (forthcoming).

opponent who wishes to claim that it's not a good explanation needs to explain how it's different from the other examples.

Additionally, there are two important features that make this explanation attractive: in the first place, because God's choice is hypothesized to be free and rational, the hypothesis can explain how our universe is just one possibility among many, and yet it is not just arbitrary or random that our particular universe exists.[28] In the second place, because God is hypothesized to be a necessary being, this does not just push problems back a step but rather provides, as Leibniz put it, "a sufficient reason where one [can] end the series" of explanations (Leibniz [1714] 1989a, §8).

3.3.2 A Non-necessitating Explanation

We ordinarily think the universe could have been different than it is. For instance, this book didn't have to exist. In fact, the human race and the planet Earth didn't have to exist. Going even further, as we'll see in the next section, there are reasons from within physics for supposing that the basic structure of spacetime could have been different. Almost all theists (including myself) also think the fundamental laws of physics themselves could have been different. However, some naturalists (including Graham; see Oppy 2013b, §1) dispute this, so we won't rely on that assumption here.

The fact that things could have been different creates a puzzle, because many kinds of explanations are *necessitating*. A **necessitating explanation** explains something in such a way as to *require* it to be true, so that it couldn't have been otherwise. For instance, you can explain why the stuff in that glass contains hydrogen by noting that the stuff in that glass is in fact water. If that stuff is water, it *must necessarily* contain hydrogen (otherwise it wouldn't be water), so this is a necessitating explanation.

We want an explanation of History as a whole that is not necessitating. When someone chooses between alternatives on the basis of reasons, the reasons explain the choice. However, if the choice is free, then this explanation is not necessitating: the other alternatives were still, in some sense, open.[29]

---

28. The idea that free and rational choice serves as a kind of mean between the extremes of necessity and arbitrariness is a key theme in Leibniz. See Leibniz ([1710] 2005, §§345–349).
29. For a detailed discussion of this kind of explanation, see Pruss (2006, ch. 7).

The concepts of freedom and of acting for reasons involve numerous difficult philosophical issues that can't really be addressed here. However, these are concepts we use, and need to use, in everyday life, and rejecting these concepts would be a high price to pay for the naturalist. Further, we regularly explain people's actions in terms of their reasons while still thinking other options were possible for them. For instance, in a criminal trial prosecutors typically try to prove that the defendant had a *motive* (that is, a reason) to commit the crime, and this motive is thought to *explain why* the defendant (allegedly) committed the crime, but even if the defendant had a motive, the defendant didn't *have to* commit the crime. Regardless of what particular theories of free will we might endorse, naturalists and theists should agree that the reasons for a free choice provide a non-necessitating explanation of the choice.

> My claim here is about the *logic* of reasons-explanation, not about the metaphysics of free will. In other words, does the success of a reasons-explanation require that the agent's appreciating those reasons metaphysically necessitates the agent's making that choice? Philosophers with a wide range of views on the metaphysics of free will should be able to agree that the answer is 'no': the prosecutor's explanation of the defendant's (alleged) action does not involve a metaphysically necessary connection between the motive and the choice. Further, philosophers with a wide range of views on the metaphysics of free will can agree that just because you have a reason (motive) to do something does not mean you are unable to make a different choice.

The naturalist will no doubt object that, even if we accept this kind of explanation in the ordinary human case, there are special problems about applying this logic to the traditional God. It is part of traditional theism to hold that God is morally perfect. The idea that God is perfectly rational also has some basis in traditional theism, insofar as traditional theists usually believe that God has good reasons for creating this kind of universe, and that God has good reasons for not (yet) putting an end to the suffering in the world. In fact, it seems pretty plausible that no morally perfect being could allow suffering without a very good reason. Of course, most traditional theists would be quick to admit that they are rather baffled as to what these reasons might be. Nevertheless, they might say, because we trust God we believe there must be *some* good reason, even if we can't see it. So the idea that God is perfectly rational—that is, that God never acts without a reason and always does what God has most reason to do—seems pretty plausible from the perspective of traditional theism.

Classical theists typically go further than this, and claim that God is *necessarily* morally perfect and *necessarily* perfectly rational. That is, according to classical theism, it is impossible that God act in a way that is inconsistent with moral or rational perfection. It seems to follow from this that God does not have multiple options but can only choose the best. In other words, we appear to have arrived back at Leibniz's optimism. In fact, matters are even worse than this, since we seem to have arrived at the conclusion that God is not free. If God is not free, then it seems that it makes no sense to thank God. You don't thank someone for a gift if that person has no choice but to give it to you.[30]

This objection seems to me to present the most formidable challenge to the internal coherence of theism. Other difficulties, like the problem of evil, raise questions about whether theism can fit coherently within a broader worldview, but this objection leads us to question whether the traditional concept of God makes sense in the first place.

I have not seen any solution to this problem that seems to me to be fully satisfactory. Nevertheless, I don't think it's time to give up on theism.

In the first place, the concept of freedom itself is extremely murky, and theism doesn't bring along with it a particular theory of freedom. The theist could endorse just about any theory of freedom. Further, since the classical theist thinks that God is radically different from any created being, the classical theist will not think that God is free in precisely the same way that a human being can be free. Rather, God is free in some greater, higher way. What this implies is that my little sketch of the objection above is radically oversimplified. Before we could begin to evaluate the objection, we

---

30. William Rowe (2004) has given a forceful presentation of this objection, together with a critical examination of several theistic replies.

would need to say a lot more about how we understand divine freedom, divine moral perfection, and so on. There are theories of divine freedom, moral perfection, and so forth that avoid these consequences.[31] Although I've admitted that these theories don't seem to me to be *fully* satisfactory, nevertheless they save theism from internal contradiction. Additionally, the fact that these theories exist gives reason to hope that philosophers will be able to continue to improve on them. In other words, although the problem is very difficult, it seems to me that struggling with the objection is a productive endeavor and not a hopeless waste of time.

In the second place, there is room to question just how strong a notion of possibility we really need. I am sometimes tempted to think (in my most Leibnizian moments) that it's enough that God considered several options, chose between them on the basis of reasons, and no matter which one God chose that one would have become actual (see Leibniz [1710] 2005, §45). If someone claims that God couldn't *really* choose the other options, maybe we shouldn't be so worried. It's not like something outside God is *forcing* God to choose a certain way, and it's not like God is overcome by some kind of irrational desire to choose against God's better judgment. If God can't choose otherwise, it's just because of God's deep-seated commitment to the good. These kinds of commitments don't take away freedom (see Pearce and Pruss 2012, 409–412).

The deeper problem with this strategy, though, is that we seem to be running headlong into Leibniz's optimism, his implausible insistence that this is the best of all possible worlds. This second approach, then, is not fully satisfactory, but perhaps these reflections on the nature of divine freedom could be combined with the first approach to yield a theory that provides some plausible explanation of how God might choose a world like this one.

Third and finally, although classical theists have usually held that God is necessarily morally and rationally perfect, this is not actually included in my thesis (CT), and the argument from (CT) to this traditional conclusion is complex and contains disputable steps. So, at least for purposes of the present debate, even if I had to admit that the necessary being mentioned in (CT) was not necessarily morally and rationally perfect, this would not undermine my argument for

---

31. See above, note 12.

the claim that *some kind of God or other* exists. If the being in question acts freely on the basis of reasons—whether the being acts *perfectly* or not—that will suffice for my argument.

I conclude, then, that the problem of divine freedom is a serious one but should not, at least at this point, be regarded as fatal to my thesis (CT). More work is needed to describe the kind of freedom and rationality mentioned in (CT), and it will be difficult to hit on precisely the right notions. Our general idea, though, is that we can explain History in something like the way we explain human actions by appeal to reasons for action. This hypothesis has not, at this stage, been *shown* to be incoherent.

3.3.3 An Ultimate Explanation

Finally, I return to necessary existence. According to Leibniz ([1714] 1989a, §8), God is "a necessary being, carrying the reason of its existence with itself," and it is for this reason that theism provides a uniquely satisfying ultimate explanation of the universe, "a sufficient reason where one [can] end the series" of explanations. I said above that I would not be using the **Principle of Sufficient Reason**—which states that everything that stands in need of explanation has an explanation—as a premise in my argument. However, we also saw that Graham is committed to the view that the fewer brute facts a worldview has, the better. Many classical theists, including Leibniz, have thought that a worldview that includes a necessarily existing God is capable of reducing the number of brute facts to *zero*.

So far we've seen that History can be seen as grounded in God's choice, and God's choice can be explained by God's reasons. The remaining question is: why was there a God, faced with such a choice and aware of such reasons, in the first place? If we could show that the existence of God was an autonomous fact (a fact that did not stand in need of explanation), or that it followed from such a fact, then perhaps we really could reduce the number of brute facts to zero.

In §3.1, I suggested that definitions were the best candidates for autonomous facts. In §2.3, I rejected Anselm's suggestion that atheism must rest on some kind of confusion about the meaning of the word 'God'. However, if Anselm were correct, then the existence of God would follow from an autonomous fact (the meaning of the word 'God'), so perhaps we'd better take a closer look at his argument.

Anselm's basic idea is to define God as "something than which nothing greater can be thought" (Anselm, *Proslogion*, ch. 2). Now, if some atheist is thinking to herself *there is no God*, then that atheist is having a thought about God—the thought that God does not exist. Since that thought is about God, Anselm thinks, we can say that God exists in the atheist's mind. This is not (yet) to say that God *really* exists. When you imagine an ice cream cone on a hot day, Anselm would say, an (imaginary) ice cream cone exists in your mind. In the same way, God exists in the atheist's mind. But here's the thing: you don't want an *imaginary* ice cream cone, you want a *real* one, because a real ice cream cone is *better* than an imaginary one. The atheist claims that God exists *only* in the mind and not also in reality, or, in other words, that God is only imaginary. However, Anselm says, a real God, like a real ice cream cone, is better than an imaginary one! So if the atheist thinks that something than which nothing greater can be thought is purely imaginary, then the atheist is confused. We can think of a real God, and the real God we think of is greater than the purely imaginary one the atheist thinks of. Therefore, God (something than which nothing greater can be thought) exists in reality and not only in the mind.

Imaginary Existence?

Is Anselm right to say that the atheist must admit that God exists at least in the imagination? At least one present-day atheist philosopher thinks so: according to Jonathan Schaffer (2009a, 359), atheism is not best understood as the thesis that God does not exist *at all*, but rather as the thesis that God is (just) a fictional character, like Sherlock Holmes or Harry Potter. But do fictional characters exist? Many philosophers, including Schaffer, think so. After all, Sherlock Holmes is a fictional detective, and Harry Potter is a fictional wizard. How could they have these properties if they didn't exist at all? Other philosophers disagree. After all, our parents explained to us when we were young that the people in those storybooks don't (really) exist, and our parents were certainly right about this. Stacie Friend (2007) provides an overview of this debate.

Anselm set out to show that the atheist was confused, but in fact this argument has confused pretty much everyone. Even many theists have thought there was something fishy going on here. Very shortly after Anselm came up with this argument, his fellow monk Gaunilo (*Reply on Behalf of the Fool*, §6) pointed out that if we define the Lost Island as "an island than which no greater island can be thought," we appear to be able to run exactly the same argument. But it would be absurd to go looking for the Lost Island on this basis.

> You might be wondering why Gaunilo's book is called *Reply on Behalf of the Fool*. When Anselm and Gaunilo were writing, in the eleventh century, a person who openly admitted to being an atheist would face serious social and legal consequences. Many people thought the existence of God was so obvious that there couldn't really be any atheists at all. If there aren't any atheists around to argue with, why present an argument for the existence of God? With this in mind, Anselm begins his discussion by quoting a Bible verse: "The fool says in his heart, 'There is no God'" (Psalm 14:1, English Standard Version). So, according to the Bible, there really are atheists after all. Anselm's question, then, is can we use reason to prove that atheism is 'foolish', as the psalmist says? Anselm claims that his ontological argument does this. Gaunilo is not convinced and produces an argument to show that this so-called 'fool' is not so foolish as Anselm supposes!

So where does Anselm's argument go wrong?[32] Anselm's argument for God and Gaunilo's argument for the Lost Island each begin with a definition. What kind of definitions are these? We have previously distinguished real definitions from nominal definitions, but either option causes problems for the argument. In the first place, suppose it's a nominal definition. Nominal definitions are arbitrary, so the

---

32. I focus here just on the opening definition in Anselm's argument because that's the only part that will turn out to be relevant to the argument I finally endorse below. However, many other objections can be raised against Anselm's argument. For a more thorough critique of ontological arguments, see Oppy (1995).

atheist can't object to Anselm's definition of 'God'—but then, neither can Anselm object to Gaunilo's definition of 'the Lost Island'! So, assuming that the Lost Island does not exist, the argument must go wrong somewhere.

One line of thought is that nominal definitions only tell us the criteria for giving something a certain name. So if we say 'the word "triangle" means a three-sided polygon', we're just saying that nothing counts as a triangle unless it's a three-sided polygon. But if this is right, then the nominal definition version of the argument should really be seen as only talking about what it takes for something to count as God. The conclusion should be understood as holding only that *nothing counts as God unless that thing exists*. This conclusion, however, is not very interesting because nothing counts as a triangle or a tree or a unicorn unless that thing exists. This doesn't tell us whether triangles or trees or unicorns exist.[33]

Suppose, then, that the argument starts with a real definition. That is, suppose it's meant to tell us *what God really is*, and not just what we mean by the word 'God'. A real definition, unlike a nominal definition, can't just be arbitrarily made up: it's supposed to express a real fact about the world. This gives Anselm some ammunition against Gaunilo, but at the same time it gives the atheist some ammunition against Anselm. In the first place, we might say that only things that actually exist have real definitions, and God exists while the Lost Island does not. This, however, makes Anselm's argument completely useless against the atheist, since it would already assume that God exists in the very first premise, and wouldn't give the atheist any reason to accept that claim. As a second try, we might claim that only *possible* things have real definitions, and God is possible while the Lost Island is impossible.

This second line of thought is considerably more plausible. Adopting this line is unlikely to make Anselm's argument actually convincing to the atheist, but unlike the previous versions of the argument it is also not completely useless against the atheist. The atheist might have thought she could make the more modest claim that it just so happens that there's no God, but in fact (given

---

33. This line of objection is associated with Kant. For discussion, see Van Cleve (1999, §12D).

Anselm's conception of God), she must make the more ambitious claim that it is impossible for there to be a God. On the other hand, this cuts both ways: the theist might have thought he could make the modest claim that there just happens to be a God, but in fact (given Anselm's conception of God), he must make the more ambitious claim that it is necessary that there is a God. This is like a pawn swap in a chess game: it's not clear whether either side has gained an advantage, but the game has moved forward and the strategies each side needs to adopt have become clearer.

Once we've interpreted Anselm's definition as a real definition, we face another problem. It's far from clear what the real definition of God might be. There are many competing possibilities, and some of these conflict with one another. Further, classical theists have uniformly denied that we finite, mortal humans can understand what God is like in Godself in the way we would need to in order to know the real definition of God. God is a transcendent reality that infinitely exceeds our mental capacities. What this means is that God, just by knowing God's own nature, would be able to see that God must necessarily exist, but we humans lack this kind of insight.[34]

Fortunately, our friend Leibniz is prepared to come to our rescue yet again. Leibniz was a pioneer of the **modal ontological argument**, an alternative version of the argument that avoids most of Anselm's problems (see Leibniz [1684] 1989, 25).[35] This version of the argument gets its name from its use of **modal operators**, which is what logicians call words like 'possibly' and 'necessarily'. The argument goes like this:

The Modal Ontological Argument

1. Possibly, God exists.
2. Necessarily, if God exists, then necessarily God exists.
3. Therefore, God exists.

---

34. According to Thomas Aquinas (*Summa Theologiae*, Part 1, Question 2, Article 1), this is the fundamental flaw in Anselm's argument.
35. The argument has been much discussed in recent philosophy due to the influential work of Alvin Plantinga (1977, 85–112).

There is some dispute about the correct logical rules for the use of modal operators, but most philosophers today accept that this argument is valid. Here's why. Philosophers often think of possibility and necessity in terms of possible worlds.

> A **possible world** is a *complete* way things could be. For every question about the past, present, and future, each possible world has its own answer.

For instance, there are 'nearby' possible worlds at which various teams won the 2019 Women's World Cup: there are England worlds and Sweden worlds and China worlds, and so on. Further out, there are worlds at which Bhutan won, although in the actual world Bhutan did not field a team. Further out still, there are worlds at which Yugoslavia won, although in the actual world Yugoslavia did not exist in 2019. And so on. We say something is possible if there's *at least one* possible world (way things could be) where it's true. We say something is necessary if it's true in *every* possible world. In other words, a necessary claim is one that would be true no matter what. For every way things could possibly be, the necessary truths stay true.

Now consider the modal ontological argument. According to premise 1, there is at least one world—call it W—where it is true that God exists. This isn't saying that there's actually a place 'out there' where God exists, but only that God existing is a way things could be. However, according to premise 2, necessarily, if God exists then necessarily God exists. In other words, every world where God exists is a world where God necessarily exists. Now, W is such a world. So it's true in W that God exists in every possible world. But one of those possible worlds is the actual world. So God exists in the actual world, which is just to say that God exists.

Here's another way of thinking about what happens in the argument. We're here in one world, looking out at all the ways things could be and (according to premise 1) we can 'see' a world, W, where God exists. Now, according to premise 2, every world that can be 'seen' from W must *also* be a world where God exists. But if we can 'see' them, then they can also 'see' us. Our world is possible from the perspective of W, but every world possible from the perspective of W is a world where God exists, so God exists in our world. (Don't forget: all this talk about 'seeing' and 'perspective' is just a metaphor. Possible worlds aren't real places; they're ways things could be.)

> **Modal Logic**
>
> Modal logic is the study of the rules of reasoning with modal operators. The most widely accepted system of modal logic today is known as 'S5'. The characteristic axiom of S5—the axiom that distinguishes it from other systems—states that whatever is possible is necessarily possible. The leading competitor to S5 is S4. The system S4 replaces S5's characteristic axiom with a weaker axiom, which states that whatever is necessary is necessarily necessary.
>
> The version of the modal ontological argument we've been discussing is valid in S5 but invalid in S4. The reason it is invalid in S4 is that S4 allows what's possible to vary from one world to another. What the premises of the argument tell us is that there is a world W where God exists and *in that world* it's true that God exists necessarily. This means that every world that's possible *according to* W is a world where God exists. But S4 does not allow us to assume that the actual world is one of the worlds possible according to W. As a result, S4 will not allow us to conclude that God exists in the actual world.
>
> The details of the dispute about the axioms of modal logic are complex and highly technical. James Garson (2018) provides a good overview of the debate and a statement of the axioms of the various competing systems. Pruss and Rasmussen (2018, ch. 2) make the case for S5 as the correct logic for metaphysical possibility and necessity. Graham and I both agree with the majority of philosophers today in endorsing S5.

This argument isn't likely to convince any atheists because, as we saw above, they are likely to reject its first premise. But remember that what started us off on this discussion of ontological arguments was the question of whether the existence of God might be an autonomous fact, or be immediately explained by some autonomous fact. Regardless of whether the atheist is convinced by the modal ontological argument, we can now see how this explanation can go. Whether or not Anselm is right about the real definition of God, it might well be the case that necessary existence is included in or follows from God's real definition. This would certainly support premise 2 of the modal ontological argument and, depending on our theory of real definitions, it might also support premise 1.

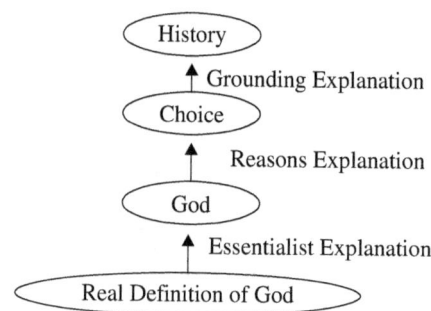

Real definitions are autonomous facts. So God's real definition would be an autonomous fact and the modal ontological argument would show us how that autonomous fact explains God's existence. Similarly, we might think that God's real definition explains why God is a free and rational being faced with a certain choice. Even if we don't know God's real definition, we have good reason to hypothesize that it has these features because this will enable it to do the theoretical work that it needs to do. The modal ontological argument might not persuade any atheists, but it does show how the existence of God can be explained by an autonomous fact, namely, the real definition of God.

The overall structure of the explanation contained in (CT), then, includes several stages: History is explained by God's choice; God's choice is explained by God's reasons; God's existing and having those reasons is explained by God's real definition; God's real definition is an autonomous fact. Voilà! No brute facts.

3.3.4 Conclusion

I conclude, then, that (CT) provides an explanation of History. This explanation is especially appealing insofar as it makes possible the elimination of brute facts while still allowing that the world could have been otherwise.

How should the atheist respond? Recall from §3.1 that the atheist could just accept premise 2 of the Positive Argument. In the first place, the atheist could reject premise 1 instead, though I already offered some defense of that premise. In the second place, the atheist could reject premise 2n of the Negative Argument, and so hold that although this is a point in favor of theism, it's not a point that favors theism *over naturalism*. In the third place, the atheist could admit that I've put some points on the board with these arguments and hope to get even at a later stage in the debate.

Supposing that the atheist does want to attack premise 2, there are several issues left open. One issue is the very coherence of God choosing (perfectly) freely yet (perfectly) rationally. Another is the question of what God's reasons for creating this world *actually are*. This question is particularly difficult in light of the fact that this does not appear to be the best of all possible worlds, and it seems that God should have had lots of reasons *against* creating this particular world. Additionally, we have admitted that we don't know the real definition of God and are just constructing a hypothesis about what that real definition must be like in order to explain what needs to be explained. Finally, some atheists might challenge the broader metaphysical framework in which this explanation takes place, including our assumptions about grounding and real definitions and so forth.

Nevertheless, I have shown in this section that *within a particular theistic worldview* (one that includes grounding and real definitions and such), it is possible that History be explained in such a way as to leave no residue of brute facts. Further, the structures of explanation I've used are not introduced for the special case of God but rather are kinds of explanation used within the natural world. I've argued that the naturalist needs these patterns of explanation just as much as the theist does. While I have not been able to spell out all the details of my explanation of History, I have shown what the general strategy of the explanation would look like. This provides us with excellent reason to accept premise 2 of the Positive Argument.

3.4 Naturalism Can't Explain History (Defense of Premise 2n)

Even if the naturalist admits that (CT) provides an explanation of History, she is likely to think that it does so at extravagant cost. Remember that explanatory comprehensiveness is not the only value at work in worldview comparison. Worldviews are also to be preferred to the extent that they are simpler. The theistic worldview I've described accepts the existence of a supernatural being who is utterly unlike anything in the natural world. It's reasonable to ask: is this really the price we have to pay to explain History?

The answer is 'yes'. Here's why.

Any explanation of History must be a non-causal, non-necessitating explanation. It must be non-causal because all causes are part of History and so a causal explanation of History would be circular. It must be non-necessitating because the causal history of the universe could have had a totally different structure from our actual History.

We've already discussed a few kinds of non-causal explanations. I argued that naturalists should accept certain kinds of grounding explanations, for instance. Most philosophers think that grounding explanations necessitate: necessarily if the clay is shaped this way with these intentions and regarded as such by the art world, then a statue exists. This certainly seems to be the case in the key examples that motivate naturalists to accept grounding: if the physical facts are such and such, then *necessarily* the biological facts are thus and so. Grounding, therefore, doesn't look like a very promising strategy for a non-necessitating naturalistic explanation of History.[36]

Some philosophers have tried to come up with *statistical* explanations of why there is something rather than nothing: there are infinitely many ways for there to be something, but there's only one way for there to be nothing, so the **probability** that there would be nothing at all is infinitesimally small (van Inwagen 1996). There are, however, very serious technical and mathematical problems with this kind of approach.[37] Additionally, statistical explanations typically presuppose a background of observed patterns and natural laws, which is lacking here (Kotzen 2013). As a result, this is a problematic kind of explanation that is not actually as similar to established science as the naturalist might like.

Perhaps the naturalist might think she doesn't need a non-necessitating explanation of *all* of History. Perhaps she can allow that at least some parts of our actual History *are* necessary. From here, the naturalist could use the indeterministic causation in quantum physics to avoid the conclusion that *all* of History is necessary.

---

36. Even those philosophers who deny that grounding necessitates generally admit that the totality of fundamental facts necessitates the totality of non-fundamental facts. This (weak) kind of contingentism about grounding is no help to the naturalist. See e.g. Leuenberger (2014) and Skiles (2015).
37. For just a few of the technical difficulties involved in assigning probabilities to possible worlds, see Lewis (1986, 118–123).

This, in fact, is the course Graham has taken in previous work. According to the view Graham calls 'my favorite theory of **modality**', possibility is based on objective chance.

> **Objective chances** are the probabilities that exist in the laws of physics, like the probabilistic outcomes that occur in quantum mechanics.

According to Graham, all possible worlds are "alternative ways that the actual world could have gone, could go, or could one day go" (Oppy 2013b, 47). As Graham explicitly notes, this means that all possible worlds share the laws of the actual world and share some initial portion of the actual world.

This does allow Graham to construct an ultimate explanation that looks at least a bit similar to mine above. Graham can hold that there is an initial state of the universe that is necessary, and the first event in History (the first instance of causation) is some chancy event that leads to the development of the universe as we know it.

Suppose we ask, why does History have the structure it does? That is, why does it start out from a chancy first event, leading outward to other chancy events, and so forth? Graham will answer, it *had to* have this structure. This was, according to Graham, the only possible structure.

Why did it have to have this structure? Graham doesn't give much of an answer to that question. Then again, someone might think I haven't given much answer to the question of why God had to exist. I've given some account of divine necessity, but I've admitted that we don't have the kind of understanding of the real definition of God that would allow us to see why God has to exist.

The central problem for Graham's insistence on the necessity of the initial conditions of the physical world is that it breaks the rules of his naturalism by failing to treat 'well-established science' with due seriousness.

One of the fundamental theories in current physics is **general relativity**. This theory describes the nature and behavior of spacetime. Spacetime, according to this theory, is not an inert container for matter. Spacetime is itself an entity that interacts with material objects (Maudlin 1993). In particular, spacetime *bends* in the presence of mass. This bending affects the motion of objects within spacetime, which is the origin of what we call 'gravity'.

The equations that describe the bending of spacetime are called **Einstein's Field Equations**. A solution to these equations describes a possible way spacetime and mass could be in some region. A *global* solution describes a possible shape for the totality of spacetime.

Some solutions to Einstein's Field Equations are very strange. For instance, there are some solutions that say that if you went on a trip in a spaceship that followed just the right path, you could arrive back home *before* you left. (Time travel! See Maudlin 2012, 155–165.) The mathematician Kurt Gödel was the first to discover the existence of such solutions. His solution is in fact so bizarre that "our [ordinary] notions of 'past', 'present', and 'future' break down" (Malament 1984, 91).

Our universe looks pretty well-behaved, as far as we can tell, so there's good reason to suppose that the solution to Einstein's Field Equations that describes *our* universe is one of the boring ones and not one of these exotic ones. Still, in the several decades since these strange solutions were discovered, physicists and philosophers of physics have debated the question, do these solutions have physical significance? That is, do the laws of physics really permit the world to be this way? In particular, there has been a vigorous debate about whether the kind of backward time-travel scenario I mentioned is really physically possible (for an overview, see Arntzenius and Maudlin 2013). A background assumption of these debates is that *most* solutions to Einstein's Field Equations—the non-bizarre solutions—*do* describe physical possibilities.[38] If, then, we're taking our cues from current, well-established science, we should endorse the following principle: any solution to Einstein's Field Equations should be assumed to describe a physical possibility unless there are compelling reasons to the contrary.

One class of global solutions to Einstein's Field Equations has the universe beginning as a tiny point and expanding outward from that point, growing larger and larger forever. Physicists today believe that one of these solutions describes our universe. There are also solutions in which gravity eventually overcomes the universe's expansion and the universe starts shrinking, so that after starting

---

38. For a historical and philosophical account of debates about which solutions to Einstein's Field Equations should be regarded as representing real physical possibilities, see Earman (1995). Earman's account is now a bit dated (it was written before the discovery of dark energy) but continues to be useful.

with a Big Bang it ends with a Big Crunch, compressed back into that tiny point again. These Big Bang/Big Crunch models could go in cycles: the universe could expand and contract again and again and again, perhaps from eternity and to eternity. Finally, there are 'static' solutions—which Einstein himself initially favored (Singh 2004, 146–149)—on which the universe does not expand or contract at all. A static universe would not have a beginning or an end.

Graham's 'favorite theory of modality' implies that if the universe has a beginning, then it *necessarily* has a beginning. If current theories in physics are correct that the actual universe started from a Big Bang then, Graham's theory implies, the universe *had to* start this way. Therefore, on Graham's theory, the eternal Bang/Crunch solutions and the static solutions do not describe ways the world could be. The reasons for this are not found within physics but within metaphysics: these solutions are being ruled out by Graham's theory of modality. Contrary to his stated naturalistic position, Graham the philosopher is telling the physicists how to conduct their business.

If we are to respect the idea that all of these solutions to Einstein's Field Equations describe physical possibilities, then we need to hold that it is physically possible for the total sequence of causes and effects either to have a beginning or not. Graham's attempt to provide a naturalistic explanation of History violates this constraint.

Any explanation of History that respects current physics must be a non-necessitating explanation. Any explanation of History that is non-circular must be a non-causal explanation. Naturalism cannot provide any form of explanation that fits the bill.

3.5 Conclusion

In this section I've argued that History—the total sequence of causes and effects—stands in need of explanation. However, such an explanation could not just be a first cause that got History started. The explanation must be both non-causal and non-necessitating. My hypothesis (CT) provides such an explanation, but no such explanation is available on naturalism. This provides a good reason for favoring theism over naturalism.

It is frequently the case in worldview comparison that we have to trade off **simplicity** against explanatory comprehensiveness. (CT) introduces a supernatural being totally unlike anything in the natural world in order to achieve a comprehensive explanation of the natural world as a whole. The introduction of such a being might be thought to be a massive increase in the complexity of our worldview. Is it worth it?

Many philosophers would say 'no'. After all, most naturalists (though not Graham) are happy to admit that there must be a few brute facts left over at the end of the day. Leaving a small number of brute facts, they might say, is better than going off on metaphysical flights of fancy.

How high is the price here, in terms of simplicity, really? Although God must be totally unlike beings in the natural world, the kinds of explanation used in (CT) do have examples in the natural world. Recall that I said in §3.3 that God's choice explains History in the way the arrangement of bread and meat explains the existence of a sandwich, and God's choice is in turn explained by God's reasons in the way our free choices are explained by our reasons. It is true that the being who figures into these explanations is rather exotic, but the patterns of explanation themselves are ones we need to accept in everyday life. Further, as we have seen, there are good reasons why no being of an ordinary, mundane sort could do the kind of explanatory work we need here.

The naturalist might complain, however, that even if the theist is not introducing new kinds of explanation, the theist is introducing another kind of complexity. According to the naturalist, there is only one kind of fundamental stuff, physical stuff. God, however, is not physical, so the theist has fundamental physical stuff *plus God*, which is extra complexity.

This, however, is a mistake. According to the version of classical theism I've developed, the physical is grounded in God who is the only truly fundamental entity. So at the most fundamental level, this view not only has only one *kind* of thing, it has only one individual thing, namely, God. If the naturalist objects that I have introduced a new layer in the grounding hierarchy, this is quite correct, but when we introduce a more fundamental layer of reality that unifies and explains the layers to which we were already committed, this is not an increase in complexity. As a result, it is actually not clear that the naturalist has any advantage in simplicity at all.

I conclude, then, that classical theism has a significant advantage over naturalism with respect to explanatory comprehensiveness at little, if any, cost to simplicity. Thus, we can say at least this much: if (some version of) naturalism is among the best worldviews so far constructed by philosophers, then (some version of) classical theism is also among the best worldviews. That's certainly enough to show that God is not at all like Russell's orbital teapot.

> In this section, I have defended a version of the cosmological argument from contingency in favor of classical theism. The argument contends that classical theism provides a good explanation of the totality of causal reality, while competing naturalistic views are unable to provide such an explanation.

4 Classical Theism and Religious Belief

Most people who believe in God do not do so because of a metaphysical argument like the one we considered in the last section. Rather, most theists believe in God as part of a religious commitment. In this section, I argue that these kinds of religious commitments can also be rational and, furthermore, that consideration of the nature and origin of religious commitment can strengthen the case so far made for the existence of God.

One might expect that the central question of philosophy of religion would be "what is religion?" However, while this very difficult question has been given a great deal of attention in other academic disciplines such as anthropology, sociology, and political science (see e.g. Platvoet 1990; Schilbrack 2013; Allen and Allen 2016), it has not been a major focus in recent philosophy of religion. Instead, philosophers have mainly focused on critical examination of particular teachings of particular religions (especially Christianity). This state of affairs is unfortunate, not only because there are many interesting philosophical questions about the nature of religion, but also because the relevance to religion of the kind of metaphysical theorizing I've been doing so far can be, and has been, called into question (see e.g. Cahn 1969). For instance, one could very easily wonder, how could all this metaphysics give me a reason to attend church this week? How could it motivate me to love my neighbors?

This debate is about whether God exists, not about whether to go to church. Nevertheless, I do think it is useful to address religion here because I think that religion can provide an alternative path to rational belief in God, and that religious theism and metaphysical theism can stand in a relation of mutual support. In other words, these two kinds of belief together are stronger (rationally speaking) than either of them taken alone.

4.1 Religion, Religious Belief, and Religious Experience

Religion is such a complex and diverse phenomenon that it is probably not possible to give a definition that would apply to every form of religion. When trying to understand a phenomenon like this, an alternative to giving a definition is to examine some paradigm cases. There is a particular family of paradigm cases that are of particular interest to the present debate: the religions that are based around belief in God. Giving an account of monotheistic religion is an easier task than giving an account of religion in general, because there is more similarity among the monotheistic religions than there is among religions in general.

The monotheistic religions are selected because they are most relevant to the present debate and *not* because they are somehow 'more religious' than the other religions (whatever precisely that would mean). We should therefore be careful not to overgeneralize from the monotheistic case: the things that most or all monotheistic religions have in common will not necessarily be common to most or all religions.

My account of monotheistic religion begins from a conception of **religious experience**. Like religion, religious experience is quite diverse and varied, and it is difficult to give a general account. For now, we'll focus on what I will call 'monotheistic religious experience', or 'MRE' for short.

> **Monotheistic religious experience (MRE)** is any experience that is interpreted as experience of God.

Just as monotheistic religion is one kind of religion, so also MRE is one kind of religious experience. Again, we want to be careful not to overgeneralize. What we are interested in here is the general sort (or sorts) of experiences that people within monotheistic traditions usually interpret as experiences of God. As we will discuss below, it seems likely that people who do not belong to monotheistic traditions may have similar experiences (or even the very same experiences) and interpret them differently.

Two things should be noted about my definition of 'MRE', as compared to how philosophers normally use the phrase 'religious experience'. In the first place, MRE is, by definition, interpreted as experience of God. The capital 'G' is intentional. MRE is *mono*theistic—that is, MRE (by definition) is interpreted as experience of the one and only God. However, we should not understand this too narrowly. People have all sorts of different beliefs about what God is like, and they interpret their experience in light of these beliefs. MRE includes all of these different experiences, including those that are interpreted in terms of conceptions of God very different from the one I've been defending.

The second thing that should be noted about this definition is that MRE is not restricted to ineffable inner feelings. Philosophers often distinguish religious experience from experience or evidence of (alleged) miracles. They often assume that religious experience must be purely internal, while a miracle must be some kind of publicly observable event (see e.g. Oppy 2006a, §§7.2 and 7.4; 2013a, 35–38, 59–62). However, whether an experience is internal or external, there is still a process of *interpretation* involved in seeing this experience as an experience of God. In what follows, I will be arguing that this process of interpretation raises similar issues in both cases, so I will treat observation of events interpreted as miracles performed by God as a kind of MRE.

Note further that, on this account, MREs need not be in any way extraordinary. For instance, as a Christian I believe that I hear God speak when I read the Bible, I believe that I am joined to Christ and to the Christian community when I receive the bread and wine in the communion ritual, and I believe that I meet with God when I pray. I am committed to interpreting these experiences as experiences of God *whether or not anything extraordinary happens*. Sometimes I have a profound emotional response, but more often I don't. Nevertheless, I *interpret* these events as experiences of God. I think many believers in many different religious traditions probably want to say something similar.

These ordinary events, though quite important to Christian spirituality, don't count for much when it comes to providing rational support for Christian belief. The reason I interpret these as experiences of God is because of the beliefs about God I already hold. If religious experience is to bear any evidential weight, much of the weight will have to be borne by the extraordinary experiences. Note in this connection that, according to Christianity, the Bible is not only a means by which people experience God today, but also a record of the most important experiences of God that humans have had in the past. Christians regularly share with one another reports (what many Christian communities call 'testimonies') of experiences of God, both ordinary and extraordinary. The extraordinary experiences, past and present, provide the basis for interpreting the ordinary experiences as experiences of God.

An analogy might help. Modern physics tells us that all material objects are ultimately composed of quarks and electrons. Because I have learned this from the physicists, I am able to recognize that as I'm typing on this computer, as I'm sitting in this chair, as I'm resting my arms on this desk, I am having an experience of quarks and electrons. However, if it weren't for certain extraordinary experiences had by physicists—that is, if they hadn't rigged up very complicated experiments and seen certain unusual outcomes—I would never interpret my experience in this way. Furthermore, my experience doesn't provide much evidence for the existence of quarks and electrons. The physicists are able to explain how the quarks and electrons are built up into computers and desks and chairs, and since the theory successfully accounts for the behavior of these objects my ordinary experience might provide some degree of support for it—to the physicist. But, in the first place, *I* know very little about how all of this works, so for me this doesn't really provide evidence of quarks and electrons at all. In the second place, even the physicists would never have arrived at this theory on the basis of ordinary experience alone, without sophisticated experiments. Nevertheless, it is perfectly reasonable for me to interpret my experience in terms of this theory.

This analogy with science suggests something else: perhaps not every believer needs to have extraordinary experiences. Perhaps it is enough to put one's trust in a religious community where some extraordinary experiences have served to shape the interpretation of ordinary experiences.

We can now define **monotheistic religious belief** as belief based on MRE—either one's own MRE, the testimony of the MRE of others, or some combination of the two. We have seen that, in such a picture, extraordinary MRE will play an important role, but a large part of its role is to establish a practice of interpreting experience—even ordinary experience—as experience of God. Such a practice will be embedded in what Ludwig Wittgenstein ([1953]

2009, §23) called a **form of life**.³⁹ That is, this practice of interpreting our experiences as experiences of God will be tied to many other practices that shape our words, beliefs, feelings, and actions. It will involve not just believing that God exists, but seeing ourselves as related to God and to one another in a certain way. I use the term **monotheistic religion** to refer to this kind of embedding of MRE within a form of life.

> Monotheistic religious experience (MRE): anything that is interpreted as experience of God.
> Monotheistic religious belief: belief based on MRE or testimony of MRE.
> **Monotheistic religion**: the embedding of MRE within a form of life.

While I am not attempting to give a general account of religious experience, I do assume that the monotheistic version represents an important class of paradigm cases. I therefore assume that other kinds of religious experience will resemble the monotheistic kind to a greater or lesser degree. The exact kind and degree of resemblance will, of course, be different in different cases. The same goes for religion and religious belief.

Among the definitions of 'religion' from scholars outside philosophy that I mentioned earlier, my definition is most similar to the one given by the theologian and anthropologist Jan Platvoet. Platvoet (1990, 195) defines 'religion' as "behavior which believers interpret as communication, direct or indirect, between themselves and beings whose existence and activity cannot be verified or falsified but whom the believers believe to exist and to be active, directly and indirectly." However, Platvoet's talk of verification and falsification suggests that he sees a sharp distinction between 'falsifiable' science and

---

39. I do not mean to endorse or incorporate any more of Wittgenstein or Wittgensteinianism than the aspects I discuss in the text. For a more robustly Wittgensteinian approach to religion, see Phillips (1986). For another approach that combines Wittgensteinian elements with classical theism, see Hewitt (forthcoming).

> 'unfalsifiable' religion. Most philosophers of science and philosophers of religion today would agree that this is a massive and extremely problematic oversimplification. The division between 'scientific' and 'religious' beliefs just isn't that neat and tidy. On the 'falsifiability' conception of science, see below, §4.5.

If we engage in a form of life involving MRE, we will presumably believe that God exists. The question that faces us now is, can this kind of belief be rational? That is, can we give a rational justification for the practice of interpreting experiences—both ordinary and extraordinary—as experiences of God?

4.2 Reidian Religious Epistemology

Sometimes we know things for sure, sometimes we believe things rationally, and sometimes we believe things irrationally.

> **Epistemology** is the branch of philosophy that tries to understand when beliefs are rational and when they amount to knowledge.

In order to answer the question of whether monotheistic religious belief can be rational, we need to go a little deeper into epistemology.

According to one historically influential theory in epistemology, knowledge consists in self-evident truths—claims that are impossible to doubt—plus whatever other claims we can derive from the self-evident truths by means of **valid arguments**. This view is called 'classical foundationalism'.

> **Classical foundationalism** is the view that a belief counts as knowledge if and only if it is either self-evident or inferred from self-evident beliefs by valid arguments.
> A belief is **self-evident** if and only if it is impossible to doubt.

The reason this view is called 'foundationalism' is that the self-evident truths form a foundation for knowledge, and the rest of our knowledge is like a structure built on this foundation.

How do we identify self-evident truths? René Descartes ([1641] 1993), perhaps the best known advocate of classical foundationalism, made this proposal: try to doubt everything. If you find yourself unable to doubt something, then you've found a self-evident truth.

One problem with this procedure is that philosophers are *really* good at doubting. Descartes, for instance, found it easy to doubt the existence of the chair he was sitting in. He raised this doubt by noting that he had sometimes dreamed he was sitting in a chair when there wasn't a chair there at all (Descartes [1641] 1993, Meditation 1). Descartes reported that he was unable to doubt his own existence—after all, if he didn't exist, then who would be doing the doubting? It was in this context that Descartes wrote what are perhaps the most famous words in all of Western philosophy, "I think, therefore I am" (Descartes [1637] 1998, pt. 4; compare Descartes [1641] 1993, Meditation 2). (Doubting is a kind of thinking.) Other philosophers, however, have doubted or even denied their own existence.

> The denial of the existence of the self is a core tenet of Buddhism, and arguments for this thesis date to the very beginning of Buddhist philosophy. One such argument can be found, for instance, in the *Milindapañha*, a Buddhist scripture dating to the first century CE. A translation of the relevant portion of that text is included in the collection of Indian philosophical texts compiled by Radhakrishnan and Moore (1957, 281–284). More recently, similar arguments have been defended outside the Buddhist context by philosophers such as Peter Unger (1979).

Even if we agree with Descartes that there are some truths that cannot be doubted, there are not enough of these truths to get us anything like common sense or science. As Wittgenstein (1972, §337) pointed out, you can't very well do science while doubting whether your experiment exists! Neither theism nor naturalism can be justified within classical foundationalism, since neither theology nor science can be built up from self-evident foundations.

An alternative approach was influentially proposed by Thomas Reid (1710–1796). According to Reid, when Descartes doubts the existence of the chair he's sitting in, he's using reason to cast doubt on the senses. That is, he's making a philosophical argument for the claim that the senses are unreliable. The trouble with this is, unless human reason is reliable, philosophical arguments made by humans are no good. But if our senses don't work correctly, why should we think our reason works correctly? As Reid ([1764] 1997, 169) memorably puts it, our senses and our reason "came both out of the same shop," so if one is faulty, the other probably is too. On the other hand, if one is reliable the other probably is too.

In this way, Reid seeks to defend the reliability of the faculties of the human mind.

> The **faculties** of the human mind are its basic abilities for getting at the truth.

These faculties include the five senses and reason, as well as other abilities like memory. When Descartes uses reason to cast doubt on the senses, he's trusting one faculty (reason) and distrusting another (sensory perception), but, Reid claims, there is no justification for treating sensory perception and reason differently. Further, we can't doubt all of our faculties at once since doubting itself is a use of our faculties, and we can't use them without trusting them.

Speaking of beliefs instead of faculties, Wittgenstein (1972, §115) makes a similar point: "If you tried to doubt everything you would not get as far as doubting anything. The game of doubting itself presupposes certainty." When we doubt, we use some beliefs to cast doubt on others. For instance, Descartes uses the belief that he sometimes dreams of things that aren't really there to cast doubt on the belief that the things he's perceiving really exist. He couldn't do this, according to Wittgenstein, if he was also doubting that he had ever dreamed. However, there is no justification for treating the one belief differently from the other.

The basic thought behind Reidian epistemology is this. When we first begin to reflect on our beliefs, we notice that we already, from the time we were children, have certain beliefs and certain ways of forming beliefs. These ways of forming beliefs include forming them by trusting faculties like sensory perception, memory, and reason. There is no justification for just *starting out*, at the beginning of our investigation, regarding some of these as more reliable than others. Either all of these beliefs and faculties are guilty until proven innocent, or they are all innocent until proven guilty. If, like Descartes, we take them to be guilty until proven innocent, we'll never be able to prove anything at all, since we can't prove anything without using our faculties. So we have no choice but to regard our faculties and our prior beliefs as innocent until proven guilty.

Note that naturalists can happily accept this Reidian picture, and, indeed, Graham has previously endorsed a rather similar view (Oppy 2006a, 22–31). In fact, this seems to be very much how science works. If the scientist started out by regarding the senses, or memory, or human reason as unreliable, she could never do any science in the first place. Scientists have, of course, discovered many limitations on the reliability of human faculties—that we are subject to certain optical illusions, that our vision only picks up a tiny proportion of all the light that exists, that our reasoning is subject to certain biases, and so on. But what happens in these cases is that scientists start by assuming that our faculties are reliable *in general* and, working on this assumption, they discover that there are some cases in which our faculties are unreliable.

We have, then, no choice but to start from an attitude of trust in our faculties and our prior beliefs. As we investigate and critically reflect, we'll change some of our beliefs and we'll develop views about precisely how reliable our faculties are and in what circumstances they tend to be unreliable, but we have to regard our faculties as reliable in general.

The failure of classical foundationalism is in fact the very reason why we employ the method of worldview comparison in the first place. If it were possible to reject all of our prior beliefs and assumptions and build our worldview on self-evident foundations, we could just build up the correct worldview without having to compare it with others. In fact, this is not possible. Even the foundations of our worldview can be subjected to philosophical doubt. However, both intellectually and practically, we must operate within some worldview or other. The foundations of my worldview can be called into doubt, but I can't reject it without finding a replacement, so when these doubts arise the correct response is to ask whether some other worldview is better. Although this isn't precisely how Reid himself saw things, the Reidian argument fits well with this approach. The skeptic, according to Reid, unavoidably makes certain assumptions (for instance, the reliability of human reason), which can themselves be called into doubt. Once we recognize this, we should be able to see that, although anti-skeptical worldviews are not built up from self-evident foundations, they are nevertheless preferable to skeptical worldviews.

The Reidian argument pulls us in the direction of belief in the reliability of our faculties. We also believe that other humans have faculties basically like ours. But we have a lot of evidence that humans, including ourselves, often get things wrong. This appears to be an unavoidable tension in any worldview. Since the Reidian attitude of trust appears unavoidable, worldviews that take our faculties to be more reliable will have less tension here. So, other things being equal, we should prefer worldviews that take our faculties to be more reliable.

Recently, a number of philosophers have suggested that this general Reidian picture allows for a defense of the rationality of religious belief. The basic structure of the argument is as follows:

The Reidian Religious Argument

1. Either we should start from a position of trusting all of our faculties, or we should start from a position of distrusting all of our faculties.
2. If we should start from a position of distrusting all of our faculties, then knowledge and rational belief are impossible.
3. But knowledge and rational belief are possible.
4. Therefore, we should start from a position of trusting all of our faculties.
5. If we should start from a position of trusting all of our faculties, then many people are rational in holding religious beliefs.
6. Therefore, many people are rational in holding religious beliefs.

Note that the conclusion of this argument is not that religious beliefs are true, nor does it claim that people who reject religious beliefs are irrational. It only claims that many people who hold religious beliefs do so rationally. Since it is often possible to be rational in believing something that turns out to be wrong, the naturalist could endorse the whole argument.

Suppose, though, that the naturalist does want to reject the argument. Where should she begin? While other premises of the argument could be questioned, by far the most controversial premise is premise 5.

I use the term **Reidian religious epistemology** to refer to any defense of the rationality of religious belief that is based on the Reidian Religious Argument. Different versions of Reidian religious epistemology differ mainly in how they defend premise 5. By far the most influential version is due to Alvin Plantinga.[40] However, the version I defend here mainly builds on the work of William Alston (1991) and Linda Zagzebski (2012). Compared with Plantinga, Alston and (especially) Zagzebski place much greater emphasis on the role of the religious *community* in the justification of religious belief, and I will follow them in this.

Think, for a moment, about how **sensory perception** informs us about the world. At first glance, it might seem that there's nothing very complex or confusing here: I know there's a table in front of me because I can see it. Case closed. But in fact things are much more complicated than this. In the first place, even if I was looking right at the table and my eyes were working properly, I still wouldn't know there was a table if I didn't know what a table was. Take another example: if I don't know the difference between elm trees and oak trees, then I can't know that there's an elm in front of me just by looking. However, someone who knows about trees could do this. The same is true for senses other than sight: some people can know by smelling that there's a chrysanthemum nearby, but others only know that there's some kind of flower.

What all of this shows is that gaining information about the world by means of our senses requires a complex process of interpretation, and this process of interpretation is at least partly something we learn.

This phenomenon is even more pronounced in modern science. Although scientific experiments are meant to test scientific theories, scientists have to use theories to interpret the results of their experiments. (In philosophy of science, this is known as **the theory-ladenness of experiment**.) For instance, the Higgs boson was first observed in 2012 at the Large Hadron Collider in Switzerland. What actually happened was that, over the course of several months, a lot of data was written onto a lot of hard drives by a lot of very complicated machines. A gigantic team of physicists analyzed that data and determined that the data meant that these

---

40. For a brief presentation of Plantinga's argument, see Plantinga (1981). For the full details, see Plantinga (2000).

Higgs particles were being created inside the experiment. Showing that this is the meaning of the data requires (at least) a shelfful of graduate-level physics textbooks. If the ideas in those textbooks are wrong, then that's not what those data mean.

This is an extreme example, but the same is true in much simpler cases, including the sorts of experiments you might have done in high school or college science labs. For instance, it's often necessary to know the temperature at which an experiment took place because this might affect the results. You measure temperature by looking at a thermometer. You have background theoretical beliefs about what temperature *is* and how and why the thermometer measures it. (Perhaps these beliefs aren't very detailed at all; perhaps you just believe the thermometer works because your teacher said so.) There are also background theories that explain why this factor might be relevant to the experiment. These background theories are needed in order for you to observe the outcome of the experiment. Even if it were possible to use just your senses, without interpretation, this would not allow you to observe (for instance) that the Bunsen burner increased the temperature of the water in the beaker at a rate of 1 °C per minute. By the time you make that observation, you've already done a lot of interpretation.

These interpretations are part of what Alston calls a 'doxastic practice'. ('Doxastic' means 'having to do with beliefs'.)

> A **doxastic practice** is a way of forming and revising beliefs.

Usually, these practices are taught and learned in a community, and they include practices for taking in data, interpreting it, drawing preliminary conclusions, revising or rejecting those conclusions in light of new evidence, and so forth. We are all engaged in a doxastic practice of trusting sensory perception. However, our actual doxastic practice around sensory perception includes a lot of interpretation, and also includes procedures for recognizing that we have been the victim of an illusion or hallucination in certain cases. This practice is *communal*: I don't just trust my own sensory perception; I also trust others to tell me what they are perceiving.[41]

---

41. Zagzebski (2012, ch. 3) provides a strong defense of this kind of trust in others as essential to rationality.

Religious communities have procedures for interpreting religious experience, and, as Alston (1991) argues at length, these procedures look a lot like the doxastic practice of trust in the senses. The doxastic practice of trusting the senses, the naturalist must agree, is a rational one. (If it weren't, we wouldn't be able to believe in science, but believing in science is what naturalism is all about.) As a result, the naturalist has no basis for saying that the religious doxastic practice is irrational. To put this in terms more similar to the Reidian Religious Argument, trusting our faculties and beliefs means taking the doxastic practices we have inherited to be rational and reliable (in the absence of evidence to the contrary), but many people have inherited the doxastic practice of interpreting some experiences as experiences of God, so this doxastic practice must also be regarded as rational and reliable (in the absence of evidence to the contrary), at least by those who have inherited it.

If this is right, then people who have inherited a doxastic practice of interpreting experiences as experiences of God, or who belong to a community that engages in this practice, have reason to trust this practice. Trusting this practice means accepting both my own MRE and the testimony of the MRE of others. To put this in simpler terms, people who have been raised in a monotheistic religious community, or are currently members of a monotheistic religious community, are rational to trust the community's (purported) experience of God unless there are strong reasons for supposing that experience to be misleading. This is no different from the way we trust our practice of interpreting our sensory data unless and until it can be shown to be wrong.

This line of reasoning suggests that those who are part of this doxastic practice of religious experience are rational to accept it, and those who aren't part of that practice are rational to reject it. This still assumes that one side is right and the other side is wrong but, as I said above, false beliefs can often be held rationally. Rationality isn't a matter of being right all the time; it's a matter of doing the best you can with what you've got. For comparison, even the best poker player will sometimes lose if she's dealt a series of bad hands. Being an excellent poker player is about doing the best you can with the cards you're dealt. Rationality is like that as well.

In fact, though, we can go a little further because I argued above that taking human faculties to be unreliable creates tension in worldviews. The atheist must regard these very widespread religious doxastic practices as radically unreliable. This is a cost to any atheistic worldview. We can put this in the form of an argument as follows:

> **The Argument From Religious Experience**
> 1. If one worldview takes human faculties to be more reliable than another worldview takes them to be, this is a reason to prefer the first worldview over the second.
> 2. If one worldview takes MRE to be reliable and another worldview doesn't, then (other things being equal) the first worldview takes human faculties to be more reliable than the second.
> 3. Only theistic worldviews can take MRE to be reliable.
> 4. Therefore, other things being equal, there is a reason to prefer theistic worldviews over non-theistic ones.

The central point here is that the atheist is effectively stuck holding that all the people who report MRE are either hallucinating, lying, or radically misinterpreting their experience. However, the atheist (and particularly the naturalist) has to start from the assumption that human faculties are generally reliable, just like the theist does. As a result, the atheist is effectively making a special exception for MRE, and this generates tension within atheistic worldviews.

4.3 The Problem of Hallucination

There is a really obvious problem with the Argument from Religious Experience. People report MRE in favor of conflicting views of the world: one tradition says that God speaks through the Quran, another says God speaks through the Bible, and the adherents of these traditions make conflicting claims about God. Although Christians and Muslims (for example) agree about many things, they also disagree about other things. If they really disagree, they can't both be right.

Further, in addition to MRE, religious experience is used to support views that conflict even with basic monotheism. Some people report experiencing a multiplicity of gods, while others report experiencing an impersonal Absolute or some other ultimate reality that (according to them) is not God.

Since there are disagreements among religions, and many conflicting claims are supported by religious experiences, everyone has to say that religious experiences are sometimes misleading. This is part of the more general issue that, as I mentioned above, nobody can say that human faculties are *perfectly* reliable, so every worldview has to live with some tension on this point.

To make matters worse (for the theist), the naturalist has a pretty good explanation of why humans have these religious experiences. Researchers in the cognitive science of religion have argued that religious experience is due to a hypersensitive agency detection system.

> The **cognitive science of religion** is a research program that tries to understand the origins of religion through empirical study of the function and evolutionary origins of the human mind.

The human mind, these researchers say, is hard-wired to detect agency, that is, to tell the difference between inanimate objects like rocks and things like tigers that do things *on purpose*. We need this system in order to survive. Now imagine you are an ancient human living in the jungle. You hear a rustling noise behind you, and you wonder: is it just the wind, or am I being stalked by a tiger? If you guess that it's just the wind and you're wrong, you get eaten. If you guess it's a tiger and you're wrong, you survive. So one kind of error is worse than the other. As a result, it is suggested, it's beneficial for humans to 'err on the side of caution' by seeing agency *everywhere*. For this reason, we tend to interpret natural phenomena as though they were done *by somebody* with a *purpose* in view. This, it is claimed, is the origin of religion and religious experience: we naturally think that events in nature were done by somebody on purpose, but they weren't done by anybody we can see, so we interpret them as having been done by someone invisible (i.e. some kind of god or God).

More on the Cognitive Science of Religion

One of the earliest versions of the story I've just told can be found in David Hume's *Natural History of Religion* (Hume [1757] 2007, §§2–3). Barrett (2000) provides a brief and

> (relatively) philosophically neutral overview of contemporary theories in the cognitive science of religion. Views on the relevance of these theories for the philosophy of religion differ widely. Some philosophers, such as Dennett (2006), see this research as undermining the rationality of religious belief; others, such as Braddock (2018), argue that the research actually *supports* the rationality of religious belief; and still others, such as De Cruz and De Smedt (2015), argue that the evidence is equally amenable to theistic and naturalistic interpretations.

What's nice about this story (for the naturalist) is that it gives a unified account in terms of a general theory for why human faculties would be unreliable in this particular instance. Since every worldview has to face the tension created by the imperfect reliability of our faculties, the best way to minimize this tension is to have some general theories that explain why our faculties, though generally reliable, are unreliable in some particular cases. This story does just that, explaining why our generally reliable faculties give unreliable information about a supernatural person or persons.

This points to an important general feature of the doxastic practices we employ in interpreting our experience: they rely on background theories.

> A **background theory** is a collection of assumptions about the world, our place in it, and the operation of our faculties that we use to interpret experience.

Background theories are especially important for telling the difference between reliable and unreliable experience. For instance, if I seem to see a pink elephant in my living room, I'll conclude that I'm hallucinating because every plausible background theory I know makes hallucinations more common than pink elephants in living rooms. This is true even if I have no idea what might be causing me to hallucinate in the present case. If I've been warned that a medication I'm taking can cause hallucinations in a certain percentage of patients, I'll come to this conclusion much more easily, about matters much less strange than pink elephants.

Background theories don't just apply to cases of out-and-out hallucination, but also to less serious forms of misperception. For instance, we know that the weather feels hotter when it's humid, so our background theory can explain why I might perceive an 80°F day in Pennsylvania to be hotter than a 90°F day in Arizona.

The naturalist appears to be in really good shape here. In the first place, it's part of her background theory that there just couldn't be any such thing as God, so religious experiences can't be reliable. God, for the naturalist, is like a pink elephant (or an orbital teapot). Second, the naturalist has an explanation of why these unreliable experiences occur. Hence, for the naturalist, MRE is very much like seeing a pink elephant after taking a medication that has hallucination among its known side effects: there's excellent reason for supposing that experience is unreliable, there's an explanation for why it's unreliable, and that explanation does not make human faculties *generally* unreliable. Given all of this, the naturalist is in a position to continue rejecting MRE as unreliable even if she has MRE herself!

> MRE is experience that is interpreted as experience of God. The naturalist, of course, doesn't think there's a God out there to be experienced, but she could still have experiences of God in the way I might have an experience of a pink elephant (although I don't believe the pink elephant is there). The experience gets interpreted first and then, on the basis of that interpretation, gets rejected as hallucinatory.

What the theist really needs is an alternative background theory. If the theist's background theory allows religious experiences to be generally reliable, this will be a point in its favor. However, it also needs to explain the existence of conflicting religious experiences, and this will involve admitting that religious experiences are not *perfectly* reliable.

Here's a summary of where we are: religion involves a doxastic practice in which some experiences are interpreted as experiences of God. When we first begin to reflect on our beliefs, we are already engaged in various doxastic practices. It is appropriate to regard these practices as innocent until proven guilty. Some people, when they begin to reflect, are already engaged in a religious doxastic practice. However, religious doxastic practices yield massively conflicting results (the different disagreeing religions), so they can't all be perfectly reliable. Why do they sometimes go wrong? The naturalist has a nice explanation of this, in terms of hypersensitive agency detection, and this explanation implies that religious experiences are *wholly* unreliable and should be *entirely* discounted. In other words, the naturalist purports to have proven religious doxastic practices guilty. If, however, the theist can come up with an alternative theory, she may yet come out ahead. A theory that explained why religious experience is *sometimes* misleading while still holding that it was *generally* reliable would allow for more trust in human faculties, and this would be a point in its favor.

4.4 The Reliability of Religious Experience

The **doxastic practice** of trust in sensory perception is our process of interpreting input from the senses in order to form or revise beliefs. As part of this practice, we sometimes conclude that certain sensory experiences are illusory, hallucinatory, or prone to misinterpretation, and so we don't form the beliefs we normally would. The pink elephant is an example of this. When witnesses to an event disagree, we often go looking for reasons to discount some of the witnesses and believe others. In this process, we employ two kinds of background beliefs: beliefs about what the world is like, and beliefs about the circumstances in which our senses are most (and least) reliable. Beliefs about the reliability of the senses may be based on beliefs about how the senses actually work, but they don't have to be. They could just be formed by trial and error, without much theory. For instance, you don't need to know much about the functioning of the eye in order to recognize that humans don't see very well in the dark.

When interpreting sensory experience, we often take these two kinds of factors together: I have a prior belief about the likelihood of pink elephants in living rooms, and a prior belief about the likelihood of hallucination, and I compare them with one another. Of course, the likelihood that I would hallucinate a pink elephant in my living room (when I haven't taken any drugs or anything) is very small, but the likelihood that there would actually *be* a pink elephant in my living room is even smaller. So I draw the conclusion that I'm hallucinating.

Imagine, now, a person just beginning to question the religious worldview she's inherited. She knows that many people have very different beliefs about God from her community, and many other people don't believe in God at all. She learns about naturalistic worldviews and the cognitive science of religion, and how an alternative worldview can provide explanations of why and how religious experiences are illusions or hallucinations. What should she do?

Well, in the first place, notice that her own (current) worldview includes the existence of God, so she doesn't think this is like the pink elephant case. However, if she is impressed with the coherence, simplicity, and explanatory power of some naturalistic worldview, she might start to wonder whether she *should* think that religious experience is like the pink elephant case, as the naturalist does. The only way to answer this question is to elaborate a theistic worldview and show that such a view can compete with naturalism when it comes to coherence, simplicity, and explanatory power. This, however, is precisely what I did in presenting my defense of classical theism. So this particular problem is neutralized: God, once again, is not a pink elephant (or orbital teapot).

There's still a second kind of problem, though: does work in the cognitive science of religion show that religious experience is unlikely to be reliable? I admitted above that the cognitive science of religion shows that *within a naturalistic worldview*, there can be a compelling explanation of religious experience. However, that doesn't mean that this work gives the theist any reason to doubt the reliability of religious experience. The naturalistic explanation of religious experience *assumes from the beginning* that there isn't really any immaterial person out there and tries to explain why people think there is. If there really is a God, then our agency detection system isn't so hypersensitive after all, since God is at work in nature as an agent acting for reasons. That's not to deny that people sometimes think there's a tiger when it's only the wind, but the problem is not nearly so widespread as the naturalist takes it to be.[42]

Religious disagreement presents bigger problems. Different monotheistic religious communities make radically different claims about God, and all base their claims on the community's (alleged) experience of God. Further, there are, of course, communities that are *not* monotheistic. All of these different communities have

---

42. For a detailed and empirically informed argument to the effect that theists can reasonably regard the natural mechanisms of religious belief formation as reliable, see De Cruz and De Smedt (2015, esp. ch. 9).

different procedures for evaluating religious experience and forming beliefs on the basis of it.

This presents two different problems. First, the fact that religious experience supports conflicting claims may cast doubt on its reliability. Second, we may worry that there can be no justification for 'picking a side' in the conflict among religions: why regard one religion's claims as more likely to be true than another's?

Note, however, that sensory perception also often supports conflicting claims, particularly when combined with testimony and memory. Witnesses to a crime disagree about what they saw. Split pea soup looks distinctly unappetizing (visually) but tastes delicious. And so on. Reason, too, can support radically conflicting claims. Philosophers purport to use reason to answer life's big questions, but philosophers never agree about anything.

When there are conflicts based on sensory perception (or testimony thereof), we have procedures for determining which source of information is likely to be more reliable. When reason appears to support conflicting claims, we go back and examine the arguments more carefully. Are there equivalent procedures for religious experience?

Religious communities do have such procedures. Communities have beliefs about the circumstances in which God is typically experienced, and the vehicles through which that experience comes (e.g. the Christian sacraments or the reading of the Bible), and they also test the content of those experiences against the community's previous experience of God (including those recorded in their sacred texts) and other beliefs about God. This, again, is not so different from sensory experience. The community's procedures will often determine that religious experiences had outside the community are not reliable.

Note, however, that there is no need to rule *all* outside experiences hallucinatory. Perhaps some religions include the belief that God is never experienced by outsiders, but there is no reason religions *must* hold this. Christians, for instance, generally believe that God is constantly extending invitation to those outside the Christian community, and so Christians should expect many non-Christians to have experiences of God. There is no need to claim that one's own religious community has a monopoly on authentic religious experience and, indeed, it is better for the religious believer *not* to claim this because (as I've been arguing) worldviews that take our faculties to be more reliable are to be preferred. A religious picture that allows more religious experiences to be authentic is going to be in better shape than one that rejects most of them.

Indeed, this can be extended even beyond the bounds of MRE. It may be the case that what someone interprets as an experience of a plurality of gods, or of an impersonal Absolute, or of the oneness of the universe, or whatever, is in fact a misunderstood experience of God.

Still, as we said above, no one can take *all* religious experiences to be reliable, because religious experiences are used to support beliefs that conflict. For instance, a follower of Judaism cannot take a vision of Jesus to be an experience of God, a Christian cannot hold that Muhammed really transcribed the words of God when he wrote down the text of the Quran, and so on. More generally, a religious believer will usually take religious experience to support the correctness of his own religion and the incorrectness of the others.

Recall, though, that religious experience, like sensory experience, requires interpretation. We have already said that different religions have different procedures for interpreting their experience. As a result, we need to distinguish between *authentic religious experience* and *reliable religious experience*.

Authentic religious experience is experience of God (regardless of how it is interpreted).

Reliable religious experience is religious experience that leads to the formation of true beliefs.

It seems pretty clear that these two can come apart, precisely because religious experience gets interpreted against the background of prior beliefs. The Bible is not a story in which God reveals everything all in a flash. It's a story in which people interpret their experience of God against their own cultural background and gradually revise their beliefs as a result of this encounter. The same is true for most reports of MRE: people don't usually claim that they suddenly know *everything* about God as a result of their experience, any more than you would claim that you suddenly know *everything* about groundhogs because you just saw one on the lawn. The religious believer can and should hold that many unreliable religious experiences are nevertheless authentic—that is, many people really do have experiences of God, even if not all of the beliefs they form on the basis of those experiences are accurate. Of course, the religious believer won't want to hold that God regularly manifests Godself to people in ways that lead them further astray, compared to where they started, but that doesn't imply that all the beliefs people form on the basis of authentic religious experience are going to be accurate.

Even authentic experience of God (just like sensory experience) is interpreted on the basis of prior beliefs and cultural background, and there's no guarantee of getting everything right.

What's nice about this picture is that it enables the theist to say that most people who report religious experiences really do experience *something*, even if the interpretation of that experience goes wrong at some later stage. From the perspective of the Reidian argument that says we need to assume the reliability of our faculties this is a nice result, because it implies that the error occurs only at the level of interpretation and can be corrected by revising or replacing the background theory. By way of comparison, consider this (true) story. I recently read on Wikipedia that there are no antelope in North America.[43] I thought to myself, "but that's not true! There are pronghorn antelope in Oregon. *I've seen them myself*, and so have lots of people I know." So off I go to the Wikipedia page for 'Pronghorn',[44] where I am informed that the so-called 'pronghorn antelope', which does indeed live in Oregon and look basically like I remember, is (according to the biologists) not really an antelope at all! Well that's no problem. It would have taken a source more reliable than Wikipedia to convince me that I and all those other people hallucinated or misremembered or whatever. It's a lot easier to convince me that the thing we saw wasn't an antelope. The experience was authentic (there was really an animal there) but misinterpreted (it wasn't an antelope). Although this is a failure of my doxastic practice, it's an easily corrected failure and one that doesn't make me trust my eyes or my memory any less.

> **Authentic but Unreliable Experience**
>
> Experience is authentic but unreliable when it is experience of a really existing object, but it nevertheless results in false beliefs because of misinterpretation. I maintain that most religious experience is authentic, but it is very difficult to interpret and, for this reason, can often be unreliable. This is my explanation for the plurality of religions.

---

43. https://en.wikipedia.org/wiki/Antelope#Distribution_and_habitat (accessed August 15, 2019).
44. https://en.wikipedia.org/wiki/Pronghorn (accessed August 15, 2019).

The misinterpretation of religious experience might be harder to correct than the misinterpretation of pronghorn experience, both for lack of reliable sources for that correction and because religion is so much more deeply rooted in people's lives. However, a worldview that makes most religious experience authentic, even if it's often misinterpreted, is a worldview that takes our faculties to be more reliable and hence is to be preferred over one that thinks all religious experience is illusion or hallucination. A classical theistic worldview can do this: although people often form false beliefs about God because they interpret their experience in light of their cultural background and other beliefs, it is (usually) really God that they are experiencing.

4.5 Resolving Conflicts

A problem still remains, though: in light of competing claims purporting to be justified by religious experience, how should we actually decide what to believe? I am just as culturally bound and prone to misinterpretation as anyone else, and my community is just as culturally bound and prone to misinterpretation as any other community.

For purposes of the present debate, this question is not crucial. We could be agnostic between the competing theistic traditions and hold that *some kind of God or other* is experienced in all of them, and therefore some kind of God or other exists. Nevertheless, for a person who seeks to form beliefs on the basis of religious experience, there are significant advantages to working within some particular tradition.

The key point here is that, as with sensory perception, the doxastic practice of religious experience is based on a *social* process of evaluating and interpreting that experience. One needs to be able to compare one's experience against that of others, and one needs a set of procedures for evaluation and interpretation. This is just like the scientific case: you start out by believing that there's such a thing as temperature and that it's reliably measured by thermometers and so on just because that's what you've always been told. As you learn more and as you interact with the world, you find that this matches up with your own experience. But you never would have been able to make sense of your experience if it hadn't been for the presuppositions you inherited from your parents and teachers and so forth. Scientists, philosophers, and ordinary folks can and should question the ideas they inherit, but this kind of questioning is not a matter of throwing out the entire inherited tradition and starting anew. It's a matter of considering revisions to the inherited tradition. Sometimes the revisions are extreme, like the transformations of our concepts of time and space in relativity theory, but Einstein was still revising a view of the physical world he had inherited from Newton and friends, not starting over from scratch. In the same way, an interpretive tradition and an interpretive community are needed if we are to make much progress in making sense of religious experience.

On the Reidian picture I've been defending, our inquiry doesn't begin from nowhere. It begins from within a particular set of beliefs and practices to which we are already attached. We then proceed to subject these beliefs and practices to rational scrutiny and compare them with others to see if others are any better. This applies just as much to religion as to anything else.

The major problem faced in the religious case, however, that differentiates it from the scientific case is that there are many different well-developed religious traditions that differ radically from one another and that claim the same kinds of support. How are we to decide between them?

The method of worldview comparison works just as well here as it does anywhere else. A person who has inherited a particular religious worldview is rational in holding that view as the default or treating it as her starting point, but, when she recognizes that it is subject to doubt, she ought to ask whether any of the other worldviews is better. This will involve asking which of these worldviews does the best job of making sense of her own religious experience (if any) and that of others. But it also involves comparisons of coherence and simplicity.

This is another place where classical theism can help. I've argued that classical theism is an attractive and well-developed metaphysical theory about God. Once we are confronted with the attractions of naturalistic worldviews (and I freely admit that naturalism has its attractions), it is rational to continue to regard (some) religious experience as reliable only if we are able to elaborate an alternative worldview that is similarly attractive and allows these experiences to be reliable. Classical theism is (a component of) such a worldview. What this means is that one of the ways we can judge between religious traditions, or one of the ways we can consider revising our own religious worldview, is by seeing how well the interpretation of religious experience within that tradition fits together with classical theism (or some other attractive metaphysical view of God).

The interaction between this kind of metaphysical theorizing and the teachings derived from the community's encounter with God can be understood as analogous with the interaction between theory and observation in the sciences. Theories are constructed 'from the armchair', but they are not constructed in total ignorance of the observations that have already been made. The theorist tries to come up with a picture that is elegant in its simplicity and also captures as much of the existing data as possible. According to a picture popularized by Karl Popper ([1963] 1972), the theory is then tested by an experiment, and if the experiment doesn't line up with its predictions, the theory is rejected. However, philosophers of science (and working scientists) today recognize that the reality is much more complicated than this. In the first place, as we saw above, we must use theories to interpret the experiments. In the second place, rejecting the theory is not the scientist's only option when conflicting experimental results are reported or observed. Rather than outright rejecting the theory, it's possible to tweak it. Rather than rejecting or tweaking the theory, you might hypothesize that there was some additional factor present that wasn't taken into account. For instance, when the motion of a planet doesn't exactly match Einstein's predictions, an astronomer's first thought will be that there is some other massive body out there whose gravity is affecting the planet's motion. This seems far more likely than the hypothesis that Einstein's very well-confirmed theory is wrong. Finally, one can write off certain observations as experimental error or, in extreme cases, even as fraud. Scientists sometimes do just deny the (alleged) results of an (alleged) experiment, and sometimes part of the reason for doing so is that they clash too much with our well-confirmed theories. The relation between theory and experiment is in this way a kind of dialogue or negotiation.

I suggest that an analogous method should be employed in bringing metaphysical theorizing about God into contact with religious traditions in the course of worldview construction. The religious tradition represents the community's interpretation of its encounter with God. Typically, the tradition itself already includes a great deal of theorizing about this encounter. Metaphysical theorizing and religious experience (including its interpretation) represent two routes for shaping our thinking about God, and the better they can be brought into harmony, the more compelling the resulting worldview will be.

Classical theism is a theory about the ultimate nature of reality developed by philosophers and theologians, and it differs in some ways from the beliefs about God held by ordinary Jewish, Christian, and Muslim believers. What, then, is the relationship between classical theism and religion? To answer this question, I have given an account of monotheistic religious belief as belief based on (what is taken to be) experience of God, and argued that such belief can be rational. However, as I went on to argue, monotheistic religious belief faces certain challenges that can be overcome only by positioning it within an intellectually satisfying worldview, such as that provided by classical theism. For this reason, I claim, classical theism and monotheistic religious belief taken together can enjoy stronger rational support than either of these kinds of belief taken separately.

5 Conclusion

Graham and I agree that the method of worldview comparison provides the correct approach for the philosophy of religion. The criteria for comparison include simplicity, coherence, and explanatory comprehensiveness. The question of the present debate is, do theistic worldviews or naturalistic worldviews fare better in this comparison?

In §3, I argued that certain kinds of theistic worldviews have greater explanatory comprehensiveness than naturalistic worldviews, and this gain in explanatory comprehensiveness comes at little or no cost to simplicity.

In §4, I argued that worldviews that see human faculties as more reliable are (other things being equal) more coherent (i.e. have less tension) than worldviews that attribute less reliability to human faculties. The naturalist must say that all monotheistic religious experiences (and probably most other religious experiences) are unreliable. The theist, I argued, can say that most religious experiences are authentic—that is, they are really experiences of a divine reality. It must be admitted that religious experiences are prone to misinterpretation, but this, I argued, is the least bad kind of unreliability. So the theist can take our faculties to be more reliable than the naturalist.

Theism is superior to naturalism with respect to explanatory comprehensiveness and the reliability of our faculties, and it performs about as well as naturalism on the other criteria. This is sufficient reason for favoring theism over naturalism.

> Theism and naturalism are two competing families of worldview. According to theism, the natural world is created by a God who stands outside that world. According to naturalism, the natural world is all there is. I have argued that naturalism necessarily leaves the totality of the causal order unexplained, while a certain form of theism provides a satisfying explanation. Additionally, theism is able to treat religious experience as generally reliable, while naturalism must regard it as generally involving illusion or hallucination. These two advantages provide adequate reason for favoring theistic worldviews over naturalistic ones.

Chapter 2

Are There Any Gods?

Graham Oppy

Contents

1 Argument — 93
2 Familiar Arguments — 96
   2.1 *Kalām* Cosmological Argument (Tied to T1) — 97
   2.2 Fine-Tuning Argument (Tied to T4) — 97
   2.3 Argument From Horrendous Evil 1 (Tied to A7) — 99
   2.4 Argument From Horrendous Evil 2 (Tied to A7) — 99
   2.5 Argument for Impossibility of Omnipotence (Tied to A2) — 100
3 Naturalism — 102
4 Necessity — 104
5 Existence — 107
6 Causation — 109
7 Causal Principles — 110
8 Existence of Natural Reality — 112
9 Fundamentality — 113
10 Commitments — 115
11 Analogical Language — 117
12 Definition — 119
13 Properties — 120
14 Abstraction — 122
15 Mathematics — 123
16 Science — 125
17 Evolution — 126
18 History — 128
19 Testimony — 129

DOI: 10.4324/9781003216797-4

20	Miracles	131
21	Religious Experience	133
22	Religion	134
23	Mindedness	136
24	Consciousness and Intentionality	138
25	Reason	140
26	Freedom	142
27	Morality	144
28	Flourishing	146
29	Meaningfulness	147
30	Love	149
31	Art	151
32	Play	153
33	Suffering	155
34	Death	157
35	Salvation	159
36	Infinity	161
37	Perfection	162
38	'Foundational' Simplicity	164
39	Heart's Desire	166
40	Disagreement	167

Our topic is the existence of gods. I am an atheist; I believe that there are no gods. In particular, I say that God—the one and only god—does not exist. My contribution says some things on behalf of atheism. Since the definition of 'atheism' and related terms is controversial, here is a brief summary of how I use the key terms: **atheism**: there are no gods; **theism**: there is at least one god; **monotheism**: there is exactly one god: God; **atheist**: believes atheism; **theist**: believes theism; **monotheist**: believes monotheism; **agnostic**: undecided between atheism and theism; and **innocent**: has never considered whether atheism or theism.

1 Argument

Am I *arguing* there are no gods? Maybe; that depends on what we mean by 'arguing'. Some say that, if I am to argue that there are no gods, I need to provide at least one *argument* that has the conclusion that there are no gods.

An **argument** is a bunch of claims, one of which is the **conclusion** and the rest of which are the **premises**, concerning which it is said that the conclusion is appropriately supported by the premises.

Except in the simplest cases, the argument may be presented as a **derivation** that takes you from the premises to the conclusion, justifying each interim conclusion along the way by appeal to established rules of derivation.

Suppose that I were to give you an argument in this sense: a bunch of premises supposed to support the conclusion that there are no gods, and perhaps a derivation too. How might I expect you to respond? Suppose, first, that you do not believe all of the premises. Then—without taking any other considerations into account—you will say that the argument does nothing for you; no matter what you already think about the conclusion, this argument gives you no reason to revise your opinion. Suppose, on the other hand, that you do believe all of the premises. Then, if you do not dispute the contention that they support the conclusion, you will say that you already suppose that there are no gods. However, if it turns out that you believe all the premises, do not dispute the contention that they support the conclusion, and yet do not believe the conclusion, then you will have some thinking to do! You have two live options: either you change your mind about the premises or else you change your mind about the conclusion.

Suppose that you do not already believe atheism, and I give you an argument for atheism. Now suppose you believe all of the premises and see that the premises support the conclusion. While it is not out of the question that you respond to my argument by accepting atheism, it is much more likely that you will change your mind about the premises. And, most likely, responding in this way will be reasonable. There are countless different **worldviews**—systems of belief—that posit gods; if you come to think that your current worldview is deficient, it seems reasonable for you to move to a nearby worldview that is not deficient. Rejecting a premise that you currently accept for a slightly different premise will usually be much less dramatic than changing your mind about whether there are gods.

Perhaps you are already persuaded that there is not much point tabling such arguments. But there is more. People who believe that there are gods are very diverse. Apart from belief in gods, there is very little on which they all agree. Even among professional philosophers, there is massive disagreement on the truth of the premises in every argument about gods put forward thus far, in which it is agreed that the conclusion is supported by the premises. That is, we already know that all of the intelligent, reflective, well-informed philosophers on one side of the disagreement about the existence of gods reject at least one of the premises in each of the best arguments we have to date on the other side of the disagreement. Taking all of this into account, it seems that it would just be an act of bad faith for me to present already tabled arguments for the conclusion that there are no gods.

Perhaps you think I should come up with *new* arguments for atheism. While we cannot rule out the possibility that, at some point, philosophers will come up with better arguments about gods than we currently have, it is highly unlikely that we are going to see such arguments any time soon. The current stock of arguments consists of tweaks and minor modifications to arguments that have been around for a very long time. It is not news to anyone that theists do not believe premises anywhere in the neighbourhood of the disputed premises in the current stock of atheistic arguments.

While there is more to add to what I have said here,[1] I have said enough to explain why I shall not be offering arguments, in the sense specified above. So what will I be doing instead? What I do is sketch a worldview that allows you to see, at various points where you might think that there is some need to bring gods into the picture, why, given the worldview, there is no need to bring gods into the picture *there*. You might think of this as, in some sense, an argument for atheism. But this 'argument' is open-ended: no matter how much space is allotted to me, I cannot hope to discuss *all* of the points where you might think that there is need to bring gods into the picture.

> Theory is prior to argument: your views about which claims are true properly determine your views about which arguments are sound. Where there is theoretical disagreement, we should not suppose that trading arguments—sets of premises and conclusions—will resolve that disagreement. Given that what we really care about is the disagreement about claims rather than the disagreement about arguments, we should focus our discussion directly on the disagreement about claims.

---

1. See, for example: Oppy, G. (2011) 'Über die Aussichten erfolgreicher Beweise für Theismus oder Atheismus' in J. Bromand and G. Kreis (eds.) *Gottesbeweise*. Berlin: Suhrkamp Verlag, 599–644. (Available in translation—as 'Prospects for Proofs of the Existence of God'—at *Academia.edu*.)

2 Familiar Arguments

Before I turn to setting out my worldview, I illustrate the claims I have just made with some brief remarks about some familiar arguments for and against the existence of gods and, in particular, God.

Here are some claims that many monotheists—and hence many theists—make about God. This list is indicative, but not exhaustive. In later sections, I shall refer to these claims as T1–T15.

1. God caused our universe to exist.
2. God is responsible for the beauty, order, and structure of our universe.
3. Numbers are ideas in the mind of God.
4. God chose the values of fundamental physical constants.
5. God works miracles.
6. God is encountered in religious experience.
7. Belief in God is more or less universal.
8. God caused the emergence and continuing presence of consciousness in our universe.
9. Our beliefs are reliable because God designed our cognitive faculties.
10. There are objective moral facts because God legislates them.
11. Life has meaning because God is its architect.
12. Evil is objectively horrifying because it is an affront to God.
13. God is a perfect being.
14. Belief in God is the pathway to salvation.
15. We can reject external world scepticism[2] only because we can know that God is no deceiver and God created us and our world.

Each of these claims—and many more not listed—connects to a family of arguments for the existence of God. I shall briefly discuss two examples.

---

2. According to the stories told by some philosophers, *external world sceptics* deny that we have good reason to suppose that there is a world outside our minds. In his *First Meditation*, Descartes provides arguments from sense-deception, dreams, and deceitful demons that some might take to show that it is doubtful whether there is a world outside our minds.

2.1 Kalām Cosmological Argument (Tied to T1)

1. Whatever began to exist had a cause of its beginning to exist. (Premise)
2. Our universe began to exist. (Premise)
3. (Therefore) Our universe had a cause of its beginning to exist. (From 1, 2)
4. If our universe had a cause of its beginning to exist, that cause was God. (Premise)
5. (Therefore) God exists. (From 3, 4)

Many theists suppose both that our universe began with God's act of creation and that there is a single causal network to which all causal things belong: everything posterior to God's act of creation has a cause. Theists who believe these things accept all three premises in this argument.[3]

However, I say that it is necessary that some initial part of our universe exists; consequently, I say that it is impossible that our universe has a cause. So I reject the conjunction of the first two premises. Depending upon how we interpret 'began to exist', either it is not true that our universe began to exist or it is not true that whatever began to exist has a cause of its beginning to exist (with the universe constituting the sole exceptional case).

2.2 Fine-Tuning Argument (Tied to T4)

1. The fine-tuning of the initial state of the universe is due either to necessity, or chance, or God. (Premise)
2. The fine-tuning of the initial state of the universe is due neither to necessity nor to chance. (Premise)
3. (Therefore) The fine-tuning of the initial state of the universe is due to God. (From 1, 2)
4. (Therefore) God exists. (From 3)[4]

Some but not all cosmologists suppose that our universe is fine-tuned: had the values of various fundamental physical constants

---

3. See, for example: Craig, W. (1979) *The Kalām Cosmological Argument*. New York: Barnes & Noble.
4. See, for example: Craig, W. (2003) 'Design and the Anthropic Fine-Tuning of the Universe' in N. Manson (ed.) *God and Design*. London: Routledge, 155–177.

been ever so slightly different, either our universe would have existed for no more than a few seconds or else it would have always consisted of nothing but empty space. Either way, it would not have contained atoms, molecules, proteins, plants, animals, human beings, oceans, planets, stars, galaxies, and so on.

Many theists suppose that our universe began with God's act of creation. By their lights, if the initial state of the universe that God created is fine-tuned, then the fine-tuning of that state is due to God, and not to either necessity or chance. Theists who believe that our universe is fine-tuned and who believe these further things accept both of the premises in this argument.

However, I say that, if the initial state of the universe is fine-tuned, then that fine-tuning is a matter of necessity. While I think that it remains an open question whether the universe has a fine-tuned initial state, I reject the second premise in this argument *even if* the universe does have a fine-tuned initial state.

Here are some claims that many atheists make. Again, this list is indicative, not exhaustive. In later sections, I shall refer to these claims as A1–A15.

1. Nothing could be perfect.
2. Nothing could be omnipotent.
3. Nothing could be omniscient.
4. Nothing could be perfectly good.
5. Nothing could be both perfectly just and perfectly merciful.
6. There could not be a cause of natural reality.
7. God could not permit the horrendous evil of our universe.
8. God would not permit the horrendous evil of our universe.
9. God would not permit the distribution of non-resistant, non-culpable non-belief[5] of our universe.
10. There is no evidence that God exists.
11. God could not make a universe as imperfect as ours.
12. God would not make a universe as spatiotemporally vast as ours.

---

5. Non-resistant, non-culpable non-belief manifests in those who would believe if provided with minimally adequate reasons for believing but who have not been provided with any such reasons. To take one example, there were non-resistant, non-culpable non-believers in God in the Shang and Zhou dynasties. See: Chang, R. (2000) 'Understanding *Di* and *Tian*: Deity and Heaven from Shang to Tang Dynasties' *Sino-Platonic Papers* 108.

13. God would not make a universe as ugly as ours.
14. God would endow theistic belief with less meagre moral fruit than it has in our universe.
15. God would not make a universe that contains the biological sub-optimality found in our universe.

Each of these claims—and many more not listed—connects to a family of arguments against the existence of God. Again, I shall briefly discuss a few examples.

2.3 Argument From Horrendous Evil 1 (Tied to A7)

1. If God exists, God is omnipotent. (Premise)
2. If God exists, God is perfectly good. (Premise)
3. A good thing eliminates horrendous evil as far as it can. (Premise)
4. There are no limits to what an omnipotent being can do. (Premise)
5. There is horrendous evil. (Premise)
6. (Therefore) God does not exist. (From 1–5)

Some atheists have supposed that all of the premises in this argument are true: the first two premises are true by definition, the fifth premise is undeniable, and the remaining premises are conceptual truths that no one can seriously dispute.[6]

However, theists typically reject the third and fourth premises. They say that a good omnipotent being strives only for a satisfactory balance between very great goods and horrendous evils. They also say that not even an omnipotent being can alter the logical connections that hold between goods and evils: for example, not even an omnipotent being can change the fact that there is no overcoming of adversity if there is no adversity to overcome.

2.4 Argument From Horrendous Evil 2 (Tied to A7)

1. There are horrendous evils that God could eliminate without thereby losing any greater goods or permitting other evils equally bad or worse. (Premise)

---

6. See, for example: Mackie, J. (1955) 'Evil and Omnipotence' *Mind* 64: 200–212.

2. God would eliminate any horrendous evil that God could eliminate without thereby losing any greater goods or permitting other evils equally bad or worse. (Premise)
3. (Therefore) God does not exist. (From 1, 2)

Some atheists have supposed that both of the premises in this argument are true: the first premise just seems obvious—how could things not have been made better if God had intervened to prevent the Holocaust?—while the second premise is a conceptual truth that no one can seriously deny.[7]

Theists typically reject the first premise but differ in their views about the extent of our knowledge of the very great goods that would be lost if God were to eliminate all horrendous evil from our universe. Some theists, 'theodicists',[8] think that we know exactly what the great goods that would be lost are (perhaps freedom, or opportunities for soul making); other, 'sceptical'[9] theists suppose that we know no more than that there are great goods that would be lost.

2.5 Argument for Impossibility of Omnipotence (Tied to A2)

1. Necessarily, for any x, if there is a possible task that x cannot perform, x is not omnipotent. (Premise)
2. It is a possible task for one to make something too heavy for one to lift. (Premise)
3. (Therefore) Necessarily, for any x, if x cannot make something too heavy for x to lift, x is not omnipotent. (From 1, 2)
4. Necessarily, for any x, if x is omnipotent, it is impossible for there to be something too heavy for x to lift. (Premise)
5. Necessarily, for any x, if x can make something too heavy for x to lift, then it is possible that there is something too heavy for x to lift. (Premise)

---

7. See, for example: Rowe, W. (1979) 'The Problem of Evil and Some Varieties of Atheism' *American Philosophical Quarterly* 16: 335–341.
8. A *theodicy* is an explanation or justification of God's permission of the amounts and kinds of suffering and evil that are found in our universe.
9. *Sceptical theism* is the view that we do not have—or should be in doubt whether we have—what it takes to know or understand why God permits the amounts and kinds of suffering and evil that are found in our universe.

6. (Therefore) Necessarily, for any x, if x can make something too heavy for x to lift, x is not omnipotent. (From 4 and 5)
7. (Therefore) Necessarily, for any x, x is not omnipotent. (From 3 and 6, by excluded middle)[10]
8. If God exists, God is omnipotent. (Premise)
9. God does not exist. (From 7, 8)

Some atheists have supposed that all of the premises in this argument are true. There is no reason in this context to challenge excluded middle. The first premise is true by definition: if there are things you cannot do, then you are not omnipotent. The second premise is obviously true. I can go to the gym and pile up weights until I have something too heavy for me to lift: if there were a prize available to those able to make something too heavy for them to lift, I'd be a contender! The third premise is also true by definition: you are not omnipotent if there are things that are too heavy for you to lift. The fourth premise is obviously true. The fifth premise is, once more, true by definition: it is standard to say that God is omnipotent, omniscient, and perfectly good.[11]

Theists typically reject the first premise: given that we are understanding 'possible task' in a way that makes the second premise true, we should not be thinking that omnipotence requires the ability to perform every possible task. (Some theists say that we should not think of God's power in terms of omnipotence: for those theists, the crucial point about God's power is that God has and exerts power over everything else. Perhaps, though, we should think that omnipotence just is having and exerting power over everything else.)[12]

---

10. **Law of Excluded Middle**: for any proposition, either that proposition is true or its negation is true; for any proposition p, either p or not p. Here is an instance of the law of excluded middle: either Melbourne is north of Sydney or Melbourne is not north of Sydney.
11. See, for example: Rowe, W. (1993) *Philosophy of Religion*. Belmont, CA: Wadsworth, 7.
12. See, for example: Geach, P. (1973) 'Omnipotence' *Philosophy* 48: 7–20; Sobel, J. (2004) *Logic and Theism*. Cambridge: Cambridge University Press, 345–368; Hill, D. (2005) *Divinity and Maximal Greatness*. Abingdon: Routledge; and Oppy, G. (2005) 'Omnipotence' *Philosophy and Phenomenological Research* 71: 56–84.

The familiar arguments discussed here conform to the claim that I made in §1: in every case, these arguments contain premises that are rejected by proponents of best worldviews that reject the conclusions of those arguments. Moreover, there is no secret in this: anyone who has made a serious effort to familiarise themselves with best extant competing worldviews knows that this is the case. And it is not just that I have made canny choices in my examples: there are no extant arguments on either side that are any more successful than the familiar arguments that I have considered here.

3 Naturalism

I turn now to the promised worldview sketch. The sketch speaks directly to the claims in the above lists. From the sketch, you can see that I reject all of the claims on the first list but accept at least some of the claims on the second list. Moreover, from the sketch, you can see that I do not believe in any gods: it is not just God that finds no home in my worldview.

The worldview I am sketching is **naturalistic**. 'Naturalism' and its variants have very different meanings in different mouths. I have meant different things by 'naturalism' and its variants in my earlier writings. So I need to explain what I mean here by my worldview being 'naturalistic'.[13]

Naturalistic worldviews satisfy the following three conditions:

1. *Natural reality exhausts causal reality*: All causal entities are natural entities and all causal properties are natural properties.
2. *Mindedness is late and local*: Minded entities are either relatively recently evolved biological organisms or else downstream causal products of the activities of such organisms (e.g. groupings of such organisms, institutions created by such organism,

---

13. For alternative conceptions of naturalism, see, for example: Hornsby, J. (1997) *Simple-Mindedness*. Cambridge, MA: Harvard University Press; Kim, J. (1998) *Mind in a Physical World*. Cambridge, MA: MIT Press; Kornblith, H. (2002) *Knowledge and Its Place in Nature*. Oxford: Oxford University Press; and Price, H. (2011) *Naturalism Without Mirrors*. Oxford: Oxford University Press.

artificial intelligences whose origins lie in the activities of such organism, and so on).
3. *Nothing is divine*: There is no part of causal reality that is divine, sacred, or worthy of worship.

Minded entities are entities that are conscious, perceive their immediate environments, act, believe, desire, intend, think, imagine, remember, learn, predict, feel, empathise, suffer, reason, calculate, communicate, and so forth.

Our universe is a network of causally related items. Ordinary causal talk suggests that causation is primarily a relation between *events*: for example, the striking of the cue ball by the cue causes the cue ball to roll down the table. However, events are changes to objects: for example, there is nothing more to the striking of the cue ball by the cue than the occurrence of connected changes to the cue, the cue ball, the table, the air in the immediate vicinity, and so on. It will serve us well enough to say that our universe is a network of causally related *objects*. Then, as a matter of definition, *causal reality* is the sum of causally related objects; and *natural reality* is the sum of natural objects.

Natural causal entities and natural causal properties are those causal entities and causal properties recognised in ideal, completed, true science. We do not have—and will never have—such science. However, current well-established science is the best guide that we have to such science. It is not controversial that current well-established science does not recognise angels, centaurs, demons, fairies, ghosts, ghouls, goblins, gods, mermaids, spirits, unicorns, vampires, werewolves, witches, yeti, and zombies, and does not allow that *ch'i*, karma, and psi play causal roles in our universe. Moreover, it is hardly any less controversial that ideal, completed, true science will not give recognition to, or make allowance for, these things.

How extensive is the causal domain? I'm not sure. Perhaps the universe in which we live exhausts the causal domain; perhaps the causal domain extends to a multiverse, of which our universe is but a tiny part. Nothing in the discussion to come turns on how extensive the causal domain is. Since it will make exposition easier, for the most part I shall pretend that, necessarily, if naturalism is true, the universe in which we live exhausts the causal domain.

I am a naturalist. My naturalism commits me to the claims that there are no gods and that God does not exist. Gods, and God, are typically held to be divine, and sacred, and worthy of worship. God, and Gods, are typically held to be non-natural causal agents. Gods, and God, are never held to be recently evolved biological organisms or downstream causal products of such organisms. In other words: atheism is a direct consequence of naturalism.

4 Necessity

The worldview that I am sketching includes claims about how causal reality is, how causal reality could be, and how causal reality must be. *Actual* causal reality is the way things are. Merely *possible* causal reality is some other way that things could have been. What is *necessary* in causal reality is what must be true in causal reality, or what is true in causal reality *no matter what*. Actuality, possibility, and necessity are *modalities*: *modal* metaphysics studies these modalities.

I begin with a set of claims about necessity. I am not sure whether I should insist on this set of claims. However, for the purposes of the following discussion, I shall take them to be correct:

1. For non-modalised p, if p is necessary, then there is nothing on which p's necessity depends, and there is no explaining why p is necessary.
2. For non-modalised p, if is necessary, then p's necessity explains why p, even though p's being so is neither dependent on its necessity nor on anything else.
3. There are cases where p's being necessary is a logical consequence of q's being necessary. None of these is a case of dependence.
4. Dependence is asymmetric: there are no cases where p depends on q and q depends on p.
5. Dependence is modal: if p depends on q, then it is possible to have q without p.
6. If p depends on q, then p is (at least partially) explained by q.
7. There are two types of explanation of non-modalised p. Non-modalised p may be explained by its necessity. Non-modalised p may be explained by its dependence on non-modal q.

Illustrations: (a) My existence depends upon the existence of my parents: it is possible that my parents existed and yet I did not, but not possible that I existed and yet my parents did not. (b) Given that 2 + 2 = 4, it is necessary that 2 + 2 = 4, but there is nothing that explains why it is necessary that 2 + 2 = 4. No doubt, we can derive that 2 + 2 = 4 from some suitable axioms for arithmetic. In that case, that it is necessary that 2 + 2 = 4 is a logical consequence of the necessity of the axioms. But, since we have no explanation of the necessity of the axioms, we have no explanation of why it is necessary that 2 + 2 = 4. However, that 2 + 2 = 4 is explained by its being necessary that 2 + 2 = 4. While no necessity is explained, necessities that we get via logical consequence come for free. While all necessity is 'brute', only 'primitive' necessities are theoretical costs.

Here are two fundamental principles in my modal metaphysics.

1. *Shared history*: necessarily, any possible way for causal reality to be shares an initial history with the way the causal reality actually is. Take any possible causal reality: if you trace its history back far enough, its history coincides with actual history.
2. *Chance divergence*: necessarily, the only way that possible causal histories diverge from actual causal history is by having chances play out differently.

Suppose that a possible history diverges from actual history at a given point. In the actual history, the outcome of the relevant chance process is A; in the merely possible history, the outcome of the chance process is B. What makes the process a chance process is that there is no explanation of why it issues in A rather than B. We do have an explanation of why we actually get A: we get A because it is the possible outcome of the process that actually eventuated. But, in the merely possible history, there is an explanation of why they get B: they get B because it is the possible outcome of the process that eventuates. There is simply nothing available to explain why the chance process actually issues in A rather than B, and why, in the merely possible history, the same chance process issues in B rather than A. Some people suppose that there are quantum chances; some people suppose that there are free choice chances or free act chances.

Here are two *conservation* principles in my modal metaphysics:

1. *Conservation of naturalness*: necessarily, if, at some point, causal reality is entirely natural, then causal reality remains entirely natural at all subsequent points.

2. *Conservation of non-naturalness*: necessarily, if, at some point, causal reality is at least partly non-natural, then causal reality remains at least partly non-natural at all subsequent points.

Finally, here are two conditional principles in my modal metaphysics:[14]

1. *Shared fundamental laws*: necessarily, any variations in fundamental laws across ways causal reality could be are due to differences in the outcomes of chance processes.
2. *Shared fundamental powers*: necessarily, any variations in fundamental powers across ways causal reality could be are due to differences in the outcomes of chance processes.

One consequence of these claims is that the characteristic tenets of naturalism are all necessary truths: it is necessary that natural reality exhausts causal reality, that minds are late and local, and that nothing is divine.[15]

Given what I have already said about my worldview, you can see that I accept A1 ('Nothing could be perfect'), A2 ('Nothing could be omnipotent'), A3 ('Nothing could be omniscient'), A4 ('Nothing could be perfectly good'), and A5 ('Nothing could be perfectly

---

14. For competing accounts of modal metaphysics, see, for example: Chalmers, D. (2012) *Constructing the World*. Oxford: Oxford University Press; Egan, A. and Weatherson, B. (eds.) (2011) *Epistemic Modality*. Oxford: Oxford University Press; Gendler, T. and Hawthorne, J. (eds.) (2002) *Conceivability and Possibility*. Oxford: Clarendon; Kment, B. (2014) *Modality and Explanatory Reasoning*. Oxford: Oxford University Press; Kripke, S. (1980) *Naming and Necessity*. Cambridge, MA: Harvard University Press; and Lewis, D. (1986) *On the Plurality of Worlds*. Oxford: Blackwell.
15. Many philosophers insist on a distinction between *metaphysical* modality and *natural* modality. People who draw this distinction suppose that the laws and/or boundary conditions that characterise our universe are contingent (i.e. not necessary). I demur. In my view, there is no gap between metaphysical modality and natural modality. Of course, we can imagine—or falsely believe—that the laws and/or boundary conditions are other than they actually are. But imagination and false belief are not good grounds for bloating our ontological inventory. The only ontological possibilities that we need are those that are required for objective chances. Other possibilities are merely doxastic or epistemic: they do not require any ontological investment.

just and perfectly merciful'). If it is necessary that all minds are late and local, and so on, then nothing could be perfect, omnipotent, omniscient, perfectly good, or perfectly just and perfectly merciful.

Some—but not all—theists accept an account of necessity that is quite similar to the account that I have given. Of course, they disagree with my claim that the characteristic tenets of naturalism are necessary; instead, they claim that the characteristic tenets of theism are necessary. On that competing theistic view, it is necessary that God exists; and necessary that, if natural reality exists, then it is caused to exist by God; and necessary that God is minded; and necessary that God is divine, and worthy of worship. But, despite these differences, the structure of my naturalistic account of necessity and those competing theistic accounts of necessity is much the same.

5 Existence

The worldview I am sketching includes some claims about existence.[16]

Actualism: While there are no merely possible things, it could have been that there are things that do not actually exist. For example, while it is true that there is no such thing as my fifth sibling, it could have been that I had a fifth sibling. But, by my lights, it is not true that there is a fifth sibling of mine that is such that it could have existed.

Nowism: Everything that there is now exists now: there are no merely past things now, and there are no merely future things now. While there are no merely past things now, in the past there were things that do not exist now. For example, while it is not

---

16. For competing accounts of existence, see, for example: Prior, A. (1957) *Time and Modality* Oxford: Clarendon; Quine, W. (1953) *From a Logical Point of View*. Cambridge, MA: Harvard University Press; Routley, R. (1980) *Exploring Meinong's Jungle*. Canberra: Research School of the Social Sciences; Salmon, N. (1981) *Reference and Essence*; and Thomasson, A. (1999) *Fiction and Metaphysics*. Cambridge: Cambridge University Press.

true that Bertrand Russell exists now, it was once the case that Bertrand Russell existed. But, by my lights, it is not true that Bertrand Russell is now such that it was once the case that he existed.

Existentialism: Everything that there is exists; there are no non-existent things. While there are no impossible things, there are philosophers who believe that there are impossible things. For example, Meinong believed that the round square has being even though the round square does not exist. But, by my lights, it is not true that there is a round square that is such that Meinong believed, of it, that it had being.

Realism: Everything that there is really exists; there are no merely fictional things. While there are no fictional things, there are stories according to which there are fictional things. While there is no such thing as Santa Claus, there are stories according to which Santa Claus lives at the North Pole, delivers presents to children at Christmas, and so forth. But, by my lights, it is not true that Santa Claus is such that at least some of what the stories say of him is true.

While what I have said here leaves open the question whether only presently existing things exist, I am inclined to deny that only presently existing things exist. If general relativity were the final word on spacetime, we would have pretty good reason to be four-dimensionalists. But, at the very least, we do not have good reason to think that general relativity is the final word on spacetime. Nothing I shall say turns on the truth—or falsity—of four-dimensionalism.

The claims that I have made about what there is—actualism, nowism, existentialism, and realism—reflect more fundamental theoretical commitments. We do best, I think, not to postulate any objects beyond natural reality and its past, present, and future denizens. Rather than stocking other domains—modal space, imaginative space, abstract space, and so forth—with additional entities, we should interpret talk that appears to commit us to further entities in ways that make it clear that we are not committed to any such entities.

6 Causation

The worldview I am sketching include some claims about causation. Most of these claims are not controversial. The claim about transfer of conserved quantities is both controversial and relevant to disputes between theists and naturalists about, for example, the possibility that God's creative act is causal.[17]

The causal relation has some formal properties.

1. *Causation is irreflexive*: it is impossible for anything to be a cause of itself. (More generally, it is impossible for anything to explain itself. 'A because A' is always an explanatory solecism.)
2. *Causation is transitive*: if A is a cause of B and B is a cause of C, then A is a cause of C.

The causal relation has some non-formal properties.

1. Causation necessarily involves *transfer of conserved quantities*. Necessarily, every causal interaction involves transfer between objects of quantities that obey fundamental conservation laws: mass/energy, momentum, angular momentum, charge, and so forth. One consequence here is that it is impossible for something to be a cause without itself being causally acted upon.
2. Causation is sometimes *indeterministic*. Where causation is indeterministic, it is chancy: there is a distribution of objective chances over possible causal outcomes. Chance distributions need not be flat.

There are interesting questions about the relationship between causation and time. Although I regard these as nothing more than speculative hypotheses, I am inclined to think that (a) causation is more fundamental than time; (b) there are non-temporal parts of natural reality; and (c) where there is temporal order,

---

17. For more extensive discussions of causation, see, for example: Fales, E. (1990) *Causation and Universals*. London: Routledge; Mackie, J. (1974) *The Cement of the Universe*. Oxford: Oxford University Press; Mellor, D. (1995) *The Facts of Causation*. London: Routledge; Paul, L. and Hall, N. (2013) *Causation*. Oxford: Oxford University Press; Pearl, J. (2000) *Causality*. Cambridge: Cambridge University Press; Salmon, W. (1998) *Causality and Explanation*. Oxford: Oxford University Press; and Tooley, M. (1987) *Causation*. Oxford: Clarendon.

there is perfect alignment between causal priority and temporal priority in the following sense: if A causes B, then A is temporally prior to B.

> While theists will not accept my claim that causation necessarily involves transfer of conserved quantities, many theists will be sympathetic to the claim that causation is sometimes indeterministic. In particular, theists (and non-theists) who suppose that we have libertarian freedom are committed to the claim that causation is indeterministic. Perhaps some of those theists (and non-theists) will object to the claim that indeterministic causation is chancy: however, it seems to me that the postulation of chance distributions is required in order to make sense of indeterministic causation.

7 Causal Principles

The worldview I am sketching includes some fundamental causal and explanatory principles. These principles are not particularly controversial.[18]

1. *Contingent Beginning*: Necessarily, when a contingently existing thing begins to exist, there is a cause of its beginning to exist.
2. *Contingent Ending*: Necessarily, when a contingently existing thing ceases to exist, there is a cause of its ceasing to exist.
3. *Contingent Continuation*: Necessarily, when a contingently existing thing continues to exist, there is an explanation of its continuing to exist. Often, the explanation is the absence of any cause of its ceasing to exist.

---

18. For more extensive discussion of relevant matters, see, for example: Cartwright, N. (1999) *The Dappled World*. Cambridge: Cambridge University Press; Earman, J. (1986) *A Primer on Determinism*. Dordrecht: Reidel; Eells, E. (1991) *Probabilistic Causality*. Cambridge: Cambridge University Press; Skyrms, B. (1980) *Causal Necessity*. New Haven, CT: Yale University Press; Suppes, P. (1970) *A Probabilistic Theory of Causation*. Amsterdam: North-Holland; and van Fraassen, B. (1989) *Laws and Symmetry*. Oxford: Clarendon.

4. *Change*: Necessarily, when there is change in a thing, there is an explanation of that change. Except in special cases, when there is a change in a thing, there is a cause of that change.
5. *Absence of Change*: Necessarily, when there is no change in a thing, there is an explanation of that absence of change. Typically, the explanation is the absence of any cause of change in that thing.

The occurrence of every event, and the existence of every thing, has *an* explanation. The occurrence of some events, and the existence of some things, is necessary: this necessity provides the occurrence of those events and the existence of those things with an explanation. The occurrence of *some* events and the existence of *some* things is contingent, but necessitated by the occurrence of other events and the existence of other things: this necessitation by the occurrence of those further events and the existence of those further things provides the occurrence of those contingent events and the existence of those contingent things with an explanation. The occurrence of *other* contingent events and the existence of *other* contingent things are chance consequences of the occurrence of other events and the existence of other things: the occurrence of those further events and the existence of those further things, together with the outplaying of chance, provide the occurrence of those contingent events and the existence of those contingent things with explanations.

Even though the occurrence of every event and the existence of every thing has an explanation, there is explanatory incompleteness. When there is outplaying of chance, nothing explains why the outplaying of chance yields one outcome rather than another. If the production of A rather than B by C is a matter of chance, then, while there is an explanation of why A occurs, there is no explanation of why C produces A rather than B. If the production of A rather than B by C is a matter of chance, then, while there is an explanation of why A exists, there is no explanation of why C produces A rather than B. These kinds of contrastive facts about production of chance outcomes are 'brute' contingencies: unexplained fundamental facts.

Perhaps you might think it would be better to suppose there is no brute contingency. Not so. If you think everything is necessary, then, given the claims already made, you should think there is no causation or explanation: nothing depends on anything. If you think there is only deterministic causation, then you should locate brute contingency in your boundary conditions: the fundamental laws, the fundamental powers, the initial conditions, the conditions 'at infinity', and so forth.

> In this section, I have committed myself to a reasonably strong *principle of sufficient reason*. In my view, the occurrence of every event, and the existence of every *thing*, has an explanation. Nonetheless, I also insist that there is explanatory incompleteness. In particular, I say that contrastive facts about production of chance outcomes are unexplained—and hence fundamental—facts. If it is a matter of chance that C produced A rather than B, then there just is no explaining why C produced A rather than B. If there were such an explanation, then it would not be a matter of chance that C produced A rather than B.

8 Existence of Natural Reality

We now have enough on the table to see that I reject T1 (God caused our universe to exist) and accept A6 (There could not be a cause of natural reality).[19]

Why does natural reality exist? Because (a) it was necessary that natural reality exist initially; and (b) nothing has subsequently caused natural reality to cease to exist.

Could something cause natural reality to cease to exist? Since there is nothing external to natural reality, nothing external to natural reality could cause it to cease to exist. However, it may be an empirical question whether something internal to natural reality could cause it to cease to exist. Suppose that, at some point, the expansion of the universe ceases, and the universe begins to contract. Could it go on contracting until it simply ceases to exist?

We currently have reason to believe that nothing internal to the universe could cause it to go out of existence. If that belief is correct,

---

19. For alternative views, see, for example: Craig, W. (1979) *The Kalām Cosmological Argument*. London: Macmillan; Goldschmidt, T. (ed.) (2013) *The Puzzle of Existence*. New York: Routledge; Leftow, B. (2012) *God and Necessity*. Oxford: Oxford University Press. Leslie, J. (1979) *Value and Existence*. Totowa: Rowman and Littlefield; O'Connor, T. (2008) *Theism and Ultimate Explanation*. London: Wiley Blackwell; and Rundle, B. (2004) *Why Is There Something Rather Than Nothing?* Oxford: Oxford University Press.

then it is necessary that the universe goes on existing. On this view, we can simplify our answer to the initial question: natural reality exists because it is necessary that natural reality exists.

We now have answers to a range of other related questions. Why are there causal things (rather than no causal things)? Because there must be. Is there a cause of the existence of natural reality? No: there could not be a cause of natural reality. Is there an explanation of the existence of natural reality? Yes: natural reality exists because it must. And so on.

We also now have enough on the table to see that I reject T2: 'God is responsible for the beauty, order, and structure of our universe'. I say that our universe has the beauty, order, and structure that it is has because it is necessary that it have that beauty, order, and structure. And there is no explanation of this necessity: this is where explanation does and must terminate.

> The claims made in §§4–8 entail denial of key premises in standard cosmological and teleological arguments for the existence of God. These claims entail that natural reality exists of necessity; and these claims entail that natural reality has whatever beauty, order, and structure it has of necessity. Theists typically make similar claims about God: God exists of necessity, and has whatever beauty, order, and structure God has of necessity. This observation reinforces the points that were made in §§1–2.

9 Fundamentality

There is no one thing that is fundamental or that 'grounds' everything else. There is a range of different 'grounding' relations; accordingly, there is a range of ways in which different things are fundamental.[20]

---

20. For competing views, see, for example: Aizama, K. and Gillett, C. (eds.) (2016) *Scientific Composition and Metaphysical Ground*. Basingstoke: Palgrave Macmillan; Bliss, R. and Priest, G. (eds.) (2018) *Reality and Its Structure*. New York: Oxford University Press; Koons, R. and Pickavance, T. (2017) *The Atlas of Reality*. Malden, MA: Wiley-Blackwell; Savellos, E. and Yalcin, Ü. (eds.) (1995) *Supervenience*. Cambridge: Cambridge University Press; and Thalos, M. (2013) *Without Hierarchies*. New York: Oxford University Press.

1. **Composition:** Composition is ambiguous between constitution and parthood. Some things are *constituted* from stuff: for example, some statues are constituted from clay. Some things have other things as *parts*: for example, wheels are parts of cars. In cases of constitution, we sometimes say that the stuff is more fundamental than the thing. In part/whole cases, we sometimes say that the parts are more fundamental than the whole, and we sometimes say that the whole is more fundamental than the parts.
2. **Realisation:** We distinguish between *realiser* properties and *role* properties. For example, my role property of being an eligible voter is realised by my property of being an Australian citizen, whereas your role property of being an eligible voter may be realised by your property of being a citizen of some other country. Sometimes, we say that realiser properties are more fundamental than role properties. Other times, we say that role properties are more fundamental than realiser properties.
3. **Determination:** Sometimes, being F is a way of being G. When this happens, we may say that being F is a determinate of the determinable being G. Sometimes we say that determinates are more fundamental then determinables. Other times, we say that determinables are more fundamental than determinates. A thing cannot be a particular colour unless it is coloured; a thing cannot be coloured unless there is some particular colour that it is.
4. **Supervenience:** Necessarily, the As supervene on the Bs if and only if (1) it is impossible for there to be change in the As without change in the Bs; (2) it is possible for there to be change in the Bs without change in the As; and (3) it is possible for there to be change in the As. Supervenience is an asymmetric modal dependence relation. For example, my hairstyle supervenes on the distribution of hair on my head. My hairstyle can change. My hairstyle cannot change without some change in the distribution of hair on my head. The distribution of hair on my head can change without any change in my hairstyle: the loss of a single hair does not change my hairstyle.

Every composite thing has a physical composition, many composite things also have a chemical composition, some of those composite things also have a biological composition, and so on.

Every realised thing has a physical realisation, many realised things also have a chemical realisation, some of those realised things also have a biological realisation, and so on.

All supervenient things are supervenient on physical things, many supervenient things are supervenient on chemical things, some of those supervenient things are supervenient on biological things, and so on.

The claim that there is a range of different 'grounding' relations is controversial. Some theorists suppose that there is a single 'Grounding' relation that orders everything according to fundamentality. I think that the important notion here is really one of *relative* fundamentality: the As are more fundamental than the Bs with respect to a given grounding relation.

10 Commitments

One aspect of the comparative assessment of worldviews is assessment of their comparative simplicity. All else being equal, if one worldview is less complicated than another, the first worldview is better than the other.

Assessment of the comparative simplicity of worldviews takes into account ontological, ideological, and theoretical commitments. All else being equal, a worldview that is committed to fewer things and fewer kinds of things is better than a worldview that is committed to more things and more kinds of things. All else being equal, a worldview that employs fewer undefined primitive expressions is better than a worldview that employs more undefined primitive expressions. All else being equal, a worldview that is committed to fewer and less complicated fundamental principles is better than a worldview that is committed to more and more complicated fundamental principles.

One difficulty in the accounting of ontological commitments is that it is not straightforward to explain exactly how we count things and kinds of things. Suppose, for example, that, as naturalists may suppose, every composite thing has a physical composition from physical things, and all properties of things supervene on the physical properties of things. Suppose, further, that there are physical simples: physical things that have no non-trivial physical parts. Might naturalists claim that the only things to which they have ontological commitments are physical simples and the physical kinds to which those physical simples belong? Given the claims about composition and supervenience, it seems right for the naturalist to say that there is some sense in which other things and other kinds of things are nothing over and above physical simples and the physical kinds to which physical kinds to which physical simples belong.

Even if we accept that naturalists can reasonably insist that the only things to which they have ontological commitments are physical simples and the physical kinds to which those physical simples belong, it is clear that naturalists have ideological commitments that far outrun the ideological commitments incurred by the language that they use to describe physical simples and the physical kinds to which those physical simples belong. Consider cats. First, consider a particular cat: Tibbles. While Tibbles has a physical constitution from physical simples that changes over time, it is not possible to give a definition of Tibbles in terms of that physical constitution. Second, consider the kind *cat*. While the distribution of cats in the universe supervenes on the distribution of physical simples in the universe, it is not possible to give a definition of 'cat'—or 'Tibbles'—in terms of spatiotemporal arrangements of physical simples. Relative to the vocabulary adequate to describe and categorise physical simples, 'cat' and 'Tibbles' are undefined primitive expressions. Moreover—though this is perhaps slightly more controversial—'cat' and 'Tibbles' are undefined primitive expressions relative to the vocabulary adequate to describe and categorise chemical complexes, biochemical complexes, and so on.

One difficulty in the accounting of theoretical commitments is that it is not straightforward to explain exactly how we count and assess the complexity of theoretical commitments. Given that we are thinking of worldviews as theories, we can imagine having axiomatisations for worldviews. If we had an axiomatisation for a worldview, we could take the worldview to be the logical closure of the given collection of axioms. Then, perhaps, we might think that we can take the axioms to carry all of the genuine commitments of the worldview: anything that is a logical consequence of the axioms is something that we get for free. But, apart from anything else, one insuperable difficulty for this line of thought is that we cannot axiomatise our worldviews. When we are thinking about how to count and assess the complexity of theoretical commitments, we need an approach that does not advert to the comparative complexity of axiomatisations.

Despite the problems that we have just noted, it is not hopeless to suppose that, at least in some cases, we can assess the comparative simplicity of worldviews. The most important point to note is that there is an enormous amount of agreement in best worldviews on ontology, ideology, and theory. Best worldviews incorporate ontology, ideology, and theory from common sense and science, and add some rounding out. When we focus on the rounding out, it may seem that there is massive disagreement. But, when we look at the bigger picture, we see that there is a small island of disagreement floating in a vast sea of agreement.[21]

> When we assess the comparative merits of worldviews, we balance two types of considerations. On the one hand, we want to minimise all of our commitments: ontological, ideological, and theoretical. On the other hand, we want to maximise the breadth and depth of the explanations that we give. We cannot concentrate on one of these tasks to the exclusion of the other. The simplest theory is the empty theory: the theory that says that there is nothing. Of course, this theory fails miserably when it comes to explanation. The theory with the greatest explanatory breadth and depth is one that explains every merely coincidental feature of the world. Of course, this theory also fails miserably when it comes to minimising commitments. Trading off the two demands is no straightforward matter.

11 Analogical Language

Use of language can be univocal, equivocal, or analogical. Worldviews that take talk about some things to be merely analogical incur a theoretical cost that is not borne by worldviews that do not accept

---

21. For further discussion, see, for example: Azzouni, J. (2004) *Deflating Existential Consequence*. Oxford: Oxford University Press; Heil, J. (2003) *From an Ontological Point of View*. Oxford: Oxford University Press; Sider, T. (2011) *Writing the Book of the World*. Oxford: Oxford University Press; and Sober, E. (2015) *Ockham's Razor*. Cambridge: Cambridge University Press.

this analogical talk. Worldviews that take certain predicates to be used analogically take that predicate on those uses to be an ideological primitive. For example, whatever is the status of 'good' when it is not used merely analogically of things, merely analogical use of the word 'good' creates an additional ideological primitive. *All else being equal*, this is a clear reason to prefer those worldviews in which there is no merely analogical use of predicates.[22]

Perhaps some may wish to invoke a doctrine of ontological simplicity in response to this point. If we suppose that the subjects of predication are simple, then we may suppose that there is no corresponding ontological inflation that proceeds from the ideological inflation that follows on the heels of the doctrine of analogical predication. But, even granting, at least for the sake of argument, the intelligibility of the claim that a subject of predication is simple, this observation is completely beside the point. Perhaps—perhaps—you can use the claim that a subject of predication is simple to minimise the additional primitive *ontological* commitments of the worldview; but the additional primitive *ideological* commitments of the worldview remain as they were.

It may be worth noting here that even if you can use the claim that a subject of predication is simple to minimise additional primitive ontological commitments, it remains the case that there is an additional primitive ontological commitment in worldviews that are committed to that subject of predication that is absent from worldviews that do not have a commitment to that subject of predication. *All else being equal*, this too is a clear reason to prefer worldviews that do not have the commitment in question to worldviews that do have this commitment.

> It is very common for theists to claim that language requires 'stretching' in order for it to be applicable to God. The point that I have made in this section is *not* that this 'stretching' is intrinsically objectionable. We all regularly 'stretch' terms; we all make use of

---

22. For competing viewpoints, see, for example: Alston, W. (1989) *Divine Nature and Human Language*. Ithaca, NY: Cornell University Press; McFague, S. (1983) *Metaphorical Theology*. London: SCM Press; Scott, M. (2013) *Religious Language*. London: Palgrave Macmillan; Soskice, J. (1985) *Metaphor and Religious Language*. Oxford: Clarendon; and White, R. (2010) *Talking About God*. Aldershot: Ashgate.

metaphors and so forth. Rather, the point that I have made in this section is that all such 'stretching' in the articulation of theories is theoretical cost: the use of a 'stretched' term is an addition to our ideological commitment beyond the commitment that we incurred in the use of the 'unstretched' term.

12 Definition

If a predicate F is adequately *defined* within a theory, then the theory has as a logical consequence a sentence of the following form:

Necessarily, for all x, x is F if and only if S(x),

where the non-logical vocabulary in S(x) is primitive, or explicitly defined in terms of primitives, or explicitly defined in terms of primitives and vocabulary explicitly defined in terms of primitives, and so forth.

Most of our non-compound predicates are primitive. Consider '. . . . is human'. I doubt that there is anyone who knows how to specify an S(x) for which (1) it is true that *necessarily, for all x, x is human iff S(x)*, and (2) it is plausible that *necessarily, for all x, x is human iff S(x)* is a definition of '. . . is human'. Certainly, most people cannot do this. The traditional Aristotelian definition—*necessarily, for all x, x is human iff x is rational and x is an animal*—is obviously unsatisfactory. Consider a human zygote: it is neither rational nor an animal, but it is human.

Plausibly, in order to define a thing, you specify its essential (i.e. its necessarily intrinsic) properties. (The intrinsic properties of a thing are the properties of that thing that can be specified without referring to the properties of anything else, that is, anything other than a thing and its parts.) But we are typically ignorant of the necessarily intrinsic properties of things. One property that is necessarily intrinsic to being human is having a particular genome. But, of course, for any living thing, one property that is necessarily intrinsic to being that kind of thing is having a particular genome. To give a definition, for any living thing, you need to give a specification of *its* genome. Very few among us can do that. (There are more than three billion DNA base pairs in the human genome.)

What holds generally for non-compound predicates holds in particular for load-bearing non-compound predicates in philosophy. One of the major lessons of the analytic enterprise during the past century or so is that we do not have explicit definitions for '... is known', '... is believed', '... causes ...', '... is art', '... functions ...', '... is a species', '... is good', '... is right', and so on. Philosophy neither begins nor ends with definitions.[23]

> Some people (typically not well acquainted with recent philosophy) suppose that philosophy is primarily concerned with definition. However, in practice, the most significant role for definition in philosophy is the *stipulation* of precise meanings for terms for particular, local, limited purposes. It is very easy for philosophers to end up at cross-purposes because they use key terms in different ways. But there is no prospect that philosophers will be brought to continuing universal agreement on the use of those key terms.

13 Properties

Some philosophers think that, just as many of the terms we use refer to objects, so many of the predicates that we use express properties. On this view, objects and properties properly belong to a complete ontological inventory of reality. According to these philosophers, there are not only sub-atomic particles, atoms, molecules, organisms, planets, stars, galaxies, and so on, but there is also whiteness, solidity, individuation, exemplification, and so forth.

Strictly speaking, I deny that there are properties. Nonetheless, I accept that property-talk is perfectly legitimate: it is fine to use nominalisation, the word 'property', and second-order quantification. However, I take it that property-talk merely allows us to have verbal

---

23. For further discussion, see, for example: Horty, J. (2007) *Frege on Definitions*. New York: Oxford University Press; Jackson, F. (1998) *From Metaphysics to Ethics*. Oxford: Oxford University Press; Sidelle, A. (1989) *Necessity, Essence and Individuation*. Ithaca, NY: Cornell University Press; and Williamson, T. (2008) *The Philosophy of Philosophy*. Malden, MA: Blackwell.

formulations for claims that would otherwise remain incomplete: there is no ontological commitment that goes along with property-talk.[24]

Quine argued that 'truth'-talk is acceptable because, but only because, it allows us to have verbal formulations for claims that would otherwise remain incomplete. Consider: *Everything that the Pope says is true*. We can treat this claim as committing us to no more than we would be committed to if we were able to complete the following claim: *If the Pope says that grass is green then grass is green; and if the Pope says that cows are purple, then cows are purple; and*. . . . In particular, according to Quine, we should not suppose that 'truth'-talk creates any increase in our ontological, ideological, or theoretical commitments.

I say that 'property'-talk is acceptable because, but only because, it allows us to have verbal formulations for claims that would otherwise remain incomplete. Here is an example to illustrate what I have in mind. Suppose that I think that Napoleon was a great general. You ask me: why do you think that Napoleon was a great general? It would be nice if I could complete the following definition: *necessarily, for any x, x is a great general if and only if*. . . . If I could say that *necessarily, for any x, x is a great general if and only if x is F and . . . and x is G*, then I could answer your question. I could say *Napoleon is F and . . . and Napoleon is G*. But, of course, I do not know how to complete the definition of what it takes to be a great general. Instead, what I say is *Napoleon has all of the properties of a great general*. If pressed, I can add *Necessarily, for any x, x has all of the properties of a great general if and only, for all properties F, if F is one of the properties of a great general, then x is F*. According to me, we should treat these claims as committing us to no more than we would be committed to if we were able to complete the claims: *necessarily, for any x, x is a great general if and only if x is F and . . . and x is G* and *Napoleon is F and . . . and Napoleon is G*. According to me, we should not suppose that this 'property'-talk creates any increase in our ontological, ideological, or theoretical commitments.

---

24. For discussion of competing naturalist views, see, for example: Armstrong, D. (1978) *A Theory of Universals*. Cambridge: Cambridge University Press; Mellor, H. and Oliver, A. (eds.) (1997) *Properties*. Oxford: Oxford University Press; Molnar, G. (2005) *Powers*. Oxford: Oxford University Press; and Wetzel, L. (2009) *Types and Tokens*. Cambridge, MA: MIT Press.

I think that it is fine to include, in your canonical notation, linguistic constructions whose function is merely to increase expressive power, while also supposing that there are no theoretical costs attached to the use of those linguistic constructions in the formulation of your theories.

> On one way of understanding these terms, 'realists' claim that there are properties while 'nominalists' deny that this is so. Given this way of understanding those terms, I am a nominalist. It is worth noting that nothing that I have said here commits me to any of the familiar metaphysical variants of nominalism: *sentence* nominalism, *class* nominalism, *resemblance* nominalism, and the like. Just as Quine's account of truth is a non-metaphysical account of truth, so my account of predication is a non-metaphysical account of predication.

14 Abstraction

Candidate abstract objects are legion: algebras, arbitrary objects, attributes, characteristics, classes, contents, fictional objects, functions, generic objects, groups, impossibilia, incomplete objects, inconsistent objects, institutions, intensional objects, intentional objects, mappings, mere possibilia, numbers, patterns, properties, propositions, rings, sets, states, structures, types, universals, utilities, values, and so on.

What I said in the previous section about properties goes for abstract objects in general. Speaking strictly, I deny that there are any abstract objects. However, I say that abstract-object-talk is acceptable because, but only because, it allows us to have verbal formulations for claims that would otherwise remain incomplete.[25]

---

25. For a view close to my own, see: Yablo, S. (2001) 'Go Figure: A Path Through Fictionalism' in P. French and H. Wettstein (eds.) *Midwest Studies in Philosophy* 25: 72–102; and Yablo, S. (2005) 'The Myth of the Seven' in M. Kalderon (ed.) (2005) *Fictionalism in Metaphysics*. Oxford: Clarendon. For competing views, see, for example: Bealer, G. (1982) *Quality and Concept*. Oxford: Oxford University Press; Campbell, K. (1990) *Abstract Particulars*. Oxford: Blackwell; Hale, B. (1987) *Abstract Objects*. Oxford: Blackwell; Katz, J. (1988) *Realistic Rationalism*. Cambridge, MA: MIT Press; and Parsons, T. (1980) *Non-existent Objects*. New Haven, CT: Yale University Press.

There are various grounds that lead people to commit to abstract objects; there are various grounds that lead people to commitments that go beyond the natural objects that compose our universe. On the one hand, there is *ignorance* and *inability*: these justify the use of linguistic constructions that appear to involve commitments but are really nothing more than devices to increase expressive power. And, on the other hand, there is *error* and *fantasy*: these create the need to report the sayings and attitudes of those who have mistaken commitments, or who feign commitments, or the like. I maintain that ignorance, inability, fantasy, and error in others are never grounds for taking on theoretical commitments.

In the previous section, I mentioned one way of understanding the terms 'realist' and 'nominalist'. On another way of understanding these terms, 'realists' claim that there are abstract objects, while nominalists deny that this is so. Given this second way of understanding these terms, I am (also) a nominalist. Among theists, Thomists are particularly noted for their commitment to realism—and their rejection of nominalism—in both of the indicated senses.

15 Mathematics

Given that there are no abstract objects, there are no mathematical objects. Nonetheless, there are mathematical truths: we have mathematical objectivity without mathematical objects.

The key driver of mathematical knowledge (i.e. knowledge of mathematical truth) is mathematical proof. What we know is what we can derive, (ultimately) starting from mathematical claims that are obviously (necessarily) true.

Not all (current) mathematical belief is mathematical knowledge: at least some mathematics is (currently) conjectural. The most that we can say about claims in these parts of mathematics is that they are necessary if true. It is an open, debated question whether it might become the case that all mathematical belief is mathematical knowledge. Some set theorists (e.g. Hugh Woodin) are inclined to answer this question affirmatively; many other set theorists are inclined to answer it negatively.

Our ability to do mathematics is part of our biosocial evolutionary heritage. There is no gene for mathematics; there is no neural architecture dedicated particularly to mathematics. General purpose intelligence that developed for other, essentially social, reasons was co-opted to the solving of problems (e.g. about fair division of resources) and subsequent social scaffolding enabled a general ratcheting up of mathematical competence. Neither the earlier parts of this story (which remain somewhat conjectural) nor the later parts of this story (which are recorded in well-known, detailed histories of mathematics) raise any problems for naturalistic explanations of mathematical knowledge, mathematical competence, and the existence of institutional supports for the preservation and development of both mathematical knowledge and mathematical competence.

We now have enough on the table to see that I reject T3: 'Numbers are ideas in the mind of God'. According to me, there are no numbers—and, more generally, there are no abstract objects. On the approach I favour, it cannot be that numbers are ideas in the mind of God.[26]

> My rejection of the claim that numbers are ideas in the mind of God is over-determined. The main reason that I reject this claim is that I reject the existence of God: if God does not exist, then it cannot be that numbers are ideas in the mind of God. However, a secondary reason that I have for rejecting the claim that numbers are ideas on the mind of God is that I deny that there are numbers: if there are no numbers, then, of course, it is not true that numbers are ideas in the mind of God.

---

26. For competing naturalist views, see, for example: Bigelow, J. (1988) *The Reality of Numbers*. Oxford: Clarendon; Chihara, C. (2004) *A Structuralist Account of Mathematics*. Oxford: Oxford University Press; Colyvan, M. (2001) *The Indispensability of Mathematics*. New York: Oxford University Press; Maddy, P. (1990) *Realism in Mathematics*. Oxford: Clarendon; and Resnick, M. (1997) *Mathematics as a Science of Patterns*. New York: Oxford University Press.

16 Science

On a very rough account, *science* is a collective enterprise of data driven description, prediction, and understanding in which universal expert agreement functions as regulative ideal. The role of universal expert agreement as regulative ideal entails that:

1. Reproducibility, parsimony, and consilience are fundamental scientific values.
2. There are strict protocols governing the conduct of experiments and the collection and analysis of data.
3. There are significant institutions devoted to protecting the integrity of scientific investigation, publication, recognition, and reward.

Given that universal expert agreement functions as regulative ideal, expert scientific consensus has—and ought to have—significant *authority*, and being a scientific expert is—and ought to be—a matter of significant *prestige*. Where there is expert scientific consensus about claims and methods, everyone else ought to coordinate their opinion to that scientific opinion. Of course, this procedure is fallible: expert scientific consensus can be mistaken. But, (a) such mistakes are rare, (b) such mistakes are typically corrected by subsequent scientific developments, and (c) any alternative method for forming beliefs about scientific matters has way less to recommend it.

In any scientific domain, around the core on which there is expert scientific consensus, there is a region in which no expert consensus about claims—and, in some cases, methods—has yet formed. This region includes, at least, all of the claims that are current subjects of investigation by researchers in those scientific domains. For claims in this region, it is fine for non-experts to speculate; however, non-experts should certainly be careful not to mistakenly suppose that there is expert consensus where no expert consensus has formed.

In philosophy, there is no core of settled expert opinion about claims or methods. (This is what distinguishes philosophy from other domains of inquiry. Typically, other domains shade into philosophy at their outer boundaries. In those bounding zones, it becomes unclear whether there is any prospect of expert agreement on claims and methods.) According to some, in domains where there is no settled expert opinion about claims or methods, we should all be universal agnostics. However, according to me, in these domains, all are free to stick to their guns: we can all reasonably agree to disagree in these domains.[27]

> My views about the nature of science and philosophy are controversial. I take it that, where there is properly constituted expert consensus, there is knowledge: the beliefs on which there is expert consensus are known by those experts. Moreover, I take it that, speaking loosely, the properly constituted expert consensus is explained by the truth of that on which there is consensus. For example (and speaking strictly), there is a consensus among expert physicists that there are electrons *because* there are electrons.

17 Evolution

There is expert scientific consensus on broad-scale features of the history of our universe, our planet, and our species. Our universe is about 13.7 billion years old; our planet is about 4.5 billion years old. Living organisms first appeared on earth more than 3.7 billion years ago. Human beings share a common evolutionary history with all currently living organisms. Our closest cousins are bonobos and chimpanzees, with which we share about 99% of our DNA. Our lineage diverged from the lineage of bonobos and chimpanzees between 4 million and 7 million years ago; the lineages of bonobos and chimpanzees diverged about 1 million years ago. Anatomically modern humans (*Homo sapiens*) diverged from other hominid

---

27. For more on the nature of science, see, for example: Chalmers, A. (1982) *What Is This Thing Called Science?* Brisbane: University of Queensland Press; Godfrey-Smith, P. (2003) *Theory and Reality*. Chicago, IL: University of Chicago Press; and Ziman, J. (2000) *Real Science*. Cambridge: Cambridge University Press. For more on the nature of philosophy, see, for example: Blackford, R. and Broderick, D. (eds.) *Philosophy's Future*. Malden, MA: Wiley-Blackwell; Dummett, M. (2010) *The Nature and Future of Philosophy*. New York: Columbia University Press; and Stoljar, D. (2017) *Philosophical Progress*. New York: Oxford University Press.

lineages (e.g Neanderthals) somewhere between 0.8 million and 0.3 million years ago, and began to exhibit behavioural modernity somewhere between 50,000 and 80,000 years ago. There is nothing in this broad-scale history that raises any problems or questions for naturalism.

The claim that our universe is *fine-tuned*—that is, that if certain fundamental dimensionless physical constants did not lie within very narrow ranges, then our universe would not have come to contain subatomic particles, atoms, molecules, organisms, planets, stars, and so forth—is not accepted by all expert cosmologists because of lack of consensus about which dimensionless physical constants are fundamental. Our current most fundamental physical theories—general relativity and quantum mechanics—are jointly inconsistent; we do not yet have a satisfactory quantum gravitational theory. It remains an open question what are the fundamental physical constants in correct fundamental physical theory.

Suppose, however, that there are fine-tuned constants in fundamental physical theory. There are two options. Either the values of those constants are fixed at all points in the evolution of causal reality, or there is some point in the evolution of causal reality where there is a transition from the values of those constants not being fixed to the values of those constants being fixed. In the former case, the values are necessary; in the latter case, the fixing of the values is the result of the outplaying of chance. Either way, there is an explanation for the constants taking the values that they do. Of course, in the latter case, there is no contrastive explanation—no explanation of why the outplaying of chance brought the constants to take the values they do rather than other values that they could have taken. (As foreshadowed in my discussion of the Fine-Tuning Argument, this section points to the core of my response to T4: 'God chose the values of fundamental physical constants'.)[28]

---

28. For more about evolution, see, for example: Charlesworth, B. and Charlesworth, D. (2003) *Evolution*. Oxford: Oxford University Press; Kaufmann, S. (1993) *The Origins of Order*. New York: Oxford University Press; Mayr, E. (2001) *What Evolution Is*. New York: Basic Books; and Pallen, M. (2009) *Evolution*. London: Rough Guide. For more about fine-tuning, see, for example: Manson, N. (ed.) (2003) *God and Design*. London: Routledge; and Rickles, D. (2014) *A Brief History of String Theory*. Berlin: Springer.

Teleological arguments for the existence of God have typically drawn on details from either biology or cosmology. As noted above, in the light of expert consensus among biologists, there is nothing in the biological details to give naturalists pause: there is nothing non-natural about the evolutionary pathway that has been traced out on earth over the past four billion years. And, while the cosmological details are contested, there is no advantage in introducing something non-natural to our account of the origins of natural reality in order to accommodate the values taken by the fundamental physical constants.

18 History

Extant material artefacts—including, in particular, diverse textual repositories—ground expert consensus on many aspects of the history of humanity over the past few thousand years. However, the conjectural nature of much of this kind of historical investigation means that there is less expert consensus than some suppose.

There are many significant difficulties involved in the assessment of ancient textual materials. In some cases, texts are fragmentary. In some cases, texts have been significantly rewritten in succeeding centuries. In all cases, the language of the texts is unfamiliar, and the contextual assumptions of the authors hard to reconstruct. In many cases, the genres of the texts are hard to discern, as are the historically prevailing standards governing texts written in those genres. Even texts that purport to be histories present manifold challenges: every author—and every reader—has biases, allegiances, deficits of knowledge and understanding, and so forth.

Where historians are interested in past events—not merely past attitudes to past events—the conclusions they draw from their readings of ancient texts are properly constrained by current (twenty-first century) expert consensus in, for example, anthropology, archaeology, astronomy, biology, chemistry, climatology, demography, ecology, economics, geography, geology, hydrology, linguistics, neuroscience, palaeontology, physics, psychology, and sociology. Good historians are properly moved to dismiss reports in ancient texts of, for example, the *existence* of angels, centaurs, demons, fairies, ghosts, ghouls, goblins, gods, mermaids, spirits, unicorns, vampires, werewolves, witches, yeti, and zombies; the *performance* of clairvoyant, levitational, precognitive, prophetic, telekinetic, and telepathic acts by mediums, oracles, prophets and shaman; the *occurrence* of gods impregnating human beings, gurus understanding the speech of animals, prayers causing rain in times of drought, statues drinking milk, trees moving on human command, virgins giving birth, warriors blinding enemies with handfuls of dust, and water buffaloes reciting religious texts; and the *outworkings* of *ch'i*, karma or psi. Such things do not exist; such events do not occur. Such things have never existed; such events have never occurred.[29]

> One familiar kind of objection to naturalistic worldviews draws on historical documentation of events that are supposed incapable of naturalistic explanation. These objections are never advanced by historians working under the norms that govern *other* serious academic historical research. For example, *The Cambridge History of Religions in the Ancient World* (2013, two vols.) contains not a single suggestion that there is historical documentation that presents even a *prima facie* challenge to entirely naturalistic histories of religion.

19 Testimony

The following generalisation is *approximately* true: for any people A and B, and any claim that p, if A says that p to B, and B does not already believe that p, then B will adopt the belief that p. We are all disposed to unquestioningly believe what other people tell us except when we take relevant defeating conditions to obtain. In a wide range of circumstances, it takes cognitive effort to resist just taking on board what other people tell us; consequently, in a wide range of circumstances, we do not resist. For example, typically, when you

---

29. For expansion of these very brief remarks, see, for example: Bentley, M. (ed.) (1997) *Companion to Historiography*. London: Routledge; Hewitson, M. (2014) *History and Causality*. New York: Palgrave Macmillan; Sachsenmaier, D. (2011) *Global Perspectives on Global History*. Cambridge: Cambridge University Press; and Tucker, A. (ed.) (2009) *Companion to the Philosophy of History and Historiography*. Cambridge: Cambridge University Press.

ask a total stranger for the time, and they give you an answer after looking at their smartphone, you just believe what they tell you.

The defeating circumstances are mostly obvious. If B does not understand what A says, then B will not come to believe what A tells them. (If A speaks a language that B does not understand, then B will not come to believe what A tells them.) If B thinks—rightly or wrongly—that A could not be a reliable informant on the subject matter at hand because of deficits in A, then B will not come to believe what A tells them. (B might have doubts, well-founded or ill-founded, about A's intelligence, expertise, trustworthiness, and so forth. Any such doubts might bring it about that B does not come to believe what A tells them.) If B thinks—rightly or wrongly—that A could not be a reliable informant on the subject matter at hand because of features of that subject matter, then B will not come to believe what A tells them. (B might think that the subject matter is properly given non-cognitivist construal; if so, B will not suppose that what A says is so much as a candidate for belief.) If B thinks that the stakes are sufficiently high, then, even if B has no doubts about A and the subject matter, B might think that independent corroboration is required before credence can be given to what A says. (If B is a patient, and A is a medical expert, B might be well-advised to get a second opinion if A is telling B that B's death is imminent.)

The following generalisation is also *approximately* true: for any person A, for any claim that p that belongs to the store of common human knowledge, if A believes that p, then A believes that p on the basis of testimony. Almost everything that any given person knows about archaeology, anthropology, astronomy, biology, chemistry, computer science, cosmology, decision theory, demography, ecology, economics, education, environmental science, game theory, geology, geo-informatics, history, information theory, jurisprudence, linguistics, logic, mathematics, musicology, physics, political science, psychology, sociology, statistics, systems theory, and so forth is known by that person on the basis of testimony: what teachers have told them, what they have read in textbooks, what they have read in encyclopaedias, what they have gleaned from Wikipedia, and so on.

When testimonial claims—claims that are grounded solely in testimonial considerations—are called into question, attention properly turns to matters of defeat. Do we have reason to believe that we have (enough) independent testimonial sources? Do we have reason to believe that we are correctly interpreting our testimonial sources? Do we have reason to believe that our original testimonial informants were reliable with respect to the claim at issue? Do we have reason to believe that the testimony is sufficiently weighty given what is at stake? And so on. These questions are among the most important questions to ask in connection with all *historical* religious texts.[30]

> It is easy to underestimate the importance of testimony to individual belief. Other people are the source of almost everything that any person believes. Whether a person believes well is thus mostly dependent upon whether their sources believe well: if, for example, you have no idea how to identify who are the experts with respect to a given subject matter, then it is very likely that you will not believe well in connection with that subject matter. The most important components in good education are (1) learning how to identify the genuine experts for those domains in which there are experts and (2) learning how to identify domains in which there are genuine experts.

20 Miracles

Were there miracles, they would be events caused by the actions of non-natural (i.e. not fully or entirely natural) agents. However, there neither are nor could be miracles because there neither are nor could be non-natural agents.

There are many reports of alleged miracles: there are many reports of events that are said to be the result of the actions of non-natural agents. Often enough, the people giving these reports genuinely believe what they report; much of the time, the people

---

30. Further things to read in connection with general considerations about testimony include, for example: Axelrod, A. (1984) *The Evolution of Cooperation*. New York: Basic Books; Coady, A. (1992) *Testimony*. Oxford: Oxford University Press; Fricker, M. (2007) *Epistemic Injustice*. Oxford: Oxford University Press; Goldman, A. (1999) *Knowledge in a Social World*. Oxford: Oxford University Press; Lewis, D. (1969) *Convention*. Cambridge, MA: Harvard University Press; and Surowiecki, J. (2004) *The Wisdom of the Crowds*. New York: Anchor.

giving these reports are reasonable in believing what they report. In particular, those who acquire their belief in miracles from those whom they reasonably take to be trustworthy, and reliable informants about such matters are often enough reasonable in believing as they do. The testimony of those who reasonably believe in miracles in the way just described is *evidence* that properly enters into the deliberations of anyone who is weighing the question whether there are miracles.

If the only relevant evidence that we had was the testimony of those who reasonably believe in miracles—and if there were not too much conflict in that testimony—then, plausibly, it would be reasonable to accept that testimony and reject naturalism. But, of course, there is lots of other relevant evidence, some bearing directly on miracles, and the rest bearing on naturalism. Even the most casual investigation of miracle claims discloses immediately that the vast majority of them pivot on knavery and folly. Against this backdrop, miracle claims are immediately dismissible unless they are supported by compelling testimony from a significant number of sufficiently credible, independent, direct witnesses. Where there are doubts about the testimonial independence, credibility, and motivations of witnesses, and questions about the number of witnesses and their epistemic distance from the alleged events, one ought not accept testimony to miracles. But, as Hume observed long ago, there has not been a single miracle claim in human history that is supported by compelling testimony from a significant number of sufficiently credible, independent, direct witnesses.

We now have enough on the table to see that I reject T5: 'God works miracles'. Those who believe in miracles typically insist that claims to miracles on behalf of gods other than the ones in which they happen to believe are mistaken. Given that those who believe in miracles are committed to explaining away the *vast majority* of miracle claims, no disadvantage accrues to those who insist on explaining away *all* miracle claims.[31]

---

31. For further discussion of miracles, see, for example: Earman, J. (2000) *Hume's Abject Failure*. Oxford: Oxford University Press; Fogelin, R. (2003) *A Defence of Hume on Miracles*. Princeton, NJ: Princeton University Press; Levine, M. (1989) *Hume and the Problem of Miracles*. Dordrecht: Kluwer; and Twelftree, G. (ed.) (2009) *Companion to Miracles*. Cambridge: Cambridge University Press.

When we assess historical reports of miracles, we must try to determine how many independent reports we have. One mistake that we should definitely guard against is counting mere reports of reports among the independent reports that we have. If we have a single source that reports that 500 people witnessed an event, then we have just one report of that event. This remains true even if some of the 500 people are named, and we have independent evidence that people bearing those names existed at the time at which the event is alleged to have occurred.

21 Religious Experience

Reported religious experience includes (a) experience generated by religious practice; (b) experiences generated entirely by natural phenomena; (c) dreams and visions; and (d) ecstatic, numinous, unitive, and salvific experiences. None of these kinds of experiences poses explanatory or interpretative challenges to naturalism.

Experiences generated by religious practices are explained by the existence of those practices. Experiences generated by natural phenomena are explained by those phenomena and the prior existence of religious beliefs. Dreams and visions—of which religious dreams and visions are a special case—are not yet fully understood, but no experts seriously suppose that we need to invoke non-natural entities in order to explain non-religious dreams and visions. Ecstatic, numinous, and salvific experiences are explained by a combination of religious practices, religious beliefs, and the central explanatory elements in naturalistic accounts of dreams and visions.

Unitive experience is the most interesting case. Naturalists report having experiences of being at one with nature. They also report having other hard-to-interpret experiences: shivers down the spine, surprising variations in mood and affect, feelings of being watched, intimations that they are looking at things from completely new perspectives, and so on. There is absolutely no reason why naturalists should not suppose that all of this is susceptible of fully satisfying explanation in terms of cognitive neuroscience and biosocial evolutionary history.

We now have enough on the table to see that I reject T6: 'God is encountered in religious experience'. Those who believe in gods typically claim that their gods are encountered in their religious experience but deny that the gods of others are encountered in the religious experience of others. Given that those who believe in gods are committed to explaining away the claims of those who insist on religious experience of *other* gods, there is no disadvantage that accrues to those who seek to explain away *all* claims to religious experience of gods.[32]

> One significant advantage that accrues to naturalism is the uniformity of the accounts that it gives of reports of miracles and religious experiences. Everyone disputes most reports of miracles and most non-naturalistically interpreted reports of religious experiences. But only naturalists reject all reports of miracles and all non-naturalistically interpreted reports of religious experience. Others indulge in special pleading for a small set of reports of miracles and non-naturalistically interpreted reports of religious experience that hold significance for their own religions.

22 Religion

Recent work in cognitive anthropology supports something like the following definition of 'religion':[33] **Religions** are communal displays of costly commitments to the satisfaction of non-natural causal beings (e.g. gods and/or ancestor spirits) and/or the overcoming of non-natural causal regulative structures (e.g. cycles of reincarnation, reward, and punishment) resulting from evolutionary canalisation and convergence of (1) widespread belief in non-natural causal agents and/or non-natural causal regulative structures; (2)

---

32. For further discussion of religious experience, see, for example: Boyer, P. (2001) *Religion Explained*. New York: Basics Books; Guthrie, S. (1995) *Faces in the Clouds*. New York: Oxford University Press; James, W. (1902/2012) *The Varieties of Religious Experience*. Oxford: Oxford University Press; and Taves, A. (2000) *Fits, Trances and Visions*. Princeton, NJ: Princeton University Press.
33. See Atran, S. and Norenzayan, A. (2004) 'Religion's Evolutionary Landscape: Counterintuition, Commitment, Compassion, Communion' *Behavioural and Brain Sciences* 27: 713–770.

hard-to-fake public expressions of costly material commitments—offerings and/or sacrifices of goods, property, time, and/or lives—to the satisfaction of those non-natural causal agents and/or the overcoming of, or escape from, those non-natural causal regulative structures; (3) mastering of people's existential anxieties—for example, catastrophe, death, deception, disease, injustice, loneliness, loss, pain, and want—by those costly commitments to the satisfaction of those non-natural causal agents and/or the overcoming of, or escape from, those non-natural causal regulative structures; and (4) ritualised, rhythmic, sensory co-ordination of all of the above in communion, congregation, intimate fellowship, and the like.

The religions of the world exhibit both interesting similarities and interesting differences.

Here is an example of a similarity: many religions are committed to sky fathers and earth mothers. Why is this? Plausibly, as Smith (2019)[34] suggests, because of the universal significance of rain for human beings: without rain, nothing grows. Here is an obvious explanation for this datum: the sky (father) inseminates the earth (mother) with rain. This point of similarity across religions is explained by relatively superficial features of human beings and their environments.

Here is an example of a difference: no two religions agree on their metaphysical and ritual teachings. Why is this? Plausibly because those teachings are *all* products of human imagination that have no foundation or grounding in reality. There are no non-natural agents; there are no non-natural causal regulative structures. *A fortiori*, there is no satisfying non-natural agents; *a fortiori*, there is no overcoming or escaping from non-natural causal regulative structures.

Adherents of any particular religion claim that their religion is special: it alone has metaphysical and ritual teachings that are grounded in reality. Claims of privileged status for the scriptures, traditions, and authority of a particular religion inevitably rely on claims about testimonial privilege: in the case of their religion alone, the testimonial credentials of the original witnesses to the relevant metaphysical and ritual teachings survive critical scrutiny.

---

34. Smith, T. (2019) *The Methods of Science and Religion*. New York: Lexington Books.

Naturalists are uniquely well-placed to explain *all* of the similarities and differences exhibited by the religions of the world: their account of the religions of the world is entirely uniform and even-handed.

We now have enough on the table to see that I reject T7: 'Belief in God is more or less universal'. It is very plausible that, throughout most of human history, no one has believed that there is exactly one god. Over the past few thousand years, belief that there is exactly one god has become more common; but even today, a very significant part of the population of the world does not believe that there is exactly one god. The distribution across time and space of the belief that there is just one god fits very nicely with the naturalist view that that belief fails to track the truth.[35]

> Given what we know about evolution, human history, testimony, reports of miracles, reports of religious experience, and the distribution of religious belief across time and space, it is overwhelmingly probable that monotheism is a late and local development among human beings. Moreover, naturalism is uniquely well placed to explain the similarities and differences between human religions, the sequence of emergence of human religions, and the roles that appeals to reports of miracles and reports of religious experience play in interreligious disputes.

23 Mindedness

Expert scientific consensus tells us that human beings are relatively recently evolved biological organisms. Every human organism has its origins in the fusion of a human sperm with a human ovum. In every human organism, there is antenatal development of biological systems, including neural systems, whose operations are required

---

35. For more about religion, see, for example: Atran, S. (2002) *In Gods We Trust*. Oxford: Oxford University Press; McCauley, R. (2011) *Why Religion Is Natural and Science Is Not*. Oxford: Oxford University Press; Norenzayan, A. (2013) *Big Gods*. Princeton, NJ: Princeton University Press; Talmont-Kaminski, K. (2013) *Religion as Magical Ideology*. Durham: Acumen; and Tremlin, T. (2006) *Minds and Gods*. Oxford: Oxford University Press.

for continuing postnatal existence and flourishing. In every human organism, those biological systems eventually cease working, never to resume. The death of every human organism is followed by decay: eventually, all traces vanish.

Expert scientific consensus allows that minded organisms are properly described using a range of mental vocabulary. Minded organisms are *conscious*, have *agency*, *perceive* their immediate surroundings, *believe, desire, intend, think, imagine, remember, learn, predict, feel, empathise, suffer, reason, calculate, communicate*, and so on. There are contemporary and historical cases where it is controversial whether given organisms are minded. But there are clear cases of non-minded organisms that lack nervous systems: bacteria, amoeba, paramecia, and so on. And there are clear cases of non-minded non-organisms: cups, tables, trains, towns, continents, gas giants, solar systems, galaxies, and so forth. It remains controversial whether there can be minded non-organisms (e.g. androids).

Expert scientific consensus tells us that we have no reason to suppose that we need to appeal to anything beyond biological processes in organisms, the local environments of those organisms, and the local, social, and biological evolutionary histories of those organisms, in order to explain the proper application of mental vocabulary to those organisms. For minded organisms to be *conscious* just is for those organisms to be engaged in certain kinds of neural processing. For minded organisms to be *perceiving* their environments just is for those organisms, in those environments, to be engaged in certain kinds of neural processing that have been appropriately shaped by local, social, and biological evolutionary history and that are appropriately causally related to those environments. For minded organisms to be *believing* just is for those organisms to be engaged in a particular kind of neural processing that is appropriately related to (a) other kinds of neural processing, such as desiring and intending; (b) perceiving; and (c) behaviour. All other mental vocabulary admits of similar naturalistic explanations.[36]

---

36. For more on naturalistic accounts of mindedness, see, for example: Armstrong, D. (1968) *A Materialist Theory of Mind*. London: Routledge; Hohwy, J. (2013) *The Predictive Mind*. Oxford: Oxford University Press; Kim, J. (1998) *Mind in a Physical World*. Cambridge, MA: MIT Press; Metzinger, T. (2009) *The Ego Tunnel*. New York: Basic Books; and Millikan, R. (1984) *Language, Thought, and Other Biological Categories*. Cambridge, MA: MIT Press.

On my account of mindedness, it is clear that human beings are minded, but it is also clear that there might be many other kinds of things that are minded. Here are some possible (but contentious) examples: (1) non-human organisms, (2) groups of human beings, (3) human organisations and institutions, (4) artificial intelligent agents, and (5) aliens. In at least some of these things, it need not be that neural processing plays any role in their mindedness. The accounts that I have given in the text merely concern what it is for human beings to be minded.

24 Consciousness and Intentionality

Some philosophers think that there are thought experiments that (decisively) defeat the naturalistic account of mindedness that I just sketched.

According to some philosophers, the functionalist account of believing (desiring, intending, etc.) is shown to be mistaken by thought experiments in which the functioning is preserved but other essential features of mindedness are absent. According to Searle,[37] there is no *understanding* in the **Chinese Room**. According to Block,[38] there is no *consciousness* in the **China Brain**. According to Block,[39] there is no *intelligence* in **Blockhead**. My way with these thought experiments is very short: the scenarios they describe are all impossible. The Chinese Room and Blockhead are impossible on combinatorial grounds: they require that the Chinese Room and Blockhead contain more discrete bits of information than there are atoms in the visible universe. The China Brain is impossible on grounds of finite signal transmission times: there is no way that a behaviourally normal human organism could have its brain replaced by the China Brain.

---

37. Searle, J. (1980) 'Minds, Brains, and Programs' *Brain and Behavioural Sciences* 3: 417–424.
38. Block, N. (1978) 'Troubles With Functionalism' *Minnesota Studies in the Philosophy of Science* 9: 261–325.
39. Block, N. (1981) 'Psychologism and Behaviourism' *Philosophical Review* 90: 5–43.

According to some philosophers, the naturalist account of consciousness is shown to be mistaken by thought experiments in which the neural processing is present but consciousness is absent. According to Chalmers,[40] I could have the very same neural processing that I in fact have without its being true that there is something that it is like to be an organism in which that neural processing occurs. My way with this example is also very short: it is impossible for there to be an organism in which there is that kind of neural processing and yet for which it is true that that there is nothing that it is like to be that organism. It is true that it could be that I put vegemite into my mouth and taste nothing because there is some malfunction in my taste receptors or in my processing of signals from my taste receptors. But, if everything is in working order, then it is impossible for me to put vegemite into my mouth without there being something that it is like for me to be tasting that stuff, there and then.

According to some philosophers, the naturalistic account of mindedness is shown to be mistaken by thought experiments in which agents know all of the natural facts and yet are ignorant of some mental facts. According to Jackson,[41] when Mary leaves the **black-and-white room**, she knows all of the relevant natural facts and yet does not know what red looks like. I am sceptical that this scenario is possible; I'm sceptical that anyone could know all of the relevant natural facts. But, even pretending that the scenario is possible, I deny that there is any challenge to naturalistic accounts of mindedness here. Until Mary leaves the black and white room and sees some things that (*ex hypothesi*) she knows to be red, Mary does not have the ability to identify that things are red just by looking at them—that is, without relying on her prior knowledge that those things are red coloured. Mary's knowing what red looks like just is her ability to identify that things are red merely by looking at them (given suitable conditions, normal functioning, etc.).

We now have enough on the table to see that I do not accept T8: 'God caused the emergence and continuing presence of consciousness in our universe'. Given that for organisms to be conscious just is for them to be engaged in certain kinds of neural processing, there is nothing about the distribution of consciousness in our

---

40. Chalmers, D. (1996) *The Conscious Mind*. New York: Oxford University Press.
41. Jackson, F. (1982) 'Epiphenomenal Qualia' *Philosophical Quarterly* 32: 127–136.

universe that is not satisfactorily explained within the confines of evolutionary theory.[42]

> It is common for objectors to naturalistic accounts of consciousness and intentionality to complain that they cannot see how it could possibly be that consciousness and intentionality are just engagement in neural processing. It is not much less common for aficionados of naturalistic accounts of consciousness and intentionality to insist that they cannot see how it could possibly be that consciousness and intentionality are anything other than engagement in neural processing. As in the wider dispute between naturalists and theists, the important thing to remember is to begin with sufficiently well-worked-out versions of competing accounts, and then to assess the relative theoretical virtues of those competing accounts. It is generally easy to criticise someone else's philosophical theory if you are not simultaneously subjecting your own views to exactly the same kind of critical scrutiny.

25 Reason

Recent psychological investigation supports the claim that our reasoning capacities are subserved by two distinct bases. Base 1 is fast, automatic, frugal, heuristic, possibly modular, and acquired by biology in concert with exposure and experience. Base 2 is slow, controlled, expensive, located in central processing, and acquired by enculturation and formal tuition. Base 2 is too expensive to be

---

42. For more on naturalistic accounts of consciousness, see, for example: Baars, B. (1988) *A Cognitive Theory of Consciousness*. Cambridge: Cambridge University Press; Dennett, D. (1991) *Consciousness Explained*. Boston, MA: Little, Brown; Prinz, J. (2012) *The Conscious Brain*. Oxford: Oxford University Press; and Schwitzgebel, E. (2011) *Perplexities of Consciousness*. Cambridge, MA: MIT Press. For more on naturalistic accounts of intentionality, see, for example: Chalmers, D. (1996) *The Conscious Mind*. New York: Oxford University Press; Dretske, F. (1988) *Explaining Behaviour*. Cambridge, MA: MIT Press; Levine, J. (2001) *Purple Haze*. Cambridge, MA: MIT Press; and Stich, S. (1983) *From Folk Psychology to Cognitive Science*. Cambridge, MA: MIT Press.

always available. We all rely on Base 1 when we are tired, or emotional, or when Base 2 is exhausted by extended use, or when there are no cues or prompts for Base 2.

Aspects of Base 1 are directly selected: fast, automatic, frugal heuristics are keyed to evolutionary success. A range of basic logical and mathematical techniques are built into Base 1 (e.g. some simple Boolean operations). But Base 1 heuristics lead to diverse inferential errors that have been demonstrated and recorded in psychological experiments: anchoring, availability, backfire effect, base rate neglect, confirmation bias, conjunction fallacy, Dunning-Kruger effect, frequency illusion, fundamental attribution error, gambler's fallacy, halo effect, hindsight bias, hot-hand fallacy, insensitivity to sample size, pareidolia, stereotyping, and so on.

Base 2 is directly selected as central processing: its evolutionary development correlated with increase in complexity of human social organisation, development of language, and competitive advantage accrued by human beings who were better predictors of the behaviour of other human beings. However, capacity to engage in reflective logical and mathematical reasoning is a culturally and educationally scaffolded by-product that extends the logical and mathematical techniques embedded in Base 1.

Human reason is a distinctively social achievement. The institutions of science—the consequences of the role of universal expert agreement as regulative ideal—create the possibility of scientific rationality. Individually, each of us is prone to Base 1 inferential errors at varying levels of frequency; but collectively, at our best, we have institutional resources that enable us to rise above that susceptibility.

Across a broad range of commonsense domains, our cognitive faculties—perception, memory, *a priori* intuition, sympathy, introspection, testimony, moral sense, and so forth—are reliable: they yield a preponderance of truth over falsity. Across a further extended range of scientific domains, our cognitive faculties are reliable only if they are keyed to the deliverances of scientific experts. And elsewhere—for example, in religion, politics, philosophy, and other domains where disagreement is rampant—our cognitive faculties are unreliable: most of the religious, political, and philosophical opinions of most of us are simply false.

We now have enough on the table to see that I do not accept T9: 'Our beliefs are reliable because God designed our cognitive faculties'. Our beliefs are reliable just where evolutionary theory leads us to expect them to be reliable; and our beliefs are unreliable in ways that are hard to fathom if our cognitive faculties are designed by God.[43]

> It is very important not to mythologise *individual* human capacities for reason and reasoning. Even when we exercise our abilities to draw on the resources afforded by historical collaborative investigation, our individual efforts at reasoning regularly go awry. We do not need elaborate psychological experiments to show that this is so: we need only consider rampant extant disagreement in spheres where many people make sustained deployment of System 2. Naturalism has a ready, plausible explanation for these features of our reasoning; it is not clear that any alternative to naturalism has a similarly ready and plausible explanation.

26 Freedom

Here are two basic claims about freedom. (1) *Free choice*: Necessarily, people choose freely just in case they choose according to their standardly acquired beliefs, desires, intentions, and so forth in the absence of defeating conditions. (2) *Free action*: Necessarily, people act freely just in case they act on their standardly acquired beliefs, desires, intentions, and so forth in the absence of defeating conditions.

Defeating conditions for both free choice and free action include, for example, addiction; trauma; the effects of subliminal advertising; direct causation of one's beliefs, desires, intentions, and so forth by someone else, as, for example, in brainwashing and certain kinds of torture; and external constraints, such as being imprisoned or having a gun held to one's head.

---

43. For more on naturalistic accounts of reason, see, for example: Byrne, R. (1995) *The Thinking Ape*. Oxford: Oxford University Press; Gigerenzer, G. (2007) *Gut Feelings*. London: Allen Lane; Kahneman, D. (2011) *Thinking Fast and Slow*. London: Penguin; Kahneman et al. (1982) *Judgment Under Uncertainty*. Cambridge: Cambridge University Press; and Rolls, E. and Deco, G. (2010) *The Noisy Brain*. Oxford: Oxford University Press.

Note that, given the key tenets of my naturalism, it is standardly *not* the case that there are other agents who have direct causal responsibility for our beliefs, desires, intentions, and so forth. However, there are many non-naturalist worldviews on which it is standardly the case that there are other agents who have direct causal responsibility for our beliefs, desires, and intentions. On my account of freedom, on those worldviews, we do not have freedom of choice and freedom of action.

Note, too, that my account of freedom of choice and freedom of action is *compatibilist*: it says nothing about whether, for example, we have the capacity to choose and do other than what we actually choose and do *given the circumstances in which we choose and act*, where those circumstances include the beliefs, desires, intentions, and so forth that we actually have. What matters for my freedom of choice and freedom of action is that my choices and actions depend in the right way on my standardly acquired beliefs, desires, intentions, and so forth. Had my standardly acquired beliefs, desires, intentions, and so forth been different in the right way, then I would have made different free choices and performed different free actions.[44]

> In §6, I noted that I hold that causation is indeterministic: there are at least some cases where causation is chancy. Thus, although my account of freedom is compatibilist—that is, it could be consistently put together with a view according to which causation is deterministic—the worldview that I am presenting is not deterministic. However, even though I allow that some macro-causation is chancy, I am here taking no stance on the question whether our mental causation is typically deterministic.

---

44. For more on naturalistic accounts of freedom, see, for example: Dennett, D. (1984) *Elbow Room*. Cambridge, MA: MIT Press; Holton, R. (2009) *Willing, Wanting, Waiting*. New York: Oxford University Press; Levy, N. (2011) *Hard Luck*. New York: Oxford University Press; Mele, A. (2017) *Aspects of Agency*. New York: Oxford University Press; and Wolf, S. (1990) *Freedom Within Limits*. New York: Oxford University Press.

27 Morality

According to the worldview that I am sketching, true moral principles are necessarily true. Given that true moral principles are necessarily true, there is no explaining why they are necessary. However, because they are necessary, their necessity explains why they are true. Moreover, given that the necessity of some moral claims is a logical consequence of the necessity of other moral claims, our commitment is limited to a small number of *primitive* moral principles.

Here are two examples of true moral principles. (1) *Killing*: it is morally wrong to kill, except in special circumstances. (2) *Torture*: it is morally wrong to torture babies for fun. Note that while it is outright morally wrong to torture babies for fun, it is morally wrong to kill only if special circumstances do not apply.

Some circumstances in which it is not morally wrong to kill are readily identified. Some killing in self-defence, and in defence of kith and kin, and by police and military personnel, is not morally wrong. Other circumstances in which it may not be morally wrong to kill are less clear-cut. Perhaps some killing—of non-human animals—for commercial, industrial, and recreational purposes, is not morally wrong. Perhaps some voluntary euthanasia, some abortion, and some state-authorised killing of those guilty of particular offences against the state (e.g. treason) is not morally wrong.

It is easy to extend the list of fundamental moral *proscriptions*: it is outright morally wrong to engage in sexual assault; it is morally wrong, except in special circumstances, to lie or steal; and so on. It is also easy to make a list of moral *prescriptions*: it is outright morally required that we collectively make adequate provisions for the least fortunate among us; it is morally required, except in special circumstances, that we obey the laws of the land; and so forth.

Just as there are moral truths couched in the language of wrongs and obligations, there are moral truths couched in the language of rights and freedoms. Here is an example. *Freedom*: each person is provisionally entitled to the maximum amount of freedom that is consistent with the following two conditions: (a) everyone else has provisional entitlement to that same degree of freedom and (b) the provisional entitlement to freedom of each is limited equally by the rights and provisional entitlements to freedom of everyone else. A person's entitlement to freedom is reduced from their provisional entitlement in proportion to their violations of the rights and freedoms of anyone else; a person's entitlement to freedom is their provisional entitlement to freedom unless that is reduced for the reason just given.

According to the worldview that I am sketching, there is no priority of the good over the right, of the right over the virtuous, of the virtuous over the good, and so on. Familiar moral reasoning draws on a mix of consequentialist, deontological, and virtue-theoretic considerations: we are properly motivated to virtuously pursue what is good under the circumscription of what is right. Consequently, there is no simple algorithm to which moral reasoning reduces: even the most apparently straightforward practical moral judgments require keeping a number of different balls in the air.

We now have enough on the table to see that I reject T10: 'There are objective moral facts because God legislates them'. I say that there are objective moral facts because there must be. And I say that there is no explanation of why there must be objective moral facts. I think that there are independent difficulties for the view that there are objective moral facts because God legislates them. But these are not my primary reasons for rejecting T10.[45]

> It is not uncommon for theists to claim that naturalists can have no adequate account of morality. I think, on the contrary, that the main difficulty that naturalists face is in choosing between attractive competing accounts of morality. Some naturalists are eliminativists about morality; some naturalists are fictionalist about morality; some naturalists are reductivists about morality; and some naturalists are (primitive) realists about morality. Each of these positions has its attractions. On balance, I favour realism; I do not see that realism about moral truth is any more problematic than realism about mathematical truth.

---

45. For more on naturalistic accounts of morality, see, for example: Enoch, D. (2011) *Taking Morality Seriously*. Oxford: Oxford University Press; Foot, P. (2001) *Natural Goodness*. Oxford: Clarendon; Parfit, D. (2011) *On What Matters*. Oxford: Oxford University Press; Scanlon, T. (1998) *On What We Owe to Each Other*. Cambridge, MA: Harvard University Press; and Wong, D. (2006) *Natural Moralities*. Oxford: Oxford University Press.

28 Flourishing

I have some sympathy for Aristotle's account of human flourishing. According to Aristotle, flourishing human beings are members of communities that aim to bring about the flourishing of their members. Further, according to Aristotle, the flourishing of members of communities consists in their exercise of moral and intellectual virtues: flourishing people have genuine friendships; possess and exercise both theoretical and practical wisdom; and act with courage, self-control, liberality, munificence, magnanimity, patience, amiability, sincerity, wit, and justice in pursuit of worthwhile individual and collective ends. Finally, according to Aristotle, flourishing human beings are not subject to certain kinds of liabilities: flourishing human beings are not impoverished, unhealthy, victims of misfortunes such as bereavements, and so on.

I think that Aristotle is right to emphasise that communities—from neighbourhoods to nations—should aim at the flourishing of all of their members. I think that Aristotle is right to say that flourishing people have genuine friendships; social isolation is perhaps the greatest enemy of human flourishing. While I think that it is reasonably close to the mark to say that flourishing people exercise virtue in pursuit of worthwhile ends, I think that it is closer to the mark to say that flourishing people find meaning in collective pursuit of worthwhile ends. Perhaps there is something to be said for the exercise of the virtues that Aristotle mentions, to the extent that one has the capacity to exercise them; but one can lead a flourishing life even if one has little or no capacity to exercise many of the virtues on Aristotle's list. Finally, I think that Aristotle's attitude towards 'liabilities' is no more than partially accurate. It is clearly true that loneliness, stress, low self-esteem, lack of self-control, ignorance, and poverty can count against human flourishing and, in their most crippling forms, almost certainly will. Typically, flourishing people belong to networks of flourishing people and have meaningful relationships with people in those networks. Typically, flourishing people have appropriate emotional responses to themselves and others. Typically, flourishing people do not have fantastic beliefs about themselves and the world in which they live. Typically, flourishing people do not engage in self-destructive behaviour, excessive risk-taking, and so forth. But, for some—perhaps even most—people, overcoming 'liabilities' is central to their flourishing: typically, whether we flourish is determined, at least in part, by how we deal with the inevitable curve balls that are thrown at us.[46]

> I am happy to take the characterisation of the good life for human beings to be the central focus of moral and ethical philosophy. I take this to be a question about how we should best live *together*. Perhaps one important aspect of human flourishing is that we so organise ourselves that we collectively apportion worthwhile and satisfying employment in equal measure to all.

29 Meaningfulness

Some people think that, if naturalism is true, human life is meaningless. At some point in the distant future, there will be no direct or indirect traces of human beings or any other living things; there will be no direct or indirect traces of the earth, the solar system, and the Milky Way; there will be no traces of things and kinds of things we value; and there will be no valuable things. From then on, our universe will be cold, lifeless, and empty. But, if that is what the future holds, then what we do now makes no difference: our lives are completely without meaning.

I see no reason to deny that the future of the universe will be like this: cold, lifeless, and empty. But I also see no reason to say that it follows from this that our lives are without meaning and that it makes no difference what we do.

Whether our lives and actions have traces in the far distant future is irrelevant to the meaning and value of our lives and actions in exactly the same way that whether our lives and actions register *now* in far-distant locations (e.g. in the Andromeda galaxy) is irrelevant to the meaning and value of our lives

---

46. For more on virtue and flourishing from a naturalistic perspective, see, for example: Annas, J. (1993) *The Morality of Happiness*. Oxford: Oxford University Press; Hursthouse, R. (1999) *On Virtue Ethics*. Oxford: Oxford University Press; Snow, N. (2010) *Virtue as Social Intelligence*. New York: Routledge; and Swanton, C. (2013) *The Virtue Ethics of Hume and Nietzsche*. Oxford: Wiley-Blackwell.

and actions. What matters for the meaningfulness and value of our lives and action is what happens here and now, not what is registered about what happens here and now in far-off times and places. If I belong to a community that aims to bring about the flourishing of its members, and I am not crushed by overwhelming misfortune, and I exercise moral and intellectual virtue in the pursuit of worthwhile individual and collective ends, then my life is both meaningful and valuable, and the meaning and value of my life are in no way dependent on registration of my existence and deeds in far off times and places.

Some may say that, although I have made a case that human life is not meaningless if naturalism is true, it is nonetheless the case that human life is *ultimately* meaningless if naturalism is true. While it is not altogether straightforward to explain this complaint, perhaps the central thought is that, if naturalism is true, then there is no 'grand moral narrative' in which we are players: the naturalistic story of the universe may be an epic of sound and fury, but it has no moral significance for anyone, and, in particular, it has no moral significance for us.

Naturalists agree that, if naturalism is true, there is no 'grand moral narrative' in which we are players: there is no afterlife, there is no cycle of rebirth, there is no moral scorekeeping that determines our destinies after we die, and there is no cosmic conflict between good and evil in which we play important roles. But naturalists insist that, far from being inimical to flourishing, naturalistic belief conduces to it. As we noted above, flourishing people typically do not have fantastic beliefs about themselves and the world in which they live. Many naturalists have followed Nietzsche in supposing that belief in 'grand moral narratives' conduces against rather than in favour of genuine flourishing.[47]

---

47. For more on naturalistic accounts of meaningfulness, see, for example: Blackburn, S. (2001) *Being Good*. New York: Oxford University Press; Dworkin, R. (2000) *Sovereign Virtue*. Cambridge, MA: Harvard University Press; Frankfurt, H. (2004) *The Reasons of Love*. Princeton, NJ: Princeton University Press; Raz, J. (2001) *Value, Respect and Attachment*. Cambridge: Cambridge University Press; and Wolf, S. (2010) *Meaning in Life and Why It Matters*. Princeton, NJ: Princeton University Press.

Naturalists typically distinguish between different kinds of meaningfulness. We should all want something like lives in which we (a) are not crushed by overwhelming misfortune; (b) belong to communities that aim to bring about the flourishing of their members; and (c) exercise, according to our capacities, moral and intellectual virtue in the pursuit of worthwhile individual and collective ends. But we should not want to be players in fantastical, grand moral narratives of the kinds typically provided by religions.

30 Love

Some people think that there is no place for love in naturalistic worldviews; often, such people stereotype naturalists as cold, impersonal, unemotional, detached, arrogant, angry, quarrelsome, resentful, unforgiving, uncharitable, deceitful, untrustworthy, and over-represented among those with autism spectrum disorders.

Proper objects of love are many and varied: people, objects, principles, goals, causes, and so on. While some might think that naturalists are incapable of loving objects, principles, goals, causes, and the rest, I assume that most will grant that naturalists can and do love all of these kinds of things in the same way that non-naturalists do. Of course, where non-naturalists claim to love non-natural things, naturalists will demur: it makes no sense to express love for what you take to be non-existent things. Naturalists do not love angels, centaurs, demons, fairies, ghosts, ghouls, goblins, gods, mermaids, spirits, unicorns, vampires, werewolves, witches, yeti, and zombies. But that naturalists do not love *these* things is perfectly consistent with naturalists' loving all manner of unproblematically existent things.

Love of people takes many forms: spousal love, other familial love, romantic/erotic love, friendship, hospitality, and so on. While there are differences in the extent to which various virtues figure in these kinds of love, we expect loving relationships to feature intimacy, affection, delight, admiration, commitment, loyalty, concern, honesty, selflessness, kindness, benevolence, charity, altruism, and so on. Moreover, while there are differences in the extent to which various vices can undermine these kinds of love, we expect loving relationships not to feature vanity, self-centredness, mania, obsession, codependence, deceit, dishonesty, disdain, disloyalty, indifference, and so forth.

It follows from what I have already said about morality, flourishing, and meaningfulness that love is one of the central ingredients in human flourishing and the meaningfulness of human lives. Engagement in collective pursuit of worthwhile ends typically requires both love of objects, principles, goals, causes, and so forth, and love of people. Not everyone who flourishes engages in every kind of loving human relationship, but few who flourish engage in no kinds of loving human relationships.

There is simply no evidence that naturalists have any diminished capacity for engagement in loving human relationships. Like everyone else, naturalists typically love their parents, their spouses (if they have spouses), their children (if they have children), their friends, and others whom it is appropriate for them to love. There is also no reason to suppose that naturalists have a diminished theoretical or practical capacity to understand love: intellectual, emotional, and affective capacities are distributed across naturalists in the same way that they are distributed across other categories of people. Finally, there is no good reason to suppose that naturalism provides a distorted or impoverished conception of love. While there is much more to say about the virtues that are characteristic of love and the vices that can undermine it, there is not even *prima facie* reason to suppose that my naturalistic sketch cannot accommodate everything else that has been left unsaid.[48]

> Love—in its many different forms—is no less important to naturalists than it is to non-naturalists. It was a standing trope of eighteenth-century dystopian fictions about communities of atheists—in the works of Swift, Pope, Fielding, Gibbs, Cowper, and many others—that they are simply incapable of love. (There is a very nice discussion of this in James Reeves, *Godless Fictions in the Eighteenth Century: A Literary History of Atheism* (Cambridge: Cambridge University Press, 2020.)) But history has revealed this trope to be a baseless calumny.

---

48. For more on naturalistic accounts of love, see, for example: LaFollette, H. (1996) *Personal Relationships*. Cambridge: Blackwell; Nussbaum, M. (1996) *Love's Knowledge*. Oxford: Oxford University Press; Soble, A. (1990) *The Structure of Love*. New Haven, CT: Yale University Press; Solomon, R. (1988) *About Love*. New York: Simon & Schuster; and Tuomela, R. (1995) *The Importance of Us*. Stanford, CA: Stanford University Press.

31 Art

The *fine* arts (e.g. painting, sculpture, architecture, music, theatre, dance, ballet, opera, photography, film, installations) and the *literary* arts (e.g. poetry, prose, fiction) have a range of intended functions—entertainment, therapy, communication, political instruction, consciousness-raising, propaganda, advertising, and so forth—that are subserved by fundamental human interests in symmetry, harmony, rhythm, balance, beauty, mystery, ambiguity, imagination, ritual, symbolism, expression, interpretation, pleasure, and the like. The dividing line between these arts and the *applied* and *decorative* arts (e.g. jewellery, ceramics, and interior design) is not particularly well-defined: applied arts and decorative arts are subserved by much the same range of interests and have much the same range of intended functions, albeit typically with less emphasis on political instruction and consciousness-raising.

Given the breadth of fundamental human interests that subserve the arts, there is no straightforward story to tell about the historical development of those interests. Some of those interests may have been selected for by merely biological evolution: perhaps this is true, for example, of interests in visual symmetries and auditory rhythms, both of which are found in a wide range of other organisms. Some of these interests may be spandrels: by-products of interests selected by merely biological evolution. However, it is overwhelmingly plausible that most of these interests have emerged from complex interplay of biological and social evolution over the past few million years. Human beings have practised applied arts, decorative arts, and fine arts for at least 50,000 years.

There is no serious challenge to naturalism in our *consumption* of art. On the one hand, there is no challenge to naturalism in the *functions* of art: entertainment, therapy, communication, political instruction, consciousness-raising, propaganda, advertising, and so forth. It is not puzzling, given naturalism, why people seek out entertainment, therapy, and communication; it is not puzzling, given naturalism, why people find themselves subjected to political instruction, consciousness-raising, propaganda, and advertising. On the other hand, there is no challenge to naturalism in the fundamental interests that subserve the functions of art. It is not puzzling, given naturalism, why people are prone to boredom, illness, ignorance, and so on; it is not puzzling, given naturalism, why people are interested in symmetry, harmony, rhythm, balance, beauty, mystery, ambiguity, imagination, ritual, symbolism, expression, interpretation, pleasure, and the rest.

There is also no serious challenge to naturalism in our *production* of art. Production of works of art requires creativity, imagination, and development and exercise of technical skills; production of works of art enables expression of emotion, interpretation of experience, and understanding of self, others, and the universe in which we live; production of significant—excellent, highly regarded—works of art can bring important social benefits—kudos, reputation, fame, wealth, power—to those involved in that production; and so on.

Some people suggest that it is an objection to naturalism that, whereas there is much great art that takes up religion and religious themes, there is more or less no art—let alone great art—that addresses naturalism and naturalistic themes. This is not a serious objection to naturalism. The *hypothesis* of naturalism is a philosophical claim that may not lend itself to artistic explanation. But that is no more an objection to the hypothesis of naturalism than the claim that the intermediate value theorem does not lend itself to artistic explanation is an objection to the intermediate value theorem. When we look at particular arts, we find significant contributions by naturalists in proportion to their representation in the general population. Consider, for example, the following small sample from among the many naturalists who have made significant contributions to literature in the past couple of centuries: Douglas Adams, Kingsley Amis, James Baldwin, Bertolt Brecht, Italo Calvino, Anton Chekhov, Joseph Conrad, Greg Egan, George Eliot, Maxim Gorky, Robert Graves, A. E. Housman, Henrik Ibsen, Franz Kafka, Philip Larkin, Stanislaw Lem, Primo Levi, Sinclair Lewis, Jack London, Somerset Maugham, Iris Murdoch, Marcel Proust, George Bernard Shaw, Gore Vidal, Kurt Vonnegut, Tom Wolfe, and Virginia Wolfe.

Some people suggest that there is serious challenge to naturalism in our *evaluation* of art, and, more generally, in our practices of aesthetic evaluation. However, according to the naturalistic worldview that I am developing, aesthetic claims go the same way as moral claims. True aesthetic claims are necessarily true. Because true aesthetic claims are necessarily true, there is no explaining why they are necessary. But the necessity of aesthetic claims explains why they are true. And because the necessity of some aesthetic claims is a logical consequence of the necessity of other aesthetic claims, our commitment is limited to a small number of primitive general aesthetic principles.

Consider Mozart's piano concerto in D minor. It is true that it is beautiful. It is necessarily true that it is beautiful: there is no possible world in which Mozart's piano concerto in D minor exists and is not beautiful. It is either a primitive truth that Mozart's piano concerto in D minor is beautiful, or else a logical consequence of primitive truths that Mozart's piano concerto in D minor is beautiful. There is a relevant difference between aesthetic claims and moral claims; typically, there is more 'setting up' that is required in order for particular people to be able to recognise the truth of aesthetic claims. On the whole, people are straightforwardly sensitive to true claims about what is good and bad, right and wrong, fair and unfair, just and unjust, and so on. However, whether people are sensitive to true claims about what is beautiful depends, to a much larger degree, on whether they have acquired facility to appreciate the kind of beauty that is at issue. People typically have many more aesthetic blind spots than they have moral blind spots.[49]

> As in the case of morality, it is not uncommon for theists to claim that naturalists can have no adequate account of arts and aesthetics. It seems to me that this claim is plainly false. There are no particular difficulties for naturalists in our production, consumption, appreciation, evaluation and understanding of art. This is true even in the case of *religious* art.

32 Play

Basic sources of pleasure and enjoyment in mammals include food, exercise, hygiene, sleep, sex, and *play*. While it is not fully settled why mammals engage in play, plausible suggestions that might fit into the overall explanation include to practice behaviour, to build global connections in the brain, to clear up excess brain cells in the cerebrum, and to develop flexibility and avoid false endpoints in the

---

49. For more on naturalistic engagements with art, see, for example: Budd, M. (2008) *Music and the Emotions*. London: Routledge; Carroll, N. (1999) *Philosophy of Art*. New York: Routledge; Danto, A. (2013) *The Transfiguration of the Commonplace*. Cambridge, MA: Harvard University Press; Kivy, P. (1980) *The Corded Shell*. Princeton, NJ: Princeton University Press; Walton, K. (1990) *Mimesis as Make-Believe*. Cambridge, MA: Harvard University Press.

acquisition of useful skills and traits. (Perhaps, in some mammals, play also establishes dominance hierarchies in young adults.)

From a naturalistic standpoint, it is straightforward to understand the *evolution* of play in mammals: there are obvious advantages to being a kind of creature that can and does engage in play. Moreover, from a naturalistic standpoint, it is straightforward to understand the *significance* of play: it just is one of the basic sources of pleasure and enjoyment in life. Human beings play and have fun—engage in spontaneous active diversionary behaviours—because these are basic sources of pleasure and enjoyment; and these are basic sources of pleasure and enjoyment for human beings for the same kinds of reasons that these are basic sources of pleasure and enjoyment for other mammals.

Humour is a basic element in many kinds of fun. Typically—but not always—humour involves both verbal and non-verbal elements. Verbal humour may involve puns, jokes, riddles, anecdotes, limericks, bloopers, and so on. Non-verbal humour may involve oddities or exaggerations of size, sound, location, facial expression, non-verbal behaviour, and so forth. While some kinds of humour may be harmful—aggressive humour, self-defeating humour, schadenfreude, taunting, and so forth—many kinds of humour have clear beneficial effects for individuals and groups. Smiling and laughing are important for both psychological and physical well-being: they promote coping, relieve stress, defuse negative emotions, improve group morale, enhance creativity, and so on.

Plausibly, humour is another basic sources of pleasure and enjoyment in human beings and other mammals. If that's right, then, from a naturalistic standpoint, it is straightforward to understand both the evolution of humour in human history and the significance of humour for individual human beings. Humour, like play, contributes to the individual and collective flourishing of human beings; humour, like play, clearly has an evolutionary history that relies on a complex interplay between biological and social features of human individuals and human groups.[50]

---

50. For more by naturalists on humour, see, for example: N. Carroll (2007) *Comedy Incarnate*. Malden, MA: Blackwell; T. Cohen (1999) *Jokes*. Chicago, IL: University of Chicago Press; W. Chafe (2007) *The Importance of Not Being Earnest*. Amsterdam: John Benjamins; J. Morreall (2009) *Comic Relief*. Malden, MA: Wiley-Blackwell; and R. Provine (2000) *Laughter*. Harmondsworth: Penguin.

We now have enough on the table—in my discussion of flourishing, meaningfulness, love, art, and play—to see that I reject T11: 'Life has meaning because God is its architect'. There are many dimensions that give life meaning; none of those dimensions has anything to do with God. I think that there are independent difficulties for the view that life has meaning because God is its architect. But those are not my primary reasons for rejecting T11.

> It is common enough for theists to claim that naturalists cannot adequately explain play, or art, or love, or meaning, or flourishing, and so on. However, it seems to me that naturalistic explanations that find evolutionary origins for these things have a satisfying depth and complexity that theistic explanations that eschew appeal to evolutionary origins plainly lack. Of course, these evolutionary origins are not the whole story, but they are a very important part of the whole story.

33 Suffering

At least locally, our universe is filled with horrendous suffering. Some of the horrendous suffering of humans and other animals is due primarily to *natural* causes: bushfires, crop failures, droughts, earthquakes, epidemics, floods, hurricanes, meteor strikes, plagues, tornadoes, tsunamis, and so on. Some of the horrendous suffering of humans and other animals is consequent upon the actions of *moral* agents: genocide, mass murder, pack rape, torture, war, and so forth. Some of the most horrendous suffering of humans and other animals is due to the combined effects of natural causes and moral agents (e.g. droughts in war-ravaged countries). It is plausible that the capacity for suffering appeared in our corner of the universe more than 500 million years ago; the amount of horrendous suffering that has occurred in our corner of the universe is nigh incomprehensible.

The distribution of horrendous suffering across time and place in our corner of the universe has a straightforward naturalistic explanation provided by evolutionary big history. At least until very recently, every bushfire, every drought, every earthquake, every flood, every hurricane, every meteor strike, every tornado, every tsunami, and every other natural disaster had an entirely naturalistic causal explanation. At least until very recently, the suffering of every sentient organism had an entirely naturalistic explanation in terms of some among a range of entirely natural causes: natural disaster, attacks from predators, invasion by viruses and bacteria, the deleterious effects of ageing, and so on. Moreover, in more recent times, the only additional factor that needs to be added to these explanations is the activity, and the consequences of the activity, of human beings.

Horrendous suffering is *bad*. Really, genuinely bad. Intrinsically bad. Moreover, intentionally engineering horrendous suffering is *wrong*. Really, genuinely wrong. Necessarily wrong. Where horrendous suffering arises from merely natural causes, there is nothing that it is to blame for the horrendous suffering: there is nothing to which we can point the finger and say 'This is at least partly your fault!' Such horrendous suffering is intrinsically bad, but there is no further dimension to our assessment of it. However, where horrendous suffering arises from the activities, and the consequences of the activities, of human beings, there is a further dimension to our assessment; there may be something that is to blame for the horrendous suffering: we may be able to point the finger and say 'This is at least partly your fault!' Moreover, in cases where there is intentional engineering of horrendous suffering, we will typically be justified in judging that we are dealing with the worst possible kind of case. If there is no difference in the intrinsic badness of two cases of horrendous suffering, but just one of those cases involves intentional engineering of the horrendous suffering, then we shall rightly think that that case is worse.

One consequence of the position that I have just outlined is that the supposition that non-natural agents are responsible for engineering cases of horrendous suffering makes those cases *worse* than they would be if there were no such engineering by non-natural agents. It is a positive feature of naturalism that it does not say that there are non-natural agents who are responsible for horrendous suffering that we would otherwise say is due to none but natural causes.

We have enough on the table to see that I reject T12: 'Evil is objectively horrifying because it is an affront to God'. I agree that horrendous suffering is objectively bad, and that intentionally engineering horrendous suffering is objectively wrong. But it is necessary that horrendous suffering is objectively bad, and it is necessary that intentionally engineering horrendous suffering is wrong. Since these things are necessary, they cannot depend upon God's affront—or anything else.[51]

> Given the correctness of what I have said in previous sections (in particular, §§3, 8, 17, and 23), it is clear that naturalism has no problem accounting for the data about suffering on earth over the past 500 million years. In particular, naturalism does not require new postulates—additional ontological, ideological, and theoretical commitments—in order to give a satisfactory account of that data.

34 Death

As I noted in §21, a biological organism dies when the biological systems that are essential to its being alive switch off for the last time. In most cases, these systems (neural, cardiovascular, pulmonary, etc.) finally switch off at more or less the same time. However, there are some cases in which some but not all of these systems have switched off for the last time, where it is not clear whether we should think that the organism is still alive. Having *all* of the relevant systems switch off for the last time is sufficient for death, but may not be necessary.

Given what I said in §26, there is nothing more to the mindedness of organisms than the presence of neural processing in those organisms: it is impossible for any aspects of the mindedness of an organism to survive the death of that organism. According to my naturalism, for any given organism, the existence of that organism begins at some point after its conception and ends with its death. There is no afterlife. There is no beforelife. There is no cycle of reincarnation. Moreover, these claims are all true of necessity. There cannot be an afterlife. There cannot be a beforelife. There cannot be a cycle of reincarnation.

---

51. For more by naturalists on suffering, see, for example: Anderson, R. (2014) *Human Suffering and Quality of Life*. Dordrecht: Springer; Davies, J. (2012) *The Importance of Suffering*. New York: Routledge; Halpern, C. (2002) *Suffering, Politics, Power*. Albany: State University of New York Press; Mayerfeld, J. (2002) *Suffering and Moral Responsibility*. Oxford: Oxford University Press; and Scarry, E. (1988) *The Body in Pain*. Oxford: Oxford University Press.

Given what I said in §22, there can be no 'transfer' of mindedness between organisms, no 'uploading' from the 'neural hardware' of one organism that is then 'downloaded' to the 'neural hardware' of another organism. Maybe it is possible to exchange the 'neural hardware' of two organisms or to replace the 'neural hardware' of one organism with the 'neural hardware' of another organism. However, 'neural hardware' is subject to the same vicissitudes as other bodily parts: such replacement would lead, at most, to modest extensions of the life spans of 'neural hardware'.

Death is nothing to be regretted. You did not exist before the biological systems that are essential to your being alive switched on for the first time; you will not exist after the biological systems that are essential to your being alive switch off for the last time. Your not existing after your death is no more to be regretted than your not existing before your conception. Which is just to say that neither is to be regretted at all: it makes no sense to regret what you take to be necessarily so.

For similar reasons, death is nothing to be feared. *Dying* may be a different matter. For many people, dying brings the most pain that they ever endure. Moreover, often enough, people know that they are dying and so have reduced resources for dealing with that pain: for example, at least by naturalist lights, they cannot then properly look forward to any pain-free future states. The right response here, at least by naturalist lights, is to accept that your death might be painful. It is one of the facts of life that some deaths are painful. Until your time comes, you have no way of knowing whether your death will be painful nor—if it will be painful—how painful it will be. You gain nothing by worrying about this before your dying comes. Before you start to die, there is much else in which you do far better to invest your emotional and intellectual energy.[52]

---

52. For more by naturalists on death, see, for example: Bradley, B. (2009) *Well-Being and Death*. Oxford: Oxford University Press; Feldman, F. (1994) *Confrontations With the Reaper*. Oxford: Oxford University Press; Kagan, S. (2012) *Death*. New Haven, CT: Yale University Press; Luper, S. (2012) *The Philosophy of Death*. Cambridge: Cambridge University Press; Rosenberg, J. (1998) *Thinking Clearly About Death*. Indianapolis: Hackett; and Yourgrau, P. (2019) *Death and Non-existence*. Oxford: Oxford University Press.

Given the correctness of what I have said in previous sections (in particular, §§3, 8, 17, 21, 23, 26, and 33), it is clear that naturalism has no problem accounting for the data about death. Moreover, there is no reason to think that naturalists cannot have liveable attitudes towards their own deaths and the deaths of those near and dear to them.

35 Salvation

In many religions, teachings about death and the meaning of life connect to teachings about salvation. In particular, in many religions, post-mortem fate is tied to achievement of salvation. Those who are saved are rewarded in heaven or escape from samsara; those who are no saved are punished in hell or remain in the cycle of birth and death.

As I noted in the previous section, according to my naturalism, these teachings about salvation are necessarily false. There cannot be an afterlife. There cannot be a beforelife. There cannot be a cycle of reincarnation. There cannot be reward in heaven. There cannot be punishment in hell. There cannot be release from—nor continuation in—an ongoing cycle of birth and death. It cannot be that the central purpose of life is to gain reward in heaven. It cannot be that the central purpose of life is to escape from the cycle of death and rebirth.

If naturalists assign a credence—a probability—to the claim that there is salvation, and value to their being saved given that there is salvation, what should that credence and value be? I think that naturalists should assign zero credence to the claim that there is salvation: given that they think that salvation is impossible, there is no other probability that it makes sense for them to assign to salvation. And I think that naturalists should refrain from assigning a value to their being saved given that there is salvation, for here we are asking naturalists to assign a value that is conditioned on something that naturalists take to be impossible. But there is simply no sensible way for naturalists to do that.

Does this mean that my naturalists hold that salvation is ruled out *a priori*? Not at all. Commitment to naturalism is justified by the judgment that, among worldviews, naturalism makes the best trade-off between minimising commitments and maximising breadth and depth of explanation. That judgment is *a posteriori*: it depends upon taking all relevant evidence into account. There is nothing in the commitment to naturalism that rules out a change of mind: a naturalist could come to think that some non-naturalistic worldviews makes a better fist of the trade-off between minimising commitments and maximising breadth and depth of explanation. My naturalists maintain only that it is necessary *a posteriori* that there is no salvation.

There is a distinctive feature of my naturalism that is worth noting here. I maintain that decision between worldviews is not well-modelled by Bayesian machinery. This is not because Bayesian decision theory is nowhere applicable—when it comes to, for example, my choice about whether or not to carry my umbrella, Bayesian modelling gives a perfectly accurate representation of my reasoning. Rather, the central point is that there is a limit to the scope of application of the Bayesian machinery. When I choose between worldviews, I am not choosing between **alethic** possibilities, but those are the only kinds of possibilities over which it makes sense to assign probabilities. Mere **doxastic possibilities**—things that it is possible for people to reasonably believe—simply are not appropriate bearers of probabilities in domains of theory choice.[53]

> There are many reasons why naturalists do not choose to take Pascal's wager. One distinctive reason that emerged in the preceding discussion is that naturalists assign zero credence to the claim that God exists, because they think that it is impossible (a posteriori) that God exists. Given that you assign zero credence to the claim that God exists, and given that you assign higher utility to not believing that God exists than to believing that God exists given that God does not exist, it falls out immediately that your expected utility for not believing that God exists is higher than your expected utility for believing that God exists. So Pascal's wager does not even make it to the starting gate.

---

53. For more by naturalists on salvation, see, for example: Blackmore, S. (1993) *Dying to Live*. Amherst, VA: Prometheus; Dworkin, R. (2013) *Religion Without God*. Cambridge, MA: Harvard University Press; Martin, M. and Augustine, K. (eds.) (2015) *The Myth of an Afterlife*. Lanham: Rowman & Littlefield; and Scheffler, S. (2016) *Death and the Afterlife*. Oxford: Oxford University Press.

36 Infinity

It is currently an open question whether the volume of our universe is finite or infinite. If the volume of our universe is finite, then it may be potentially infinite: it may go on increasing without limit forever. Equally, if the volume of our universe is finite, it may not be potentially infinite: it may go on increasing asymptotically forever, or it may, at some point, cease increasing (and perhaps even start decreasing).

If the volume of our universe is infinite, then it may be that our universe contains infinitely many stars. However, even if our universe contains infinitely many stars, it is impossible that our universe contains infinitely large hotels, or libraries that hold infinitely many books, or infinitely many mobsters who conspire to kill a single victim, or machines that exhaustively check Goldbach's conjecture in finite time, or machines that print out a complete decimal representation of pi in finite time, and so on.

If, as I have been pretending, our universe exhausts the causal domain, then the history of the causal domain is finite. However, if our universe does not exhaust the causal domain, it may be that the history of the causal domain is infinite, as it is on some of Antony Aguirre's cosmological models. However, even if the history of the causal domain is infinite, it is impossible that there is someone who has been writing since infinity past, or someone who has counted backwards from infinity, or the like.

It is currently an open question whether the number of different possible physical configurations that might be contained in a given finite volume of spacetime—say, one cubic light year in one year—is finite or infinite. If there are infinitely many such possible configurations, then there are infinitely many possible worlds. If there are only finitely many such possible configurations, then there may still be infinitely many possible worlds, or there may be only finitely many possible worlds. However, even if there are infinitely many possible physical configurations in finite volumes of spacetime, it is impossible that our universe contains an infinitely divided stick, or a switch that is flicked infinitely often in a finite period of time, or a piece of string that successively shaped into every possible regular n-gon in a finite period of time, and so forth.[54]

---

54. For more by naturalists on infinity, see, for example: Barrow, J. (2005) *The Infinite Book*. New York: Vintage; Huemer, M. (2016) *Approaching Infinity*. London: Palgrave Macmillan; Oppy, G. (2006) *Philosophical Perspectives on Infinity*. Cambridge: Cambridge University Press; and Rucker, R. (2004) *Infinity and the Mind*. Princeton, NJ: Princeton University Press.

Considerations about infinity figure prominently in many debates about the existence of God. Given the claims I made in §§3 and 4, it is an open question whether natural reality is infinite in certain respects. In particular, it remains unsettled whether natural reality has an infinite past, an infinite future, an infinite volume, and an infinite number of separate domains ('universes'). However, given those earlier claims, I think it *is* settled that most of the things discussed in 'paradoxes of the infinite' do not—and could not—exist: infinite hotels, infinite libraries, and so forth.

37 Perfection

Idealisations and approximations serve many useful purposes. Scientific calculations may only be analytically tractable when modelling takes certain quantities to be infinite. The use of idealisations and approximations does not entail commitment to the instantiation of those idealisations and approximations in the universe. Idealisations and approximations are features of models that allow us to get predictions and explanations that are good enough for particular practical ends.

Talk about *perfect* things, *maximal* things, and *ideal* things is rarely intended to carry commitment to the existence of such things. Compare with talk about *average* things. It may be true that the average household has 1.8 children, but it would be a strange kind of error to seek out the address of the average household (because, say, you want to prosecute the heads of the household for what must be a fairly awful kind of child abuse).

Is there a perfect organism? No! Could there be a perfect organism? No! Is there a maximal organism? No! Could there be a maximal organism? No! Is there an ideal organism? No! Could there be an ideal organism? No! Necessarily, organisms have evolutionary histories that fit them for some environments and purposes and do not fit them for other environments and purposes. Organisms are not kinds of things that admit of perfection, or maximality, or ideality.

Is there a perfect human being? No! Could there be a perfect human being? No! Is there a maximal human being? No! Could there be a maximal human being? No! Is there an ideal human being? No! Could there be an ideal human being? No! Necessarily, human beings have evolutionary histories that fit them for some environments and purposes and do not fit them for other environments and purposes. Human beings are not kinds of things that admit of perfection, or maximality, or ideality. What goes for perfection, maximality, and ideality goes also for near perfection, near maximality, and near ideality. Organisms, including human beings, are not kinds of things that admit of near perfection, near maximality, and near ideality.

What about greatness? Is there a greatest human being? Could there be a greatest human being? Is there a greatest possible human being? Could there be a greatest possible human being? Pretend that we have an agreed scale that generates a partial ordering of possible human beings according to their greatness: for any two possible human beings A and B, either A is greater than B, or B is greater than A, or neither is greater than the other. Even under this pretence, it is not obvious that there is a greatest human being, or that there could be a greatest human being, or that there is a greatest possible human being, or that there could be a greatest possible human being. Given plausible incommensurabilities, it may well be that there are relatively few cases where we can say with confidence that one possible human being is greater than another possible human being.

What goes for human beings goes for organisms and for beings in general. At best, naturalists should be loath to allow that there is or could be anything that fits the description 'the greatest possible being'. Moreover, since it is obvious that naturalists suppose that it is impossible for there to be anything that is omnipotent, or omniscient, or perfectly good, and so forth, it is obvious that naturalists suppose that it is impossible for there to be anything that has some or all of these 'perfections'. By naturalist lights, there cannot be anything that fits the description 'being that has every perfection'.

We now have enough on the table to see that I reject T13 ('God is a perfect being') and that I accept A1 ('Nothing could be perfect').[55]

---

55. There is a very large critical literature on ontological and cosmological arguments. For some of what naturalists have to say about the claim that there is a perfect being, see, for example: Mackie, J. (1982) *The Miracle of Theism*. Oxford: Clarendon; Oppy, G. (1996) *Ontological Arguments and Belief in God*; Rowe, W. (1975) *The Cosmological Argument*. New York: Fordham University Press; Sobel, J. (2004) *The Logic of Theism*. Cambridge: Cambridge University Press; and (at least by my lights) Slote, M. (2011) *The Impossibility of Perfection*. Oxford: Oxford University Press.

Given the claims that I made in §§3 and 4, it is clearly controversial to suppose either that there is, or that there could be, a greatest being (or a maximal being, or a perfect being, or the like). More importantly, even if there is, or could be, a greatest being (or a maximal being, or a perfect being, or the like), this fact has no particular interest to us. It is not the case, for example, that a greatest being (or a maximal being, or a perfect being, or the like) would be worthy of worship, or divine.

38 'Foundational' Simplicity

Some non-naturalists claim that their non-naturalism should be preferred to naturalism because their non-naturalism provides the simplest non-natural 'foundation' for natural causal reality. Naturalists demur. Setting any other relevant considerations aside, it is clearly simpler to suppose that natural causal reality has no non-natural 'foundations': whatever 'foundations' there may be are all to be found within natural causal reality.

Some non-naturalists claim that their non-naturalism should be preferred to naturalism because they provide the simplest 'foundation' for causal reality. Naturalists demur. When we compare the simplicity of naturalism and its non-naturalistic competitors, we consider all of the ontological, ideological, and theoretical commitments of those worldviews. If a worldview includes the claim that A is a non-deterministic cause of B in circumstances in which any of $B_1, \ldots, B_n$ could have been non-deterministically caused by A, then it is part of the 'foundation' of that worldview that A caused B rather than any of $B_1, \ldots, B_n$.

Science identifies 'boundary conditions' in naturalistic accounts of natural causal reality: roughly speaking, laws, initial conditions, and 'comparative' outcomes of indeterministic causation. Everyone is required to suppose that the 'comparative' outcomes of indeterministic causation are brutely contingent, so we can set further consideration of them aside. Naturalists suppose that laws and initial conditions are either necessary—and so brutely necessary—or else brutely contingent. My own preference is to take them all to be brutely necessary.

Non-naturalists might think to improve on naturalism by explaining laws and initial conditions in terms of something else, thereby making them neither brutely necessary nor brutely contingent. Moreover, they might undertake to do this without making other additions to the 'foundations' that outweigh the gains that can be made by insisting that laws and initial conditions are both contingent and completely explained. Naturalists are, to say the least, sceptical that this trick can be turned.

On the one hand, there will be utterly new commitments—ontological, ideological, theoretical—that are incurred by the postulation of whatever is alleged to do the explaining of the laws and initial conditions. Typically, these commitments of non-naturalistic theories turn out to be significant; obviously enough, they never turn out to be *null*.

On the other hand, there will be new theoretical commitments—ontological, ideological, theoretical—that are incurred in the detailed postulations that are designed to explain why the laws and initial conditions are as they are rather than any other way that they could have been. No explanation that claims that the laws and initial conditions are as they are because some non-natural agents wanted them to be as they are is more economical in its commitments than the naturalistic alternative: we get no better explanation of why the laws and initial conditions are as they are, and we have the additional theoretical costs associated with the postulation of those non-natural agents.[56]

> Some theists suppose that theism has an advantage over naturalism because it postulates a particular simple 'foundational entity': a 'foundation' for everything else. I think that naturalists should claim that the initial part of natural reality provides a 'foundation' for everything else that is simpler than any non-natural 'foundation' could be. I also think that, whether or not the naturalistic 'foundational' entity is simpler than the theistic 'foundational' entity, it is still the case that naturalism is simpler than theism: there is much more to the 'foundations' of theories than the 'foundational' entities that they postulate.

---

56. One important target of the views developed in this section is Rasmussen, J. (2019) *How Reason Can Lead to God*. Downers Grove, IL: InterVarsity Press. On any view on which human beings act with libertarian freedom, that human beings act as they do *rather than* in other ways that they could do, is foundational. More generally, on any view on which there are unexplained comparative facts, those unexplained comparative facts are foundational: if, for example, God could have had different creative intentions, then that God has *these* particular creative intentions rather than *those* is foundational.

39 Heart's Desire

Some may suppose that, whether or not we have reason to *believe* that there are non-natural causal agents, structures, and pathways to afterlives and salvation, we have reason to *desire*, *hope*, or *have faith* that there are such pathways.

I think that we have no reason to desire, or have faith that what we take to be impossible exists or obtains. Since my naturalists give zero credence to the hypothesis that there are non-natural causal pathways, my naturalists have no desire, hope, or faith that there are such pathways. This is *not* to say that, instead, they desire, hope, or have faith that there are no such pathways. Rather, it is to say that those who give zero credence to the hypothesis that there are no such pathways simply have no attitudes of desire, hope, faith, and so on towards that hypothesis. From my naturalist standpoint, it makes as much sense to desire, or hope, or have faith that that there are (or are not) such pathways as it does to desire or hope or have faith that pure water is (or is not) two parts hydrogen to one part oxygen.

Some friends of non-natural causal pathways claim that my naturalists *do* have other attitudes towards these non-natural things: they *hate* them, *fear* them, are filled with *disgust* by them, and so forth. My naturalists demur. It makes exactly as much sense to suppose that my naturalists hate, fear, or are filled with disgust by such pathways as it does to suppose that my naturalists hate, fear, or are filled with disgust by the Easter Bunny.

Of course, matters are complicated here by the fact that we do have genuine emotional and affective reactions towards what we take to be (impossible) fictions. When we are in the cinema, we are afraid of Godzilla; when we read *Boating for Beginners*, we are amused by the travails of Gloria Munde; and so on. But emotional and affective responses to what we take to be fictions involve elements of imagination and pretence that are absent from our emotional and affective reactions to things that we take to be real: we do not run screaming from the cinema when we are afraid of Godzilla, but we would run screaming from a real-world Godzilla. My naturalists do not deny that they have just these kinds of emotional and affective responses to stories about non-natural pathways that they have to other kinds of fictions; but they insist that any such emotional and affective responses are 'screened off' from action in the same kind of way that emotional and affective response to fictions are 'screened off' from action. Even if the fear that I experience in the movie theatre has some impact on my behaviour after I leave the cinema—perhaps, for example, I have elevated levels of anxiety—it simply will not be correct to say that I am afraid of Godzilla. If I have been spooked, it is my going to the movie that has spooked me, not the merely fictional title character. If naturalists get 'worked up' in conversations with non-naturalists about what they take to be non-existent non-natural entities, any negative emotions that they are exhibit are directed either towards the non-naturalist *storytellers* or the non-naturalist *storytelling*; they are certainly not directed towards the non-existent non-natural entities that figure in the stories told.

We now have enough on the table—in my discussion of salvation, infinity, and heart's desire—to see that I reject T14 ('Belief in God is the pathway to salvation') and arguments like Pascal's wager that are premised on claims in that vicinity.[57]

> There has been a recent flurry of interest in the question whether naturalists should want theism to be true. I think that it should not be the case that naturalists want theism to be true. But I also think that it should not be the case that naturalists want theism to be false. Given the views that I take naturalists to hold, it seems to me that naturalists should have no desires concerning the existence of God: once you have assigned credence zero to hypotheses, it makes no sense for you to have desires in connection with those hypotheses.

40 Disagreement

In the preceding sections, I have briefly discussed naturalism, necessity, existence, essence, causation, natural reality, fundamentality, primitive commitments, analogical language, definition,

---

57. For further discussion of naturalistic attitudes towards God, see, for example: Kahane, G. (2011) 'Should We Want God to Exist?' *Philosophy and Phenomenological Research* 82: 774–796; and Nagel, T. (1997) *The Last Word*. Oxford: Oxford University Press.

mathematics, science, evolution, history, testimony, miracles, religious experience, religion, mindedness, consciousness, intentionality, reason, freedom, morality, flourishing, meaningfulness, love, art, play, suffering, death, salvation, infinity, perfection, foundational simplicity, and heart's desire. My aim has been to say enough to make it clear that I think that there is nothing in any of these topics that provides *me* with a good reason to suppose that there are gods.

In the back of my mind, there is a large collection of valid arguments for the existence of at least one god. What I have said in the preceding sections suffices to indicate which premises I reject in all of those many valid arguments. There are, of course, also many invalid arguments for the existence of at least one god, but the invalidity of those arguments alone suffices to establish that those arguments are unsuccessful.

From the claims in the preceding sections, it is easy to assemble valid arguments for the conclusion that there are no gods. Here is one modest example:

1. Necessarily, any possible way for causal reality to be shares an initial history with the way that causal reality actually is. (Premise: *Shared History*)
2. Necessarily, if, at some point, causal reality is entirely natural, then causal reality remains entirely natural at all subsequent points. (Premise: *Conservation of naturalness*)
3. Necessarily, if, at some point, causal reality is at least partly non-natural, then causal reality remains at least partly non-natural at all subsequent points. (Premise: *Conservation of non-naturalness*)
4. Causal reality is currently entirely natural. (Premise: *Naturalism*)
5. Necessarily, gods are non-natural causal entities. (Premise: *Definition of gods*)
6. (Therefore) Necessarily, there are no gods. (From 1–5)

I do not think that any real interest attaches to this argument, or to any other similar argument that could be generated from the claims tabled in the preceding sections. Here is why.

Suppose—at least for the sake of argument—that there is no inconsistency between the claims tabled in the preceding sections.

Let N be the collection of all of these claims, and let [N] be their logical closure.[58] Let G be the claim that there are no gods, and let [N]/G be what you get when you remove G from [N]. It is obvious that there are infinitely many logically inconsistent sets of sentences {[n], ~G}, where [n]⊂[N]/G. That is, it is obvious that there are infinitely many not utterly trivially valid arguments of the form [n] ∴ G. All of these arguments contain none but premises that I accept. Most of them are beyond my powers to discover. By my lights, it would be a complete waste of my time for me to seek to discover more of them. Sure, I think that these arguments are sound. But my judgment that these arguments are sound depends upon my judgment that the claims in N are true. If someone disagrees with me about one of the claims in [k], then the argument [k] ∴ G is not such as ought to persuade that person to accept that G. The mere fact of disagreement about one of the claims in [k] is sufficient to utterly disarm the argument [k] ∴ G for the one who disagrees about one of the claims in [k]. Perhaps there are 'nearby' arguments that cannot be so readily dismissed, but it is up to the arguer to establish that this is so in any given case.

Given the number of claims that I have made in the preceding sections, it would not be surprising if those claims are jointly logically inconsistent. On the other hand, it is worth noting that there is a great deal of modularity in the naturalism that I develop: what I say in almost any one of the sections might be adjusted without requiring significant adjustments in any of the other sections. Moreover, it should be said upfront that it would be astonishing if, in each of the cases, I have developed the best naturalistic standpoint that it is possible to take on the matter at hand. Nonetheless, it is important that effort is invested in developing comprehensive presentations of worldviews. In particular, there is no prospect of comparing the merits of competing worldviews unless we all make the best efforts that we can to get *all* of our controversial commitments into full view.

The attempt to get all of a given worldview on the table is particularly important from the standpoint of the assessment of naturalistic worldviews. Each additional non-naturalistic

---

58. Given a set of claims S, the logical closure of S is the set of all claims that are entailed by subsets of S. If a set of claims S is logically closed, then anything that is entailed by claims in S is itself in S.

commitment—ontological, ideological, theoretical—that is found in a non-naturalistic worldview is an additional reason to suppose that naturalistic worldviews are less theoretically committing than that non-naturalistic worldview. Failure to disclose the non-naturalistic commitments of a non-naturalistic worldview is simply an attempt to cook the books. So, too, is any attempt to insist that a decision between naturalistic and non-naturalistic worldviews can be made by paying attention to some small, carefully selected range of the relevant data. We relied on this critical point in our discussion of the idea that we can choose between worldviews on the basis of the comparative simplicity of their 'foundation'; we can apply it, in equal measure to any suggestion that we can choose between worldviews on the basis of their comparative success in explaining this or that particular piece of data.

Naturalism seems like the plainest common sense to me. But I know full well that it does not seem like that to most people. While since the beginning of the twentieth century there has been modest growth in the percentage of the population that is naturalist—particularly in prosperous democracies—it remains the case that there are many more non-naturalists than there are naturalists. Moreover, I expect that it will continue to be true for years to come—perhaps even for as long as there are human beings—that there are many more non-naturalists than there are naturalists.

I say that naturalism is true; I do not say that non-naturalistic belief is *irrational*. Sure, there are naturalists and non-naturalists who are irrational in their worldview beliefs. But, even among those who come closest to being experts on decision between worldviews, there is disagreement over naturalism and non-naturalism. By any ordinary standards, there are serious, thoughtful, reasonable, reflective, informed, intelligent naturalists and serious, thoughtful, reasonable, reflective, informed, intelligent non-naturalists. Moreover, there is no prospect that the differences that divide these naturalists and non-naturalists will be resolved any time soon: there is no prospect that, one day soon, all serious, thoughtful, reasonable, reflective, informed, intelligent people will come down on the same side in the debate over naturalism and non-naturalism.

Perhaps unlike many other parties to the discussion, I do not think that it matters very much if there is ongoing difference of opinion over naturalism and non-naturalism. By my naturalistic lights, the stakes are not very high: most non-naturalistic belief is intrinsically harmless. True, some non-naturalistic worldviews embed toxic political and social views, but exactly the same is true of some naturalistic worldviews. High stakes challenges lie elsewhere: acting responsibly in the face of climatic and other environmental emergencies (e.g. global warming, pollution, habitat loss, biodiversity loss, ocean conservation); working to reduce inequalities of wealth, particularly by investing in shared public goods (e.g. food security, water security, health, education, gender equality, the broad sweep of human rights); facing up to the serious challenges posed by governmental and corporate corruption (e.g. opposition to the undermining of established democratic institutions, protection of whistle-blowers, guarantee of genuine press freedom); and so on.

There remain two pieces of unfinished business. First, I have said nothing about T15 ('We can reject external world scepticism only because we can know that God is no deceiver and God created us and our world'). Obviously, no one who accepts my worldview is an external world sceptic. Moreover, it seems obvious to me that the worldview of any external world sceptic is much worse than the worldview of naturalists like me. Sure, I have some false beliefs about the world, and, in those cases, the external world sceptic avoids errors that I make. But I have lots of true beliefs about the world—and, in every one of those cases, the external world sceptic misses out on the truth.

Second, I have said nothing about A7–A15. Since I think that it is impossible that there are gods—and, in particular, I think that it is impossible that God exists—I think that A7–A9 and A11–A15 are modal and counterfactual claims with impossible antecedents. Further, I think that modal and counterfactual claims with impossible antecedents are trivially true. So I think that A7–A9 and A11–A15 are all trivially true. Given that it is impossible that God exists, any claim of the form 'God cannot. . . .' is true. Given that it is impossible that God exists, any claim of the form 'God would not . . .' is true. God neither could nor would permit the horrendous evil of our universe; God neither could nor would permit the great goods of our universe. Finally, I reject A10. There are various claims that are such that, if they were our total evidence, would give us at least some reason to believe that God exists. For example, if the only evidence you have is that a whole lot of people believe that God exists, then that is some evidence that God exists. Of course, in this particular case, this is not even our total evidence about what people believe concerning God: once we take into account the full sweep of belief concerning God across space and time, that evidence offers no clear support to any stance that one might take concerning God's existence. My verdict is that the total evidence supports naturalism over theism: the best trade-off of minimisation of commitments against maximisation of explanation gives the palm to naturalism. This verdict does not require me to say that there is no evidence that, considered in isolation, favours theism over naturalism.[59]

> Kenny's opening statement contains many boxed *historical* notes; my opening statement does not. This might be taken to be evidence for an important difference in our philosophical approaches. As Kenny remarked to me when we discussed this, it is not a coincidence that it turns out that it is more common for theistic philosophers than it is for atheistic philosophers to take a historically grounded approach. However, as with everything else in philosophy, the devil is in the details. Given what I am trying to do in my opening statement, I am not concerned about historical antecedents for the position that I am staking out. However, that is not to say that there are no interesting antecedents for my claims in either the freethought literature of the eighteenth and nineteenth centuries or in the scholastic literature on disputations. Certainly, you should *not* be taking me to be suggesting that you would profit less from reading Meslier, or Holbach, or Hume than you might from reading me.

The naturalism that I have outlined here is what seems to me, at the time of writing, to be the best worldview. I am sure that my sketch can be greatly improved. I am sure that there are many non-optimal steps that I have taken. Moreover—and importantly—I do not think that it is irrational for people to adopt worldviews wildly different from the naturalistic view that I have outlined. Despite the long history of dispute between theists and naturalists, we are still learning how to properly conduct these disputes, and we seem to have arrived no closer to any kind of resolution of our differences.

---

59. Since I have written previously on at least some of the themes touched on here, it is probably worth ending with a brief list of other books I have written that you can go to next if you want more of the same: *Arguing About Gods* (Cambridge: Cambridge University Press, 2006); *The Best Argument Against God* (Basingstoke: Palgrave, 2013); *Describing Gods* (Cambridge: Cambridge University Press, 2014); *Reinventing Philosophy of Religion* (Basingstoke: Palgrave, 2014); *Naturalism and Religion* (New York: Routledge, 2018); *Atheism and Agnosticism* (Cambridge: Cambridge University Press, 2018); and *Atheism: The Basics* (New York: Routledge, 2019). Unsurprisingly, the further back you go, the more different the views that are defended in these books are from the views that I defend now. If you are likely to consider only one of the books on this list, then the one that I would commend to you is *Atheism: The Basics*.

First Round of Replies

Chapter 3

Reply to Graham Oppy

Kenny Pearce

Contents

1 Good Arguments — 177
2 Explanation and Necessity — 183
   2.1 Explanation in Ethics and Mathematics — 185
   2.2 Explaining Necessities — 187
   2.3 The Cost of Brute Necessity — 190
   2.4 How Classical Theists Can Avoid Brute Necessity — 194
   2.5 Theism, Naturalism, and the Explanation of Necessary Truths — 200
3 Miracles and Religious Experience — 202
4 Theism and Simplicity — 208
   4.1 Ontological Simplicity — 209
   4.2 Ideological Simplicity — 211
   4.3 Comparative Simplicity — 216
5 Conclusion — 217

According to a frequently repeated (but probably apocryphal) story, Napoleon Bonaparte once criticized the great mathematical physicist Pierre-Simon Laplace for failing to include any mention of God in his book *The System of the World*. Laplace is supposed to have replied, "I have no need for this hypothesis."[1]

---

1. So far as I have been able to determine, the earliest version of this story is found in De Morgan (1915, 2:1–2), who (writing about a century after the purported event) says simply that "[this] anecdote is well known in Paris."

Following in Laplace's (purported) footsteps, Graham's opening statement declines to defend any *direct* argument against the existence of God. Instead, Graham outlines a naturalistic worldview and considers numerous places where theistic philosophers, religious apologists, and ordinary religious believers have thought God was needed. Graham denies that his worldview exhibits any 'God-shaped holes'. According to Graham, naturalism is complete and satisfying as it stands and has no need of any supernatural hypotheses.

Unsurprisingly, I disagree.

Claims T1–15

Graham enumerates 15 specific claims made by many theists about the various places where God might be 'plugged in' to a worldview. These claims are not a *definition* of theism, and not every theist will endorse them all. In particular, I do not endorse them all. The arguments in my opening statement explicitly relied on just one claim from Graham's theistic list:

T6. God is encountered in religious experience.

Given what I said about the universe's dependence on God, the reader may (correctly) infer that I endorse a couple of others:

T2. God is responsible for the beauty, order, and structure of our universe.

T4. God chose the values of fundamental physical constants.

I also indicated that I would like to endorse one more claim:

T13. God is a perfect being.

However, I said that my arguments might still succeed in showing that some kind of God exists, even if we can't get quite as far as T13 (see §§2.3 and 3.3.2 of my opening statement).

On the other hand, I explicitly *rejected* one claim on Graham's theistic list:

T1. God caused our universe to exist.

I rejected this view because I hold that causation is a feature of the internal structure of our universe, while God stands outside the universe as its *ground* (see Pearce 2017a, 2017b).

I'll have more to say about T3, T10, and T12 (on ethics and mathematics) in §2.4, below. I'll have more to say about T5 and T6 (on miracles and religious experience) in §3. For reasons of space, I will not be addressing the other claims on Graham's list. For the record, I reject T7, T8, and T15. I think T9, T11, and T14 are highly ambiguous, and that they are true on some interpretations and false on others.

My opening statement offered two main arguments for theism. The first argument claimed that theism offers benefits to **explanatory comprehensiveness** by enabling us to give an explanation of History (the sequence of causes and effects) as a whole. The second argument was that theism offers benefits to internal **coherence** because it allows for a treatment of religious experience that takes human **faculties** to be more reliable.

Graham's opening statement addresses a wide variety of philosophical issues. For reasons of space, my reply will focus on those aspects of Graham's statement that have the most direct bearing on my arguments. The most foundational of these is Graham's contention that it is a waste of time to offer arguments at all. Second, Graham defends some controversial views about explanation and necessity that, if true, would undermine significant elements of my **cosmological argument**. Third, Graham suggests that the naturalist is in fact in a better position than the theist to provide an explanation of the purported evidence for miracles and religious experience. Fourth and finally, Graham argues in a number of places that naturalism is simpler than theism in a variety of ways. I address each of these issues in turn.

1 Good Arguments

In my opening statement I emphasized the extent to which I agree with Graham about the methodology of **worldview comparison**. However, Graham's statement brings to light some points of disagreement. The most important of these concerns the role of arguments.

In *Arguing About Gods*, Graham began from the assumption that "the proper function of arguments is to bring about reasonable belief revision" (Oppy 2006a, 10). More precisely, according to the account Graham gave there, an argument aims to bring the audience to accept the conclusion and to do so reasonably. Arguments are successful if and only if they have this effect. Working from this starting point, Graham undertook a wide-ranging survey of arguments about the existence of God and arrived at the conclusion that "there are no successful arguments that have as their conclusion that there are—or that there are not—orthodoxly conceived monotheistic gods" (414). This, as Graham tells us, is hardly a surprising conclusion since there are many examples of apparently reasonable people who are well-informed about the facts and have considered the arguments and yet hold opposite views.

More recently, Graham has defended an even stronger position. According to Graham, there are structural reasons why there could not possibly be a successful argument for or against the existence of God (Oppy 2015). At the very beginning and very end of his opening statement, Graham offers further support for this position. According to Graham, since no argument for or against theism could possibly be successful, there is no point giving arguments in a debate about the existence of God.

I agree that successful arguments (in Graham's sense) are few and far between. In particular, I know of no arguments for or against the existence of God that are successful (in Graham's sense). That includes my own arguments. But I don't think it follows from this that there's no point giving arguments. To see why, let's draw some distinctions. (We're philosophers, it's what we do.)

Logicians, who study the structure of **valid** reasoning, usually consider arguments in a very abstract way. For the logician, an argument is just a set of claims (the **premises**) that allegedly support another claim (the **conclusion**). Logicians want to know whether the premises really do support the conclusion. The premises of an argument might be totally bizarre, but when we're doing logic we just assume they're true and try to figure out whether they support the conclusion.

When we actually *use* arguments, in philosophy or elsewhere, there's more than just logic going on. An argument is offered to a particular audience who is thinking about whether the conclusion is true. Sometimes the audience might just be yourself: you might be thinking about whether (for instance) you should believe that God exists, and you might try to present yourself with the best arguments on each side. Other times, you might offer arguments to some other people who are considering whether to believe a certain claim.

Whether an argument is good or successful or persuasive clearly depends on what the audience already believes. Keeping this in mind, we can give the following definitions:

> An argument is **strongly successful** if and only if, upon considering the argument, *all* members of the audience are rationally obligated to endorse the conclusion.
> An argument is **moderately successful** if and only if, upon considering the argument, *some* members of the audience are rationally obligated to endorse the conclusion.
> A person is **rationally obligated** to endorse a claim if and only if it would be irrational of him not to endorse it.

I agree with Graham that there are very few strongly or moderately successful arguments in philosophy. Some conceptions of God are incoherent—for instance, those that succumb to the **Stone Paradox**—and so there are strongly successful arguments against *those precise conceptions* of God. However, the theist can always give a better analysis of omnipotence (see Pearce and Pruss 2012) or find some other way of talking about divine power (see Geach 1973; Sobel 2004, ch. 9; Hill 2014). As a result, these types of arguments cannot be converted into strongly, or even moderately, successful arguments against theism *in general*.

More generally, faced with a valid argument, the audience has the option of rejecting one (or more) of the premises rather than accepting the conclusion.

In real life, most people—and in particular most philosophers—are pretty firmly attached to their beliefs about God. They are much more attached to these beliefs than to the premises of most of the arguments for and against the existence of God. So real people aren't very likely to be persuaded by philosophical arguments about God. If they don't already believe the conclusion, they'll probably find a premise to reject.

In response to this issue, Peter van Inwagen (2006, 44–47) has suggested an alternative criterion for the success of arguments. I will call this 'weak success'.

> An argument is **weakly successful** if and only if the argument would persuade an audience of ideal agnostics.
> An **ideal agnostic** is a perfectly rational and well-informed person who cares about the question in dispute but is (at the

beginning of the debate) perfectly neutral between the two sides of the debate in which the argument is offered.

Van Inwagen admits that it is usually rationally acceptable to reject one of the premises of an argument. He also admits that when it comes to arguments about the existence of God, this is what almost everyone will actually do. However, according to van Inwagen, instead of considering what people are rationally obligated to do, or what real people will actually do, we should consider how a perfectly fair and neutral audience *would* respond.

The trouble with van Inwagen's criterion is that our aim in philosophy is to improve our beliefs (make them more rational) and help others to do the same. But we do not and should not start out as ideal agnostics on most of the questions we discuss. As a result, van Inwagen's ideal agnostics just don't seem relevant to our philosophical project.

I concede, then, that Graham is right about three things. In the first place, when we give arguments, we aim to convince the (really existing) audience of the conclusion. In the second place, the audience almost never *has to* endorse the conclusion—they can instead reject one or more of the premises. In the third place, in debates about the existence of God, almost everyone *will in fact* choose to reject a premise rather than changing sides on the question of whether God exists.

Still, when you see a valid argument for a claim you don't already believe, you have to do *something* with it. The fact that you don't have to endorse the conclusion, and most members of the audience won't endorse the conclusion, does not make the argument pointless.

So what am I doing when I give an argument? I'm pointing to a **tension** in certain **worldviews** and suggesting a way of resolving it. The argument doesn't say, 'you have to endorse this conclusion!' It says, 'you have to endorse this conclusion, *if* you want to hold on to these premises'. If the (entire) audience responds, 'why on earth would I want to hold on to those premises?!' then the argument is no good. But if the response is 'I prefer to pay the price of rejecting one of the premises, rather than endorsing the conclusion', then the argument has done some useful work. The question is whether rejecting a premise amounts to a *cost*, from the audience's perspective.

In sum, here is my account of good arguments:

> **Good Arguments**
>
> An argument presented to an audience exposes an alleged tension in the audience's worldview(s) and suggests the conclusion as a way of resolving (or easing) that tension.
>
> An argument is good if and only if:
>
> 1. It exposes a genuine tension in one or more worldviews actually held by at least some members of the audience.
> 2. At least some members of the audience would be rational to respond to that tension by endorsing the conclusion.

For an argument to be good (in my sense), it is not required that endorsing the conclusion is the *only* rational response to the argument. Nor is it required that the actual audience in fact responds by endorsing the conclusion, or that some hypothetical audience would respond by endorsing the conclusion. What's required is that the argument points to an actual problem for the audience and endorsing the conclusion is one way the audience (rationally) *could* address that problem.

I say that a good argument *exposes a tension* in the audience's worldview. The most extreme case is the case where the audience is committed to endorsing all the premises and denying the conclusion of a valid argument. In this case, the argument identifies an actual **contradiction** in the worldview in question. These cases are relatively rare. Much more common are cases where there are some reasons within the worldview for finding the premises attractive and the conclusion unattractive. For instance, the naturalist is committed to thinking that (other things being equal) the more things a worldview can explain, the better. But naturalism does not allow History to be explained, while theism does. The naturalist wants more things to be explained, but doesn't want to accept the kind of non-naturalistic metaphysics that is necessary for explaining History—she's pulled in both directions. Many naturalists have seen this point and thought that accepting a few **brute facts**, although it's a cost, is better than giving up naturalism. In claiming that my cosmological argument is a good argument, I am claiming that it could also be rational for someone to go the other way and endorse theism (or some other form of non-naturalism) in order to avoid commitment to brute facts. I'm not claiming that this is the *only* rational response, and I'm also not claiming that anyone will actually choose this course.

I maintain that, despite the scarcity of successful arguments in philosophy, there are lots of good arguments. The arguments I've given in my opening statement are examples.

If arguments aim to persuade the audience of the conclusion, but even good arguments rarely do that, then what are good arguments good *for*? They're good for building better worldviews, by identifying tensions and considering the possible strategies for easing or eliminating those tensions.

It seems to me that the root of the disagreement between Graham and me here is that Graham is making a restrictive assumption about the context in which arguments are offered and the audiences to whom they are offered. Graham thinks of arguments as offered in a 'dispute' where one person's job is to affirm a certain claim and the other person's job is to deny it (again, see Oppy 2015). Think, for instance, of this debate. It's my job here to defend the existence of God. Part of that job is putting together the best possible theistic worldview. Suppose that, in this context, Graham presents a valid argument against the existence of God. If that happens, then either I already reject one of the premises, or else I haven't done my job. Certainly the best possible theistic worldview will reject at least one premise of *any* valid argument for atheism!

Of course, we mere mortals never do our job *perfectly*. As a result, it's always possible that, in a real debate between real people, an opponent might point out a tension, or even a contradiction, in a worldview. Graham admits that this is a useful role arguments can play. But in this case, even if I succeed in locating a tension in Graham's worldview that could be resolved by adopting theism, there's no point in my suggesting that he take *that* route to resolve the tension—rejecting theism is his job here! Since he's good at this job, he'll *always* find some other premise to reject, rather than endorsing theism.

In response to this I say, first, that a debate in which each party has an assigned role is far from the only context in which arguments are used. In fact, it is a rather artificial and unusual context. In the second place, even in this artificial context, the audience to which I present my arguments is not really Graham—it's *you*, the reader.

When we recognize these two facts, then we see that it is *not* pointless to suggest one particular resolution to a tension over others. An audience who has not been assigned the task of rejecting that suggestion might take the suggestion after all. You, the reader, are such an audience. Probably (hopefully) no one has told you that it is your job, in reading this book, to take one side come what may. Furthermore, even if, as suggested above, the audience doesn't take the suggestion, there can still be a point to suggesting one particular resolution over the other possibilities. It challenges the audience (and, in this case, the opponent) to explain their particular reasons for not wanting to go that route, and to identify the route they want to take instead.

> Graham is right that there are no successful arguments for or against the existence of God. When presented with an argument for or against the existence of God, you have the option of rejecting a premise rather than accepting a conclusion. It does not follow from this that there are no *good* arguments for or against the existence of God. Arguments may serve to expose tensions in worldviews and suggest ways of dealing with those tensions. Arguments can serve this useful purpose even if they don't force anyone to accept their conclusions.

2 Explanation and Necessity

Both my worldview and Graham's allow that all **contingent** facts (facts that could have been otherwise) have explanations. In my opening statement (§3.4), I argued that Graham achieves this result only by restricting the scope of possibility in ways that are inconsistent with straightforward interpretations of modern physics. Setting this worry aside, Graham and I have two general disagreements about explanation. In the first place, Graham holds that "contrastive facts about production of chance outcomes are 'brute' contingencies: unexplained fundamental facts" (§7). Second, Graham holds that all necessities are brute.

The first of these disagreements is not terribly important to our debate. Both Graham's worldview and mine hold that the contingent facts are ultimately explained by some necessary facts. This requires some form of **indeterminism** in the explanation—that is, the same necessary facts could have led to different contingent facts. Graham thinks that when this kind of indeterminism is present, contrastive explanation is impossible, and this is a kind of brute contingency. I disagree. I maintain that there are no contrastive facts. Consider these two sentences:

1. The electron was measured with spin up rather than spin down.
2. The electron was measured with spin up and not spin down.

I maintain that these two sentences express precisely the same fact. Sentence 1 emphasizes or draws attention to the contrast between the spin up measurement and the alternative spin down measurement. But the actual fact about the world that it expresses is the same fact expressed by sentence 2.

In general, we can explain why A and B by explaining why A and explaining why B. These are both non-contrastive explanations. So if we explain why the electron was measured with spin up and we explain why it was not measured with spin down, then there is nothing left unexplained. Graham agrees that causes non-contrastively explain their effects even under indeterminism. The prior state of the experimental apparatus caused the electron to be measured spin up, and also at the same time caused it not to be measured spin down. Thus, the prior state of the experimental apparatus explains why the electron was measured spin up and not spin down—no brute facts (see Pruss 2006, §7.6).

A Further Note on Contrastive Explanation

I am not denying that there is a difference between contrastive and non-contrastive explanation. My view is that there are no contrastive *facts*, and therefore the absence of contrastive explanation does not lead to brute facts. The difference between contrastive and non-contrastive explanation is a feature of human explanatory practices and not of the objective explanatory relations between facts. Some philosophers have argued that contrastive explanation is (at least sometimes) possible even under indeterminism (see Clarke 1996; Hitchcock 1999). Whether this is true need not concern us here.

The reason this disagreement is not very important is that my view about contrastive explanations and indeterminism could easily be adopted by a naturalist, and if Graham adopted it then he too would be able to avoid brute contingency. On the other hand, Graham's view about contrastive explanations and indeterminism could easily be adopted by a theist, and if I adopted it then I would be stuck with brute (contrastive) facts just like Graham. As a result, thinking about this question won't help us decide between theism and naturalism.

The second disagreement is much more important. Graham admits a lot of necessary truths to his worldview—not just all of logic and mathematics (§15), but also all of ethics (§27) and aesthetics (§31), as well as the laws of nature and boundary conditions of the universe (§4). The view that none of these things can be explained is intrinsically implausible and flatly inconsistent with the way mathematical and ethical reasoning is actually conducted. Further, this feature of Graham's worldview involves a massive (in fact, infinite) multiplication of primitives, and therefore it comes at a heavy cost with respect to the criteria of worldview comparison. Many worldviews—including many theistic worldviews—are able to avoid these costs.

2.1 Explanation in Ethics and Mathematics

Ethics and math provide lots of examples of explanations of necessary truths. Marc Lange (2010, 308–310) discusses the following simple mathematical example. Consider the number keys on a typical calculator, arranged like this:

$$
\begin{array}{ccc}
7 & 8 & 9 \\
4 & 5 & 6 \\
1 & 2 & 3
\end{array}
$$

Pick any row, column, or diagonal you like and hit the number keys first in one direction then the other, to get a number like 789987, 753357, and so forth. Every number typed in this way is divisible by 37 (as you can verify by playing with a calculator). This is *weird*, and it seems quite mysterious—like the sort of thing that ought to have an explanation!

In fact, this phenomenon *does* have an explanation. The series of numbers in a row, column, or diagonal on a calculator has the form

$(a, a + d, a + 2d)$. For instance, if we go across the top row, we set $a = 7$ and $d = 1$. If we go across the diagonal from the top left to the bottom right, we set $a = 7$ and $d = -2$. And so on. Now, we can express any number formed by this procedure as: $10^5 a + 10^4(a + d) + 10^3(a + 2d) + 10^2(a + 2d) + 10(a + d) + a$. Factoring out a and d, we get $(10^5 + 10^4 + 10^3 + 10^2 + 10 + 1) a + (10^4 + 2*10^3 + 2*10^2 + 10)d$, which is equal to $111111a + 12210d$, which is equal to $1221(91a + 10d)$. It follows that every such number is divisible by 1221, which is in turn divisible by 37.

This, obviously, is a toy example that would not be of too much interest to real mathematicians. However, the crucial feature of the example is that we know *that* the claim is true (by checking each number individually) before we know *why* it is true. There are real examples in the history of mathematics in which someone proved *that* a certain theorem was true but mathematicians thought it was still mysterious *why* that theorem was true (Pincock 2015). As Frans and Weber (2014) note, because of cases like this, "There is an increasing consensus among philosophers of mathematics and mathematicians that mathematical explanations exist." This consensus is based on examination of the practice of mathematics. As Penelope Maddy (1997) has argued at length, there is no good reason why naturalists, who give such deference to the practice and conclusions of scientists, should take a different attitude to mathematicians. So, contrary to Graham, there is excellent reason for naturalists (and everyone else) to accept the existence of explanations within mathematics.[2]

Similar considerations apply to morality. Although Graham's worldview allows for explanations of why particular individual actions are right or wrong, Graham holds that there can be no explanations of moral *principles* (see §27 of his opening statement). However, it is commonplace to appeal to more general moral principles to explain less general moral principles. One of Graham's examples of a moral principle is, "It is morally wrong to torture babies for fun." Why is this true? Because it's morally wrong to torture *anyone* for fun. Why is that true? Because it's morally wrong to take pleasure in causing suffering to others. Why is that true? Because suffering is *bad*. There are many philosophical

---

2. For an overview of recent philosophical work on explanation in mathematics, see D'Alessandro (2019).

difficulties in spelling out the details of these explanations, including the difficulty of understanding precisely how wrongness relates to badness in the last stage of the explanation. There is also the difficult question of whether all of this could ultimately be explained in non-moral terms. But the fact is, as Mark Schroeder (2005, 1) has put it, "Moral theories do not purport merely to tell us which things we ought to do. They also try to tell us *why* we ought to do them. Moral theories, that is, generally have explanatory ambitions." Perhaps Graham thinks that moral theory, as understood by Schroeder, is just a mistake—that there can't be any such thing as a moral theory in this sense. But Graham's denial that moral principles ever stand in explanatory relations to one another isn't just throwing out moral theory, it's also throwing out a large part of our ordinary reasoning about what we ought to do. We often can and do give explanations of moral principles.

2.2 Explaining Necessities

Why does Graham deny that necessities can be explained? He does not really say. To see what might be motivating Graham's line of thought here, we need to look in a little more detail at the account of explanation and dependence he gives in §4.

According to Graham, every **non-modalized** claim (every claim that does not contain **modal operators** like 'possibly' or 'necessarily') has an explanation, and these explanations are of two kinds. If a claim is **contingent**, then we explain it by pointing to something on which it depends. If a claim is necessary then we explain it by pointing out that it is necessary. So, Graham says, we can explain why 2 + 2 = 4 by pointing out that it is necessary that 2 + 2 = 4. However, according to Graham, "there is nothing that explains why it is necessary that 2 + 2 = 4" (§4).

I find this conclusion of Graham's a bit surprising. According to most systems of modal logic—including the system S5, which Graham and I both accept[3]—whatever is necessary is necessarily necessary. In particular, if it is necessary that 2 + 2 = 4, then it is necessary that it is necessary that 2 + 2 = 4. Now, according to Graham if we ask 'why does 2 + 2 = 4?' the answer is 'it had to be

---

3. On S5 and other modal systems, see the digression "Modal Logic" in my opening statement, §3.3.3.

that way, it could not have been otherwise'. But if we ask 'why is it necessary that 2 + 2 = 4?' it seems that we can give just the same answer. Why does this count as an explanation in the first case but not the second?

It seems to me that this is not an adequate explanation in either case. Think about the examples I gave in the previous subsection. Would the calculator mystery be dispelled if we simply said 'every number formed that way *must* be divisible by 37, it could not have been otherwise'? I think not. Similarly, if we ask why it's wrong to torture babies for fun, is 'it *had to* be that way, it could not have been otherwise' an adequate answer? Again, I think not.

Recall, though, that according to Graham there are just two types of explanations: necessity explanations and dependence explanations. So if we think the necessity explanations are inadequate or unsatisfying, at least in some cases, then all we've got left is dependence. However, it follows directly from Graham's account of dependence that no necessary truth (whether modalized or non-modalized) depends on anything.

Graham maintains that "Dependence is modal: if p depends on q, then it is possible to have q without p" (§4, claim 5). Graham illustrates this by pointing out that it's possible for his parents to exist without him existing, but impossible for him to exist without his parents existing. Now, if every instance of dependence follows this model, then no necessary truth depends on anything. For instance, if the fact that 2 + 2 = 4 depended on the fact that my left shoe exists, then it would have to be possible for my left shoe to exist without 2 + 2 being equal to 4. But this is impossible. And what goes for the existence of my left shoe goes for every other fact whatsoever. Since 2 + 2 *must* be equal to 4, no matter *how* things are, it follows from Graham's modal criterion that 2 + 2 = 4 does not (and could not) depend on anything at all. Since 2 + 2 = 4 can't depend on anything, either it is explained by its necessity or it is not explained at all.

But why should we hold this view about dependence? Graham does not say.

In my opening statement, I argued that both naturalists and theists should accept the existence of **grounding** relations. It is widely accepted by theorists of grounding that these relations do not obey Graham's conditions for dependence. Indeed, the authors of the *Stanford Encyclopedia of Philosophy* article on "Metaphysical Grounding" write: "Proponents of grounding *all* agree that grounding isn't a purely modal relation" (Bliss and Trogdon 2016, §5, emphasis added). This claim, like (almost?) all claims of universal agreement in philosophy, turns out to be false. (Graham is a counterexample.) Nevertheless, *most* grounding theorists do agree that grounding relations cannot be defined just in terms of possibility and necessity. Here's a famous example to explain why.

In one of Plato's dialogues, the character Euthyphro claims to be an expert on piety. When Socrates asks Euthyphro to explain what piety is, Euthyphro says that what's pious is whatever is loved by the gods. So far, so good.[4] But then Socrates asks a tricky question (as philosophers do): "Is the pious being loved by the gods because it is pious, or is it pious because it is being loved by the gods?" (Plato, *Euthyphro* 10b).

A certain translation of this problem into classical theism has come to be known as the *Euthyphro Dilemma*.

> **The Euthyphro Dilemma**
>
> According to classical theism, it is necessary that God exists and is perfectly good. Since it is necessary that God is perfectly good, it is necessary that God *approves of*—and perhaps even *commands*—all right actions. But does God approve of right actions because they are right, or are they right because God approves of them?

This does indeed look like a dilemma for the classical theist.

> A **dilemma** is a case where there are exactly two options, and both of them look bad.

If the theist says God approves of right actions because they are right, then it looks like there's a moral law that is somehow *superior* to God, telling God what to do. On the other hand, if the theist says that right actions are right because God approves of them, then we get the result that whatever God approved of would be right just

---

4. Well, not exactly. As Socrates points out, according to Greek mythology, the gods all love different things! (Plato, *Euthyphro* 6b–8a).

because God approved of it, even if (for instance) God approved of torturing babies for fun. On such a view, the claim that God is good is trivial—it doesn't actually tell us anything about what God is like.[5]

> I've focused here on the concept of *rightness*, but parallel dilemmas arise for other moral concepts, including *wrongness, goodness, badness*, and so forth. Are bad things bad just because God doesn't like them? And so on.

We will return to this dilemma in §2.4, below. My present point, though, is that if Graham were right, then there would be no dilemma at all, since these 'because' claims would turn out to be nonsense. On Graham's view, one necessary truth can never be more basic or fundamental than another, and one necessary truth can never be based on or grounded in another. The question here is not whether this view about God and ethics is correct. The question is whether the use of the word 'because' in the Euthyphro Dilemma makes sense. If the Euthyphro Dilemma makes sense (and it does), then Graham is wrong about explanation, necessity, and dependence.

> **A Meta-puzzle**
>
> I just said that, according to Graham's view, there would be no dilemma *since* the 'because' claims would be nonsense. But 'since' is a synonym of 'because'—it indicates an explanatory relation. Graham's view implies that *necessarily* there is no dilemma here, and therefore the only reason why there is no dilemma is the fact that necessarily there is no dilemma. This illustrates just how difficult it is to think or argue about necessary truths without presupposing that they sometimes stand in explanatory relations.

2.3 The Cost of Brute Necessity

We've now seen that there are compelling examples of explanations of necessities in math, ethics, and elsewhere. We have also seen that the idea of a necessary truth having an explanation makes sense. It follows from this that the multiplication of brute necessities is a cost to a worldview. How significant is this cost?

---

5. But for a recent defense of this view, see Harrison (2017).

Graham's doctrine of **brute necessity** incurs two kinds of costs: a cost to **theoretical simplicity** and a cost to explanatory comprehensiveness. Both costs are enormous. In fact, they are literally *infinite*.

Graham describes the value of theoretical simplicity like this: "All else being equal, a worldview that is committed to fewer and less complicated fundamental principles is better than a worldview that is committed to more and more complicated fundamental principles" (§10). Graham notes, but does not attempt to solve, a serious difficulty for his approach: he has no account of what makes a principle *fundamental*.

I suggest that a theoretical commitment is fundamental if and only if, *according to the worldview itself* that commitment has no explanation. In the terms I borrowed from Dasgupta (2016), a worldview's fundamental theoretical commitments include both those claims it takes to be brute and those claims it takes to be autonomous.

It might be objected that on this approach a worldview can avoid fundamental theoretical commitments just by *declaring* that some claim has an explanation without actually bothering to *provide* any such explanation.

I don't think this is a problem. Such a maneuver will incur costs elsewhere in the criteria of worldview comparison. In the first place, even if a claim has an explanation, it may still incur **ontological commitments** and **ideological commitments**. Additionally, worldviews include some kinds or patterns of explanation and exclude others. Can the alleged explanation fit neatly into one of the patterns of explanation already recognized within the worldview? Trying to force an explanation into a pattern where it doesn't fit neatly will create **tension** in the worldview. Introducing a new pattern of explanation will incur ideological and theoretical costs. Finally, the claim that something has an explanation is itself a theoretical commitment, and may turn out to be fundamental.

Worldviews include claims about what explains what. These claims, just like all the other claims included in a worldview, may incur commitments and exhibit tensions. So claims about explanation can't be added for free any more than any other claims. But adding claims about explanation does have a benefit: if, according to the worldview, a theoretical commitment has an explanation, then that commitment doesn't count against theoretical simplicity. Thus, a worldview that includes harmoniously within itself patterns of explanation that allow many things to be explained will gain a substantial benefit in theoretical simplicity at modest expense to ideological simplicity. This is because the fundamental theoretical commitments that count against theoretical simplicity are only those commitments that, according to the worldview itself, lack explanations.

Still, it might be that all worldviews (or at least all worldviews that don't have fatal flaws elsewhere) have infinitely many fundamental theoretical commitments. For instance, my worldview takes real definitions to be autonomous facts. There is a real definition for every kind of thing that could possibly exist. So my worldview has a separate fundamental theoretical commitment for every possible kind of thing.

There are difficulties in comparing the number and complexity of fundamental theoretical commitments, given that they will generally be infinite. Here, though, I'm just trying to evaluate the net cost of Graham's principle of brute necessity. That principle implies that *every* necessity claim is a *separate* fundamental theoretical commitment. But Graham and I agree that all the truths of logic, all the truths of pure mathematics, and all moral principles are necessary. So Graham's principle adds infinitely many fundamental theoretical commitments.

Some of these commitments are very complex. For instance, consider the following theorem selected at random from a textbook in mathematical logic:

> There is an unsatisfiable set of second-order sentences every finite subset of which is satisfiable.
>
> (Enderton 2002, 285)

The claim that this theorem is necessarily true is among Graham's fundamental theoretical commitments, as are plenty of far more complicated logical and mathematical theorems.

Now, it should be noted that Graham is already committed to rejecting my explanation-based account of theoretical simplicity. According to Graham, "While no necessity is explained, necessities that we get via logical consequence come for free. While all necessity is 'brute', only primitive necessities are theoretical costs" (§4). Graham, however, explicitly denies that these case of logical consequence are cases of either dependence or explanation.

Graham does not explain what makes some necessities 'primitive' (or fundamental) and others not. In his discussion of necessary truths in §4, he notes that 2 + 2 = 4 is a logical consequence of the axioms of arithmetic. Presumably these axioms are the primitive necessities. However, in §10, Graham *rejects* the idea that we measure the complexity of a worldview's theoretical commitments by comparing axiomatizations.

I agree with Graham that only fundamental theoretical commitments count against the theoretical simplicity of a worldview. I maintain that a theoretical commitment is fundamental if and only if it is taken to be unexplained. Graham is committed to rejecting this account of fundamental theoretical commitments, but he has so far not explained what kind of alternative picture he endorses. If my account of theoretical simplicity is correct, then Graham's principle of brute necessity is infinitely costly.

In addition to these costs in terms of theoretical complexity, Graham's principle of brute necessity incurs an infinite cost in terms of explanatory comprehensiveness. Remember, on Graham's own account (in Oppy 2018a, §2.3), when we compare worldviews, we favor those that can explain more of the data on which the worldviews agree. These necessary truths are part of that data—we all agree about the truths of mathematics, for instance, and we all agree that these truths are necessary. So any worldview that can explain these data will (other things being equal) have an infinite advantage over Graham's worldview.

It might be objected that I'm engaged in 'double counting' here. I said that when a worldview takes a claim to have an explanation, that claim doesn't count against the worldview's theoretical complexity. Now I'm saying that worldviews also, separately, get credit for explaining more of the data.

Here I want to draw a distinction. What matters for theoretical simplicity is which of the claims to which a worldview is committed can in principle be explained, according to the worldview itself. What matters for explanatory comprehensiveness is how much of the agreed-upon data can actually be explained by the defender of the worldview. In evaluating explanatory comprehensiveness, a sketch of an explanation counts for something, and a well-worked-out explanation counts for more, but a mere assertion that some (unknown) explanation exists counts for nothing.

There are general patterns of explanation that allow us to explain infinitely many mathematical facts. Since our lifespan and attention span are finite, any human mathematician can only give finitely many of them. But we're not simply *asserting* that they exist. The mathematicians actually know how to construct them. Graham is committed to rejecting all of these explanations. So, again, the cost to explanatory comprehensiveness is infinite.

2.4 How Classical Theists Can Avoid Brute Necessity

I maintain that some necessary truths depend on others. Some necessary truths are more basic or fundamental than others. In particular, the facts about God and God's nature are the most fundamental of all necessary truths.

Graham's list of claims commonly endorsed by theists includes:

> T10. There are objective moral facts because God legislates them.

We've already seen one problem for this kind of view: the **Euthyphro Dilemma**. If the moral facts stem from divine legislation, *why* does God legislate as God does? Could God legislate differently? How, on this view, can moral facts really be *necessary*?

On the other hand, if God doesn't just legislate the moral facts, then how can God be truly sovereign? Aren't the moral facts now superior to and independent of God? And so on.

Remember our definition of a dilemma:

> A **dilemma** is a case where there are exactly two options and both of them look bad.

The two options are called the 'horns' of the dilemma. When someone presents an alleged dilemma for your worldview, there are two ways to respond:

> To **embrace one horn** of a dilemma is to argue that one of the two options isn't so bad after all.
> To **split the horns** of a (supposed) dilemma is to argue that it isn't really a dilemma at all; actually, there is a third option.

Faced with the Euthyphro Dilemma, the most popular option for theists has been to try to split the horns. That is, theists have tried to say that morality *somehow* depends on God, but God doesn't just arbitrarily make up the moral principles.

Historically, the most popular strategy for doing this is a theistic form of **virtue ethics**. However, I do not accept this view. I prefer an alternative Kantian approach (see Kant [1785] 2012).

Theistic Virtue Ethics

The general idea of virtue ethics is that the most basic kind of moral evaluation is the evaluation of a person's character. Virtues are morally good traits of character like courage, compassion, self-control, and so on. Good or right actions are the kinds of actions that virtuous people would perform.

In ancient Greek, the word for 'virtue' is the same as the word for 'excellence'. What it is for a thing to be excellent depends on what kind of thing it is. An excellent knife is one that cuts well, for instance. The virtues are the traits possessed by excellent human beings.

Not all forms of virtue ethics are theistic. The sketch I've just given is based on Aristotle (*Nicomachean Ethics*) and these ideas about human excellence are central to the (broadly) Aristotelian account of human flourishing Graham endorses (see §28 of his opening statement).

Nevertheless, there is a good reason why virtue ethics has been particularly popular among theists. Theistic virtue ethics can split the horns of the Euthyphro Dilemma as follows. When God creates, God must have some conception or idea of what God is creating. So when God creates humans, God has some understanding of *what it is to be human*. But to understand knives is also to understand what makes some knives excellent and others not. So God's prior understanding of what it is to be human includes understanding of what it is to be an excellent human. And this is the nature of human virtue. So, on this view, part of what it is to be human is to be the sort of being who *ought to be* courageous, compassionate, self-controlled, and so on. Maybe God could have created other beings for whom courage was of no value, but those beings wouldn't be human.

On this view—which was endorsed, for instance, by Aquinas (*Summa Theologica*, II-Iq71)—God does not just arbitrarily make up ethics. When God decides to make humans, God thereby, necessarily, decides to make beings who ought to be courageous, and so forth. Nevertheless, it's up to God to decide to make beings whose excellence is of this sort.

My main objection to this traditional version of theistic virtue ethics is that it makes real definitions normative. On

> this kind of view, the nature of *humanity* isn't just a matter of what a human is, but what a human should be. Insofar as an individual human doesn't precisely match up with the nature of *humanity*, this view takes that individual to be defective. I think this is implausible as an account of real definitions and of the foundations of ethics, and that it has bad consequences for applied ethics and for philosophy of biology.

Immanuel Kant (1724–1804) is one of the most obscure writers in history. There are endless debates about what Kant really thought (about ethics or anything else). Here I will briefly outline a moral theory *inspired by* Kant without trying to say what Kant really thought. The basic idea is that we can derive the moral facts from *what it means to act for a reason*. If I choose to eat the chocolate cake in front of me *because* chocolate cake is delicious, I regard the deliciousness of chocolate cake as a reason for eating chocolate cake—not just for me here now, but for everyone always and everywhere.

Really, of course, things are more complicated than this. Even though chocolate cake is delicious, there are lots of situations in which I would think that eating it was not the thing to do. For instance, perhaps I baked this cake for my wife's birthday and we planned to cut into it together this evening. Then I definitely shouldn't eat it now. Or perhaps it's not even my cake—maybe I'm looking at it in the display case at a bakery. Then I shouldn't eat it without paying for it, at least. Or maybe I've already eaten two pieces of chocolate cake today and haven't gotten any exercise in the past month due to the COVID-19 lockdown order. Then, once again, I shouldn't eat the cake.

Furthermore, deliciousness is not an objective property of the cake itself. Some people do not enjoy chocolate cake. It's not as though those people have somehow misunderstood the nature of chocolate cake. Rather, anything that is delicious is delicious *to someone*. Chocolate cake is delicious *to me* insofar as my sensory systems respond to it in a certain way. If chocolate cake is not delicious *to you*, then you don't have the reason I do. Nevertheless, according to the Kantian theory, we can't really understand something as a *reason*, rather than an irrational urge, unless we take it to have some kind of universal validity. When I take the deliciousness of the cake as a reason to eat it, I thereby judge that everyone *in the same situation as me* has a reason to eat chocolate cake. What, precisely, counts as *the same situation*?

My judgment that eating the cake is the thing to do incorporates all kinds of conditions. In Kantian ethics, this kind of practical judgment is called a *maxim*.

> The **maxim** of an action is the practical judgment that drives it. This judgment includes all the features of the situation that the person regards as relevant to the appropriateness of the action.

According to Kantian ethics, we act wrongly when our maxim is *inconsistent*—that is, when we don't *really* (consistently) think that this is the thing to do *every time* these circumstances happen. For instance, if I make up excuses for why it's ok for *me* to lie in these circumstances, but I wouldn't accept those same excuses from others, I'm acting wrongly.

One of the nice features of this theory is that it preserves a kind of moral **autonomy**. Kant says, "a person is subject to no other laws than those he gives to himself" (Kant [1797] 2017, 19). We make laws for ourselves when we make the practical judgments that are our maxims.

At the same time, the Kantian view preserves a kind of moral objectivity. I can't make up just any rules because of the way I'm constrained by consistency. Kant ([1781] 1998, A46/B63–A49/B66) uses the following comparison. When you are doing constructions with a compass and straight edge in geometry, you're just *making up* the shapes, and you can make them up however you want. Nobody's stopping you. But just try to make up a two-sided polygon. It can't be done! In the same way, nobody's stopping you from making up a system of moral rules that permits lying and stealing and so on. Nevertheless, you can't make up such a system. If you try (Kant claims), you'll find that you're not really willing to apply those same rules consistently to everyone, and so your maxims are contradictory.

Kant on Geometry and Ethics

I've been trying to give the general idea of Kantian ethics without resorting to any of Kant's impenetrable jargon. But for readers who are familiar with Kant and Kantian ethics,

> the following clarification may be in order. (If you don't speak Kantianese, this digression will clarify nothing and should be skipped.)
>
> Kant actually uses the example of a two-sided polygon in the course of arguing that geometry consists of synthetic *a priori* necessary truths. There is nothing internally contradictory in the concept of a two-sided polygon and yet, according to Kant, just by sitting and thinking we can see that there couldn't be such a thing. Kant says that we do this by trying to *construct* such a polygon 'in the mind's eye', as it were (see Van Cleve 1999, §3A).
>
> Now, Kant also says that the categorical imperative is "an a priori synthetic practical proposition" (Kant [1785] 2012, 33). I think that interpreting Kant's account of the categorical imperative in light of his general account of the synthetic *a priori* supports a *constructivist* reading of Kant's ethics. On this view, we build ethics in something like the way you build shapes with a (real or imaginary) compass and straight edge. The constructivist version of Kantian ethics I describe in the text is particularly influenced by the work of the present-day Kantian ethicist Christine Korsgaard (1996b).
>
> For present purposes, of course, it doesn't matter whether this was Kant's real view—it's *my* view and I arrived at it by reading Kant and Korsgaard, whether or not I have interpreted them correctly!

Another nice feature of this theory is that it makes morality much less *mysterious*. How could there be universal moral rules that necessarily apply always to all people? Because all people *make these rules for themselves* every time they act for reasons. (Note: this is yet another example of an explanation of a necessary truth.) A being that doesn't (ever) act for reasons isn't a person and therefore is not subject to moral rules. We, on the other hand, are subject to moral rules, but only because we made those rules for ourselves.

This has been a brief sketch of a very complicated theory. The theory faces lots of problems, and there are specialists who spend their whole careers debating whether those problems can be solved. I'm not one of those specialists. As an interested bystander to that debate, I'm hopeful that some version of Kantian ethics, roughly along the lines I've outlined, can be made to work.[6]

The general Kantian approach to ethics is compatible with either theism or naturalism. However, the Kantian approach is one way for a classical theist to split the horns of the Euthyphro Dilemma. According to the Kantian view, everyone who acts for reasons is subject to the moral law—but only because everyone who acts for reasons necessarily legislates the moral law for herself. That God is a being who acts for reasons is at the core of my version of classical theism. Thus, I see God as a Kantian moral agent whose goodness consists in God's adherence to the law God legislates for Godself. But the fact that the moral law is self-legislated does not make it arbitrary.

The Euthyphro Dilemma is a problem for God's relation to the moral truths, but analogous problems arise for necessary truths in general (Morris and Menzel 1986, 358; Hanrahan 2009, 384–385; Tweedt 2013). It is foundational to my version of classical theism to consider God as a being who chooses freely and rationally. If God just makes up the necessary truths, what kind of reasons could God possibly have for making 2 + 2 equal to 4 rather than 5? How could that possibly be a rational, rather than arbitrary, decision? On the other hand, if God does not make up the necessary truths, then aren't the necessary truths somehow *superior* to God, *constraining* God's power and freedom?

Here, again, I want to split the horns. The Kantian agent is subject only to the laws that she make for herself. Yet, insofar as she is a being who acts for reasons, she cannot avoid making the moral law for herself. The moral law has its origin within the agent, not outside, and for this reason the moral law is not a constraint on the agent's freedom but rather the fullest expression of it.

In the same way, I maintain, all of the necessary truths have their origin within God, yet insofar as God is a rational being it is impossible that God should have made different necessary truths. God *values* or *endorses* the laws of ethics, logic, mathematics, and so on in such a way that, necessarily, God chooses in accord with them. Yet because God's choices are guided by God's values, this limitation on God's possibilities for choosing should not be understood

---

6. For more on Kantian ethics, see Korsgaard (1996a, 1996b, 2009), Wood (1999), and O'Neill (2013).

as a constraint that diminishes God's freedom (see Pearce and Pruss 2012, 410–412).

The necessary truths arise from God's nature as a rational being. For this reason it is true, on my view, that *if God were irrational, there might be true contradictions* (Pearce 2017a, 8). But necessarily God is perfectly rational, and necessarily there are no true contradictions.

How precisely do the necessary truths arise from God's nature? The general picture is that, in making a free and rational decision about whether and how to create, God *necessarily* endorses the necessary truths as laws of thought that (like the moral law) God makes for Godself.

> **More on God and Math**
>
> Graham lists among beliefs commonly held by theists:
>
> T3. Numbers are ideas in the mind of God.
>
> In recent philosophy of religion, two versions of this claim have been discussed. According to the first version, *theistic conceptual realism*, God's ideas are uncreated but nevertheless dependent on God. According to the second version, *theistic activism*, God creates these ideas by God's conceptual activity (Panchuk 2016, §1). Thomas Morris and Christopher Menzel, who originally coined the term 'theistic activism' as a name for their theory, explicitly argued that numbers and similar objects are *caused* by God (Morris and Menzel 1986, 355). (Menzel 1987 provides further details on how the theory can deal with math.) Since I deny that creation is causal, it is unclear whether my view counts as a version of theistic activism or theistic conceptual realism. I hold that the necessary truths are true because, in creating, God acts for reasons and thereby adopts the necessary truths as laws of thought.

2.5 Theism, Naturalism, and the Explanation of Necessary Truths

Leibniz ([1714] 1989b, §§43–44) thought that these kinds of considerations about how to explain necessary truths gave rise to another argument for the existence of God. We can express the argument like this:

1. Some affirmative truths are necessary.
2. All affirmative truths depend on the existence of some being or collection of beings.
3. A necessary truth could not depend on a contingent being or collection of contingent beings.
4. (Therefore) There is a necessary being.

The restriction to *affirmative* truths is meant to rule out negative truths, such as *there are no unicorns*.

Premise 1 is clearly true, and Graham (like most other naturalists) also accepts it. Premise 2 seems pretty plausible. Statements are generally statements *about* something, and typically if that something doesn't exist, then the statement will be false. Premise 3 must certainly be true if it is possible that no contingent beings exist.[7] Even if it is necessary that at least some contingent beings exist, you might still think that plausible explanations of necessary truths will obey premise 3. It follows that there is a necessary being on whom the necessary truths depend. According to Leibniz, this is God.

The naturalist has a number of responses available to the above argument. Graham rejects premise 2. He accepts premise 3, but only because he thinks necessary truths can't depend on *anything*. Note, however, that Graham also accepts the *conclusion* of this argument, since he holds that some initial segment of the material universe is necessary.

Graham, then, could try to ground the necessary truths in the facts about the necessary initial segment of the universe. Alternatively, since he rejects premise 2, he could hold that at the root of each domain of necessary truths (mathematics, ethics, aesthetics, etc.) are just a few brute necessities that explain the rest. For instance, the axioms of set theory might be brute necessities and explain the rest of mathematics.

In his comments on math (opening statement, §4) and ethics (§27), Graham suggests that he wants to adopt something like this second course. However, without an account of what makes some necessities 'primitive' or 'fundamental' and others not, it is unclear how he can avoid the explosion of theoretical commitments described above. Furthermore, the infinite cost to explanatory

---

7. For debate about this, see Efird and Stoneham (2013), Lowe (2013), and Rodriguez-Pereyra (2013).

comprehensiveness is a necessary and unavoidable consequence of denying that necessities can be explained.

At the end of the day, I do think that theism does a better job than naturalism at explaining the necessary truths. In particular, I think that my theistic worldview, which takes only definitions as autonomous and nothing as brute, provides a simple and highly coherent approach to the explanation of necessary truths. But I also think that Graham's doctrine of brute necessity is an unforced error. Naturalists don't have to endorse this doctrine, and in the game of worldview comparison the costs of endorsing it are literally infinite.

> According to Graham, all necessities are brute. This view does not just run contrary to intuition; it also runs contrary to the practice of moral reasoning and mathematical investigation. Furthermore, in the game of worldview comparison, the costs of Graham's principle of brute necessity are literally infinite. Graham holds this view in part because he denies that one necessary truth can depend on another. This claim about dependency relations is implausible. Once we reject it, we can see that classical theism can provide an attractive and highly unified picture of the dependence of necessary truths on God.

3 Miracles and Religious Experience

In §§20–21 of his opening statement, Graham argues that naturalists can reasonably hold that reports of **miracles** and **religious experience** can be given naturalistic explanations. I don't contest this point. Naturalistic explanations of the phenomena are possible. If you think you have strong reasons for endorsing naturalism, then it will be reasonable for you to endorse those naturalistic explanations.

In my opening statement, I argued that endorsing one of these naturalistic explanations amounts to endorsing a form of skepticism. The **external world skeptic** takes our senses to be unreliable and refuses to form beliefs on the basis of the senses. In just the same way, the naturalist takes religious experience to be unreliable and refuses to form beliefs on the basis of religious experience. This is an unfortunate place for the naturalist to be, but it's only a tension and not a contradiction in naturalism.

Recall that I included in **monotheistic religious experience (MRE)** anything that is interpreted as experience of God. There are significant problems about what is sometimes called **special divine action**—that is, acts of God that somehow go beyond God's creating and sustaining the ordinary course of nature. My argument does not require me to solve any of these problems. Even if God only creates and sustains the ordinary course of nature and does nothing else, it might still be correct to interpret some experiences as experiences of God. Indeed, once we have appreciated God's role in creating and sustaining the universe, it might be correct to interpret *all* experiences as experiences of God (see Berkeley [1710] 2002, §148). Of course, many theists have religious commitments to special divine action. Nevertheless, for present purposes, that issue may be set aside.

What's the Problem With Miracles?

David Hume ([1748] 2003, §10) influentially defined a miracle as "a violation of the laws of nature." However, there are serious problems with the idea that God violates the laws of nature.

In the first place, God has *decreed* the natural order. When God said, "let there be water!" God decreed that there should be a certain sort of stuff—stuff that flows downhill and doesn't separate to let the Israelites walk through on dry land. Thus, it would appear that, if God decrees that the Red Sea should part for the Israelites, God is *undoing* God's own previous decree. However, it is impossible that any decree of God's should be undone. It is also impossible that God, having made a decree, should have a change of mind (see Maimonides, *Guide*, ch. 2.29; Aquinas, *Summa Contra Gentiles*, chs. 3.98–99; Spinoza [1670] 2007, 82–83).

In the second place, theists generally take the beauty and orderliness of nature as evidence for the existence of God. But if orderliness is evidence *for* God, then disorderliness is evidence *against* God. On Hume's definition, a miracle would be a disorderly event. A forceful presentation of this argument has been given by Christine Overall (1985). (Also see Spinoza [1670] 2007, 84–87).

> These two problems are *internal* to theism and were familiar to theistic philosophers long before the rise of modern science. (However, modern science does create *some* new problems about miracles; see McDermid 2008.) One traditional line of response is that miraculous events are not *contrary* to nature, but *above* nature (Aquinas, *Summa Contra Gentiles*, chs. 3.100–101). This distinction obviously requires some spelling out, but it accounts for why theologians and theistic philosophers have often not liked Hume's talk of 'violations' (see Larmer 1985).
>
> Graham does not follow Hume's definition. Instead, he defines a miracles as "events caused by the actions of nonnatural.... agents" (§20).
>
> I have argued that God's activity of creating and sustaining the natural causal order is not itself causal. As a result, my argument does not require the occurrence of miracles in either Hume's sense or Graham's. I think an account of miracles that avoids the above problems is possible, but I will not attempt that here since I don't need it for my argument.

The real question is, is it reasonable to interpret some of our experiences as experiences of God? If you start out by assuming theism, you'll probably think the answer is 'yes'. If you start out by assuming naturalism, you'll probably think the answer is 'no'. Graham offers some specific reflections about exactly how the naturalist is likely to understand these sorts of experiences. I do not think these reflections undermine my claim that the naturalist's attitude to religious experience amounts to an unfortunate form of skepticism.

Graham notes that religious experience is often produced by religious practice, and that a person's prior religious beliefs often influence the kind of religious experiences that person has. Further, Graham notes, many religious experiences involve dreams and visions. There are unsolved scientific problems about dreams and visions, but certainly these can be given a neurological explanation.

Let's concede, for the sake of argument, that all of this is true and that religious experiences are not the product of special divine action. Still, Graham has yet to identify any important difference between religious experience and ordinary sensory experience.

First, sensory experience is the product of sensory practices. If you want to know whether it's raining, you engage in the practice of looking out the window. Second, as I argued at length in my opening statement (§4.2), our interpretation of sensory experience depends on our prior beliefs about the world. Third, sensory experience has a neurological explanation.

It will no doubt be objected that there is this difference: the objects perceived are the causes of the neurological processes that explain our sensory experience.

But why do we think this? Couldn't something else be causing these electrochemical processes in my brain? Perhaps I am a **brain in a vat**, and have no eyes at all, and my optic nerve is being stimulated by electrodes.

Note that these kinds of scenarios (notoriously) can't be disproven empirically. Whatever signals my body is capable of sending to my brain, electrodes would also be capable of sending. At the conclusion of his opening statement (§40), Graham writes, "it seems obvious to me that the worldview of any external world sceptic is much worse than the worldview of naturalists." That seems obvious to me too. The reason Graham gives is that the skeptic, by distrusting her senses, avoids error but has no chance of getting at the truth. It's worth the risk of being wrong in order to have a chance of being right.

Graham, in other words, adopts the Reidian attitude of trust in our faculties. No reason has been given for assuming that sensory experience is hooked up to the world in the right way to yield true beliefs while religious experience isn't. If we assume from the outset that what seem to be experiences of apples come from real apples, then we should also assume from the outset that what seem to be experiences of God come from a real God. Of course, either kind of experience might be shown to be misleading after further investigation, but in both cases trust should be the default attitude.

Graham does say something that can be construed as a response to this line of argument. He says, "Given that those who believe in gods are committed to explaining away the claims of those who insist on religious experience of *other* gods, there is no disadvantage that accrues to those who seek to explain away *all* claims to religious experience of gods" (opening statement, §21). In other words, according to Graham, even if we start from the Reidian attitude of trust, we will end up rejecting religious experience because it leads to contradictory results (all of the competing religions).

Since Graham says something very similar about miracles (§20), he appears to be endorsing the following general principle:

> If you are already committed to explaining away the vast majority of the x's, then no further disadvantage accrues if you decide to explain away all of the x's.

This general principle is incorrect. Here's an example to explain why.

For a study published in 2017, researchers conducted genetic analysis on fish purchased from 26 sushi restaurants in Los Angeles. They ordered halibut 43 times, but according to their genetic analysis, *every single sample* of halibut was fake (Willette et al. 2017). There is lots of *apparent* halibut in Los Angeles sushi restaurants—it's listed on menus, you can find people who remember eating it, and so on. But we must explain away the vast majority of this apparent halibut. According to the study, about 89% of it is flounder and the remaining 11% is made up of various other types of fish.

Having read this study, I'm now committed to explaining away the vast majority of halibut sushi claims (at least in Los Angeles). Does it follow that I incur no further cost by explaining away *all* of the halibut claims? Should I deny the existence of halibut? Certainly not. Should I deny the existence of halibut sushi? Again, no. Should I deny the existence of halibut sushi in Los Angeles restaurants? Even here, I should probably exercise some caution. It's not too unlikely that there is real halibut sushi in *some* Los Angeles restaurant sometimes, even if 43 samples from 26 restaurants are all fake.

The point here is that even if we have to explain away the vast majority of claims of a certain sort, there are still broader costs and benefits to be considered in deciding whether we should try to explain them *all* away. Do we have other reason to believe in halibut? Yes. Do we think that halibut, if it existed, is the kind of thing people would sometimes taste? Again, yes. If halibut really exists, is it likely that it's sometimes made into sushi? Once again, yes.

It turns out that neither restaurant menus nor the testimony of restaurant-goers is a reliable source of information about halibut sushi. Nevertheless, it's a reliable source of information about *halibut or flounder or something like that*. The exact details of how we should think about these alleged halibut sushi experiences, and what exactly might be revealed by them, will be dependent on other elements of our worldview. But the fact that most of what people experience isn't halibut doesn't show that we shouldn't take these halibut sushi experiences seriously as a source of evidence about the world. The experiences are usually misdescribed by those who experience them, but they are *authentic* experiences nonetheless.

If someone claimed that everyone who reports having eaten halibut sushi was hallucinating or misremembering or lying, I would regard this as a skeptical hypothesis. The Reidian attitude of trust would lead me to reject it, at least in the absence of extraordinary evidence. On the other hand, the researchers' conclusion that most people who think they ate halibut actually ate flounder does not involve any kind of radical distrust in the senses, or memory, or testimony. The researchers used all three of these faculties in the course of their investigation. Their conclusion implies that these faculties are prone to certain kinds of error, but it doesn't undermine the general attitude of trust. (This is the same point I was making with the antelope example in §4.4 of my opening statement.)

Let's return to the case of religious experience, which is not exactly like halibut sushi. The two have this in common: there are a quite substantial number of first-person reports, but most of these reports must be mistaken at least to some degree. Scientific studies are based on sensory evidence, so the halibut case involves a conflict between two sources of sensory evidence. People judged based on color, texture, and flavor that they were eating halibut, but the evidence of the gene sequencing process (which is also known by means of the senses) disagrees. In the religious experience case, we likewise have a variety of reports of experience that conflict with one another.

A further similarity: Graham apparently agrees that people who report religious experience are (often) sincerely reporting a real experience of some sort. The same is true, of course, of people who claim to have eaten halibut sushi.

I claim that the cases have yet another similarity: in both cases, people who form false beliefs generally do so by misinterpreting their experience. I claim that it would be objectionably skeptical (and problematic in various other ways) to hypothesize that people just periodically *hallucinate* experiences of eating halibut sushi. People eat flounder and think it's halibut because that's what they've been told. Similarly, in the case of religious experience, people experience God and interpret that experience in light of their total worldviews. Preserving in this way the authenticity of religious belief makes for a more robustly anti-skeptical worldview.

The vast majority of people who claim to have eaten halibut sushi in Los Angeles restaurants are mistaken. The claim they make is false, and must be explained away. In the same way, because different religions make conflicting claims on the basis of religious experience, it must be the case that most claims people make on the basis of religious experience are false. These claims must be explained away. But it does not follow from this that no cost is incurred by explaining religious experience away *entirely* and regarding it as *wholly* unreliable. The hypothesis that people mistake flounder for halibut is to be preferred over the hypothesis that people hallucinate halibut. In precisely the same way, in the case of religious experience, the hypothesis that people often misunderstand what they experience is to be preferred over the hypothesis that their experience is some kind of hallucination. Furthermore, just as one might hope to develop a more discerning palate and learn to distinguish halibut from flounder, so also one might hope that the right kind of religious training and practice might lead one to interpret religious experience more accurately.[8] It is this last hope that justifies us in deciding to place our bets on a particular religious tradition.

> Naturalism involves a kind of skepticism about religious experience. When it comes to the senses, Graham doesn't argue that they are reliable; he just assumes it. So do I. But Graham has not identified any difference between sensory experience and religious experience that justifies trusting the one and distrusting the other. If we assume from the outset that what seem to be experiences of apples come from real apples, then we should also assume from the outset that what seem to be experiences of God come from a real God.

4 Theism and Simplicity

In this final section, I discuss a number of points Graham makes about theism and simplicity. Graham distinguishes three kinds of simplicity: ontological, ideological, and theoretical. I discussed

---

8. For an illuminating discussion of the kind of knowledge that might be gained through participation in religious practices, see Cuneo (2014).

theoretical simplicity above (§2), so here I will focus on ontological and ideological simplicity.

4.1 Ontological Simplicity

Ontological simplicity takes into account the basic things and kinds of things that a worldview takes to exist. In this comparison, we consider both how many things and kinds of things the worldview recognizes, and also how complex these things and kinds of things are.

My version of theism has only one primitive ontological commitment; namely, God. Everything that exists is ultimately grounded in God. Since there's only one individual thing (God) that is ontologically primitive, there's also only one *kind* of thing that's ontologically primitive. This is a version of priority monism.

> **Priority monism** is the view that, although many things exist, they are all grounded in one thing.

There are also naturalistic versions of priority monism. The best known version of priority monism in philosophy today is due to Jonathan Schaffer (2009b, 2010), who argues that spacetime is the only fundamentally real entity.

Graham, however, rejects priority monism (opening statement, §9). He believes that there are many ontologically primitive things. So Graham's version of naturalism has many more primitive ontological commitments than my version of theism.

We should also compare the complexity of primitive ontological commitments. Here, the relevant type of complexity is ontological. That is, it's not a matter of how complicated our thinking about the fundamental things is (that comes under ideological and theoretical complexity). It's a matter of how complex the fundamental things themselves are.

The medieval classical theists had an extreme view of God's ontological simplicity. According to philosopher-theologians like Avicenna (*Metaphysica*, chs. 21–26), Maimonides (*Guide*, chs. 1.35, 1.50–52), and Aquinas (*Summa Theologiae*, Iq3), there is no ontological complexity of any kind in God. When we say of a human judge that she is both just and merciful, we identify two different attributes that she has. So there are, in this case, three things: the judge, her justice, and her mercy. Not so with God, according to these thinkers: God's justice just is God's mercy, which just is God.

On this basis, Maimonides even goes so far as to say God has no attributes! And this is only the beginning. Avicenna famously argued God's essence is the same thing as God's existence, which is the same thing as God. He was followed in this by Maimonides, Aquinas, and others. Further, according to these thinkers, God's act of creating the universe just is God. And so on.

From the perspective of ontological simplicity, this is positively *lovely*. I'm not sure it makes any sense.[9]

Even if the full-strength classical doctrine of divine simplicity does make sense, this kind of ontological simplicity is clearly paid for with ideological and theoretical complexity. It's not for nothing that Christopher Hughes (1989) gave his book on Aquinas the title *On a Complex Theory of a Simple God*!

Still, without defending the full-strength classical doctrine of divine simplicity, we can say that God is simple in a number of ways. God, for instance, is not made out of parts. We can also say that God's omnipotence is one unified feature of God rather than a collection of many powers (see Pearce 2019). Similarly, we can say that God does not have many separate items of knowledge but that God knows all possible things in a single cognitive act. Additionally, there is reason to think that omnipotence entails omniscience and perfect rationality (see Pearce and Pruss 2012, 411–412). Further, on the account of the foundations of morality given above, perfect rationality entails moral perfection. There may be similar relations between other divine attributes. So, although I'm not prepared to defend the idea that God's essence just is God, still I think that God's essence is highly unified, and this is a kind of ontological simplicity.

Graham hasn't told us much about his fundamental ontological commitments. In §10, he suggests that the basic ontological commitments of naturalism *might* be physical simples. Presumably, he means fundamental particles like electrons. Electrons, the physicists tell us, have a number of puzzling features; for instance, their position and momentum are indeterminate (expressed by **probabilities** rather than precise numbers), and it can even be indeterminate whether an electron has been created by a particular interaction. Even stranger is the fact that it can be indeterminate whether an

---

9. For a valiant attempt at making sense of the classical doctrine of divine simplicity, see Brower (2009).

electron we observe at a later time is the same one we observed earlier. What precisely this means for the nature of reality is disputed (see French and Krause 2003; Bokulich 2014; Wolff 2015; Glick 2017; French 2019). In order to judge the complexity of Graham's fundamental ontological commitments, we would need to know how he interprets quantum physics. (Of course, I'm committed to quantum weirdness too, but I don't take it to be ontologically fundamental.)

Here's the point: on both Graham's view and mine, the primitive ontological commitments exhibit some puzzles and complexities. It's not totally obvious whose ontological commitments are simpler. But one thing is clear: Graham is primitively ontologically committed to an enormous multitude of individual things, belonging to several different categories. I am primitively ontologically committed to just one thing: God.

4.2 Ideological Simplicity

In comparing the ideological simplicity of worldviews, the question is, which worldview contains fewer "undefined primitive expressions" (Graham's opening statement, §10); that is, words or concepts that can't be analyzed in simpler terms. These words or concepts are the worldview's primitive ideological commitments.

The central attributes of God employed in my explanation of History are *mental* attributes: God makes a free and rational choice. I don't think we can paraphrase this kind of mental state talk away, so these sorts of concepts are among the primitive ideological commitments of my view.

Graham evidently thinks he can paraphrase away talk of *minds*. This is why he talks about *mindedness* and *minded organisms* (see §23 of his opening statement).

Graham's rejection of minds as separate entities is clearly good for the ontological simplicity of his view. I don't think it makes any difference to ideological simplicity because I don't think the concept *mindedness* is any simpler than the concept *mind*.

According to Graham, "Minded organisms are *conscious*, have *agency*, *perceive* their immediate surroundings, *believe*, *desire*, *intend*, *think*, *imagine*, *remember*, *learn*, *predict*, *feel*, *empathise*, *suffer*, *reason*, *calculate*, *communicate*, and so on" (§23). Graham claims that all of these activities can be explained biologically. This is certainly in some sense true: in actual organisms (such as humans), these activities occur *because of* certain biological facts, and biologists have a reasonably good (though still imperfect) grasp of what those facts are. What kind of explanation is this? How complete is it? What consequences does this have for the nature of minds or mindedness? These are difficult questions on which Graham and I will likely disagree, but there is not space to address them here.

Graham claims that "For minded organisms to be *conscious* just is for those organisms to be engaged in certain kinds of neural processing" (§23). Presumably, though, this is a metaphysical claim about what consciousness really is, and not an analysis of our concept of consciousness. Even if there is some sense in which some complicated neurological description tells us what consciousness *really is* (at least for organisms with brains like ours), we won't be able to replace our concept of consciousness with this neurological concept (see Levine 1983; Loar 1990).

In addition to consciousness, Graham holds that at least some minded organisms have reason (§25) and freedom (§26).

Since Graham has a primitive ideological commitment to these mental concepts, my appeal to God's free and rational choice appears not to incur any additional primitive ideological commitments beyond those present in Graham's worldview.

Graham offers an objection to this claim: when theists apply these concepts to God, he says, they use them *analogically*, and when concepts are used analogically this incurs a new ideological commitment (§11).

In my opening statement (§2.1), I noted that classical theists have historically held that language must be somehow 'stretched' to talk about God. This is what's meant by 'analogy' in this context.

> **Analogy** is the use of a concept in a new context in a way that changes its meaning.
> **Univocity** is the use of a concept in the normal or original way, without shifting or stretching its meaning.

Analogy and Metaphor

Many theistic philosophers have thought it was important to distinguish between analogy and metaphor in our talk about God. Aquinas, for instance, argued quite explicitly that when

> we call God 'good', we speak analogically but not metaphorically (Aquinas, *Summa Theologiae*, Iq13a3). The difference, roughly speaking, is supposed to be that when we use metaphor—as, for instance, if one says 'God is my rock' (see Psalm 18:2)—we say something that, taken literally, is false. On the other hand, when we say 'God is good', we're applying the word 'good' in a context very different from the context in which we originally learned the word. This new context somehow shifts the word's meaning. However, according to Aquinas, we're not just speaking metaphorically here: the thing we say is (somehow) literally true.
>
> It is not possible to make this distinction precise without developing detailed theories of metaphor and analogy. Furthermore, both metaphor and analogy are ways of using words to talk about things other than their usual objects. Finally, the distinction between metaphor and analogy in classical philosophical theology does not match the distinctions drawn in theories of metaphor and analogy today. For these reasons, we won't worry about this distinction here.

The concept of *free and rational choice* is also an ideological commitment of Graham's view. He thinks humans sometimes make free and rational choices. Does my application of this concept to God incur a new primitive ideological commitment? There are three possibilities here:

1. This instance of concept application is univocal.
2. This instance is analogous but does *not* incur an additional primitive ideological commitment.
3. This instance is analogous and *does* incur an additional primitive ideological commitment.

In my opening statement I endorsed the view that God is **atemporal**. It's hard to see how a being who is outside time could make a free and rational choice in precisely the same sense that a human does. The temporal element of our experience seems to be essential to our choosing. So (1) seems unlikely to work here.

Option (2) can be divided into two versions:

2a. Analogous predication does not incur additional ideological commitments.
2b. Although analogous predication incurs additional ideological commitments, in this particular case these commitments are not *primitive*: the analogy can be spelled out in terms of other concepts to which we are already committed.

I think either of these options might be made to work. Here's a reason for endorsing (2a). According to what is perhaps the most historically popular theory of analogical talk about God, when we think about (for instance) God's mercy, we employ the very same concept *mercy* that we employ when thinking about humans. However, when we apply the concept to God, we know it isn't picking out the exact same kind of thing it normally does (see Aquinas, *Summa Theologiae*, Iq13a3–6). Since there's no additional concept here, one might think, whatever additional complexity we're incurring is ontological, not ideological. Of course, we'll have an ideological commitment to the mechanism of analogy itself. But it might be argued that we need that mechanism for non-theological reasons anyway. In fact, Lakoff and Johnson (1980) have famously argued that "[o]ur ordinary conceptual system, in terms of which we both think and act, is fundamentally metaphorical in nature." They think of metaphor as involving a kind of stretching of concepts similar to what one finds in classical theories of analogy. Elizabeth Camp (2006, 159), while expressing skepticism about Lakoff and Johnson's radical thesis, concedes that "[t]he claim that metaphor is unavoidable may well be true for thought about unfamiliar or mysterious topics, such as computers or particle physics."

It seems to me that the biggest difficulty with this view is making sense of its account of analogy (or metaphor). It's easy to see how you can use a *word* to refer to different objects than normal (you could call your cat 'mercy'), but if the concept you have in mind is the concept of *mercy*, doesn't it follow that you are thinking about mercy—in the ordinary, everyday sense? The answer to this question depends on difficult issues about the nature of concepts.

Suppose, then, that we turn to (2b) instead. The idea here would be that, although the concept *free and rational choice* is applied to God analogically, this analogy can be spelled out in univocal terms.

Analogy and metaphor have been studied extensively by philosophers, literary critics, linguists, psychologists, and cognitive scientists. Many of these theorists are skeptical of the idea that analogies and metaphors in general can be spelled out in literal and univocal terms (Davidson 1978; Walton 1993; Reimer 2001).[10] Could some literal and univocal expression be found precisely equivalent to what Elton John meant in saying of Marilyn Monroe that she lived her life "like a candle in the wind"? If you think not, go back to (2a): you're committed to the claim that we need an account of irreducible analogical thought and speech for non-theological purposes. But suppose you think that, in general, we can spell out analogies and metaphors in literal and univocal terms. This would be to provide an analysis or definition of our concepts. We would therefore avoid new primitive ideological commitments.

I think there is reason to hope that the application of the concept of *free and rational choice* to God can be spelled out in literal and univocal terms. For instance, I think the concept of *having reasons* can probably be applied to God in the same sense that it is applied to humans. So we may be able to say, without resorting to analogy, that *History is occurring because God has certain reasons*. This might be the beginning of a literal and univocal spelling out of the analogy contained in my official formulation of classical theism.

Option (3) is to bite the bullet and admit that we've incurred an extra primitive ideological commitment. Nevertheless, we can claim that the kind of ideological commitment incurred by the analogical extension of a concept is 'cheaper' than the commitment incurred by introducing a totally new concept. For instance, in classical physics it's part of the concept of a wave that it has to propagate in a medium. A wave of water, for instance, is a pattern of movement in the water. You couldn't just have the wave without any water. Eventually, though, physicists started to think that light might be a wave that could propagate through empty space with no medium at all. They stretched the concept *wave* to apply to things that don't only propagate in a medium. Since this altered the concept, it incurred a new ideological commitment. But the commitment wasn't *totally* new because it was an analogical extension of a concept the physicists already had.

---

10. For a discussion of this issue in the context of Jewish theology, see Lebens (2019).

I would be most satisfied with a solution of type (2b). In my own research on this topic, I think I've made some progress in this direction for the particular notions of God's power and God's free and rational choice (see Pearce and Pruss 2012; Pearce 2017a, 2019), but this is admittedly still a work in progress.

I've focused here on the notion of free and rational choice because that's the notion that figures centrally in my explanation of History. However, we need to answer the same question for *every* concept we want to apply to God, and we might not give the same answer every time.

As far as I can see, Graham's worldview isn't committed to any extra ideology.

I conclude, then, that Graham's worldview has a modest advantage in ideological simplicity over my worldview as it currently exists. However, it's possible that further work on the divine attributes might narrow this gap, or even close it entirely.

4.3 Comparative Simplicity

In §2, I argued (among other things) that my worldview has an enormous (indeed, infinite) advantage over Graham's when it comes to theoretical simplicity. In §4.1, I argued that, although it's not clear whose fundamental ontological commitments are simpler, I have only one fundamental ontological commitment, while Graham is committed to many things and kinds of things. Finally, in §4.2, I conceded that Graham's worldview likely has a modest advantage in ideological simplicity. This is certainly not enough to offset the theoretical complexity of Graham's worldview. As a result, in addition to the other advantages outlined in my opening statement, my particular version of theism is, on the whole, simpler than Graham's particular version of naturalism.

> We saw in §2 that my worldview is infinitely theoretically simpler than Graham's. In this section, I've argued that Graham does not have significant advantages in either ontological or ideological simplicity. My worldview is a version of priority monism, which gives it a significant advantage in ontological simplicity. Graham might be right that some of the things I say about God are analogical, and perhaps this incurs some cost in ideological simplicity. However, I have argued that this cost is not severe.

5 Conclusion

Graham contends that his worldview stands in no need of any supernatural hypotheses. In a way, I agree: there certainly are internally coherent versions of naturalism. At the same time, I reject Graham's claim that there is no work for theism to do in constructing a simple, coherent, and explanatorily powerful worldview. Indeed, we've now seen quite a number of reasons for favoring my version of theism over Graham's version of naturalism.

Chapter 4

Reply to Kenny Pearce

Graham Oppy

Contents

1 Argument   219
2 Worldview Comparison   220
3 Kenny's Negative Argument   222
4 Kenny's Positive Argument   224
5 Brutes   229
6 Religious Experience   232
7 Concluding Remarks   237

There is much on which Kenny and I agree. Under the broadly Reidian epistemology that we both accept, this is to be expected. If we did not agree on most commonsense and scientific matters, then our commitment to the broadly Reidian epistemology would be called into question. But, even on questions in philosophy—where, as Kenny points out, there is nothing like the widespread agreement that we find on questions of science and common sense—Kenny and I agree about quite a lot. While I shall not be focussing in these comments on areas in which we do agree, it is important to remember just how much there is on which we do agree.

There is also much on which Kenny and I disagree. In particular, there is much on which Kenny says that we agree, but we do not. Before turning to other matters, I shall point to a couple of important places where this is so.

DOI: 10.4324/9781003216797-7

I Argument

While many philosophers agree with Kenny that philosophers support their positions over the positions of others with arguments, I deny that this is generally so. In my view, except in very special cases, positions *cannot* be supported over other positions by arguments. Unsurprisingly then, I think that, except in very special cases, philosophers *do not* support their positions over the positions of others with arguments. Of course, this is not to deny that some philosophers benightedly take themselves to be supporting their positions over the positions of others with arguments. (Remember that an argument is a collection of claims, one of which is the conclusion, and the rest of which are the premises. An argument may—but need not—be accompanied by a derivation of the conclusion from the premises in which each step in the derivation is justified by appeal to appropriate rules of derivation.)

A position is a theory: a set of claims closed under the taking of consequences. If a position has absurd consequences, then it has a serious flaw. One philosopher can use a derivation to show that another philosopher's position has absurd consequences. In that case, all else being equal, the first philosopher has an argument that the position of the first philosopher is better than the position of the second philosopher. This is the special case in which a philosophical position is supported over another position by an argument. Note that, in this case, the argument of the first philosopher has, at its premises, only claims that are accepted by the second philosopher, and, as its conclusion, something that is recognised even by the second philosopher to be absurd.

Suppose that two philosophers A and B have positions that do not have absurd consequences. Suppose that A maintains that p, B maintains that not p, and it would be absurd to maintain that both p and not p. Suppose that A constructs an argument for p. It must be that, given our assumptions, if p is a consequence of the premises in the argument that A constructs, then B does not accept at least one of the premises in A's argument. Suppose, for example, that q is one such premise: A maintains that q, and B maintains that not q. If we accept that A's asserting that p does not support the position of A over B, then we should also accept that A's argument with q among its premises and p as its conclusion does not support the position of A over B, since, in asserting that argument, A does no more, with respect to q, than to merely assert *it*. If A cannot make the case for the superiority of the position of A over the position of B by merely insisting that p, then A cannot make the case by merely insisting on an argument with p as conclusion and q among its premises.

If you have a theory that you take to be true, then you suppose that there are countless arguments that you take to be sound. Exhibiting some of these arguments does nothing to support your theory. The soundness of these arguments is not *evidence* that your theory is true. Moreover, your taking the arguments to be sound cannot be your *reason* for taking the theory to be true. After all, in assessing the soundness of the arguments, you have to assess the truth of the premises—but the premises just are the claims that belong to your theory.

2 Worldview Comparison

Kenny suggests that worldview comparison is a two-stage process: first, we check for *internal coherence*, and then we check for *simplicity* and *explanatory comprehensiveness*. According to Kenny, a worldview is (a) more internally coherent if its 'different pieces fit [more] neatly together'; (b) more simple if it 'posits fewer things, or fewer kinds of things, or is . . . more elegant and less convoluted'; and (c) more explanatorily comprehensive if it 'explains more things and leaves fewer unexplained'.

I say that worldview comparison is a three-stage process. First, we try to articulate the worldviews as far as we can, to the same level of detail and with the same degree of care. Second, we check to see whether the worldviews fail on their own terms: do the worldviews have consequences that they themselves take to be absurd? Third, we compare how well the worldviews do in managing the trade-off between minimising theoretical commitments and maximising breadth and depth of explanation of data. In general, according to me, there is no algorithm for determining when one worldview does better than another in managing the trade-off between minimising theoretical commitments and maximising breadth and depth of explanation of data. However, there are special cases: for example, if W1 and W2 are worldviews that do not fail on their own terms, and if W1 has fewer commitments than W2, and W1 has no less breadth and depth of explanation of data than W2, then W1 is a better worldview than W2.

As I said in §10 of my initial statement, theoretical commitments are of three kinds: ontological commitments (to membership of domains of quantification), ideological commitments (to undefined predicates), and theoretical commitments (to axioms). In order to explain 'breadth and depth of explanation of data', I need to explain 'data'. The simplest—and I think best—explanation is that data is the full set of claims on which W1 and W2 agree. If you prefer to separate data from worldview, then, instead, you can take the worldviews to be just the claims on which there is disagreement.

There are three important differences between my account and Kenny's account. First, according to me, having 'different pieces fit more neatly together' is part of the minimisation of theoretical commitments. One advantage of my way of seeing things is that this makes the second stage non-comparative: it is an all-or-nothing, non-comparative matter whether a worldview has consequences that, by its own lights, are absurd. Second, according to me, 'explains more things and leaves fewer unexplained' runs together minimisation of theoretical commitments and maximisation of explanation of data. It is one thing to treat data as theoretically primitive; it is another thing to introduce theoretical primitives in order to explain data. Third, according to me, the most important part of worldview comparison is the first stage: articulating worldviews as far as we can, to the same level of detail and with the same degree of care. If we are comparing two worldviews, we want to be clear about *everything* that is in the theoretical commitments of just one of the two worldviews. There is no 'putting some runs on the board' if you have failed to declare the full range of your relevant theoretical commitments.

With these preliminaries out of the way, let us move on to the main game.

> Worldview comparison is a three-stage process: (1) articulation, (2) internal check, and (3) comparison. The most important stage comes first: you need to articulate all of the relevant commitments of the worldviews that are up for comparison before you move to the later stages. The second stage is best treated as a kind of formality: if your opponents have not demonstrated that your view fails the internal check, then your view moves on to the third stage. (Even in principle, there are limits on proving consistency.) The third stage is where there will be most detailed discussion. Except in special cases, there is unlikely to be agreement about the results at this stage.

3 Kenny's Negative Argument

Kenny claims that, whereas his theism provides an explanation of the existence—or perhaps, more strictly, the occurrence—of History, my naturalism provides no such explanation. Without charitable interpretation, this claim is just false. After all, I claim that the existence of History is necessary; there is no doubt that I do have an explanation of the existence of History. Moreover, it is hard to see that my explanation of the existence of History is in any worse shape, *qua* explanation, than Kenny's explanation of the existence of God; after all, his explanation of the existence of God is that God's existence is necessary. Given that the necessity of something explains why it is so—a claim on which Kenny agrees—he is in no position to say that my worldview affords no explanation of the existence of History.

So what is the charitable interpretation of Kenny's criticism? What he is claiming is that my worldview fails at the second stage: it is logically inconsistent. Why? Because, according to Kenny, my naturalism commits me to the claim that the existence of History is contingent, and that claim is logically inconsistent with my further claim that the existence of History is necessary. If Kenny is right about this, then, before I can rejoin the fray, I need to revise my worldview.

According to Kenny, any explanation of History that respects current physics must be a non-necessitating explanation. Why? Because in the decades since the discovery of Einstein's Field Equations, physicists and philosophers of physics have debated the physical significance of exotic solutions to those equations, premised on the assumption that a significant number of non-exotic solutions to those equations describe physical possibilities. According to Kenny, if we take our cues from current physics, we should endorse the principle that solutions to Einstein's Field Equations describe physical possibilities unless there are compelling reasons to the contrary. When I say that every possible world shares some initial history with the actual world, I am telling the physicists how to conduct their business in a way that no naturalist can, because I am saying that only one of the solutions to Einstein's Field Equations describes a physical possibility.

As I said in §3 and §16 of my initial statement, naturalists take their cues from current *well-established* science—that is, science on which there is expert scientific consensus on claims and methods. However, in domains in which there is not expert scientific consensus on claims and methods, it is fine for naturalists to speculate. Perhaps unsurprisingly, I deny that there is expert consensus that a significant number of non-exotic solutions to Einstein's Field Equations describe physical possibilities. Indeed, if there is anything approaching expert scientific consensus in this area, it is that *none* of the solutions to Einstein's Field Equations describes physical possibilities.

Although quantum mechanics and general relativity are, as Roger Penrose says, *superb* theories, they are jointly logically inconsistent. We have, as yet, no satisfactory theory of quantum gravity; we have no expert scientific consensus that general relativity accurately describes our universe at all times and at all energy levels. Sure, we do have expert scientific consensus that general relativity provides a very accurate description of our universe at all times after the inflationary era and at all sufficiently low energy levels; but it is precisely the nature of our universe in the pre-inflationary era that is of interest to us when we are thinking about the initial history of our universe.

Kenny's argument requires that my naturalism commits me to the claim that we have expert scientific consensus that solutions to the Einstein Field Equations describe possible shapes for the *totality* of History. But my naturalism simply does not commit me to that claim. Indeed, as I noted above, it is more plausible to suppose that my naturalism commits me to the denial of that claim. Of course, this is not to say that there was no point in History at which it was an open question which of the solutions to the Einstein Field Equations provided an accurate description of our universe at all sufficiently low energy levels and at all sufficiently late stages in the history of our universe. All that is required for open questions is something like epistemic possibility; but our present question concerns ontological or metaphysical possibility. This, in turn, is not to say that there were no other ontological or metaphysical possibilities for the subsequent shape of History that depended on chance outcomes in the pre-inflationary era. Open questions can pivot on ontological or metaphysical possibilities.

> Kenny's claim that my naturalism is logically inconsistent is central to the case that he makes for the superiority of his view. He claims that I cannot consistently maintain that there are solutions to the Einstein Field Equations that are not physical possibilities. However, I do claim that there are solutions to the Einstein Field Equations that are not physical possibilities; and I deny that there is anything else that I am committed to that is inconsistent with this claim.

4 Kenny's Positive Argument

Kenny claims that his theism provides a *non-causal* explanation of the existence of History. On his view, 'History is grounded in God's choice'; 'History is *distinct* from God's choice and yet *nothing over and above* God's choice'; but God's choice is not a cause of the existence of History. While grounding occurs when more fundamental things 'give rise to' less fundamental things, we can interpret this 'giving rise to' in non-causal terms. In particular, we can suppose that God's choice gives rise to the existence of History without being a cause of the existence of History.

Kenny discusses four examples of grounding: (a) the relation between a statue and its constituent clay, (b) the relation between a sandwich and the bread and meat that are its parts, (c) the relation between facts about debt and facts about fundamental physics, and (d) the relation between a waltz and the dancers who are waltzing.

(a) In examples of constitution—like the case of the statue and the clay—we are thinking about the relationship between a thing and some stuff. Many philosophers who consider this case suppose that we are instead thinking about the relation between two things: a statue and a lump of clay. In my view, that is a mistake. The clay in question might, at different times, constitute one lump, seven lumps, one statue, and seven statues. It is obvious that the one statue is *separate* from the seven lumps: there is—and can be—no overlap in the time periods at which they exist. What makes it the case that none of these things is 'separate' from the clay is precisely the fact that the clay is the stuff from which, at non-overlapping times, they are each constituted.

Kenny claims that the grounding of the statue in the clay provides a non-causal explanation of the statue's existence. However, the fact that there is something that is constituted by the clay simply does not explain why there is a statue. Sure, as Aristotle might have said, the clay is the material cause of the statue. But in order for a statue to exist, you also need formal and efficient causes: there must be a sculptor who moulds the statue from the clay according to some previously developed plan. Curiously, Kenny seems to concede this point: 'Why is there a statue? Because the arrangement of the clay corresponds to certain artistic intentions and the community regards the clay in light of these intentions. In other words, the statue exists because of certain physical, historical and relational features of the clay'. Statues do not pop into existence without efficient causes.

Even if constitution did yield non-causal explanation, it cannot be that God's choice constitutes History. Choices are things, not stuff. ('Choice' is a count noun, not a mass noun.) If History has a constitution, then there is some kind of stuff from which it is constituted. God's choice is no kind of stuff, and so not a candidate to be the stuff from which History is constituted, if, indeed, there is stuff from which History is constituted.

(b) In examples of part and whole—like the case of the sandwich—we are thinking about the relationship between a thing and other things that are parts of the given thing. The slices of bread and the slice of meat are things that are parts of the sandwich. ('Slice of bread' is a count noun, even though 'bread' is a mass noun.) If we suppose that the sandwich has an exhaustive decomposition into the slices of bread and the slice of meat, then we can certainly accept that the sandwich is *nothing over and above* those things in the following sense: it has no parts that are not overlapped entirely by those three things. Moreover, we can accept that the sandwich is *distinct* from each of its parts: while it fully overlaps each of its proper parts, none of its proper parts fully overlaps it. And we can accept that the sandwich is not *separate* from any of its parts: it fully overlaps each of its proper parts.

Kenny claims that, although it is clearly possible to give a causal explanation of the existence of the sandwich that appeals to the making of the sandwich by a sandwich-maker, it is also possible to give a non-causal explanation of the existence of the sandwich in terms of the arrangement of its parts: 'there's a sandwich because the [slice of] meat is between the two slices of bread'. This does not sound quite right to me. It is not the case that there is one question about the existence of the sandwich that is answered equally well by the causal explanation and the non-causal explanation. Rather, there are distinct questions, one of which is answered by the causal explanation, and the other of which is answered by the non-causal explanation. If we are interested in the *nature* of the thing in question—its being a sandwich—then it makes sense to advert to its parts; near enough, quite generally, sandwiches just are fillings between slices of bread. But if we are interested in the *existence* of the thing in question, then what we want to know about is its efficient causal history. (If your Mom asks you 'What is that sandwich on your bedroom floor?' it will be risky to say 'It's a slice of meat between two slices of bread'.) It is perhaps also worth noting that it seems no less possible to give a non-causal explanation of the existence and arrangement of the slice of meat and the slices of bread in terms of the existence of the sandwich: 'There is a slice of meat between two slices of bread because there is a sandwich'.

Even if part/whole relations did yield non-causal explanations, it could not be that God's choice and History stand in some kind of part/whole relation. By definition, according to Kenny, History is the total sequence of causes and effects. Parts of History are themselves causes and effects. If God's choice were part of History, then it would be a cause or effect (or a part of a cause or effect). But in that case, God's choice could not be any kind of explanation of History. For, if it were an explanation of History, then, in particular, it would be an explanation of itself. But nothing can be self-explanatory: 'A because A' is always an explanatory solecism.

(c) In examples of supervenience—like the case of facts about debt—we are thinking about quite complex relationships. As I said in §9, necessarily, As supervene on Bs if and only if (1) it is impossible for there to be change in the As without change in the Bs, (2) it is possible for there to be change in the Bs without change in the As, and (3) it is possible for there to be change in the As. In the case in which we are interested, facts about debt supervene on physical facts because (1) it is impossible for there to be change in the facts about debts without change in the physical facts, (2) it is possible for there to be change in the physical facts without change in the facts about debts, and (3) it is possible for there to be change in the facts about debts. As in the cases of constitution and part/whole, supervenience seems to licence 'nothing over and above' and 'distinct but not separate' talk.

Kenny claims, at least *inter alia*, that is it possible to give a non-causal explanation of the obtaining of facts about debt in terms of the obtaining of physical facts. That does not seem quite right to me. I think that no one is in a position to explain particular facts about debt in terms of their supervenience on particular physical facts. If I ask why Donald has a particular debt of $2 billion, the most that anyone can say by way of explanation of this fact, if they appeal to the supervenience of facts about debt on physical facts, is that, in order for this fact not to obtain, the physical facts would have to be other than they actually are. Moreover, for any other particular economic fact upon which we choose to focus our attention, exactly the same thing is true: the most that anyone can say by way of explanation of that other fact, if they appeal to the supervenience of facts about debt on physical facts, is that, in order for this fact not to obtain, the physical facts would have to be other than they actually are. Anyone looking for an informative explanation of why it is that Donald has a debt of $2 billion needs to look beyond the general supervenience of the economic on the physical.

Even if we suppose that we can get informative explanations of singular facts in terms of supervenience, it seems wrong to think that we can appeal to supervenience in order to generate a non-causal explanation of the existence of History in terms of God's choice. The reason for this is straightforward: on the kind of account of God's causing the existence of History that would most appeal to Kenny, it turns out that History supervenes on God's choice. But, if History's supervening on God's choice is consistent with God's causing History, then it seems wrong to say that to adopt the claim that History supervenes on God's choice is to adopt a *non-causal* explanation of the existence of History. Saying that there is a relation of supervenience is simply insufficient to rule out causation.

(d) I think that the relationship between the waltzing of the dancers and the waltz is part/whole. The waltz is an event that has as parts the events that are the waltzes of the dancers. If that is right, then discussion of this example goes the same way as the discussion of the sandwich, the slices of bread, and the slice of meat. Perhaps it might be suggested, instead, that the waltzing of the dancers is the stuff that constitutes the waltz itself. If that were right, then the discussion of the example would go the same way as the discussion of the statue and the clay. Either way, it seems implausible to think that we have here an alternative model for 'nothing over and above' and 'distinct but not separate'.

Given the discussion to this point, I think that it is reasonable to conclude that, whatever Kenny has in mind when he claims that History is grounded in God's choice, the grounding relation to which he is appealing is not one of the familiar grounding relations exhibited in his examples: constitution, part/whole, and supervenience. Kenny says that he is not supposing that there is just one grounding relation; he leaves it open—at least for the purposes of the argument that he develops—that grounding is a diverse family of relations. Perhaps he can have his cake and eat it: perhaps he can say that each of the particular grounding relations is a determinate of the determinable Grounding relation. But, if he supposes that among the diverse family of determinate grounding relations there is a determinate relation that is uniquely exemplified in the case of the grounding of History in God's choice, then there is a *new* bunch of unacknowledged theoretical commitments that he accrues that his naturalist opponents do not. Along with his acknowledged commitments to God, omnipotence, omniscience, perfect goodness, immutability, impassibility, atemporality, simplicity, and all of the consequences of the doctrine of analogous predication—such as the goodness of God that is distinct from the goodness of human beings—Kenny is committed to a *sui generis* determinate of Grounding exemplified uniquely in the relation of History to God's choice. (And of course, this is just the beginning of a *much* longer list: we have not heard what he has to say about angels and demons, heaven and hell, trinity, incarnation, atonement, resurrection, and on and on. In his concluding remarks, Kenny says that there is little or no difference in the simplicity of his view compared to mine. I think that is plainly false. It is true that there is very little difference in our accounts of natural reality ('spacetime and all its contents'); restricting our attention to natural reality, we have more or less exactly the same ontological, ideological, and theoretical commitments. But, whereas I have no further commitments, Kenny has many more. And that is all it takes to show that my view has fewer commitments than his.)

As I see things, Kenny and I both have an explanation of the existence of History. While I think that the existence of History is necessary, Kenny thinks that the existence of History is contingent. However, Kenny thinks that the existence of History is somehow grounded in the choice of a God whose existence is necessary. Ignoring all other considerations, Kenny's view commits to more but yields no explanatory advantage. This is *not* 'runs on the board' for Kenny.

Perhaps some readers will be tempted to object that the claim of divine necessity is more plausible than the necessity of the initial conditions of the physical universe. However, it is important to remember that considerations about plausibility play no role in the method of worldview comparison to which I subscribe and which Kenny has said that he also accepts. It is to be expected that those who are committed to theistic worldviews will find divine necessity more plausible than the necessity of the initial conditions of the physical universe. But it is also to be expected that those who are committed to naturalistic worldviews will find the claim that the initial conditions of the physical universe are necessary more plausible than the claim that there is a necessarily existing God. Our judgments about what is plausible track our worldview commitments: it would be very odd, to say the least, if our judgments about what is plausible were reversed but our worldview commitments remained the same.

Kenny's claim that only his view provides an explanation of History is central to this claim that his theism is superior to my naturalism. I insist that my view provides an explanation of History: the existence of History is necessary. I also insist that Kenny's explanation—the existence of History is contingent but grounded in God's choice—involves more ontological, ideological, and theoretical commitments than my explanation. So, if all else were equal, Kenny's view would be clearly inferior to mine.

5 Brutes

Kenny says that there can be contingency without brute contingency. I disagree. Kenny says that causes explain effects even when they do not necessitate them. I agree. But Kenny thinks that, if causes explain their effects even when they do not necessitate them, then there can be contingency without brute contingency. Of course, I disagree.

Possible worlds are total ways that things can be. The actual world is the total way that things are. Of course, the actual world is one total way that things can be. (Whatever is actual is possible.) If the actual world is the only possible world, then there is just one total way that things can be: everything is necessary. If the actual world is not the only possible world, then there are different total ways that things can be. If there is contingency, then not everything is necessary. If there is contingency, then there are other possible worlds in which the total way that things are is different from the total way that things are in the actual world.

Suppose that there is contingency. Consider two different possible worlds W1 and W2. Given that W1 and W2 are different possible worlds, there are differences between the total way that W1 is and the total way that W2 is. If there are differences between the total way that W1 is and the total way that W2 is, then either there are initial differences (in the order of explanation) between the total way that W1 is and the total way that W2 is, or there are only non-initial differences (in the order of explanation) between the total way that W1 is and the total way that W2 is.

If there are initial differences (in the order of explanation) between the total way that W1 is and the total way that W2 is, then there are brute differences between the total way that W1 is and the total way that W2 is. Suppose, for example, that W1 is initially F and not G, while W2 is initially G and not F. Then there is nothing in W1 that explains why W1 is initially F and not G, and there is nothing in W2 that explains why W2 is initially G and not F. The key point is that there is nothing available (in the order of explanation) that can explain initial differences, since there is nothing available (in the order of explanation) that is explanatorily prior to initial things.

If there are only non-initial differences (in the order of explanation) between the total way that W1 is and the total way that W2 is, then there is a first point at which there is a non-initial difference (in the order of explanation) between the way that W1 is and the way that W2 is. Suppose, for example, that at this point, W1 is F and not G and W2 is G and not F. Then, at this point, there is nothing in W1 that explains why W1, unlike W2, is F and not G rather than G and not F; and, at this point, there is nothing in W2 that explains why W2, unlike W1, is G and not F rather than F and not G. The key point is that there is nothing available (in the order of explanation) that can explain first non-initial *contrastive* differences, since there is nothing available (in the order of explanation) that is explanatorily prior to the contrastive difference between the worlds. Note that, in this case, it is *only* the contrastive difference that has no explanation: the prior explanatory order in W1 does afford resources for explaining why W1 is F and not G; and the prior explanatory order in W2 does afford resources for explaining why W2 is G and not F.

Suppose, for example, that x is the total indeterministic cause of y. Suppose that the range of things that could have been caused by x is y, . . ., z. Clearly, given that x is the total indeterministic cause of y, x is the cause of y. But, no less clearly, given that x is the total indeterministic cause of y, there is nothing that explains why x causes it to be the case that y rather than z. Consider a world identical to the actual world up until the point at which the chances play out in which x is, instead, the total indeterministic cause of z. In the nature of the case, there is no difference between the worlds to which appeal can be made to explain why, in the actual world x causes y rather than z while, in the merely possible world, x causes z rather than y.

Of course, not all contingency gives rise to brute contingency. Even in deterministic worlds, current contrastive contingent differences can be explained by prior contrastive contingent differences. That W1, unlike W2, is currently F rather than G while W2, unlike W1, is currently G rather than F might be explained by the fact that W1 was previously H rather than I while W2 was previously I rather than H, together with the facts that it must be that F given that it was H and that it must be that G given that it was I. Contingency gives rise to brute contingency only in cases of initial difference and cases in which indeterministic causes play out differently.

All indeterministic causation involves brute contingency. Hence, in particular, any indeterministic choice of a necessary being among multiple options open to it involves brute contingency. If a necessary being makes an indeterministic choice, then it is a matter of brute contingency that it makes the choice that it does rather than any of the other choices that it could have made. If we suppose that free and rational choices are indeterministic choices, then, if a necessary being makes a free and rational choice, then it is a matter of brute contingency that it makes the choice that it does rather than any of the other choices that it could have made. Suppose that W1 and W2 are identical to the point at which the necessary being makes its free and rational choice. Suppose that the necessary being chooses x rather than y in W1 and y rather than x in W2. Then, in each of W1 and W2, it is a matter of brute contingency that the necessary being chooses as it does rather than as it merely could have done. In the nature of the case, there is nothing to which appeal can be made to explain why it chose as it did rather than as it merely might have done. Introducing *this* brute contingency is a theoretical cost for the theist that is not incurred by the naturalist.

> Kenny claims that there can be contingency without brute contingency. I disagree. If there is indeterminism, then there is incompleteness of explanation. If an indeterministic process that can produce either A or B in fact produces A, then, in the nature of the case, there is no explanation why the indeterministic process produced A rather than B.

6 Religious Experience

Kenny endorses the following argument:

1. If one worldview takes human faculties to be more reliable than another worldview takes them to be, this is a reason to prefer the first worldview over the second.
2. If one worldview takes monotheistic religious experiences—that is, experiences that are interpreted as experiences of God—to be reliable and another worldview does not, then (other things being equal) the first worldview takes human faculties to be more reliable than the second.
3. Only theistic worldviews can take monotheistic religious experiences to be reliable.
4. (Therefore) Other things being equal, there is reason to prefer theistic worldviews over non-theistic worldviews.

The first premise in this argument is false. Human faculties are all imperfect. Moreover, we all know this to be so. It is true that, in a wide range of circumstances, our faculties are reliable; but it is also true that, in some circumstances, our faculties are unreliable. In a wide range of circumstances, we see what is there to be seen: but distance, smoke, inattention, intoxication, and visual impairment can all interfere with our ability to see what is there to be seen. In a wide range of circumstances, we hear what is there to be heard: but distance, ambient noise, inattention, intoxication, and auditory impairment can all interfere with our ability to hear what is there to be heard. In a wide range of circumstances, we recall what is there to be recalled; but cognitive load, inattention, intoxication, and deficits of memory retrieval can all interfere with our ability to recall what is there to be recalled, and there are various ways in which what is there to be recalled can fail to be veridical. In a wide range of circumstances, we correctly infer what is there to be inferred: but complexity, cognitive load, inattention, emotion, intoxication, and cognitive impairment can all interfere with our ability to infer what is there to be inferred. It is *only* when we are in good shape, and conditions are friendly, and the task is not too demanding, that our perceptions, memories, and inferences are fully reliable. A worldview that ascribes *more* reliability than this to our perceptions, memories, and inferences is worse than a worldview that ascribes *exactly* this reliability to our perceptions, memories, and inferences.

There is more. We endlessly update our views about exactly where we and others are reliable in our perceptions, memories, and inferences. We have different expectations for different kinds of people: neonates, children, enemies, liars, the depressed, the deluded, the demented, and so forth. Sometimes, we witness deterioration in our memories, our sensory acuities, and our abilities to perform reasoning tasks. If we learn things from recent research in psychology, we know that we are collectively prone to all kinds of cognitive misadventures: ignoring base rates, failing to recognise framing effects, overlooking regression to the mean, misestimating our own competencies, and so forth. With experience of the world, we come to know that there are many domains—including philosophy, politics, and religion—in which there is no convergence of informed opinion, and hence concerning which it would be absurd to suppose that our faculties are reliable. While we do have qualified general dispositions concerning the reliability of our faculties, there is nothing in these qualified general dispositions that supports the claim that worldviews that take religious experiences to be reliable are, other things being equal, to be preferred to worldviews that do not take religious experiences to be reliable.

Consider divinatory practices. Many religions practice alleged communication with non-natural agents. Many religions have specialists who are allegedly able to interpret omens set in the natural world by non-natural agents. Many religions have specialists who are allegedly able to divine future events with the aid of information that they elicit from, or that is disclosed to them, by non-natural agents. Many religions have prayers and rituals that are alleged to influence the course of future events via the intercession of non-natural agents. Many religions have specialists who are alleged to be in direct or indirect communication with non-natural agents.

The range of human divinatory practices is astonishingly broad. (If you have not previously investigated this topic, you might like to look up the entry on 'Methods of Divination' at Wikipedia: https://en.wikipedia.org/wiki/Methods_of_divination.) Consequently, so is the range of human divinatory experiences—that is, experiences of revelation of the future generated by methods of divination. For any human divinatory practice, there are people who take their associated divinatory experience to be reliable. If we follow Kenny, it seems that we can make the following argument:

1. If one worldview takes human faculties to be more reliable than another worldview takes them to be, this is a reason to prefer the first worldview to the second.
2. If one worldview takes divinatory experiences to be reliable and another worldview does not, then—other things being equal—the first worldview takes human faculties to be more reliable than the second.
3. Only divinatory worldviews can take divinatory experiences to be reliable.
4. (Therefore) Other things being equal, there is reason to prefer divinatory worldviews to non-divinatory worldviews.

This argument tells us, for example, that a worldview that takes cephalonomancy to yield accurate information about the future, and so prizes cephalonomantic experiences, is preferable, all else being equal, to a worldview that denies the reliability of any divinatory experiences. I disagree. I say that boiling a donkey's head is not a reliable way of gaining knowledge of the future. I expect you to agree with me on this point. The conclusion of the argument above is just plain wrong. Other things being equal, we should prefer non-divinatory worldviews—worldviews that repudiate all divinatory experience—to divinatory worldviews. No one—not even proponents of particular types of divination—supposes that your worldview *improves* as you accept more and more different kinds of divination.

It might be objected that Kenny need not reject anything that I have said to this point. True, Kenny does say that his argument from monotheistic religious experience shows that naturalists are 'stuck holding that all the people who report [monotheistic religious experiences] are either hallucinating, lying, or radically misinterpreting their experience'. Moreover, he adds that, since naturalists must suppose that human faculties are generally reliable, naturalists are required to make a 'special exception' for monotheistic religious experience. However, he goes on to note that naturalists have what by their lights looks like a pretty good explanation of religious experience, which entails that religious experiences are 'wholly unreliable' and hence to be 'entirely discounted'. His response to this is that theists have a better theory that explains why religious experience is only sometimes misleading: there are many unreliable religious experiences that are nonetheless authentic. That is, there are many religious experiences that do not give rise to true beliefs about God but that are nonetheless really experiences of God. Moreover, Kenny says that he has *already* shown that theistic worldviews 'can compete with naturalism when it comes to coherence, simplicity, and explanatory power'.

I do not think that naturalists are required to say that all people who report religious experiences are hallucinating, lying, or radically misinterpreting their experience. Some religious experience is hallucinatory; most is not. Some who report religious experiences lie; most do not. According to naturalists, those who place a theistic interpretation on their religious experience thereby form false beliefs. But, by naturalist lights, there need be no radical difference between this case and other cases where people who interpret their experience in the light of false beliefs form further false beliefs. When it comes to philosophy, politics, and religion, we *standardly* form false beliefs on the basis of the interpretation of experience in the light of already established false beliefs. Most of the big philosophical beliefs of most philosophers are false. Most of the big political beliefs of most people are false. Most of the big religious beliefs of most people are false. We all know this, because we all know how rampant disagreement is in all of these domains. By naturalist lights, there is no special sting in the claim that the theistic beliefs of theists are false.

I do not think that naturalists make a 'special exception' for monotheistic theistic beliefs. Here, if anything, the boot is on the other foot. Kenny takes 'monotheistic religious experience' to be experience that is interpreted to be experience of God. But, even among theists, religious experience is typically given a much broader interpretation. And, more importantly, across human history, far more religious experience has been non-theistic rather than theistic. This is completely uncontentious if 'God' is taken to be Kenny's God: 'the God of classical theism'. But it is hardly any more contentious if 'God' is taken to be picked out by any class of beliefs of any participants in any branch of the Abrahamic religions. When you consider the full range of religious experiences across the historically and geographically diverse kinds of Hindu, Buddhist, Daoist, Confucian, Shinto, Sikh, Jain, Bahà'i, Zoroastrian, and indigenous religions, claiming veridicality for a small subset of those religious experiences is, I think, quite clearly a case of making a 'special exception'.

Although I think that naturalists suffer no disadvantage in claiming that religious experience does not reliably generate true beliefs, I do not think that it is right to say that naturalists thereby 'entirely discount' religious experience. Naturalistic accounts of religious belief are developed in response to the full sweep of historical demographic data. Given the disagreement in religious belief that we see across time and place, it is simply not contentious that *most* religious beliefs—across the full sweep of human history—are false. Views that maintain that all religious beliefs—across the full sweep of human history—are false are clearly well-placed to explain the full sweep of historical demographic data that we have.

What about the view that claims that, although the broad sweep of religious experience has not mostly given rise to true beliefs about God, nonetheless the broad sweep of religious experience has been experience of the God of classical theism? Consider, for example, the religious beliefs of indigenous Australians prior to European colonisation. For perhaps as much as 50,000 years, indigenous Australians lived their Dreaming without having any experiences that are plausibly interpreted as experiences of the God of classical theism. Many indigenous Australian groups believed in some version of the Rainbow Serpent: a huge snake descended from a much larger being that can be seen as a dark streak in the Milky Way, present to human observers as a rainbow that moves through the rain, which swallows some people and drowns others, bestows rainmaking and healing powers on the elect and causes others to suffer infirmity, disease, and death. It does not seem unreasonable for naturalists to be sceptical of the claim that, across all those centuries, the religious experiences of indigenous Australians were misperceptions of the God of classical theism.

Kenny's defence of the claim that theists have a better theory that explains why religious experience is only sometimes misleading, by way of appeal to the further claim that he has *already* shown that theistic worldviews 'can compete with naturalism when it comes to coherence, simplicity and explanatory power', seems to me to rest on a misapplication of the method of theory evaluation on which we have presumptively agreed. The method says that you compare the *total* theories on *all* of the relevant data. In order to apply the method, you need to make a serious attempt to display *all* of the claims upon which the theories disagree; and you also need to make a serious attempt to display *all* of the data that is relevant to the assessment of the disagreement between the theories. From this standpoint, it seems to me that the worldviews that we are evaluating both have explanations of the data concerning religious experience, just as they both have explanations of the data about History. But, at most, what follows from this observation is that the worldviews are competitive when it comes to explanatory power on that data. Nothing at all follows from this point about the competitiveness of the worldviews when it comes to consistency and simplicity. And although this is not the consideration that I am primarily interested in here, nothing at all follows from this point about the competitiveness of the worldviews on other data. Moreover, it is also worth remembering that the method says that what really matters is the overall *trade-off* between minimising commitments and maximising explanation: on its own, maximising explanation is not an indication that a worldview is particularly virtuous.

> Kenny's argument from religious experience seems to me to rely on a false assumption about the extent to which we are required to suppose that our faculties are reliable. We all know that there are many domains on which our faculties are unreliable. A view that over-estimates how reliable our faculties are on such domains is worse than a view that gives an accurate estimation of how reliable our faculties are on those domains. That our faculties are unreliable when it comes to the claims of religion is obvious from the disagreement that there is on those claims. At least according to me, this problem is not resolved by claiming that there is a core of religious claims on which there is widespread agreement.

7 Concluding Remarks

Kenny claims that considerations about History and religious experience favour classical theism over naturalism. I disagree. The arguments that Kenny constructs—the positive argument from History, the negative argument from History, and the argument from monotheistic religious experience—all have premises that I reject. I deny (a) that if a theory provides a good explanation of something of which it makes sense to ask why it occurs that is a good reason to endorse the theory; (b) that naturalism cannot explain History; and (c) that if one worldview takes human faculties to be more reliable than another worldview takes them to be, that is a reason to prefer the first worldview to the second. So those arguments do not, and cannot, show that my naturalism is inconsistent. Moreover, there is nothing in the considerations to which Kenny appeals that does, or can, show that naturalists do worse than theists in managing the trade-off between minimising theoretical commitments and maximising explanation.

Second Round of Replies

Chapter 5

Reply to Graham's Reply

Kenny Pearce

Contents

1 Respect for Science   241
2 Grounding   247
3 Religious Experience, Again 249
4 What's the Point?   255

In this second reply, I will address three issues Graham raised about the substance of my arguments. First, Graham says that my negative argument against **naturalism** fails because the naturalist can consistently insist on a necessary initial segment of the universe. The bigger question raised by this issue is: what does it mean for philosophers to respect science? Second, Graham raises a number of questions about the grounding explanations used in my theory. Third, Graham raises questions about the reliability of our faculties and my account of religious experience.

In addition to these three issues about the substance of my arguments, Graham at a number of points raises general methodological concerns about what, if anything, these kinds of arguments could possibly accomplish, and how they relate to the project of worldview comparison. I will therefore conclude with some general reflections on philosophical methodology, and try to answer the all-important question: what is the point of this book?

1 Respect for Science

In my opening statement (§3.4), I argued that naturalism could not provide an explanation of History. As Graham correctly points out in his reply (§3), his **worldview**, as outlined in his opening

DOI: 10.4324/9781003216797-9

statement and his previous work, *does* contain an explanation of History. As Graham correctly discerns, my claim is that insofar as Graham takes some initial segment of History to be necessary, his worldview does not respect science in the way a naturalistic worldview (or, really, any worldview) should. This is a tension within his version of naturalism.

I think most philosophers would agree that trust in science is the chief motivation for endorsing naturalism. Certainly this is how it seems to me. Since scientific investigation has given us a quite comprehensive and well-supported picture of the world, why should we go beyond this scientific picture? Why should we add shaky metaphysics (or religion) on top of this well-grounded science? It is because of the power of this line of thought that I regard naturalism as the most significant alternative to theism.

In light of this, however, it is surprising that science plays such a limited role in Graham's particular version of naturalism. In the first place, unlike many other naturalists, Graham only says that we shouldn't go beyond science in "identifying causal entities and causal powers" (Oppy 2018a, 13). He is happy to admit facts about morality and aesthetics, for instance, that have no scientific basis. Note further that, since I think of creation in a non-causal way, my version of theism is actually consistent with this plank of Graham's naturalism: my views about God go beyond science only in the way Graham's views about math and ethics go beyond science. This is why, in §3 of his opening statement, Graham has to add additional principles, specifically about minds and God, to his definition of naturalism. Graham's principle of respect for science is just one element of his naturalism, and by itself it is not strong enough to rule out theism.

Graham also limits his principle of respect for science in another way. According to Graham, "Natural causal entities and natural causal properties are those causal entities and causal properties recognised in ideal, completed, true science." He then goes on to say that "current well-established science is the best guide that we have to such a science" (opening statement, §3). Graham connects "well-established science" with "expert scientific consensus" (§16). According to Graham, where expert consensus is lacking, where the science is not well-established, "it is fine for non-experts to speculate" (§16). Such speculation is part of what goes on in the kind of worldview construction in which Graham is here engaged.

Here, I think there are two questions on which Graham and I disagree. First, what is the scope of the expert scientific consensus concerning general relativity? Second, what kind of non-expert speculation is consistent with respect for science?

In his opening statement, Graham seems to think there is quite a lot of expert consensus. For instance, "There is expert scientific consensus on broad-scale features of the history of our universe, our planet, and our species," and this consensus includes specific claims, such as the claim that the evolutionary ancestry of humans "diverged from the lineage of bonobos and chimpanzees between 4 million and 7 million years ago" (§17). Further, according to Graham, there is "expert consensus on many aspects of the history of humanity over the past few thousand years," and this historical consensus is based partly on "expert consensus in, for example, anthropology, archaeology, astronomy, biology," and so on (§18).

These examples are not too controversial, and I agree that these are cases where there is expert scientific consensus deserving of our trust. But some of Graham's later examples of supposed expert scientific consensus are quite controversial. For instance: "Expert scientific consensus allows that minded organisms are properly described using a range of mental vocabulary" (§23). An example of minded organisms being described using mental vocabulary is the claim that human beings (such as Graham and myself) hold various *beliefs* (such as naturalism and theism). However, the naturalistic philosophers Patricia and Paul Churchland have famously argued that concepts like *belief* are the product an outmoded and unscientific 'folk psychology' that will eventually be replaced by a completed neuroscience (P. S. Churchland 1980, 1996; P. M. Churchland 1981, 1985, 1996). Contrary to Graham's claim of expert consensus, it seems that many neuroscientists agree with the Churchlands. For instance, according to one popular introductory textbook:

> Contemporary brain theory is materialistic. Although materialists, including the authors of this book, continue to use subjective mentalistic words such as consciousness, pain, and attention to describe more complex sets of actions, at the same time materialists recognize that these words do not describe single mental entities. The materialistic view argues for *measurable* descriptions of behavior that can be referenced to the activity of the brain.
> (Kolb and Whishaw 2014, 13)

This certainly seems to suggest, with the Churchlands, that "subjective mentalistic" language is a sloppy way of speaking that we will be able to abandon once we find "*measurable* descriptions" of certain complex behaviors. In other words, the authors of this textbook do not think that descriptions employing mental vocabulary are 'proper', contrary to Graham's claim of expert scientific consensus.

On the other hand, the claim that minded organisms sometimes believe things would no doubt find consensus among psychologists or cognitive scientists. But if the Churchlands are right, then psychology and cognitive science are unscientific and therefore need not be taken seriously.

I agree with Graham, against the Churchlands, that there are legitimate scientific disciplines that make use of these mentalistic concepts.[1] My point is that if the neuroscientists count as experts here, then there is not a particularly robust expert consensus around this point.

Even more controversially, Graham says:

> Expert scientific consensus tells us that we have no reason to suppose that we need to appeal to anything beyond biological processes in organisms, the local environments of those organisms, and the local, social, and biological evolutionary histories of those organisms, in order to explain the proper application of mental vocabulary to those organisms. For minded organisms to be *conscious* just is for those organisms to be engaged in certain kinds of neural processing.
>
> (§23)

Graham says similar things about other mental attributes like perceiving and believing.

In fact, however, there is no scientific consensus on the question of what specific neural processes give rise to consciousness (Chalmers 1995, §4; Crick and Koch 2003; Wu 2018). Indeed, there is no scientific consensus on what consciousness *is* (Chalmers 1995; Koch and Tsuchiya 2007; Van Gulick 2018, §2). Furthermore, Graham does not seem to recognize that the claim that consciousness *just is* a certain kind of neural processing is a much stronger

---

1 For a defense of this claim, see Kitcher (1984a).

claim than the claim that consciousness is fully explained by neural activity. All of these issues are hotly contested, and it's not obvious who are the real experts on them. Finally, some people who might seem to be experts think that all this debate rests on a confusion. For instance, the authors of the previously mentioned neuroscience textbook explicitly argue that the ordinary notion of consciousness is not scientifically useful and should be *replaced with* (not just explained by) the objective measures of the Glasgow Coma Scale (Kolb and Whishaw 2014, 12–13).

This is not to deny that many experts on the brain and/or the mind would agree with Graham's claims. It is simply to note that there is a great deal of debate about the precise meaning of these claims, the nature and strength of the alleged evidence for them, and so on. *Some* experts would reject Graham's claims outright.

What all of this shows is that Graham's criteria for expert consensus can't be too demanding. If the existence of a single person with proper credentials, or a single peer-reviewed journal article, disagreeing with a claim was enough to show that there was no expert consensus, then there would be no expert consensus about anything. Further, some of Graham's examples of (purported) expert consensus include matters on which there is active debate among people who might reasonably be regarded as experts. Indeed, they even include matters on which popular textbooks in relevant fields disagree with Graham's claims. The standards for expert consensus must, therefore, be rather low.

In light of this, it is quite surprising that Graham *denies* that there is expert consensus on general relativity (Graham's reply, §3). In general, physics is in a much more mature, settled, and rigorous state than neurology, cognitive science, or psychology. Robust expert consensus is much easier to find in physics than in most other disciplines.

Graham, however, gives a specific reason for claiming that general relativity is no threat to his account. Graham points out, quite rightly, that while there is expert consensus that general relativity is a successful theory of space, time, and gravity on certain energy and distance scales, there is *also* expert consensus that general relativity cannot be the last word on the subject. The reason for this is that straightforward attempts to combine relativistic physics with quantum physics lead to contradiction. When the density of mass-energy in a region is high, we need to use relativistic physics. When we are dealing with very small distances, we need to use quantum physics. Since there is no expert consensus on how to combine relativistic physics with quantum physics, there is likewise no expert consensus on how to deal with high mass-energy densities in very small spaces—precisely the conditions that obtained at the beginning of our universe! As a result, there is no expert consensus on the precise details of what happened in the very earliest moments of our universe.

All of this is true, but not relevant. Recall, as I mentioned in my opening statement, that one class of solutions to Einstein's Field Equations are the *static* solutions in which the universe neither expands nor contracts. In these solutions, the universe is never contracted into a tiny point, either in the past or in the future. In a universe like that, general relativity should be valid all the time.

This provides excellent reason for supposing that a static universe is physically possible. But our universe is an expanding universe, not a static one. Hence, there are at least two possibilities for the global structure of spacetime: static and expanding.

Expert consensus holds that general relativity is not the final word. But, as Graham explicitly recognizes, we humans are not and never will be in possession of "ideal, completed, true science" (§3). In other words, no scientific theory actually developed and understood by humans will ever be the final word. So the mere fact that general relativity is not the final word—and the experts agree on this—cannot prevent it from being a matter of settled scientific consensus.

Nevertheless, suppose for the sake of argument that general relativity wasn't settled science. (I have trouble supposing that while also supposing that *anything* about the relation between mind and brain is settled science, but leave that aside.) I maintain that Graham's position would still be untenable.

The reason is this: sure, where there is no expert consensus the non-expert is free to speculate. But is such speculation completely unconstrained by the state of the expert debate? I think not. Respecting scientific expertise involves more than just refraining from contradicting settled consensus. Where the science is unsettled, the non-expert's speculations should be guided by the current state of the scientific debate. It may sometimes happen that the science is so unsettled that the debate provides no meaningful guidance, but this is certainly not the case with fundamental physics today. Quantum gravity and early universe cosmology are active areas of research, and the current state of that research provides hints or suggestions about what a completed theory might look like. I'm not aware of anything that so much as hints that there might be only one possible initial segment of History, and Graham hasn't so much as suggested how any theory of quantum gravity might possibly have this result. I maintain, therefore, that this is a case of non-expert speculation that is totally unmoored from the expert debate and therefore does not display proper respect for scientific expertise.

> Respect for scientific expertise is a core value of naturalism and a value that should also be endorsed by theists. Graham thinks that it is consistent with this value for non-experts to engage in speculation about matters where the science is unsettled and that, therefore, he need not be troubled by my argument from general relativity against his modal views. However, Graham's standards for expert consensus are very low, and this makes his claim that general relativity is not settled science extremely implausible. Furthermore, non-expert speculation should be constrained by the current state of the scientific debate. Graham's speculation is not constrained in this way.

2 Grounding

In his discussion of my positive argument, Graham makes a number of points about the details of my particular examples. Let's not get too distracted by sandwiches and things. In this discussion, Graham defends two important philosophical theses. First, he denies that these kinds of grounding explanations are alternative answers to the same question that could be answered by giving a cause. Second, he argues that "whatever Kenny has in mind when he claims that History is grounded in God's choice, the grounding relation to which he is appealing is not one of the familiar grounding relations exhibited in his examples" (Graham's reply, §4).

The first point I think I can concede. I say that questions like "why does x exist?" or "why are there x's?" can be answered by giving either a cause or a ground. But it could be that that's just because those questions are ambiguous. Or it could be, as Graham seems to think, that those questions, at least in normal contexts, are asking for a cause, while a ground answers some other question. Nevertheless, a ground is a type of explanation. Furthermore, it is inconsistent to maintain that History has a cause, but one can consistently maintain that it has a ground. That's all I need for my argument.

The second point is a bit trickier. There are two questions here. The first question is, is my hypothesis intelligible? That is, can anyone understand what I mean when I say that God is the ground of History? The second question is, is God's relation to History a *new* grounding relation, one that doesn't occur anywhere in Graham's worldview? If so, I've incurred a new cost in complexity.

On the intelligibility question, I think my examples help even if the relation between God and History isn't exactly the same as the relation in any of the examples. These examples help us get a grip on the notion of grounding or ontological dependence *in general*. Once we have this notion, then we can say that God's relation to History is another one of those.

Graham doesn't appear to dispute this. Instead, he focuses on the other question: is this a totally unique relation that adds to the complexity of my worldview? I need not concede this point, and even if I did concede this point it would not undermine my argument.

First, as I noted in a digression in my opening statement ("Grounding—Big 'G' or Small 'g'?" in §3.3.1), some philosophers think that there is just one Grounding relation that accounts for all the myriad instances of ontological dependence. If Grounding can cover all of the diverse examples, it seems that it can also do the work I need it to do.

Even if we don't go the big 'G' route, there may be some more specific grounding relation that can do the trick. The example that I think is most similar is the waltz example. As Graham suggests (although he does not endorse this theory of the metaphysics of waltzes), we can think of the motion of the dancers as if it were a kind of stuff from which the waltz is constituted. Regardless of whether event constitution is the same thing as object constitution, it seems to make sense to speak of one event or action constituting another. This usage can sound a little odd in plain English, but it is fairly common in legal language. For instance, a recent decision of the US Supreme Court held that "The Ninth Circuit panel's drastic departure from the principle of party presentation constituted an abuse of discretion."[2] Never mind the rest of the legal jargon. What

---

2 *United States v. Sineneng-Smith*, decided May 7, 2020, www.supremecourt.gov/opinions/19pdf/19-67_n6io.pdf (accessed June 19, 2020).

matters for our purposes is that the panel's departure (an event) constituted the panel's abuse of discretion (another event).

Graham makes a few points here about my use of the term 'choice' for what explains History. A 'choice' does sound like a discrete event (then again, so does a 'departure'). But God's choice is atemporal and, as I admitted in my first reply (§4.2), nothing atemporal could be precisely the same kind of thing as the choices we make. Since God is atemporal, when we are talking about God there is really no distinction between discrete actions and ongoing activities. It would be more appropriate—would provide a better analogy—to think of God's choosing History as an ongoing activity, like the motion of the dancers. God's ongoing activity of choosing History constitutes the occurrence of History.

Is the relation between God's choosing History and the occurrence of History the same kind of relation as the one mentioned in the Supreme Court's holding? Is it the same kind of relation as that between the motion of the dancers and the waltz? I think it really might be. But if you are not convinced, I refer you to my previous comments about analogy (my first reply, §4.2).

> My hypothesis that God is the ground of History provides an intelligible explanation of History. The best model for this kind of grounding is event constitution—for instance, the way a waltz is constituted by the motion of the dancers.

3 Religious Experience, Again

Much of the discussion of **religious experience** in Graham's reply (§6) ignores my qualification "other things being equal." Graham and I agree that, in comparing two worldviews, we need to weigh several competing factors. For this reason, the "other things being equal" qualification is doing important work. Taking human **faculties** to be more reliable may come at the cost of **tension**, or even **contradiction**. It may come at the cost of a massive increase in complexity. It may come at the cost of being unable to explain certain data. And so on. Sometimes these costs outweigh the benefits. So we should not always prefer worldviews that take human faculties to be reliable. In particular, we should reject worldviews that take human faculties to be *perfectly* reliable. Human faculties sometimes deliver contradictory results, so taking them to be perfectly reliable leads to contradiction.

Graham and I agree that all non-skeptical worldviews begin by assuming that (at least some) human faculties are generally reliable. There's no way to prove the reliability of the senses without using the senses, no way to prove the reliability of memory without using memory, and so on (Alston 1986; Van Cleve 2003). Instead, we start out by assuming that the senses and memory and so on are *generally* reliable. Then we accumulate evidence that shows they are not *perfectly* reliable. After that, we try to figure out how reliable they tend to be and in what circumstances they are more or less reliable. Finally, we try to explain why these faculties sometimes get things right and sometimes get things wrong.

I claim that the same applies to religious experience. We should start out from the assumption that it's generally reliable and then try to figure out when, why, and how it goes wrong. In the course of this project, I say, we do not find good reason for discounting it entirely. In this, I suggest, religious experience is different from the various kinds of divinatory experiences and practices Graham mentions. When we come to examine these divinatory experiences and practices, we find excellent reason for supposing that they don't work.

How does this line of thought relate to the method of **worldview comparison**? I think that internal **coherence** of worldviews comes in degrees because worldviews sometimes have tensions that are not outright contradictions. One kind of tension in a worldview is when similar things are not treated the same. Religious experience and sensory experience are similar, but naturalistic worldviews, such as Graham's, do not treat them the same.

This is how I arrive at my principle that, other things being equal, worldviews that take our faculties to be more reliable are to be preferred. I maintain that all non-skeptical worldviews treat the senses, memory, reason, and so on as innocent until proven guilty. As a result, I hold that any non-skeptical worldview that does not extend the same courtesy to religious experience exhibits a tension.

Graham has three lines of reply to this. In the first place, he disagrees with me methodologically. This is probably why he mostly ignores my 'other things being equal' qualifier. Graham says that the second stage of his method of worldview comparison, where we "check to see whether the worldviews fail on their own terms," is "an all-or-nothing, non-comparative matter" (reply, §2). He says this is an advantage of his approach, but doesn't explain why it's advantageous. Graham, just doesn't seem to recognize what I call 'tensions' as an important category here: either the worldview works or it doesn't. I agree that if we frame the question this way, then, when it comes to religious experience, both of our worldviews work.

Presumably, Graham will want to deal with what I'm calling 'tensions' as part of the complexity of a worldview. If so, my point can be reframed: worldviews that treat human faculties as more reliable will be simpler in their **epistemology**. This is because they will endorse the very simple Reidian principle *trust your faculties* without making as many complicated exceptions to it. Such views should, therefore, be preferred, other things being equal. Of course, other things are often not equal: the simplest such view, which says we should always unquestioningly trust our faculties, is contradictory. But worldviews that apply the same simple rules to all of our faculties should be preferred over worldviews that draw more distinctions than necessary.

Graham's second line of reply is that he *doesn't* treat religious experience differently. In the first place, he treats it the same as divinatory experience. More generally, saying that most religious beliefs are false is not treating religious beliefs differently from other kinds of belief. After all, most political beliefs are false, most philosophical beliefs are false, and so on. Furthermore, Graham says, in none of these cases is he saying that people who endorse these beliefs are hallucinating, lying, or radically misinterpreting their experience. Rather, these are all "cases where people who interpret their experience in the light of false beliefs form further false beliefs." Everyone must admit that this happens very frequently (reply, §6).

Graham here misses a crucial point about what I called the *authenticity* of certain experiences. This is the point I was illustrating in my opening statement with the antelope example (§4.4) and in my first reply with the halibut sushi example (§3). The point is, in both these cases the experience was really experience *of something*. The unreliability of the beliefs was due to misunderstanding of the nature of that something.

This, I say, marks a crucial difference between different ways we might misunderstand our experience. When Macbeth hallucinated a dagger, *there just wasn't anything there at all*. This kind of hallucination involves a more radical unreliability of the senses than mistaking flounder for halibut.

There are also in-between cases, like rainbows. It's easy to think that a rainbow is a physical object located at some definite position in the sky. But in fact there's no particular place where the rainbow is: it's projected in different apparent positions to different observers. If you went to its apparent location, you wouldn't see (or feel) it at all. However, unlike Macbeth's dagger experience, rainbow experience is produced by our eyes correctly registering patterns of light.

Hallucinations (like Macbeth's dagger) and illusions (like the rainbow) do of course sometimes occur. But we are rightly resistant to the possibility that something like this is going on until we have a lot of evidence and/or some understanding of what caused the hallucination or illusion. It's easier to believe that the alleged halibut was really flounder than to believe that there wasn't anything there at all. It's also easier to believe that what you saw was a hologram or some other kind of optical phenomenon than to believe that what you saw was a figment of your own brain. It is rational for us to trust our faculties in this way and be resistant to these kinds of hypotheses. (Of course, there is also such a thing as being *too* resistant: I shouldn't believe there's a pink elephant in my living room!)

Naturalists, including Graham, are committed to saying that nearly all religious experience is either hallucination, like Macbeth's dagger, or illusion, like the rainbow.

Graham's third and final line of response is to argue that *I* am the one making special exceptions, since many people and cultures have taken their religious experience to support very different beliefs from mine. Graham writes:

> Kenny takes 'monotheistic religious experience' to be experience that is interpreted to be experience of God. But, even among theists, religious experience is typically given a much broader interpretation. And, more importantly, across human history, far more religious experience has been non-theistic rather than theistic. This is completely uncontentious if 'God' is taken to be Kenny's God: 'the God of classical theism'. But it is hardly any more contentious if 'God' is taken to be picked out by any class of beliefs of any participants in any branch of the Abrahamic religions.
>
> (Reply, §6)

Here there is a quite delicate issue: what does it mean to interpret an experience as experience of God? It certainly does not mean explicitly thinking to yourself that this experience supports my proposition (CT). It also shouldn't mean that you think your experience supports **traditional theism**. People who describe their experience in that way mostly do so because they have inherited the tradition. People outside the cultural influence of this tradition don't talk this way.

What we want, first, is for MRE to be as broad a category as possible and, second, for it to be plausible that a broad range of non-monotheistic religious experience is in fact misinterpreted experience of God. Regarding the first issue, I say that to interpret experience as experience of God is to take it to be experience of the (unique) being who satisfies some God-identifying description.

A **God-identifying description** is a description that, necessarily, is satisfied only by God (according to my view).

Here are some examples:

- The creator of the universe.
- The ground of all being.
- A being who is worthy of worship.
- The greatest of all beings.
- A perfectly and infinitely loving being.
- A perfectly just and all-knowing judge of human actions.

According to my view, all of these things are true of God and could not possibly be true of anyone else. I say that a person who interprets her experience as experience of (for instance) a perfectly and infinitely loving being, and who thinks there is only one such being, counts as having MRE even if she doesn't agree with most of the other things I say about God.

A few more things should be noted here. First, it's important that we stick to descriptions that are *necessarily* only true of God. This is because of cases like this. Arthur reports that he was abducted by aliens and one of the aliens, Slartibartfast, claimed to be the (one and only) designer of the planet earth (see Adams [1979] 1996, 108–109). Suppose that Arthur really did have some kind of experience (a dream, an acid trip, whatever). Suppose further that Arthur really believes that he met Slartibartfast, the (one and only) designer of the planet earth. Now, I believe that God is the (one and only) designer of the planet earth. Does Arthur, then, count as having MRE? No. It is metaphysically possible for the planet earth to have been designed by space aliens rather than by God, so 'designer of the planet earth' is not a God-identifying description. On the other hand, Slartibartfast himself, if he existed, would be part of the universe and therefore could not be the creator of the entire universe. So 'creator of the universe' *is* a God-identifying description.

Second, it's important that the definition of 'God-identifying descriptions' refers to what is possible *according to my view*. This is because we are trying to use religious experience in an argument for the existence of God, so we can't just start out by assuming that (for instance) necessarily God is the one and only creator of the universe.

We are now in a position to offer a more precise definition of MRE.

> **Monotheistic religious experience (MRE)** is experience that is interpreted as experience of a being who uniquely satisfies some God-identifying description.

Next: what about *non*-monotheistic religious experience? I want to say that as much of this as possible is misinterpreted experience of God. Graham suggests that it is implausible to take this view about, for instance, the religious experience of indigenous Australians prior to European contact (reply, §6). Perhaps. To evaluate just how much religious experience can be regarded as misinterpreted experience of God, we would need to do a lot of very detailed work in anthropology. We would also need to think very carefully about what kinds of misinterpretation hypotheses are plausible. However, reports that are at least somewhat similar to some of the God-identifying descriptions listed above are common, cross-cultural, and can certainly be found beyond the Abrahamic traditions.

> Monothestic religious experience is experience that is interpreted as experience of a being that uniquely satisfies a God-identifying description such as 'creator of the universe'. Such experience is quite widespread and not limited to the Abrahamic traditions. Furthermore, many reports of non-monotheistic experience sound similar enough to at least some God-identifying descriptions that it is not implausible to consider these to be misunderstood experiences of God. As a result, my argument from religious experience stands: theism takes our faculties to be more reliable than naturalism does, and this is a reason for favoring theism over naturalism.

4 What's the Point?

According to Graham, "the most important part of worldview comparison is the first stage: articulating worldviews as far as we can, to the same level of detail and with the same degree of care." Accordingly, in this process "we want to be clear about *everything* that is in the theoretical commitments of just one of the two worldviews" (reply, §2). Graham seems to think that we are not yet prepared to do a proper job of worldview comparison here because I have not yet gone on record with any views "about angels and demons, heaven and hell, trinity, incarnation, atonement, resurrection, and on and on" (reply, §4). But the trouble is, this list could go on forever. Furthermore, whatever I say about these matters, some other theistic philosopher will say something else. Given that it is not obligatory for theists to agree with me about any of these issues, how does this advance the debate about whether there is a God?

There is a precisely parallel issue on the other side. At the end of his opening statement, Graham mentioned that "there is a great deal of modularity" in his naturalism (§40). That is, almost any of the positions he takes on a variety of philosophical issues could be adjusted while still maintaining his naturalism. How, then, are his views on (for instance) the nature of art and beauty (opening statement, §31) relevant to a debate about the existence of God?

This, I suppose, is why Graham says that we want to know "the theoretical commitments of *just one* of the two worldviews" and "the full range of *relevant* theoretical commitments" (reply, §2, emphasis added). That is, we assume a broad background of agreement between the two worldviews and then focus on their points of disagreement.

I think this could be a productive philosophical approach in some contexts. However, given the extent to which worldviews *in general* are 'modular' (as Graham puts it), it is difficult for this approach to focus on one particular question or one particular point of disagreement. For instance, it could turn out that our differences over explanation, necessity, the foundations of ethics, and so on are what's really making the difference between our worldviews. It could then happen that most of the debate turns out not to have much bearing on the existence of God. (Perhaps some readers will think that's precisely what's happened in this book!)

I suggest the following alternative. Wittgenstein famously wrote, "If a lion could talk, we wouldn't be able to understand it" (Wittgenstein [1953] 2009, PPF §327). You cannot understand, and so cannot contemplate adopting, a worldview (or form of life) that is ultimately, fundamentally, completely alien to your own. As a result, when engaging in worldview comparison, you are never really thinking about throwing out and replacing your worldview. Rather, you are always thinking about *revising* it.

This debate is really directed at *you*, the reader. Hopefully, as you've been reading this book, you've given some thought to your worldview and the possibility of revising it. But even if you started out as a theist, you probably didn't start out agreeing with everything I've said about God, let alone everything I've said about every other topic we've discussed! Similarly, even if you started out as a naturalist, you probably didn't start out agreeing with everything Graham said. And this doesn't necessarily mean you've got some kind of problem. Worldviews tend to be modular. Just being a theist, or a naturalist, doesn't determine what you have to say about every philosophical question ever.

This has consequences for which commitments of worldviews should be considered relevant. It is also connected to my reasons for thinking that there *is* a point in giving arguments.

You, the reader, may have started out as a theist, or an atheist, or an agnostic. You may have had strong opinions on many other topics we've discussed, or you might never have considered them before. But the question for you is this: if you changed your belief about God, would this be an improvement? Would your worldview be getting better or worse?

In answering that question, there is a clear role for arguments. Arguments could show that certain things that are already part of your worldview support the existence of God, or that they are inconsistent with the existence of God. Arguments could show that if you change your mind about God, you would also need to change your mind about other things.

On the other hand, if you changed your mind about God, there are a lot of other things you *wouldn't* have to change your mind about. (At least, not without a lot more argument.) For instance, if you were an atheist and you became a theist, you would not have to change your mind about "angels and demons, heaven and hell, trinity, incarnation, atonement, resurrection, and on and on" (Graham's reply, §4). Perhaps considerations about the shared religious experience of a particular community over time, and their tradition of interpretation of that experience, could give you reason to believe in these kinds of things (on some interpretation). But if you think these things are implausible, you could believe in God without accepting any of them. Worldviews tend to be modular.

Now, as I indicated way back at the beginning (opening statement, §1), the hypothesis that there is a God of some sort or other is too vague for us to say very much about. In order to start thinking seriously about what it would look like for you to believe in God, you have to be at least a bit more specific about what kind of God is under consideration. For this reason, it does make sense to start outlining the core elements of some particular theistic worldview, and to look at it in comparison to some of its naturalistic competitors. If you are starting out as a naturalist, then, obviously, the most important naturalistic worldview for comparison is your own.

We've covered a lot of ground in this debate: explanation, necessity, epistemology, math, ethics, and, of course, God. Even more ground, believe it or not, was covered in extensive correspondence among the authors and the editor. And there's still a lot more to be said.

Graham has raised many astute questions for my cosmological argument, which I had previously defended elsewhere (Pearce 2017b), and for my argument from religious experience, which I have developed here for the first time. He has pressed me to confront difficult questions about the nature of the explanations involved in my view of God, about my attitude toward theological analogy, about my approach to the plurality of religions, and many other topics as well. As a result of Graham's probing questions, my worldview is now far better defined than it was when we began.

One of the challenges, and one of the benefits, of philosophy is that we are forced to try our best to see the world through other eyes. While we may not be able to inhabit a *totally* alien worldview, it is rewarding and eye-opening to try to get inside a *somewhat* alien worldview and see what things look like from there. I am fascinated by these questions and perspectives, and Graham's contributions have helped me better understand how the world looks from the perspective of a person who sees naturalism as "the plainest common sense" (Graham's opening statement, §40). Graham puts forward this point of view in a clear, careful, and detailed fashion, and in engaging with opposing views he is simultaneously an unflinching critic and a friendly one. These are among the reasons that Graham's work has been of such great help to me and many other philosophers.

Still, we all knew we weren't going to come to agreement. It wouldn't have been much of a debate if we did! My aim in this debate has not been to convince Graham. My aim has been to argue that many non-theistic worldviews—including, I hope, the worldviews of many readers—could be improved by endorsing my hypothesis (CT): *spacetime and all of its contents exist because of the free and rational choice of a necessary being.* I've focused on two specific reasons for thinking this: the explanation of History and the reliability of religious experience. It is now up to you to judge whether I've succeeded.

> The real question of this debate is whether you, the reader, could improve your worldview by changing your belief about God. Considerations of the explanation of History and the reliability of religious experience provide reason for thinking that a broad range of naturalistic worldviews could be improved by endorsing my hypothesis (CT): *spacetime and all of its contents exist because of the free and rational choice of a necessary being.*

Chapter 6

Further Reply to Kenny Pearce

Graham Oppy

Contents

1	Naturalism	260
2	Arguments	261
3	Worldviews	265
4	Theoretical Commitments	267
5	Ontological Commitments	269
6	Ideological Commitments	272
7	Comparative Simplicity	275
8	Necessity, Dependence, Grounding, and Explanation	276
9	Brute Facts	279
10	Autonomous Facts	282
11	Mathematical Explanation	283
12	God and Mathematics	285
13	Moral Explanation	286
14	Euthyphro Dilemma	287
15	Theistic Ethics	288
16	Laws of Thought	290
17	Religious Experience	292
18	Reflections	297

I agree with some of the criticisms that Kenny has made of things that I said in my opening statement. In the following comments, I shall note points of remaining disagreement, some of which arise only because of adjustments that I shall make to those earlier claims.

1 Naturalism

In his opening statement, Kenny says that the core idea of naturalism is that *the natural sciences provide the correct methods for knowing about the world*. Whether this is even approximately correct depends upon what we mean by 'world'. If by 'world' we mean everything that is the case, then, according to me, this is not even close to being right. The natural sciences do not provide correct methods for, among other things, the study of ethics, aesthetics, philosophy, metaphysics, and so on. However, if by 'world' we mean something like 'the causal order', we are closer to being right. But, in my view, the natural sciences do not provide correct methods for the social sciences, and yet it is true that the social sciences—psychology, sociology, economics, and so forth—provide correct methods for knowing about the causal order. A much better slogan for generic naturalism is something like this: *natural reality exhausts causal reality*. To accommodate Kenny's objection to this slogan, we should suppose that causal reality is understood to include its explanatory grounds, if it has any.

Kenny says that, according to me, my naturalistic worldview is complete and satisfying as it stands. Neither part of this is true. I emphasised in my opening statement that the attempted elaboration of my worldview is incomplete; and I emphasised that the little knowledge that I have floats in a vast sea of ignorance. Moreover, I also emphasised that my worldview—like the worldview of everyone else who has ever lived—is a work in progress. Philosophers perpetually change their minds on answers to philosophical questions. No one has a complete worldview; no one has a worldview that is fully satisfying.

Kenny says that, according to me, naturalistic worldviews have no need of any theistic hypothesis. I accept this; I am happy to follow in Laplace's alleged footsteps. However, contrary to the view that Kenny imputed to me in his opening statement, I think there is good reason for naturalists to take theism seriously. The obvious difference between Russell's teapot and God is that, while there is no one who believes in Russell's teapot, there is a significant part of the global population that believes in God. Moreover, as I see it, there are thoughtful, sensitive, reflective, intelligent, informed parties on both sides of the dispute between theists and naturalists. This is all that is needed in order for there to be good reason for naturalists to take theism—and theists—seriously.

> Kenny wants to attribute to me a kind of 'methodological naturalism': the natural sciences provide the correct way of knowing about the world. But I do not embrace anything like that kind of natural scientism. I do think that, in the domain of the natural sciences, it is foolhardy for non-experts not to follow expert consensus where there is expert consensus. But I think that this is true generally: it is always foolhardy for non-experts not to follow expert consensus where there is expert consensus.

2 Arguments

Kenny defends the following two claims about good arguments:

1. An argument presented to an audience exposes an alleged tension in the audience's worldview(s) and suggests the conclusion as a way of resolving (or easing) that tension.
2. An argument is good iff (a) it exposes a genuine tension in one or more worldviews actually held by at least some members of the audience and (b) at least some members of the audience would be rational to respond to that tension by endorsing the conclusion.

He says that he agrees with me that (1) when we give arguments we aim to convince a real audience; (2) the real audience is rarely rationally required to endorse our conclusion; and (3) in debates about the existence of God, almost everyone will always in fact choose to reject a premise rather than changing sides. Despite all of this, he claims that, when we give arguments, we point to tensions in worldviews and suggest ways of resolving those tensions.

> The argument does not say, 'you have to endorse this conclusion!' It says, 'you have to endorse this conclusion if you want to hold on to these premises'. If the (entire) audience responds, 'why on earth would I want to hold on to those premises?!' then the argument is no good. But if the response is 'I prefer to pay the price of rejecting one of the premises, rather than endorsing the conclusion', then the argument has done some useful work. The question is whether rejecting a premise amounts to a *cost*, from the audience's perspective.

I disagree with almost everything that Kenny says here.

On the one hand, I think that, when we act as we ought when giving arguments, we draw our target audience's attention to what we take to be, for them, unnoticed consequences of their beliefs. The reason why we give them an argument—or a derivation—is to draw attention to the fact that there is a consequence relation between some things that they already believe and something that they do not—and perhaps should not—believe. In the most interesting case, the consequence to which attention is drawn is some kind of absurdity; for example, some unacceptable contradiction. In the case in which our argument is good—that is, in the case in which our audience is committed to the premises, and the conclusion is absurd—the audience is rationally required to respond to our argument, at least in the longer term. The audience members cannot rationally just shrug their shoulders and embrace absurdity. (Notice that, if we count this as the exposition of a tension in the beliefs of our audience, it does nothing towards suggesting ways of resolving that tension. The only information that is being given to the audience is, you must revise something, somewhere!)

On the other hand, if we act in the way that Kenny suggests that we should when giving arguments, then, so long as we choose both premises and conclusion that our opponents reject, we can (almost) *always* claim that our argument has done some useful work, because there is some cost to the audience, from the audience's point of view, in the rejection of the premises that we ourselves accept. Almost always, for any claim that a worldview rejects that other worldviews accept, there will be *some* reasons for favouring the rejected claim. But those reasons are weighed when the favoured worldview is accepted. Kenny's proposal here is completely antithetical to the method for the assessment of the comparative merits of worldviews that Kenny has professed to endorse. Given that both parties recognise that they disagree on the claims in question, the proper method for assessing their disagreement is to determine which of them has the better worldview: which has the worldview that makes the better fist of trading of minimisation of theoretical commitments against maximisation of explanation of data. There is a kind of double-counting involved in thinking that, alongside the weighing of theoretical virtues that the method of worldview comparison requires, there is some additional weighing that is prompted by drawing attention to argument generated entirely from within one of the competing worldviews.

Kenny illustrates his claims about good argument with the following case:

> The naturalist is committed to thinking that (other things being equal) the more things a worldview can explain, the better. But naturalism does not allow History to be explained, while theism does. The naturalist wants more things to be explained, but doesn't want to accept the kind of non-naturalistic metaphysics that is necessary for explaining History—she's pulled in both directions. Many naturalists have seen this point and thought that accepting a few **brute facts**, although it's a cost, is better than giving up naturalism. In claiming that my cosmological argument is a good argument, I am claiming that it could also be rational for someone to go the other way and endorse theism (or some other form of non-naturalism) in order to avoid commitment to brute facts.

The cosmological argument that Kenny is referring to here has two parts, one positive (A) and one negative (B):

A. The Positive Argument

1. History stands in need of explanation.
2. Kenny's worldview provides a good explanation of History.
3. If a worldview provides a good explanation of something, this is a good reason for endorsing the worldview.
4. (Therefore) There is a good reason for endorsing Kenny's worldview.

B. The Negative Argument

1. History stands in need of explanation.
2. Graham's worldview cannot explain History.
3. If a worldview cannot explain something that stands in need of explanation, this is a good reason for rejecting that worldview.
4. (Therefore) There is a good reason for rejecting Graham's worldview.

The project in which we are embarked is an attempt to weigh the theoretical virtues of Kenny's worldview against the theoretical virtues of my worldview. Setting all other considerations aside, *even if*—contrary to fact—Kenny's conclusions here were correct, they would do nothing to provide anyone with *any* reason to prefer Kenny's worldview to mine. One way of thinking about the project of worldview comparison is that it aims to weigh all of the reasons of this kind on each side of the dispute. Since such reasons are legion, and since the method of worldview comparison will take account of them, there is nothing useful to be gained by the production of these kinds of arguments. Moreover, presenting these arguments to people who have taken on the task of trying to compare the worldviews serves no purpose that would not be served simply by asking questions like the following: Do the worldviews agree that History stands in need of an explanation? Does Kenny's worldview make inconsistent claims about the explanation of History? Does Graham's worldview make inconsistent claims about the explanation of History? Does Kenny's worldview provide an explanation of History? Does Graham's worldview provide an explanation of History? Drawing attention to the *consequence* relation that holds between the four claims in each of the two arguments plays no useful role in the project of weighing the comparative theoretical virtues of our worldviews.

Kenny claims that I make a restrictive assumption about the contexts in which arguments are offered and the audiences to whom they are offered. In his view, I assume that arguments are offered in disputes where one person has the job of affirming a particular claim and the other person has the job of denying it. According to Kenny, this is a rather artificial and unusual context and, in any case, the real audience for the arguments that he presents is made up of the readers of this book. I dispute all of this. I think that arguments are useful in any context where someone has failed to see the consequences of their commitments, particularly when there is good reason to draw their attention to those consequences of their commitments. No restrictive assumption about contexts there; certainly, no restrictive assumption of the kind that Kenny imputes to me. Moreover, given that we have invited the readers of the book to join us in the enterprise of weighing the comparative theoretical virtues of our worldviews, we have good reason not to muddy the waters for our readers by presenting them with the kinds of arguments that Kenny wants to introduce.

There is one last point about arguments that I should note. Kenny claims that I say that there are structural reasons why there could not possibly be a successful argument for or against the existence of God. I do not say this. I do say that we do not currently have successful arguments for or against the existence of God. And I do say that we should not expect to have successful arguments for or against the existence of God any time soon. But I insist that we cannot rule out the possibility that there are successful arguments for (or against) the existence of God that we have not yet discovered. There is nothing structural that rules out our coming to discover such arguments. Of course, if naturalism is necessarily true, as I suppose, then we cannot discover successful arguments for the existence of God. But that is not a *structural* consideration: it is not a logical consequence of the correct theory of argumentation that we cannot discover successful arguments for the existence of God.

> Kenny claims that good arguments expose tensions in audiences' worldviews. I disagree. Good arguments draw audiences' attentions to consequences of their worldviews that they have not hitherto noticed. Arguments have no proper role in drawing attention to disagreement between worldviews. If we make a good fist of articulating worldviews, then the disagreements are plain for all to see.

3 Worldviews

It is not clear that Kenny and I have been working with the same understanding of *worldview*. According to me, at least roughly, your worldview is your theory of everything. Your worldview includes all of your 'big ticket' commitments, but it includes lots of 'small ticket' commitments as well.

An *ideal model* of a worldview is a complete theory of everything. In order to express a complete theory of everything, we would need an expressively complete language. In order to comprehend a complete theory of everything, we would need capacities that far outstrip the capacities that we actually have.

While our worldviews are nothing like ideal worldviews, we may get some clues about how to make comparative assessments of actual worldviews by considering how to make comparative assessments of ideal worldviews. Since ideal worldviews are complete and consistent, there is only one step in the comparative assessment of ideal worldviews: we check to see which ideal worldview (or ideal worldviews) make the best fist of trading off minimisation of commitments against maximisation of explanation.

In figuring out which ideal worldviews do better with respect to minimisation of commitments, there are three dimensions to consider: ontological commitment, ideological commitment, and theoretical commitment. While, in general, it is doubtful that there is an algorithm that tells us how to weigh these three kinds of commitments, there are special cases in which it is clear that one ideal worldview is doing better than another in point of minimising commitments. For example, if one ideal worldview does better than another at minimising all three kinds of commitments, then that ideal worldview is doing better overall in minimising commitments.

In figuring out which ideal worldviews do better with respect to maximising explanation, we look to see what is, and what is not, explained by each of the competing worldviews. While it may not always be straightforward to determine which ideal worldview does better at maximising explanation, there are again special cases in which it is clear that one ideal worldview does better than another in maximising explanation. One important point to bear in mind is that what ideal worldviews are required to explain is data—claims on which they both agree. It is no advantage to a given ideal worldview that it explains things that do not figure in the commitments of competing ideal worldviews.

Even in cases where we can figure out which ideal worldviews do better than others with respect to minimising commitments, and which ideal worldviews do better than others with respect to maximising explanation, it is not always straightforward to determine which ideal worldviews do better overall. However, yet again, there are special cases in which it is clear that one ideal worldview does better than another ideal worldview. For example, if one ideal worldview does better than another both at minimising commitments and maximising explanation, then it does better overall.

So far, we have just considered ideal worldviews. When we turn to actual worldviews—which are very poor approximations to ideal worldviews—matters become much more complicated. A first difficulty is that, unlike ideal worldviews, actual worldviews are not fully articulated. If we wish to take on worldview assessment, the first—and most important—task is to try to make reasonably comprehensive articulations of worldviews. If we are comparing worldviews, but some of them have hidden commitments, then we have no hope of making a fair and accurate assessment of them. A second difficulty is that, unlike ideal worldviews, actual worldviews may well involve inconsistencies. When comparing actual worldviews, we need to winnow out inconsistencies, so that we do not put lots of effort into assessing worldviews that we can know, on independent grounds, are not among the best worldviews.

One important thing to notice in this account is that it gives no role to the notion of a *tension* within a worldview. In practice, it is probably not very accurate to represent people as having a single worldview. Rather, it is more accurate to represent people as being undecided between a range of different worldviews. In particular, wherever people are undecided about a particular claim, we can think of this as indecision between different worldviews that contain the claims that they are undecided between. Where people are genuinely torn between options, we should not think of them as having a tension in their worldview; rather, we should think of them as being undecided between different worldviews. And, when we assess their outlook, we should assess the different worldviews between which they are undecided. Often enough, in practice, it will be enough to choose a representative worldview, and proceed with its assessment. But this will not always be the case.

We are not quite done. We still have to explain how we assess theoretical commitments, ideological commitments, and ontological commitments.

> Where Kenny wants to talk about tensions in worldviews, I would much prefer to talk about indecision between competing worldviews. If I am torn on the question whether there can be causation in the absence of time, then I am best represented as being undecided between a worldview in which there can be causation in the absence of time and a worldview in which there cannot be causation in the absence of time. When we move from idealised theorising to more realistic theorising, indecision between worldviews becomes a very significant consideration.

4 Theoretical Commitments

In the case of ideal worldviews, the right way to think about theoretical commitments is in terms of *axiomatisation*: one ideal worldview does better than another in terms of theoretical commitments just in case it has a simpler best axiomatisation. The main idea here is that, from the standpoint of theoretical commitments, whatever you get by way of logical consequence from claims to which you are committed comes for free. If we want, we can call the axioms in a best axiomatisation of an ideal worldview the fundamental principles of that ideal worldview.

When we come to actual worldviews, it is not so straightforward what to say. As Kenny rightly notes, in my original presentation, I left open the question what makes principles fundamental. It seems right to say, as I said there, that we cannot axiomatise our worldviews. So, in practice, we certainly cannot use axiomatisation to determine which principles are fundamental. However, what we can say—and what we should say—is that we should treat all claims as fundamental except those that have been explicitly shown to be logical consequences of other things to which we are committed.

Kenny has what looks like a different proposal. He suggests that a theoretical commitment is fundamental iff according to the worldview itself that commitment has no explanation. On his account, at least roughly, the fundamental claims of a worldview are those that it takes to be brute and those that it takes to be autonomous.

Perhaps it will help to think about an example. Consider what an ideal worldview will say about the natural universe. It will give a complete specification of all of the following: (1) the initial state, assuming there is one; (2) the laws; and (3) the outcomes of every chance event. Moreover, on the assumption that there is scale independence, the complete specification of the initial state will consider all scales, and the complete specification of the laws will consider the laws at all scales. I maintain that logical consequence affords no possibilities to compress this information. So, on my account, we should suppose that it is all fundamental. Moreover, I take it that, except in the case of the outcomes of chance events—which Kenny will need to take to be brute—Kenny will suppose that logical consequence gets us these things from claims about what God wants them to be: God wants the initial state to be thus-and-so and God wants the laws to be thus-and-so. Again, I do not think that logical consequence affords any possibility of further compressing this information. So, I think, on Kenny's account you should suppose that it is all fundamental, because autonomous. Either way, then, I think that what falls out is that, with respect to complete accounts of the natural universe, naturalism is ever so slightly better off than theism when it comes to minimisation of theoretical commitments.

Kenny claims that my views about necessity commit me to saying that every necessity claim is a separate fundamental theoretical commitment. But that is not so. When it comes to mathematics, morality, and other domains in which there are necessary truths, our fundamental theoretical commitments are only to those claims that are not logical consequences of other claims to which we are committed. (Qualification: If p is a logical consequence of q and q is a logical consequence of p, we cannot claim that we avoid commitment to both p and q on account of these facts about logical consequence. You have to be committed to claims that have the target claims as logical consequences in order to disavow fundamental commitment to the target claims.)

> In the ideal case, it is clear, I think, that we should think about theoretical commitment in terms of axiomatisation. This leaves it open how to think about theoretical commitment in non-ideal cases. My inclination is to say that we should treat all claims as fundamental except those that have been explicitly shown to be logical consequences of other things to which we are committed (with the proviso that we must be able to show that we can recover all of the claims for which we are claiming exemption from the claims for which we are not claiming exemption).

5 Ontological Commitments

In the case of ideal worldviews, the right way to think about ontological commitments is in terms of the domain of quantification of the axioms in the best axiomatisation of the worldview. An ideal worldview is ontologically committed to everything that lies in the domain of quantification of its axioms if the worldview is true. When we compare the ontological commitments of ideal worldviews, we compare both commitments to entities and commitments to kinds of entities. While, in general, there is no algorithm that tells us how to weigh commitments to entities and commitments to kinds of entities, there are cases that yield clear outcomes. For example, if the entities and kinds of entities to which one ideal worldview is committed are proper subsets of the entities and kinds of entities to which a second ideal worldview is committed, then the first ideal worldview does better than the second ideal worldview in point of minimising ontological commitments.

In the case of actual worldviews, we again think about ontological commitments in terms of the domain over which the quantifiers used in expressing the worldview range. Actual worldviews are ontologically committed to everything that lies in their domains of quantification. Moreover, actual worldviews are fundamentally ontologically committed to everything that lies in their domains of quantification except for those things and kinds of things whose existence is a logical consequence of the existence of other things and kinds of things that lie in the relevant domain of quantification.

Kenny expresses a different view about ontological commitment. In his view, the only things that count towards the ontological commitments of a view are the things that the worldview takes to be *basic* or *fundamental*. On his own reckoning, his view is committed to just one fundamental thing (God) and just one fundamental kind of thing (being God). Moreover, on his own reckoning, Kenny claims that God is relatively simple: God has no parts, and the fundamental attributes of God are highly unified, both individually and collectively.

I think that, even by his own lights, Kenny underestimates his own ontological commitments. In order to make a complete estimation of your ontological commitments, you need to consider all of the ontological categories in which you have commitments. So far, all that Kenny has told us about is what he takes to be his fundamental commitments in the category of *objects*. But there are many other ontological categories in which you might register fundamental commitments: *events, states, powers, facts*, and so forth. Of course, we might hope to reduce some of these ontological categories to others; and we might seek to explain away some of these ontological categories, as I said I would like to be able to do with attributes, characteristics, classes, functions, groups, patterns, properties, propositions, sets, structures, types, universals, and so forth. At the very least, I think that Kenny should allow that, by his own lights, God's grounding of natural reality is among his primitive ontological commitments. And—though this is more controversial—I think that Kenny should also allow that, by his own lights, all of the instances of God's wanting the universe to have particular features are among his primitive ontological commitments.

More importantly, though, I think that Kenny's view of ontological commitment is mistaken. Consider Donald Trump. Kenny and I are both ontologically committed to Donald Trump. We both think that there is an explanatory history to Trump's existence and nature that traces back to the initial state of the universe, the laws, and the outplaying of chances. Of course, we cannot fill in all the details of that explanatory history. But we are both committed to there being an explanation of this kind; neither of us thinks that Donald Trump's existence is explanatorily fundamental. However, from the standpoint of our worldviews, it is not clear that this is sufficient to ensure that Donald Trump is not among our fundamental ontological commitments. The key question, I think, is whether the existence of Donald Trump is a logical consequence of the initial state, the laws, and the actual sequence of chance outcomes. If, as I suspect, the existence of Donald Trump is not a logical consequence of the initial state, the laws, and the actual sequence of chance outcomes, then Donald Trump will be ontologically fundamental but not explanatorily fundamental. (Note that we get the same result even if we add Kenny's further view that it is actually God's wanting the initial state, the laws, and—perhaps—the actual sequence of chance outcomes that is explanatorily fundamental. The question about logical consequence is no different under this scenario.)

Kenny notes that in my initial statement, I did not say much about my fundamental ontological commitments, in the sense in which he understands what it is for ontological commitments to be fundamental. While he allows that, on both our views, our fundamental ontological commitments exhibit puzzles and complexities, he claims that it is clear that I am fundamentally ontologically committed to an enormous multitude of individual things belonging to several different categories, while he is fundamentally ontologically committed to just one thing: God. I do not agree with this assessment. First, if we take account of the full range of ontological categories—and do not focus solely on the category of objects—then it is not clear that there is any difference in the number of things to which we are fundamentally committed. Kenny says there is one initial thing: God. I say there is one initial thing, which I will call 'the initial singularity'. I say that there are various true things to be said about the initial singularity; Kenny says that there are corresponding true things to be said about God's wanting those things to be true of the initial singularity. Either way, there is further commitment to events, states, or items belonging to other ontological categories. When we do the accounting properly, it seems that there is little difference in the number of our fundamental ontological commitments. Second, as I have argued above, Kenny's thinking about fundamental ontological commitments seems to conflate two kinds of considerations that should be kept separate: on the one hand, considerations about explanatory fundamentality, which is really the concern of our theoretical commitments; and on the other hand, ontological fundamentality, which is the proper subject of concern when we are thinking about ontological commitments. Even if—improbably—it turns out that the initial singularity is more complicated than God, the fact that Kenny's fundamental explanatory object is simpler than my fundamental explanatory object does not have the implications for choice between worldviews that Kenny takes it to have.

> Kenny and I disagree about how to determine the ontological commitments of a theory. I say that what matters, in the determination of ontological cost, is whether the existence of a given thing is a logical consequence of the existence of other things. Kenny says that what matters, in the determination of ontological cost, is whether the existence of a given thing is an explanatory consequence of the existence of other things. At this point, by my lights, Kenny is running together ontological costs and theoretical costs.

6 Ideological Commitments

Kenny claims that, while my worldview has a modest advantage in ideological simplicity, it might be that further work on divine attributes could narrow the gap or close it entirely. There are two sources of additional ideological complexity in Kenny's worldview.

One source is new primitive vocabulary that is required for the statement of Kenny's worldview but that is not required for the statement of my worldview. In particular, there is a lot of religious and theological vocabulary that is required for theorising about the Christian God that my worldview does without: *aseity, consubstantiality, hypostatic union, omnipotence, omniscience, perichoresis, substitutionary atonement*, and so forth. This vocabulary would be no theoretical cost if it were all given explicit definition, but the plain truth is that there is no agreement among theologians and believers about the explicit definitions of a very large number of words of this kind. Kenny ignores this source of additional ideological complexity in his discussion.

Another source is the use of analogy that is required for the statement of Kenny's worldview but that is not required for the statement of my worldview. As Kenny notes, it is very common for theologians and religious believers to claim that, because of the 'otherness' of God, terms that we apply to God do not apply to God in the same way that they apply to other things. We may say, for example, that God is good; but, according to may theologians and religious believers, we should not say that God is good in the same sense in which some of us, at least some of the time, are good.

Kenny discusses this second putative source of additional ideological complexity at some length. He considers four possible responses. (1) All of the vocabulary is used univocally. (2) At least some of the vocabulary is used analogously, but does not incur any new commitments. (3) At least some of the vocabulary is used analogously, but does not incur any new primitive commitments. (4) Some of the vocabulary is used analogously and, as I claim, it does incur new (primitive) commitments. Kenny is quick to reject (1), and to accept (4) would be to concede that there is, indeed, a second source of additional ideological complexity that is present in Kenny's worldview but not in mine.

As Kenny notes, in order to take the second option, we need to say that we employ the very same concept when we talk of God and when we talk of, say, humans, but that our concept does not pick out the same kind of thing when we talk of God and when we talk of, say, humans. I think that this is *prima facie* implausible. On all familiar accounts of concepts—in terms of necessary and sufficient conditions, or prototypes, or family resemblances, or theory-theory, or causal relations to things in the world—it turns out that concepts pick out things that fall under them, and hence pick out the same kind of thing no matter how they are applied. If concepts are defined by necessary and sufficient conditions, then everything that falls under a concept satisfies those necessary and sufficient conditions. If concepts are defined by prototypes, then everything that falls under a concept is suitably similar to its prototypes. If concepts are defined by family resemblances, then everything that falls under a concept is suitably similar to other things that fall under the family resemblance. If concepts are defined by the theory-theory, then concepts are defined in terms of platitudes that are true of the things that fall under the concept, and so things that fall under the concept will all satisfy a decent number of the platitudes. If concepts are defined by causal relations to the world, then there will be some external factors that unite all of the things that fall under a given concept. While I am not arguing that we can definitively rule out the claim that Kenny is considering here, I do think it is reasonable to suppose that its prospects are bleak.

As Kenny says, in order to take the third option, we need to suppose that, when terms are used analogically, the relevant analogies can be spelled out in univocal terms. This approach is unpromising from the get-go. As Kenny notes, most theorists of analogy and metaphor are sceptical of the idea that, in general, analogies and metaphors can be spelled out in literal and univocal terms. Kenny claims—perhaps plausibly—that we should think that *having reasons* applies in the same sense to God and humans. But it is not clear that this justifies the further claim that the application of the concept *free and rational choice to God* can be spelled out in literal and univocal terms. And, even if it does, there is a very large catalogue of further terms waiting to be discussed, and a long history of philosophers, theologians, and religious believers who deny that the task can be completed.

After his examination of cases, Kenny claims that, even if he has to accept that there is additional primitive ideological commitment in the analogical use of terms when applied to God, we can insist that it is cheaper to use analogical extension of concepts than it is to build totally new concepts. I do not think that this is correct. Each ideological primitive in your theory is a theoretical cost; no ideological primitive is more expensive than any other ideological primitive.

> Kenny and I disagree about the extent to which the ideological costs of his theory outweigh the ideological costs of my theory. I think that it is quite clear that his ideological costs are significantly greater than mine. On the one hand, there is a lot of theological vocabulary that my theory does without but that is essential to the statement of Kenny's views. And, on the other hand, Kenny's theory makes frequent analogical use of terms that only find univocal use in my theory. While Kenny tries to play down the theoretical costs of analogical uses of terms, I do not think that those attempts are successful.

7 Comparative Simplicity

Kenny claims that his worldview is simpler than my worldview. His assessment of the comparative simplicity of our worldviews rests on the following three claims. (1) Kenny's worldview has an infinite advantage over mine when it comes to theoretical simplicity. (2) While it is not entirely clear which worldview does better when it comes to ontological simplicity, his view has only one fundamental ontological commitment, while my worldview is committed to many fundamental things and fundamental kinds of things. (3) It may be that my worldview has a modest advantage when it comes to ideological simplicity, though it is not clear that that modest advantage cannot be overcome. I think that, if Kenny were right in these three claims, then it would be plausible to claim that his worldview is simpler than my worldview.

However, my assessment of the state of play, as displayed above, returns a different result. (1) My worldview has a slight advantage over Kenny's worldview when it comes to theoretical simplicity, because claims about God do not feature among the claims that it makes. Every worldview has a bunch of 'that is all there is' clauses: that is all the objects there are, that is all the events that there are, that is all the global states that there are, and so forth. Claims about God do not compress the information that is required to give a complete account of the natural world, but they do have additional informational content. So it is unsurprising that there is some extra theoretical complexity in Kenny's worldview. (2) My worldview has a slight advantage over Kenny's worldview when it comes to ontological simplicity. It may be true that the fundamental explanatory item in Kenny's worldview is simpler than the fundamental explanatory item in my worldview. But it is not clear that this is so; and even if it is so, it remains the case that Kenny's worldview has other fundamental ontological commitments that my worldview does not, but not vice versa. (3) My worldview has some advantage over Kenny's worldview when it comes to ideological simplicity, but it is not entirely clear how great this advantage is. Kenny is more optimistic than I am that the gap in ideological simplicity between our worldviews might be narrowed by subsequent developments. As I see it, my worldview fares a little better than Kenny's worldview on every dimension of commitment, and, in consequence, it fares a little better than Kenny's overall.

Kenny and I disagree in our overall assessment of the comparative simplicity of our worldviews. Given the discussion in the past three sections, it is clear what I think. As I see it, my view has fewer commitments in each of the three dimensions of assessment: ontological, ideological, and theoretical. Consequently, as I see it, my view has fewer commitments than Kenny's *tout court*.

8 Necessity, Dependence, Grounding, and Explanation

Kenny claims that the views that I have expressed about necessity, dependence, and explanation are 'an unforced error'. In particular, Kenny claims that my view that 'all necessities are brute' (1) entails that every necessity is a separate theoretical commitment, (2) incurs an infinite cost in terms of explanatory comprehensiveness, (3) is intrinsically implausible, and (4) is flatly inconsistent with the way mathematical and ethical reasoning is actually conducted. Moreover, Kenny says that I do not explain (5) why I deny that necessities can be explained, (6) why I maintain that dependence is modal, and (7) how I distinguish between those necessities that are primitive and those that are not.

Kenny may be right that there is an unforced error in my view. But before I consider what the consequences of that would be for me, I will first explain why I do not think that Kenny's criticisms suffice to show that there is something wrong with my views about necessity, dependence, explanation, and grounding.

We can distinguish between two different kinds of necessities. On the one hand, there are necessities that are only knowable *a posteriori*. Examples of these kinds of necessities in my worldview include the laws and boundary conditions of causal reality, and the kinds of claims that support what Kenny calls 'real definitions'—for example, the claim that water is two parts hydrogen to one part oxygen. On the other hand, there are necessities that are knowable *a priori* (e.g. the claims of logic and mathematics) or that are inferred from contingent claims in conjunction with claims that are knowable *a priori* (e.g. claims in ethics and aesthetics that are not knowable purely *a priori*). While this is not entirely philosophically uncontroversial, it is not implausible to suppose, further, that the kinds of claims that support what Kenny calls 'nominal definitions' all fall into this latter category.

In the case of necessities that are knowable only *a posteriori*, it is immediately plausible that that they have no explanation. Kenny himself gives voice to something like this intuition when he claims that real definitions are plausible candidates to be autonomous facts. On his view, it is just a mistake to ask why real definitions are true. On the view I set out in my initial statement, it is just a mistake to ask why real definitions are necessarily true. Even if I should agree with Kenny that it is only a mistake to ask why real definitions are true, we are in agreement that we have hit explanatory rock bottom when we arrive at necessities that are knowable only *a posteriori*. Moreover, I think, it is plausible that we will agree that, in cases where we have hit explanatory rock bottom, there could not be something upon which that which sits at explanatory rock bottom depends. Were there something upon which what sits at explanatory rock bottom depends, then—*per impossible*—there would be something in terms of which explanatory rock bottom could be explained.

In the case of necessities that are knowable *a priori*, it is less clear what to say about the prospects for their explanation. However, one thing that is obviously true is that some things that are knowable *a priori* are logical consequences of other things that are knowable *a priori*. But, quite generally, if B is a logical consequence of A, then anything that explains A also explains B. Hence, in particular, if one thing that is knowable *a priori* is a logical consequence of a second thing that is knowable *a priori*, and there is some third thing that explains the truth of the second thing, then that third thing also explains the truth of the first thing. Given that all of the mathematical (or logical, or ethical, or aesthetic) claims are logical consequences of a small number of mathematical (or logical, or ethical, or aesthetic) claims, the small number of things that explain the small number of mathematical (or logical, or ethical, or aesthetic) claims suffice to explain all of the mathematical (or logical, or ethical, or aesthetic) claims. Moreover, quite generally, if B is a logical consequence of A, and there is nothing that explains A—so that A is a primitive theoretical commitment—then B is not an *additional* primitive theoretical commitment. Given that all of the mathematical (or logical, or ethical, or aesthetic) claims are logical consequences of a small number of mathematical (or logical, or ethical, or aesthetic) claims, even if the small number of mathematical (or logical, or ethical, or aesthetic) claims are primitive theoretical commitments, the remaining mathematical (or logical, or ethical, or aesthetic) claims are not primitive theoretical commitments.

Given just this much, I think it is clear that I do *not* accept that every necessity is a separate theoretical commitment and that my view does *not* incur an infinite cost in terms of explanatory comprehensiveness. In particular, it is clear that, while my view does insist that necessities are unexplained, my view does not claim that everything that is unexplained is primitive. Given that logic and mathematics do admit of axiomatisation, it is quite clear in those cases what I take the primitive necessities to be; and my best guess is that Kenny would take those axioms to express autonomous facts. Moreover, while ethics and aesthetics are not typically axiomatised, there is quite broad agreement on fundamental claims in ethics and aesthetics; there is no mystery about the kinds of claims that I take to be primitive necessities in those domains.

I think—and Kenny agrees—that it is fundamental to our understanding of necessity that necessary claims are true no matter what. I also think that to say this is just to say that there is nothing upon which necessary claims depend. Kenny claims that grounding theorists are united in supposing that grounding is not a modal dependence relation. Moreover, according to Kenny, there are cases where necessities are grounded in other necessities. I think that all of the grounding relations that I need are modal dependence relations. If I can do without grounding relations that are not modal dependence relations, then my worldview has an advantage when it comes to minimising ontological and ideological commitments. In particular, if I can do without the grounding of necessities in other necessities when other worldviews cannot, then my worldview has an advantage when it comes to minimising ontological and ideological commitments.

Should I accept that Kenny is right that there is *something* wrong with the set of claims about necessity, dependence, and explanation that I set out in §4 of my introductory statement? I am not sure. Kenny claims, at one point in his discussion, that we cannot explain why $2 + 2 = 4$ by adverting to the necessity of the claim that $2 + 2 = 4$. It is not an axiom of arithmetic that $2 + 2 = 4$; rather, that $2 + 2 = 4$ is a logical consequence of the axioms of arithmetic. When we ask why $2 + 2 = 4$, we might well be asking for something like a derivation of the claim that $2 + 2 = 4$ from the axioms of arithmetic. That suggests that it is a mistake to say that there are only two types of explanation of non-modalised p: explanation that adverts to necessity and explanation that adverts to dependence on non-modalised q. That principle might be fine for necessities known only *a posteriori*, but it seems susceptible of improvement in the case of necessities knowable *a priori*.

Suppose that Kenny is right, and that my account of necessity, dependence, and explanation will not fly. What will need adjusting? As far as I can see, *the most* that will need adjusting is the account of necessities that are knowable *a priori*. I have expressed a preference for views on which we have objectivity (in mathematics, logic, ethics, aesthetics, etc.) without ontology—that is, without specifically mathematical, or logical, or ethical, or aesthetic ontology. At the very worst, I could give up on the attempt to have a view in which there is objectivity without ontology, and instead opt for some kind of Platonism in these areas. Given that Kenny already opts for ontology to explain objectivity in these areas—by way of appeal to ideas in the mind of God—it seems doubtful that this would lead to anything worse than a draw in the explanations that we offer in these domains. While I am not inclined to give up on objectivity without ontology, I do not think that the overall result of the comparison of the virtues of our worldviews would turn out differently if I were to give up on it.

> Kenny claims that my views about necessity, dependence, grounding, and explanation constitute an unforced error on my part. I am include to push back: I do not (yet?) see that Kenny is right about this. However, if it turns out that Kenny is right, the changes that would be required to my worldview would not alter the conclusions that I have reached about the comparative merits of our worldviews: by my lights, my fallback worldview is also more theoretically virtuous than Kenny's worldview.

9 Brute Facts

Kenny notes that we have a disagreement about whether contrastive facts about production of chance outcomes are brute contingencies—unexplained fundamental facts. He claims that, while this disagreement is not important to our debate, it is nonetheless the case that there are no contrastive facts about production of chance outcomes that are brute contingencies.

Kenny claims that the disagreement is not important because the best theories on either side will adopt the best view about contrastive explanation and indeterminism. If the best view is that there are no contrastive facts about production of chance outcomes that are brute contingencies, then best naturalistic theories will adopt that view. And if the best view is that there are contrasting facts about production of chance outcomes that are brute contingencies, then best theistic theories will adopt that view. However, this claim is too quick. It is not obvious that whether or not we count contrastive facts about production of chance outcomes as brute contingencies makes no difference to our assessment of the comparative theoretical merits of our theories, unless it is obvious that we both committed to similar amounts and kinds of contrastive facts about production of chance outcomes. That is not obviously so. In particular, if Kenny thinks that God's grounding of causal reality is chancy, then it seems that there is a significant amount of a kind of production of chance outcome that is present in his view and absent from mine. If that is so, then whether we suppose that contrastive facts about production of chance outcomes are brute contingencies does matter when we come to tally up the theoretical costs of our worldviews.

Kenny is, however, right to insist that we should think about different versions of our worldviews that take on the different claims that can be made about whether there are contrastive facts about production of chance outcomes. If it turns out that it makes no significant difference which way we go, then, at least for the purposes of our present discussion, we can let the matter rest.

Kenny claims that there are no contrastive facts. He invites us to consider the following two sentences:

1. The electron was measured with spin up rather than spin down.
2. The electron was measured with spin up and not spin down.

He claims that these two sentences express the very same fact. Moreover, he says, in general we can explain why A and B by explaining why A and explaining why B. Since these are both non-contrastive explanations, there is nothing left to be explained.

I agree with Kenny that we need not think that the two sentences he gives express different facts. But these two sentences do not express the kind of contrastive fact that I claim is brutely contingent. Suppose that some indeterministic process P issues in A when it could have issued in B. The kind of contrastive fact that I have in mind is something like this: *P issued in A rather than B*. In the nature of the case, you might think, there can be no explanation of why P issued in A rather than B.

As Kenny points out, it is a bit quick to suppose that you can never have an explanation of why P issued in A rather than B in cases that are indeterministic. In particular, if it was much more likely that P would issue in A than that it would issue in B, then you might take that to be some kind of explanation of why P issued in A rather than B. But, even if this is right, it remains the case that there will be lots of instances in which these kinds of contrastive facts are brute contingencies. Moreover, it is not clear that this is right. Suppose that there are millions of instances of set-ups issuing in A-outcomes and B-outcomes, but A-outcomes outnumber B-outcomes one-thousand fold. Are we happy to say that, when a set-up issues in an A-outcome rather than a B-outcome, there is no brute contingency, but when a set-up issues in a B-outcome rather than an A-outcome, there is brute contingency? If we focus on a particular case in which there is an A-outcome, bearing in mind the facts about the distribution of A-outcomes and B-outcomes, it is not so clear that we should not insist that it *is* a matter of brute contingency that the set-up issued in an A-outcome rather than a B-outcome, *even though* it was highly like that the set-up would issue in an A-outcome rather than a B-outcome.

On my view, appeal to indeterminism is always (one kind of) theoretical cost. Where you have determinism, no question of the kind 'why did P issue in A rather than B?' remains entirely unanswered. That is a theoretical virtue. But, of course, it is not the only theoretical virtue. We may—and I think we do—have good reason to suppose that some processes are not deterministic.

> Kenny and I disagree about whether, in cases of indeterministic causation, there can be an explanation of why we get one outcome rather than another from the causal process in question. Kenny thinks that perhaps, where the outcome is more likely that other outcomes, we explain it by appealing to this probability. However, I am sceptical. It seems to me that we have no explanation at all of why we got the most likely outcome, rather than one of the less likely outcomes in particular cases in which we do get the most likely outcome (not to mention cases in which we do not get the most likely outcome).

10 Autonomous Facts

Kenny claims that his worldview provides an explanation of History that eliminates brute facts while allowing that the world could have been otherwise. In his view, History is explained by God's choice; God's choice is explained by God's reasons; God's existing and having those reasons is explained by God's real definition; and God's real definition is an autonomous fact (i.e. a fact that needs no explanation).

The story that Kenny is telling here relies crucially on the following pair of assumptions: (1) God's existing and having certain reasons is explained by God's real definition and (2) God's real definition is an autonomous fact (i.e. a fact that needs no explanation). Kenny claims that a real definition tells you what something really is. In order for the real definition of God to explain God's existence and possession of certain reasons, it has to be that existing of necessity and essential possessing certain reasons are included in, or follow from, God's real definition.

But, of course, there is a very similar story that could be told on a version of my worldview that adopted Kenny's fundamental explanatory categories. We need only the following two assumptions: (1) the initial singularity's existing and having the properties that it does—including its being governed by the laws that it is governed by—is explained by the initial singularity's real definition; and (2) the initial singularity's real definition is an autonomous fact. In order for the real definition of the initial singularity to explain the initial singularity's existence and possession of certain properties, it has to be that existing of necessity and essentially possessing the properties in question are included in, or follow from, the initial singularity's real definition. But, obviously enough, if you recast my worldview in terms of real definitions, then it is simply true that, according to my worldview, existing of necessity and essentially possessing the properties in question are included in the initial singularity's real definition. So, it seems, under Kenny's fundamental explanatory categories, my worldview also eliminates brute facts in favour of autonomous facts.

Just as Kenny supposes that there is no prospect here of a modal ontological argument for the existence of God, so, too, I suppose that there is no prospect here of a modal ontological argument for the existence of the initial singularity. However, it is worth noting that it is plausible that the modal ontological argument for the existence of the initial singularity is precisely as good (or bad) as the modal ontological argument for the existence of God. This result is just the kind of result that you should have predicted given my account of what makes for good arguments.

> Kenny claims that his worldview can provide an explanation of History that eliminates brute facts while allowing that the world could have been otherwise. If this claim is correct, then it is also true that my worldview—or, at any rate, the variant of my worldview that adopts Kenny's views about autonomous facts and real explanations—allows an explanation of the existence of the universe that eliminates brute facts while allowing that the universe could have been otherwise.

11 Mathematical Explanation

Kenny provides an example of what he calls 'mathematical explanation'. Consider the 'digit' keys on a typical calculator. Pick any row, column, or diagonal, and hit the keys first in one direction and then in the other, to produce a number like 789987 or 753357. It turns out that every number produced in this way is divisible by 37. Kenny says: 'This is *weird* . . . the sort of thing that ought to have an explanation!' And there is an explanation: every number produced in this way has the form: $10^5 a + 10^4(a + d) + 10^3(a + 2d) + 10^2(a + 2d) + 10(a + d) + a = 1221(91a + 10d)$. According to Kenny, the significance of the example is that we know *that* the claim is true before we know *why* the claim is true. When we are given the explanation of why the claim is true, there is some mystery that has been dispelled.

I do not think that this example makes any difficulty for the account that I gave in my introductory statement. Here is what that account would say about this particular mathematical explanation. Giving the derivation that any number of the relevant form is divisible by 37 establishes that it is necessary that any number of the relevant form is divisible by 37. (The derivation establishes that the claim is a logical consequence of claims that we already accept are necessary.) But its being necessary that any number of the relevant form is divisible by 37 has, as a logical consequence, that the observed phenomenon (concerning the number keys on the calculator) is necessary. And then the necessity of the observed phenomenon explains its truth. As I see it, I need no new principles—beyond the ones I already have—in order to explain the observed phenomenon. Contrary to what Kenny says, I do not deny that there is mathematical explanation. Moreover, I take it that, to the extent that we feel that there was mystery to be dispelled, the explanation that I have outlined does a perfectly good job of providing it. What we could not see, prior to the production of the derivation, is that it is a logical consequence of the axioms of mathematics—together with some contingently true claims about the workings of the calculator—that any number produced in the way described is divisible by 37. Once we have seen that, there is no mystery that remains to be dispelled.

What I do deny is that we can explain why it is *necessary* that every number produced in the way described is divisible by 37. We can show *that* it is necessary by deriving it from other claims that are necessary. But, ultimately, our mathematics is founded in claims that we take to be necessary but for which we cannot give an explanation of why *they* are necessary.

Consider Hume's Principle: the claim that *the number of Fs is equal to the number of Gs iff there is a bijection between the Fs and the Gs*. Why is this principle necessarily true? I think that the necessity of this principle is primitive: it is not something that can be explained. Perhaps Kenny might say that this principle is *autonomous*: it does not need an explanation. Additionally, perhaps Kenny might say that this is because the principle is a *nominal definition* of equi-numerosity. At this point, it becomes hard to see that the division between us can make a serious difference in the assessment of the theoretical virtues of our worldviews. We both think that Hume's Principle is a theoretical primitive. We both think that Hume's Principle is necessary. Neither of us thinks that there is anything substantive to say about why Hume's Principle is necessary.

> Kenny has a neat example of mathematical explanation. I do not think that this example makes any difficulties for my account of necessity, dependence, and explanation. As I see it, our attitude towards fundamental mathematical claims is more or less the same; it is just the theoretical vocabularies that we use to describe features of those claims that varies between us.

12 God and Mathematics

Kenny commits himself to a view that is either a version of theistic activism, according to which numbers are ideas in the mind of God that are created by God, or else a version of theistic conceptual realism, according to which numbers are ideas in the mind of God that are uncreated but nonetheless dependent on God. While he says that it is unclear which of these views he does or should) adopt, he holds that necessary mathematical truths are true because, in creating, God acts for reasons and thereby adopts the necessary truths as laws of thought.

It is a bit hard to know what to make of this last claim, for reasons related to the Euthyphro Dilemma. There are at least two distinct questions. One question is why the mathematical truths are as they are. Another question is why the mathematical truths must be as they are.

How, exactly, does the fact that, in creating, God acts for reasons, explain why the mathematical truths are as they are? How, exactly, does the fact that, in creating, God acts for reasons, explain why the mathematical truths must be as they are? How, exactly, does the fact that, in creating, God acts for reasons, explain why God adopts the mathematical truths that we have as laws of thought? How, exactly, does that fact that, in creating, God acts for reasons, explain why God must adopt the mathematical truths that we have as laws of thought?

Could God, acting for reasons in creating, produce some other set of laws for thought? If not, why not? Could God, acting for reasons in creating, produce some alternative set of mathematical truths? If not, why not? If God, acting for reasons in creating, could not produce any alternative, is that not because necessity already and independently rests in the mathematical truths that we have? And, if necessity already and independently rests in the mathematical truths we have, then what is left of the idea that the mathematical truths are merely thoughts in the mind of God?

One final thought: I wonder what Kenny supposes that God thinks about the generalised continuum hypothesis. Is either it or its negation a law of thought for God?

> Kenny claims that necessary mathematical truths are true because, in creating, God acts for reasons and thereby adopts the necessary truths as laws of thought. I am not sure what to make of this.

In particular, I want to know whether God could have adopted some alternative laws of thought. If so, then the mere fact that God adopted the ones he did does not explain *why* he did this. And, if not, then it seems that there must be something else that explains why God *could not* have adopted alternative laws.

13 Moral Explanation

Kenny claims that I hold that there can be no explanations of moral principles. However, as he observes, it is commonplace to appeal to more general moral principles to explain less general moral principles. According to Kenny, my denial that moral principles stand in explanatory relations throws out a large part of our ordinary reasoning about what we ought to do.

I deny that I hold that there can be no explanations of moral principles. I say that there can be no explaining why moral principles are necessary. However, I insist that, because they are necessary, their necessity explains why they are true. Moreover, as in the mathematical case, I say that, where one moral principle is a logical consequence of a second moral principle, we can infer the necessity of the first moral principle from the necessity of the second moral principle. So, in order to explain the truth of moral principles, we need only commit ourselves to the necessity of a small—or, at any rate, relatively small—number of fundamental moral principles.

> In §27 in my initial statement, I said that, given that the necessity of some moral claims is a logical consequence of the necessity of other moral claims, our commitment is limited to a small number of primitive moral principles. That I think that there is no explaining the necessity of those primitive moral principles is not, I think, a significant objection to my view. It is hard to see how Kenny could avoid supposing that those primitive moral principles are something like autonomous facts.

14 Euthyphro Dilemma

Kenny claims that, if my views about necessity were correct, there would be no Euthyphro Dilemma because the claims that are used to frame the dilemma would make no sense. Since the Euthyphro Dilemma does make sense, I must be wrong about explanation, necessity, and dependence.

Kenny frames the dilemma as follows: according to classical theism, it is necessary that God exists and is perfectly good. Since it is necessary that God is perfectly good, it is necessary that God approves of—and perhaps even commands—all right actions. But does God approve of right actions because they are right, or are they right because God approves of them? Neither option looks promising. If God approves of right actions because they are right, then it seems that God is somehow subservient to the moral law. But if right actions are right merely because God approves of them, then it seems that the content of the moral law is ultimately arbitrary.

There is no problem here for me. Some theists (e.g. Kenny) suppose that some necessary truths are grounded in other necessary truths. The Euthyphro problem is a problem for them. They take seriously the idea that God is the foundation of morality. None of this is my problem. I think that it is impossible that morality has foundations, other than in the sense that some moral claims are logical consequences of other moral claims. The point of derivation is to exhibit logical inconsistencies in worldviews. When you do this, you work solely with claims that belong to the worldview in question. What I happen to think is irrelevant to the force (or lack of force) of the Euthyphro objection to Kenny's theism.

The mistake here is analogous to a mistake that is sometimes made in connection with discussion of logical arguments from evil. Some theists say that since 'evil' means something like 'contrary to the will of God', atheists cannot coherently defend the claim that there is evil. But, when properly interpreted, logical arguments from evil claim to derive a contradiction among claims all of which are accepted by theists. What atheists happen to think about these claims is irrelevant to the success or failure of logical arguments from evil. In the particular instance under discussion here, what matters is not whether *atheists* suppose that there are things that are contrary to the will of God, but rather whether *theists* think that this is so.

Kenny goes on to say that there is a 'meta-puzzle' that is raised by my view. According to Kenny, I am committed to the claim that there is no Euthyphro Dilemma since the 'because' claims would be nonsense. But 'since' is a synonym of 'because'—it indicates an explanatory relation. So, according to Kenny, my view implies that necessarily there is no Euthyphro Dilemma, and that, consequently, the only reason why there is no dilemma is that necessarily there is no dilemma.

Again, there is no problem here for me. I am an atheist, so, of course, no Euthyphro Dilemma arises for me. But Kenny is a theist of a kind for whom, at least potentially, the Euthyphro Dilemma is a serious problem. Why is the Euthyphro Dilemma potentially a problem for Kenny? Because there is the potential that the Euthyphro Dilemma exposes a logical inconsistency in his worldview. That Kenny and I have different views about explanation, dependence and necessity does not prevent either of us from running a *reductio* argument against the position of the other.

> Kenny claims that my views about necessity make it impossible for me to claim that theists are threatened by the Euthyphro Dilemma. This claim seems misplaced to me. What matters for the Euthyphro Dilemma is that there is a set of claims that are jointly inconsistent but all of which are accepted by those to whom the dilemma is presented. If anyone's views about necessity matter, they are those on the receiving end of the Euthyphro Dilemma; what I happen to think about necessity is obviously irrelevant.

15 Theistic Ethics

Kenny explores two ways in which theists can avoid the Euthyphro Dilemma, one of which he dismisses, and one of which he thinks might be made to work.

The view that Kenny dismisses is the view of traditional theistic virtue ethics, according to which, when God creates humans, God must have some prior understanding of what it is to be human, and hence some prior understanding of what it is to be an excellent human. Given that part of what it is to be human is to be the sort of being that ought to be compassionate, courageous, self-controlled, and so forth, God does not arbitrarily make up ethics. Rather, when God decides to make humans, God thereby necessarily decides to make beings who ought to be compassionate, courageous, self-controlled, and so forth. Kenny's objection to this approach—which I am happy to endorse—is that it makes real definitions normative; for example, the nature of humanity is not just a matter of what human being really are, but also of what they really ought to be. I agree with Kenny that it is unacceptable to suppose that those who do not measure up to what human beings ought to be are therefore properly characterised to be defective.

The view that Kenny thinks holds out some promise is a kind of Kantian ethics. On this view, when I act of a reason, the maxim of my action is the practical judgment that drives it. My maxim includes all of the features of the situation that I take to be relevant to the appropriateness of my action. Moreover, according to this view, we act wrongly when our maxim is inconsistent; that is, when we do not think that it is the right thing to do every time these circumstances occur. According to Kenny, this view preserves both moral autonomy and moral objectivity. It preserves moral autonomy because we make laws for ourselves when we make our maxims. And it preserves moral objectivity because we are constrained by consistency. If I am doing constructions with a compass and straight edge, I cannot make up a two-sided polygon. Similarly, if I am making up maxims, I cannot consistently make up maxims that permit me to lie and steal. Finally, according to Kenny, we can extend this account to God: God is a Kantian moral agent whose goodness consists in God's adherence to the law that God legislates for Godself. But, according to Kenny, the fact that the moral law is self-legislated does not make it arbitrary.

There are various questions to ask about this proposal. (1) As Kenny himself notes, there is a question about what counts as 'the same situation' as the situation in which one acts. It seems, for example, that one can take situations to be indexed to particular times and places. If my maxim has the following form—anyone who is in my position on August 3, 2020, at 6:58 p.m. at 20 Chancellor's Walk, Monash University who . . .—then it seems that there is almost no constraint that 'consistency' imposes upon the content of my maxim. But it is perfectly consistent with acting on this maxim that I am acting with practical reason. (2) It is not clear why you should give yourself the rule that you act wrongly when you act on maxims that are inconsistent in Kant's sense. Why should we think that you cannot be autonomous if you fail to give yourself *that* rule?

Even if there is some non-question-begging way of settling what counts as 'the same situation', it seems that we have not been given any good reason to think that it would be wrong to act on maxims that are inconsistent in Kant's sense. (3) The analogy between making a two-sided polygon and making maxims for yourself clearly fails if situations can be indexed to particular places and times. Maxims couched in those terms can be used to justify almost anything that it is possible for you to do. (4) Most importantly, I think, even if there were no problems with the Kantian theory, there are problems in applying this theory to God. God knows that nothing could ever possibly be in the same situation in which God is placed. Consequently, maxims framed in terms of beings placed in the same situation as God impose no constraint at all on God. The idea that God might frame these kinds of maxims is completely empty.

Kenny acknowledges that there are lots of challenges to Kantian ethical theory. Perhaps it is not unreasonable to hope that all of the challenges can be overcome. Like Kenny, I am no expert in this area: the challenges that I have mentioned are just the first that came to my mind. However, I do think that, *prima facie*, the challenges make it seem rather unlikely that Kantian ethical theory can provide a satisfactory theistic response to the Euthyphro problem.

> In §27 in my initial statement, I said that, I think that there are independent difficulties for the view that there are objective moral facts because God legislates them. We can see some of these difficulties surfacing in Kenny's attempt to argue for a resolution to the Euthyphro Dilemma grounded in Kantian ethics. As I see it, the most formidable problem lies in the idea that Kantian ethics could be applicable to God. How could thoughts about what other similarly placed beings ought to do place any constraints on God, given God's knowledge that it is impossible for there to be any other similarly placed beings?

16 Laws of Thought

Kenny provides the following argument:

1. Some affirmative truths are necessary.
2. All affirmative truths depend on the existence of some being or collection of beings.

3. A necessary truth could not depend on a contingent being or collection of contingent beings.
4. (Therefore) There is a necessary being.

As Kenny notes, I accept the first and third premises. However, in my opening statement, I definitely rejected the second premise. Kenny claims that this premise is plausible because 'statements are generally statements *about* something, and typically if that something doesn't exist, then the statement will be false'. However, I claim that, if I stick to what I said in my opening statement, then this is not so.

I am happy to accept that, in the case of necessary truths that are knowable only *a posteriori*, there is ontology on which those truths depend. The truth of the claim that the initial singularity exists depends upon the existence of the initial singularity. As Kenny notes, I am happy to accept that there is a necessary being because I think that the initial singularity is a necessary being.

However, I am resistant to the idea that, in the case of necessary truths that are knowable *a priori*, there is ontology on which those truths depend. While I am happy to acknowledge that it is by no means settled that there can be objectivity without objects, I think that there are obvious attractions in the kind of position that I sketched—very briefly—in §§ 11–13 of my introductory statement. As I noted above, if it turns out that we cannot have objectivity without objects, then I will be obliged to take on more ontology to provide truth-makers for the claims of logic, mathematics, ethics, aesthetics, and so forth. But I do not think that, in any of those cases, it is plausible to suppose that my relevant additional ontological load would be any worse than the ontological load that Kenny is already carrying.

> Discussion of Kenny's argument about the laws of thought is somewhat 'academic' in the following sense: I already accept the conclusion of the argument. However, I am inclined to reject the second premise of the argument; and so I am not inclined to think that the argument is sound. Of course, my rejection of the second premise does nothing to impugn Kenny's judgment that the argument is sound.

17 Religious Experience

According to Kenny, my treatment of religious experience involves a kind of scepticism that does not differ in any important ways from scepticism about the external world. In particular, he insists that, even by my own lights, I fail to identify any difference between sensory experience and religious experience that justifies trusting one and not trusting the other. According to Kenny, the kinds of critical things that I want to say about religious experience are no less true of sensory experience: (1) sensory experience is the product of sensory practices, (2) interpretation of sensory experiences depends upon prior beliefs about the world, and (3) sensory experience has a neurological explanation. Moreover, according to Kenny, I commit myself to the false principle that, if you are already committed to explaining away the vast majority of the x's, then no further disadvantage accrues if you decide to explain away the rest of the x's. Finally, according to Kenny, I am committed to the claim that everyone who reports religious experiences is either hallucinating, or misremembering, or lying.

Kenny claims, on the one hand, that he does not contest the point that naturalists can reasonably hold that reports of miracles and religious experience can be given naturalistic explanations, and, on the other hand, that there is an unfortunate tension in naturalistic worldviews because endorsing those naturalistic explanations amounts to endorsing a kind of scepticism. However, he also insists that I adopt what he calls 'the Reidian attitude of trust in our faculties', and that the Reidian attitude of trust must lead us to treat reports of miracles and religious experience in the same way that we treat reports of sensory experience. While Kenny claims that he is merely identifying a tension in my worldview and not an outright inconsistency, I think that it is quite clear that he thinks that there is an inconsistency in my worldview. Moreover, if I am right that there is no proper use for the notion of 'tension' in criticism of worldviews, then the only charitable way to interpret what Kenny is saying here is that my views that bear on religious experience are simply inconsistent.

It is true that I am happy to claim that we all adopt a Reidian trust in our faculties, but I do not construe this Reidian trust in the same way that Kenny construes it. Kenny claims that there is an unavoidable tension in all worldviews that arises because we believe both (1) that our faculties are reliable and (2) that we often get things wrong. I say that there need not be—and typically is not—any such 'unavoidable tension'. According to me, any sensible worldview says that we trust our faculties *except* when we recognise that we have reason not to trust our faculties. Part of what happens when we learn how to use our faculties is that we develop an appreciation of their limitations. Rather than there being reason to privilege worldviews that give a *higher* estimation of the reliability of our faculties, there is reason to privilege worldviews that give an *accurate* estimation of the reliability of our faculties. This is not scepticism; it is just plain common sense. Kenny's Reidian religious argument begins with the premise that either we should start from a position of trusting all our faculties, or we should start from a position of distrusting all our faculties. But this premise is false. What we should do is start from a position in which we collectively trust our human faculties when we should trust them, and we do not collectively trust our human faculties when we should not trust them.

Kenny's argument from religious experience contains the premise that, if one worldview takes monotheistic religious experience to be reliable and another worldview does not, then—other things being equal—the first worldview takes human faculties to be more reliable than the second. According to Kenny, our *faculties* are our basic abilities for getting at the truth: our senses of sight, hearing, touch, smell, and taste, our memories, our reason, our introspective sense, and so forth. Moreover, according to Kenny, our *experiences* are deliverances from our senses with accompanying affective and interpretative overlays. As we have already seen, Reidian epistemology enjoins us to collectively trust our faculties except when we should not. Equally, Reidian epistemology enjoins us to collectively trust our experiences except when we should not. Whether *not* taking monotheistic religious experience to be reliable requires a lower estimation of the reliability of our faculties depends entirely on whether we take ourselves to have good reason not to collectively trust monotheistic religious experience. Whether we should take monotheistic religious experience to be unreliable depends entirely on whether we should take ourselves to have good reason not to collectively trust monotheistic religious experience.

Kenny is right to reject some reasons that are sometimes given for not collectively trusting monotheistic religious experience. While we should not overestimate the extent to which sensory experience is influenced by sensory practices, I do not think that it is unreasonable to allow that sensory experience can be influenced by sensory practice. Moreover, I think that it is clearly true that interpretation of sensory experience can depend upon prior beliefs, and that sensory experience has neurological explanation. None of this gives us reason to suppose that we should not collectively trust sensory experience. Consequently, that religious experience is influenced by religious practices, depends upon prior beliefs, and has neurological explanation is not, in itself, reason to suppose that we should not collectively trust religious experience. But, of course, it does not follow from these observations that we have good reason to collectively trust monotheistic religious experience. For it remains open that there are *other* good reasons not to collectively trust monotheistic religious experience.

I think that there is good reason not to collectively trust religious experience in general. The reason for this is that, unlike in the case of sensory experience, there is no central range of cases in which there is universal agreement on the deliverances of sensory experience and on the further claim that there are no defeating conditions that apply. Sure, there are complexities that arise because of differences in language, cultural traditions, and so forth. But we all know that, in the right circumstances, we are all in agreement on claims like the following: *that person is naked; that rabbit is running away, that dinghy is filling with water, that thunder suggests that there is a storm brewing, that burning fat is absolutely putrid*, and so on. Nothing like this is true in the case of religious experience. One of the first things that we learn about religion is that religious testimony is all over the place: there is more or less nothing on which the many religions of the world agree. Accepting that religious testimony is ultimately based in religious experience, it seems like a straightforward consequence that there just is no agreement on the deliverances of religious experience. But if there is no agreement on the deliverances of religious experience, then it is not even an option to collectively trust the deliverances of religious experience.

The key point here is that where there is no convergence of opinion, we have a defeater for the reliability of the deliverances of human cognition. When it comes to beliefs formed on the basis of regular sensory experience—of the kind exhibited in the previous paragraph—we have evidence of reliability in the independent convergence of those beliefs. When it comes to beliefs formed on the basis of expert sensory experience—as we find in the core of established beliefs in any established science—we have evidence of reliability in the independent convergence of those beliefs. But, in domains where there is neither of these kinds of convergence—as, for example, in philosophy, politics, and religion—we have a straightforward defeater for the claim that the beliefs that we collectively form on the basis of experiences in those domains are reliable.

Despite Kenny's apparent insistence to the contrary, the argument that I have just given does not depend upon the assumption that if you are already committed to explaining away the vast majority of the x's, then no further disadvantage accrues if you decide to explain away the rest of the x's. As Kenny says, there are counterexamples to this principle. However, the important point on which my argument really does depend is that, while naturalism provides a uniform treatment of all of the competing interpretations of the deliverances of religious experience, Kenny applies the treatment that the naturalist provides to all interpretations of the deliverances of religious experience except his own. It is somewhat ironic that Kenny claims that naturalists make a specific exception for monotheistic religious experience in their application of Reidian epistemology to experience when, in fact, it is Kenny who makes a specific exception for monotheistic religious experience in his application of Reidian epistemology to religious experience in general.

In his opening statement, Kenny responds to this kind of worry by appealing to a distinction between *authentic* religious experience and *reliable* religious experience: in his view, all religious experience is experience of his God, even though most religious experience has given rise to false beliefs. But this move does not improve matters. If the best version of Kenny's worldview says that all religious experience is experience of God, even though most religious experience gives rise to false beliefs, the best versions of many other religious worldviews will say that all religious experience is experience of their God, or gods, or other religious ultimates, even though most religious experience gives rise to false beliefs. When we compare naturalism with religious worldviews in general, it remains the case that only naturalism provides a uniform treatment of all of the competing interpretations of the deliverances of religious experiences. And that uniformity of interpretation is itself a slight edge in theoretical simplicity.

In the discussion of religious experience, it is important not to lose sight of the larger context within which this discussion is embedded. The question is not whether it is rationally permissible for Kenny to hold the religious beliefs that he does. I granted from the get-go that it is rationally permissible for Kenny to hold the religious beliefs that he does. Rather, the question is whether (1) our treatments of religious experience give rise to inconsistencies in our worldviews or (2) there are such obvious costs involved in our treatments of religious experience that there is no way that those costs can be offset elsewhere. While there are questions that one might ask Kenny—for example, *why does an omnipotent, omniscient and perfectly good being who wants us all to know that we are loved by it provides religious experiences that are so rarely interpreted correctly?*—I do not think that what Kenny says about religious experience is either inconsistent or so obviously expensive that this alone settles the question which worldview should be preferred.

In both his opening statement and his reply, Kenny insists that naturalists are obliged to suppose that monotheists who report religious experiences are either hallucinating, or misremembering, or lying. But, in fact, naturalists are not even obliged to suppose that monotheists who report *extraordinary* religious experiences are hallucinating, or misremembering, or lying. Given that there are communal ways of interpreting ordinary experiences—for example, of shame at wrongdoing, or awe at the immensity of the night sky—as experiences of God, it would be obviously absurd to suppose that those who report those ordinary experiences, as thus interpreted, must be hallucinating, misremembering, or lying. Moreover, given that reports of extraordinary religious experiences often play foundational roles in religions and are transmitted by way of testimony across the generations, it would be equally absurd to suppose that those who accept these reports must be hallucinating, or misremembering, or lying. But, even in the face of those who themselves claim to have had extraordinary religious experiences—for example, the kind of experience that Pascal had in his 'night of fire'—we are not obliged to suppose that Pascal was hallucinating, or that his subsequent reports were either mendacious or based on lapses in his memory. Of course, naturalists will have some deflating neurological account of those experiences, but all that naturalists need to insist upon is that the beliefs formed on the basis of those experiences are *false*.

Two small footnotes to the preceding discussion. (1) Kenny claims, in his opening statement, that I have previously assumed that, while miracles are publicly observable events, religious experiences are purely internal. He cites *The Best Argument Against God* as a work in which I do this. But, on the very page he cites, this is what I say:

> The reported religious experiences of human beings [include]: (i) manifestations of religion—religious practice, religious tradition, religious organisation, religious belief, and so forth; (ii) the world's being 'seen' in religious terms—for example, people's 'seeing' God's handiwork in nature; (iii) collective witnessing of miracles; (iv) dreams and visions with religious content; and (v) 'mystical'—'spiritual', 'sacred'—experiences'.
> (59f.)

(2) Kenny rejects my 'definition' of miracles as 'events caused by the actions of non-natural . . . agents' on the grounds that God's activity of creating and sustaining the natural world is not causal. It seems to me that, if we allow that it makes sense to claim that God's activity of creating and sustaining the natural world is not causal, there is a ready fix: miracles are events caused by, or otherwise grounded in, the actions of non-natural agents. (Following Kenny's lead, I ignore any difficulties for this definition that arise in connection with the distinction between 'special' divine action and 'regular' divine action.)

> It seems that Kenny and I have rather different estimations of the reliability of our cognitive faculties. Kenny says that we should suppose that our cognitive faculties are reliable, and that we should prefer views that give a higher estimation of the reliability of our cognitive faculties to views that give a lower estimation of the reliability of our cognitive faculties. I disagree. I think that we should make an accurate estimation of the reliability of our cognitive faculties, taking account, in particular, of domains where there is no expert agreement.

18 Reflections

I close with some reflections on the preceding contents of this book. As I write this, I have not seen Kenny's final reply. So some of what I say here may be overturned by things that he says there. I begin with some negative considerations and then turn to a bunch of positive considerations.

Superficially, Kenny and I agree about how to assess arguments, about how to discuss and assess worldviews, and on the virtues of broadly Reidian epistemology. However, as we dig deeper, it turns out that we have important disagreements about all of these matters. Our differences on these matters have only become clear—or, at any rate, clearer—to me while I have been working on my second round of replies.

The disagreement about what worldviews are and how they ought to be assessed is made manifest in the different approaches that we take in our opening statements. In keeping with my views about how to proceed, I tried to give as much detail as I could of the beliefs that I hold that I take to be relevant to my belief that there are no gods. Of course, there is much that is left out, including a few sections that were in my initial draft but omitted for reasons of space. But I think my opening entry nicely conveys my conception of the spirit of the enterprise of worldview comparison. You should make clear as much as you can of your controversial commitments so that others have a fair chance of assessing how your overall trading-off of simplicity with explanation fares in comparison with other attempts to do the same thing. Where you are undecided between several different worldviews, you should try to make clear what the commitments are on each of the worldviews between which you are undecided.

Kenny's approach in his opening statement is quite different. He picks a couple of claims to which his worldview is committed and compares them with corresponding claims to which my worldview is committed. He then argues that, just focussing on these particular claims, there are reasons to think that, with respect to these claims, his worldview does better than mine does. Along the way, he notes that there are all kinds of problems for the wider worldview in which his claims are embedded—that are not matched to corresponding problems in my worldview—but he does not deign to indicate how, in fact, his worldview deals with these problems. Moreover—and consequently—he makes no effort at all to disclose the full extent of his controversial theoretical, ideological, and ontological commitments that bear on his belief in 'the God of classical theism'. To take one example: Kenny does not tell us whether he thinks that God is perfect. But the only plausible option that he canvasses in response to the problems of divine determinism and optimism is that God is not perfect. Given what Kenny actually tells us, it is not clear that his worldview is so much as consistent. And, if his worldview is consistent, he has given no indication at all of the theoretical price he pays in order to deal with the problems of divine determinism and optimism.

Given that we have been playing different games, it is likely, I think, that we are both somewhat disappointed with the outcome. I am really not too fussed about arguing whether, if we focus just on Kenny's cosmological argument and his argument about religious experience, there are reasons for thinking that some of Kenny's relevant commitments are simpler than my corresponding relevant commitments. While I do think—as I have argued in my replies—that Kenny's assessment of these local points is not correct, the far more important point is that the only game that really matters when it comes to questions about simplicity is which overall view is simpler. And we cannot have a determination on that point until Kenny discloses what his relevant commitments are. There is a wider point here. An enormous amount of recent literature in philosophy of religion has focussed on arguments for and against what is sometimes called 'restricted standard theism': a small set of claims much like the ones that Kenny claims to derive from (CT). But restricted standard theism is not a comprehensive theory: no one should care how it stacks up against some kind of 'restricted standard naturalism'. What we should care about—and what we should argue about if we are interested in continuing to argue the relative merits of theism and naturalism—is how fully elaborated theistic worldviews stack up against fully elaborated naturalistic worldviews. And we should care most about the (best versions of the) worldviews that the participants in those arguments actually have.

Even if we look past the discrepancy in the ways that we think and talk about worldviews, there is also a discrepancy in the ways that we think and talk about arguments that is an additional reason for disappointment with the outcome of our discussion. While Kenny adopts an approach to argument assessment that is commonplace in the recent literature, I think that that approach to the assessment of argument is bankrupt. According to me, if you want to give an argument to someone else, you need to make sure that they accept the premises of the argument that you give to them. Giving someone an argument with premises they do not accept is just an invitation for them to say, 'I do not accept those premises'.

While Kenny insists that an argument of this kind can point to 'tensions' in a worldview, it is clear that, on my conception of worldviews and worldview assessment, that is simply not so. Each of the arguments that Kenny gives in his initial contribution has a least one premise that anyone who read my introductory piece will know that I do not accept. By my lights, anyway, the discipline should be moving away from trading in these kinds of arguments.

While our views about Reidian epistemology are quite close, there is one important difference that has a significant impact on our discussion of religious experience. According to Kenny, Reidian epistemology maintains that we *start out* with the assumption that all of our experiences are accurate reflections of reality: 'what seem to be experiences of apples come from real apples . . . [and] what seem to be experiences of God come from a real God'. I do not think that there is any interpretation of 'start out' on which this claim is correct. It is not true that adult human beings take this as a starting assumption every time they have an experience. Nor is it true that there is a stage in life at which human beings make this assumption in connection with their experiences. As I said in my earlier discussion of this point, learning when we can and cannot trust our senses is just part of learning to use our senses. Circumstances in which we seem to have experiences of Xs that do not come from Xs are not the *typical* case, but nor are they as rare as hen's teeth.

Despite these few negative features of our discussion, there are many positives that I can take away from it. One thing that seems to me to be clearly true is that I need to think some more about the set of issues that arise in connection with the accounts that I gave of necessity, dependence, grounding, and explanation. I had not previously tried to give an account of my thinking on these topics; my attempt to give an account shows that I need to do some more thinking here. I see this as a vindication of the overall method that I endorse. Following what I take to be the correct method of comparing worldviews should lead to the improvement of all worldviews. It is typically easier for others to see the major flaws in current formulations of our own worldviews. The likely rewards for the effort of trying to make your own commitments fully explicit—at least so long as you are interacting with other people who are genuinely committed to the project of comparing the merits of worldviews—is that you will end up with an improved worldview.

Given the difference in our approaches, it is to be expected that Kenny and I differ in our ambitions for our contributions to this book. Kenny's ambition is to produce good arguments for the conclusion that his worldview is better than mine, at least with respect to the topics that he takes up: the existence of History, the interpretation of monotheistic religious experience, and so forth. My own ambition is to support the claim that it is rationally permissible to suppose that my worldview is overall more theoretically virtuous than Kenny's worldview. Whereas it seems plausible to think that Kenny expects readers to agree with the particular judgments that he makes that inform the premises of his arguments, I have made it clear that I think that it is a matter for judgment whether you think that my worldview is overall more theoretically virtuous than Kenny's worldview. That is, I think that this is a matter on which reasonable people can reasonably agree to disagree.

Although it may not be visible in the final product, there is a lot of interaction—between Kenny, Tyron Goldschmidt, and me—that lies behind the finished work. In particular, there was very extensive sharing of comments on most of the drafted material. Whatever I end up thinking about the quality of my own contribution, I get to feel good—at least in some measure—about the quality of Kenny's contribution. I think his parts of the book are great. Of course, I disagree with what he says. But, as Kenny says elsewhere in this discussion, philosophers disagree about almost everything. Kenny writes and argues with admirable skill, flair, and passion. It has been a pleasure to work on this book with him.

> A parting note for readers of this book. Thanks for coming! I hope that you have found what you were looking for when you picked up this book. Failing that, I hope that you are nonetheless satisfied with what you have found here. If you are motivated to read further into philosophy of religion, then I am certainly satisfied with the outcome.

Further Readings

Suggested Readings (Kenny Pearce)

The most important historical influence on the version of classical theism I discuss is G. W. Leibniz, *Theodicy: Essays on the Goodness of God, the Freedom of Man, and the Origin of Evil*. An open access e-text of the Austin Farrer translation, which is the same translation normally used by scholars, is available from Project Gutenberg: www.gutenberg.org/ebooks/17147.

For an overview of the classical theistic way of thinking about God and creation in Judaism, Christianity, and Islam, see David B. Burrell, *Freedom and Creation in Three Traditions* (University of Notre Dame Press, 1993).

For a defense of classical theism as a religiously adequate conception of God, see Eleonore Stump, *The God of the Bible and the God of the Philosophers* (Marquette University Press, 2016).

A good general resource for ways of thinking about God and religion in recent philosophy is Thomas P. Flint and Michael Rea, eds., *The Oxford Handbook of Philosophical Theology* (Oxford University Press, 2009).

I have previously defended my version of the cosmological argument in Kenneth L. Pearce, "Foundational Grounding and the Argument From Contingency" (*Oxford Studies in Philosophy of Religion*, 2017).

Another influential defense of the cosmological argument from contingency in recent philosophy is Timothy O'Connor, *Theism and Ultimate Explanation: The Necessary Shape of Contingency* (Blackwell, 2008). The argument is debated extensively in Tyron Goldschmidt, ed., *The Puzzle of Existence: Why Is There Something Rather Than Nothing?* (Routledge, 2013).

The contemporary discussion of grounding was kicked off by Kit Fine, "Essence and Modality" (*Philosophical Perspectives*, 1994). The concept was then debated extensively in a number of the essays in David J. Chalmers, David Manley, and Ryan Wasserman, eds., *Metametaphysics: New Essays on the Foundations of Ontology* (Oxford University Press, 2009).

Much of the literature on material constitution addresses similar questions. See especially Lynne Rudder Baker, *The Metaphysics of Everyday Life: An Essay in Practical Realism* (Cambridge University Press, 2009).

For a detailed treatment of religious experience, see William P. Alston, *Perceiving God: The Epistemology of Religious Experience* (Cornell University Press, 1991).

On related issues about trust and epistemology, see Linda Trinkaus Zagzebski, *Epistemic Authority: A Theory of Trust, Authority, and Autonomy in Belief* (Oxford University Press, 2012).

On related issues in the cognitive science of religion, see Helen De Cruz and Johan De Smedt, *A Natural History of Natural Theology: The Cognitive Science of Theology and Philosophy of Religion* (MIT Press, 2015). De Cruz and De Smedt focus on the cognitive science of arguments for the existence of God, but these arguments are in effect ways of interpreting our experience, especially since much of the reasoning here is implicit.

Suggested Readings (Graham Oppy)

I included a list of references to expressions of competing views at the end of almost every section in my initial contribution to this work. The following annotated reading list largely does not duplicate those references, and is intended as a guide to the more important issues that have been taken up in the course of our discussion.

1. *Naturalism*. A good starting point is D. Papineau, 'Naturalism', *Stanford Encyclopedia of Philosophy* (2020), https://plato.stanford.edu/entries/naturalism/. The bibliography for this article is extensive, and the links to other entries in SEP are well worth following.
2. *Worldviews*. Many philosophers eschew talk of 'worldviews', 'theories of everything', and the like. For an older view that has many similarities to the kind of view that I am defending, it is worth reading W. Quine and J. Ullian, J., *The Web of Belief* (McGraw-Hill 1978).

3. *Arguments*. My views about arguments are completely heterodox. As good a place as any to get a sense of the kind of views that I am reacting against is L. Groarke, 'Informal Logic', *Stanford Encyclopedia of Philosophy* (2017), https://plato.stanford.edu/entries/logic-informal/. D. Manley, *Reason Better* (2019), https://tophat.com/marketplace/ is, in general, a better approach to critical thinking but, by my lights, still too conservative in its approach to arguments.
4. *Reidian Epistemology*. Reid's *Essays on the Intellectual Powers of Man* (1985) is well worth a visit. Here, Reid identifies many 'First Principles' that are marked by (a) the absurdity of their denial, (b) the consent of ages and nations, and (c) independence from education and acculturation. I think that Reid is right to take these to be marks of 'First Principles', but wrong to think that the claim that God exists bears these marks or can be inferred from other principles that bear these marks.
5. *Theoretical Virtues*. The most popular current accounts of theory assessment are Bayesian. A slightly dated introduction to the field can be found in W. Talbott, 'Bayesian Epistemology', *Stanford Encyclopedia of Philosophy* (2008), https://plato.stanford.edu/entries/epistemology-bayesian/.
6. *Religious Experience*. W. James, *The Varieties of Religious Experience*, edited by M. Bradley (Oxford University Press 2012/1902) is useful background to any discussion of religious experience. On the assessment of value of religious experience, I recommend T. Smith, *The Methods of Science and Religion* (Rowman & Littlefield 2019).
7. *Existence of God*. Although it is now a bit dated, I think that J. Mackie, *The Miracle of Theism* (Clarendon 1982) remains the best comprehensive discussion of arguments about the existence of God. A more recent text that might prove useful is J. Koterski and G. Oppy, G., eds., *Theism and Atheism: Opposing Arguments in Philosophy* (Gale 2019).
8. *Philosophy of Religion*. For those looking for a good historical introduction to philosophy of religion, I would like to put in a good word for G. Oppy and N. Trakakis, eds., *The History of Western Philosophy of Religion*, five vols (Acumen). And, if you are looking for an introduction to atheism, then you might try G. Oppy, ed., *A Companion to Atheism and Philosophy* (Wiley-Blackwell 2019).

Glossary

The glossary is compiled by the authors. Where they give different definitions, each is listed with the author's initials. Words or phrases that are defined elsewhere in the glossary are marked with a *.

Abrahamic Religious Traditions Monotheistic religions* that trace their origin to Abraham, who is traditionally thought to have been born in central Asia around 1800 BCE. The largest Abrahamic religions are Judaism, Christianity, and Islam. Other Abrahamic religions include Druzism, Mandaeism, Rastafari, Samaritanism, and, if it is not counted as part of Islam, Bahá'í.

Abstract Object Non-causal objects that exist outside of space-time. If there are numbers, then, plausibly, they are abstract objects. It is philosophically contentious whether there are abstract objects.

Actual The way things are, as opposed to the ways that thing could have been, and the ways that things could not have been.

Actualism The thesis that the actual world is everything that is or everything that is real. According to actualism, there are no non-actual things; for example, there are no merely possible things and there are no impossible things. Actualism is a very contentious philosophical claim.

Agnostic Someone who has suspended judgment* about a certain claim. For instance (most relevant to the present debate), an agnostic about God* suspends judgment about whether God exists, and therefore is neither a theist* nor an atheist*.

Agnostic, Ideal *see* Ideal Agnostic

Agnosticism The position adopted by an agnostic. It is possible to be agnostic about any claim, though in the context of the present debate we usually refer to agnosticism about the existence of God* or gods*. Agnosticism about one claim will usually go together with agnosticism about other related claims.

Alethic. Concerned with truth.

Alethic Modalities are modalities whose primary concern is with truth. They contrast with epistemic, deontic, and temporal modalities. Alethic modalities include physical, metaphysical, and logical modalities. See also Contingency*; Modality*; Necessity*; Possibility*.

Analogy In ordinary language, an analogy is a comparison between one thing and another for explanatory or evaluative purposes. An analogical argument cites observed similarities between two things to support the conclusion that some further similarity exists. In classical theism*, analogy is the application of words or concepts in new contexts in a way that changes their meaning. For instance, calling God 'wise' (a word that originally applied to humans) is often thought to involve analogy. See also Use of Language, Analogical.

Analysis In ordinary language, an analysis is a process of working back to what is more fundamental by means of which something, initially taken as given, can be explained or reconstructed. In philosophy, to give an analysis of a concept* is to define the concept, that is, to provide necessary and sufficient conditions for falling under the concept.

Analytic An analytic sentence is one whose truth can be *known* merely by knowing the meanings of the constituent terms and the way that they are combined in the sentence. A standard example of an analytic truth is: *All bachelors are unmarried men*.

A Posteriori A claim is knowable only *a posteriori* if it is knowable only on the basis of experience, and, in particular, if belief in it is justifiable only on the basis of experience. The claim that, at the time of writing, Donald Trump is president of the United States is knowable only *a posteriori*.

A Priori A claim is knowable *a priori* if it is knowable independently of experience, and, in particular, if it is justifiable independent of experience. Standard examples of claims knowable *a priori* include the claims of logic* and mathematics.

Argument In its everyday sense, an argument is a disagreement in attitudes. In its standard philosophical sense, an argument is a bunch of claims, one of which is identified as the conclusion*, and the rest of which are identified as premises*. When people give or endorse an argument, they suppose that the conclusion is properly supported by the premises.

Argument, Good In one sense, an argument is good if and only if it is sound*. From the standpoint of any consistent* theory, there are countless arguments that are deemed good, in this sense, by the lights of the theory. In a different sense, an argument is good if and only if it is a successful reductio*, or, more generally, it draws attention to unnoticed consequences of a worldview*. [G.O.]

An argument is good if and only if it exposes a genuine tension* in one or more worldviews actually held by some members of the audience to which it is presented, and at least some members of the audience would be rational* to respond to that tension by endorsing the conclusion*. [K.P.]

Argument, Invalid An argument is invalid just in case it is not valid*. While we can use logical derivation* to prove that an ordinary language argument is valid, there is no general method for proving that an ordinary language argument is invalid.

Argument, Sound An argument is sound if and only if it is valid* and all of its premises* are true. It follows from the definition of a valid argument that the conclusion of a sound argument will also be true.

Argument, Successful Successful arguments draw the attention of the targets of those arguments to hitherto unnoticed consequences of their worldviews*. [G.O.]

Ordinarily, an argument is successful if and only if it brings the audience to accept the conclusion, and to do so rationally. In the case of a reductio*, an argument is successful if and only if it brings the audience to reject one of the premises*, and to do so rationally*. [K.P.]

Argument, Valid An argument* is valid if and only if the conclusion* is a logical consequence* of the premises*.

Atemporality Timelessness. Atemporal things do not belong to our temporal order. Many classical theists* believe that God* is atemporal.

Atheism The claim that there are no gods* and there is no God*. An atheistic worldview* is a consistent worldview that has, as a logical consequence, the claim that there are no gods and there is no God. Graham defends such a worldview.

Authentic Religious Experience   *see* Religious Experience, Authentic
Autonomous Fact   If it makes sense to talk about facts standing in need of explanation*, then autonomous facts are facts that stand in no need of explanation. Real definitions* are plausible candidates to be autonomous facts, if there are autonomous facts.
Autonomy   In ordinary language, autonomy is something like self-government. In Kantian philosophy, autonomy is the capacity to deliberate and to give oneself the moral law, rather than merely heeding the injunctions of others, or failing to abide by the moral law.
Axiom   In ordinary language, an axiom is a fundamental principle. Given a consistent theory*, an axiomatisation of the theory is a minimal set of claims that has all of the claims in the theory as logical consequences.
Background Theory   If a theory* is part of a worldview*, then the background theory is everything else in the worldview that is relevant to the theory, except for the parts of the worldview that are deemed to be data*. [G.O.]

A background theory is a set of assumptions used to interpret experience. For instance, when interpreting visual experience it is normally part of our background theory that visual experience is produced by light reflected from external physical objects. [K.P.]
Bayesianism   An interpretation of probability as reasonable expectation. The core of Bayesian approaches—whether to epistemology, or statistics, or something else—is the use of Bayes' Theorem*.
Bayes' Theorem   The odds version of Bayes' Theorem says that the ratio of the posterior probabilities of competing hypotheses (H1, H2) on given evidence (E) is equal to the product of the ratio of the prior probabilities of the competing hypotheses and the ratio of the likelihoods of the evidence on the competing hypotheses. In more formal notation:

$$\frac{Pr(H1 \mid E)}{Pr(H2 \mid E)} = \frac{Pr(H1)}{Pr(H2)} \cdot \frac{Pr(E \mid H1)}{Pr(E \mid H2)}$$

Black-and-White Room   A thought experiment intended to show that the physical facts do not determine the psychological facts. According to proponents of the thought experiment, someone whose experience thus far has been black and white could know all of the physical facts and yet learn something when they first see red. See Jackson (1982) for the original presentation of this thought experiment.

Blockhead A thought experiment intended to show that functionalism* is not the correct theory of mind. According to proponents of the thought experiment, a being that operates by look-up table may be functionally equivalent to you, but it does not have any intelligence. See Block (1981) for the original presentation of this thought experiment.

Brain in a Vat An imaginary being who has no sense organs and is instead attached to a computer simulation with direct stimulation of its nerve endings by electrodes. See Putnam (1981) for an influential early discussion. A similar idea was famously explored in the 1999 film *The Matrix*. *See also* Scepticism, External World.

Brute Fact A brute claim in a theory is a claim that has no explanation* in that theory. A brute fact is a true claim that actually has no explanation. Real definitions*—necessary claims that are only knowable *a posteriori*—are plausible candidates to be brute facts. [G.O.]

A brute fact is a fact that stands in need of explanation* and yet has no explanation. *See also* Autonomous Fact. [K.P.]

Brute Necessity The view that no fact of the form 'necessarily, p' has an explanation.

Canonical Notation A formal or semi-formal language that makes visible in the surface syntax all of the ontological commitments* of theories* couched in that language. Ideal expressions of worldviews* are couched in canonical notation.

Cardinality The cardinality of a set is the number of elements in the set.

Cardinality, Infinite *see* Infinite Cardinality

Causal Compatibilism *see* Compatibilism, Causal

Causal Determinism *see* Determinism, Causal

Causal Explanation *see* Explanation, Causal

Causal Reality Roughly, causal reality is the entire network of causes and effects to which we are related, and everything that is directly involved in that network of causes and effects. It is controversial exactly what causes and effects relate: objects, events, facts, states, and so forth. But we should think of all of these kinds of things—and perhaps more besides—as belonging to causal reality, if we think that there are these kinds of things.

Chance, Objective *see* Objective Chance

China Brain The China Brain is a thought experiment that is intended to establish the falsity of functionalist* accounts of mind. The thought experiment asks you whether, if the functioning of your mind were simulated by the population of a very large country, the entity doing the simulation would be conscious. See Block (1978) for a detailed presentation of this thought experiment.

Chinese Room The Chinese Room is a thought experiment that is intended to establish the falsity of digital computational accounts of mind. The thought experiment asks you whether, if your mind were simulated by digital computation, there would be any understanding going on anywhere in that simulation. See Searle (1980) for the original presentation of this thought experiment.

Classical Foundationalism According to foundationalism, all justified belief rests on justified beliefs that have not been inferred from other justified beliefs. According to classical foundationalism, the foundational beliefs are 'self-evident' or, perhaps, 'evident to the senses'. (For Descartes, the foundational beliefs are merely those that are 'self-evident'.)

Classical Theism *see* Theism, Classical

Cognitive Science of Religion The study of religious thought and behaviour from the standpoint of the cognitive sciences, including cognitive anthropology, cognitive linguistics, and neuroscience.

Coherence Coherence is, roughly, the quality of forming a unified whole. If a thing is coherent, then its parts fit well together. In the case of theories, the minimum standard of coherence is logical consistency*. [K.P.]

Commitment (of a Worldview) Worldview* commitments are of three kinds: ideological*, ontological*, and theoretical*. Primitive* commitments of worldviews are the costs that they pay in order to provide the explanations* that they provide.

Commitment, Ideological Ideological commitments of a worldview* are concepts* required to give expression to the worldview. Primitive* ideological commitments are concepts that are not explicitly defined in terms of other concepts that are required to give expression to the worldview.

Commitment, Ontological Ontological commitments of a worldview* are the members of the domain of quantification* of the ontologically committing quantifiers* used in order to give expression to the worldview. Primitive* ontological commitments of a worldview are, roughly, members of the domain of quantification of the ontologically committing quantifiers used in order to give expression to the axioms* that figure in the best axiomatisation* of the worldview. [G.O.]

The ontological commitments of a worldview are the things that exist according to that worldview. The primitive ontological commitments of a worldview are the things that, according to the worldview, exist and are not grounded* in anything more fundamental*. [K.P.]

Commitment, Primitive The primitive commitments of a worldview* are those commitments that count as costs to the simplicity* of a worldview. It is controversial what makes a commitment primitive.

Commitment, Theoretical Theoretical commitments of a worldview* are the claims that are required to give expression to the worldview. Primitive* theoretical commitments of a worldview are, roughly, the claims required to give expression of the axioms that figure in the best axiomatisation of the worldview. [G.O.]

The theoretical commitments of a worldview* are the claims that are true according to that worldview. The primitive* theoretical commitments of a worldview are those theoretical commitments that, according to the worldview, have no explanation*. That is, primitive theoretical commitments are either brute facts* or autonomous facts*, according to the worldview. [K.P.]

Compatibilism, Causal Causal compatibilism is the claim that free will and causal determinism* are logically consistent*. According to many compatibilists, you act freely when you act on your normally acquired beliefs, desires, and intentions, even if those beliefs, desires, and intentions lead to the action deterministically*. Graham endorses a version of this view.

Compatibilism, Theological Theological compatibilism is the claim that creaturely free will and theological determinism* are logically consistent. That is, according to theological compatibilism, you can still be free even if God* determines all of your choices and actions. For instance, a theological compatibilist might hold that you are free when your actions follow from your character, beliefs, values, and desires, even though all of these are created by God.

Composition Composition is a mereological* (part/whole) relation. If the As compose B, then the As are parts of B. If the

As entirely compose B, then B is a whole composed of the As. Think about a model boat built from pieces of Lego. The basic Lego blocks are parts of the boat, and the boat is wholly composed of the basic Lego blocks.

Concept Concepts are the building blocks of thoughts. Philosophers disagree about what concepts are. Some take them to be mental—or linguistic—representations; some take them to be abilities; and some take them to be abstract objects*. If you understand a word like 'square', then you have a concept of a square.

Conceptual Truth Conceptual truths are truths that require nothing more than grasp of the concepts required for their expression in order for subjects to be positioned to recognise their truth. If there are analytic truths*, then analytic truths are conceptual truths. If there are conceptual truths, then they are knowable *a priori**.

Conclusion In ordinary language, a conclusion is a decision or judgment reached by reasoning. In philosophy, a conclusion is simply a part of an argument*. A necessary condition for an argument to be a good argument* is that the conclusion of the argument is a consequence* of the premises* (the remaining parts) of the argument.

Consequence *see* Logical Consequence

Consequentialism The view that the rightness or wrongness of an action is determined entirely by the goodness or badness of its consequences. *See also* Deontologism*; Virtue Ethics*.

Consilience Consilience—also sometimes called 'convergence of evidence' or 'concordance of evidence'—is the linking together of apparently independent sources to support a given claim.

Consistency A set of claims is logically consistent if and only if those claims do not have an absurdity (in classical logic, a contradiction*) among their logical consequences*. A set of claims is logically inconsistent if and only if those claims do have an absurdity among their logical consequences.

Constitution Constitution is a relation between things and stuff. Things can be constituted of stuff, and stuff can be constituted of things. For example, in the case of a clay statue, the thing is the statue, and the stuff is the clay from which it is constituted; and in the case of clay, while clay is stuff, the molecules from which it is constituted are things. It is controversial whether there are also constitution relations between events*, actions, and so on. Constitution is sometimes thought to be a kind of grounding* relation.

Contingency A contingency is something that obtains but that might not have obtained. So, for example, a contingent event is an event that happens but that might not have happened; and a contingent object is an object that exists but that might not have existed. More carefully: if it is contingent whether A, then it is possible* that A and it is possible that not A. *See also* Necessity.

Contradiction An explicit contradiction is a claim of the form *A and not A*. A set of claims is contradictory if an explicit contradiction is among their logical consequences*. The following set of claims is contradictory: {*Steve is my friend. All my friends are good people. Steve is an atheist. No atheist is a good person*}.

Contrastive Explanation *see* Explanation, Contrastive

Cosmological Arguments Cosmological arguments are arguments for the existence of God* that appeal only to logical principles and principles concerning very general structural features of the world—for example, that there is a causal order, or a temporal order, or a modal order, or a compositional order, or the like. There are famous cosmological arguments due to Aquinas and Leibniz. Kenny defends a cosmological argument.

Credence Very roughly, credences are degrees of belief. The higher the credence that you give to a claim, the more strongly you believe it. Philosophers often suppose that they can represent credences as probabilities. With respect to any claim, credence zero is the strongest possible degree of disbelief; credence one is the strongest possible degree of belief, and credence ½ is perfect suspension of judgment.

(CT) Kenny's central thesis, the claim that spacetime and all of its contents exist because of the free and rational choice of a necessary being.

Data *see* Evidence

Definition, Nominal A nominal definition of a thing or kind of thing is an accurate account of our ordinary concept* of that thing or kind of thing. For example, a nominal definition of water might be something like this: the stuff that, on our planet, falls from the sky, fills the lakes and rivers, and is necessary for the continuation of all larger life forms.

Definition, Real A real definition of a thing, or a kind of thing, is framed in terms of the essential properties* of that thing: the intrinsic properties* that the thing or kind of thing cannot exist without. Part of the real definition of water is that it is two parts hydrogen to one part oxygen.

Deontologism The view that the rightness or wrongness of an action is determined by its conformity, or lack of conformity, to moral norms and that no consideration need be given to the goodness or badness of the consequences of the action. *See also* Consequentialism*; Virtue Ethics*.

Derivation A derivation is a series of appropriately justified steps that moves from the premises* of an argument* to its conclusion*. Very roughly, if each of the steps correctly involves taking logical consequence*, then the derivation shows that the conclusion of the argument is a logical consequence of the premises.

Determinable/Determinate The determinable/determinate relation is a specification relation among properties*. Example: colour is a determinable that has specific shades of colour (red, green, blue, etc.) as determinates; and red is a determinable that has specific shades of red (crimson, scarlet, vermilion, etc.) as determinates.

Determination A determines B if and only if necessarily* if A then B. If causation is deterministic, then, if A causes B, then necessarily, if A then B. If micro-structure determines macro-structure, then, if A is the micro-structure of B, then necessarily if A then B.

Determinism, Causal If the world is causally deterministic, then, if there was an initial state of the world, then the current state of the world is a necessary consequence of the initial state of the world. If the world is causally deterministic, then, if we were to wind back history to the initial state and let it roll again, it would unfold in exactly the same way that it did the first time around.

Determinism, Theological Theological determinism is the view that God* decides every detail of the created world, including all of our choices and actions.

Dilemma In ordinary language, a dilemma is a difficult choice between options. Typically, in philosophy, a dilemma is taken to be a difficult choice between two undesirable claims. An example given in our text is the Euthyphro Dilemma*.

Divine Having to do with God* or the gods*.
Domain of Quantification The collection of objects over which a quantifier* ranges.
Doxastic Possibility *see* Possibility, Doxastic
Doxastic Practice Doxastic practices are socially established ways of forming and evaluating beliefs given cognitive and perceptual inputs. Typically, those interested in doxastic practices suppose that different communities across space and time have different—and perhaps widely different—doxastic practices. A doxastic practice is part of a form of life*.
Einstein's Field Equations The basic equations of General Relativity*, which describe how the curvature of spacetime in a region is related to the density of mass-energy in that region.
Embrace One Horn To respond to a (supposed) dilemma* by accepting one of the two (supposedly bad) options.
Epistemic Possibility *see* Possibility, Epistemic
Epistemology The part of philosophy dealing with knowledge and rational belief.
Equivocation The use of the same word with two different meanings. For instance, 'bat' (flying mammal) and 'bat' (sporting equipment), or 'bank' (financial institution) and 'bank' (the side of a river). *See also* Use of Language, Equivocal.
Essential Property A thing has a property essentially if and only if, necessarily*, if the thing exists, it has that property intrinsically*. For example, water is essentially two parts hydrogen to one part oxygen: it is impossible for there to be water that is not intrinsically two parts hydrogen to one part oxygen.
Euthyphro Dilemma The following question, which poses difficulties for many varieties of theism*: are right actions right because God* commands them, or does God command them because they are right?
Events Events are things that happen: births, deaths, marriages, trials, tribulations, triumphs, and so forth. Many events involve changes in the properties* of things. Many events are temporally extended: they unfold over a period of time.
Evidence is typically thought of as that which justifies belief, serves as a guide to truth, is respected by rational thinkers, and serves as a neutral arbiter on contested questions. In the context of assessment of worldviews, Graham thinks of evidence, or data, as that which is agreed between the worldviews under assessment.

Evil In philosophy of religion, evil is understood very broadly to include any kind of badness or imperfection in the world.

Evil, Horrendous Marilyn Adams (2000, 26) influentially defined 'horrendous evils' as (roughly) evils that give people involved in them reason to doubt whether their lives are worth living. Horrendous evils are thought, by Adams and others, to pose particularly difficult problems for theism.

Excluded Middle The principle that every claim is either true or false.

Existentialism The view that everything there is exists. The philosopher Alexius Meinong (1853–1920) famously argued that there are non-existent objects (centaurs, for instance) among the things that don't exist. Existentialism denies this Meinongian view and instead holds that there are no centaurs and, more generally, there are no non-existent objects. Graham endorses this view. This view is unrelated to the existentialist school of philosophy famously represented by Jean-Paul Sartre.

Explanation An answer to a 'why?' question.

Explanation, Causal An answer to a 'why?' question that is framed in terms of causes. Example: Why did the glass break? I accidentally knocked it from the table with my arm. Note that some philosophers have a much broader conception of causes than others. We are not here thinking about what Aristotle called 'material', 'formal', and 'final' causes; we are here thinking about something in the ballpark of what Aristotle called 'efficient' causes.

Explanation, Contrastive An answer to a question of, roughly, the form 'why did x issue in A rather than B?' For instance, 'why did Ciara choose chocolate rather than vanilla ice cream?'

Explanation, Necessitating A necessitating explanation explains something in a way that shows that it had to be true.

Explanatory Comprehensiveness A worldview* is more explanatorily comprehensive to the extent that it includes explanations of more things. In comparing two worldviews for explanatory comprehensiveness, we only compare their explanations of the agreed-upon evidence*, that is, the claims that both worldviews take to be true.

Expressive Power Roughly, the expressive power of a language is measured by the range of claims that can be expressed in that language. Adding new ideological primitives* to a language increases the expressive power of that language. *See also* Commitment, Ideological.

External World Scepticism   *see* Scepticism, External World

Facts   Plausibly, it is a fact that p if and only if p. Some philosophers say that we should not include facts in our ontological inventory. Other philosophers say, variously, that facts are true truth-bearers, or obtaining states of affairs, or *sui generis* entities that involve objects and properties.

Faculties (of the Mind)   The mind's basic abilities for getting at the truth. Human faculties include our senses (sight, hearing, touch, taste, smell, etc.) memory, introspection, and reasoning.

Faith   Roughly, faith in God* includes some of the following: belief that God exists; belief in, or trust in, God; a feeling of existential optimism that rests in belief in God; claims to knowledge of particular revealed truths; practical commitment beyond one's evidence that God exists; and hope that one will be saved by God. It is controversial whether faith can be rational, and it is also controversial whether faith must involve belief. Some philosophers think that some of the other attitudes mentioned (e.g. trust, practical commitment, or hope) could be sufficient for faith even in the absence of belief.

Family Resemblance   According to Wittgenstein, uses of words are connected merely by 'family resemblance': a 'complicated network of similarities overlapping and criss-crossing' that cannot be expressed as a bunch of necessary and sufficient conditions.

Figuralism   According to a figuralist account of discourse that quantifies over Xs, the Xs function as representational aids in figurative descriptions of something else, the Ys, where the Ys may themselves by representational aids in figurative description of something else, the Zs, where.... Graham would like to be a figuralist about all discourse that quantifies over abstract objects.

Fine-Tuning   The mathematical equations in our best current physical theories contain certain basic constants (numbers). If these numbers were ever so slightly different, life would be impossible in our universe. The fact that these numbers need these very precise values is called 'fine-tuning'. Physicists agree that our *current* best theories contain fine-tuned constants, but many physicists hope that we might ultimately arrive at a theory that does not require fine-tuning. Some philosophers think that fine-tuning is best explained by supposing that God* chose the values of the constants. Both authors reject this argument.

Form of Life According to Wittgenstein, a language is a form of life. What this means, roughly, is that a language is not just a way of representing objective facts about the world. Instead, it provides a way of engaging with our world and our community not just intellectually but also practically, emotionally, and so on.

Foundationalism *see* Classical Foundationalism

Four-Dimensionalism The view that spacetime is an integrated whole and physical objects are extended in time as well as in the three spatial dimensions. According to this view, times that are not present are just as real as places that are not here. According to the four-dimensionalist, (living) dinosaurs really exist, but all of them are *located* in the past. Both authors endorse this view.

Functionalism The view that mental states, such as belief and desire, can be analyzed in terms of the functional role they play in the life of an entity.

Fundamentality According to many philosophers, some objects or properties or facts are *built up out of* others. The ones that do the building are said to be more fundamental; the ones that are built are said to be less fundamental. *See also* Grounding.

General Relativity A physical theory of space, time, and gravitation, based on Einstein's Field Equations*.

Generalised Continuum Hypothesis The generalised continuum hypothesis says, *if the cardinality* of an infinite* set I lies between the cardinality of an infinite set S and the cardinality of the power set* of S, then the cardinality of I is either the cardinality of S or the cardinality of the power set of S*. Set theory* can be consistently developed with the generalised continuum hypothesis and with the denial of the generalised continuum hypothesis. The continuum hypothesis says that the cardinality of the power set of the natural numbers is the cardinality of the real numbers.

God Roughly, God is the one and only god. [G.O.]

God-identifying description A description that, necessarily, is satisfied only by God.

Gods Roughly, gods are supernatural beings that have and exercise power over the natural world but that are not under the power of other categories of beings. [G.O.]

Goldbach's Conjecture The conjecture, in number theory, that every even number greater than two is expressible as the sum of two prime numbers. The conjecture has so far been shown to hold for all integers less than 4×10^{18}.

Grounding The relation, or family of relations, whereby more fundamental* things give rise to less fundamental things. Composition*, constitution*, determination*, and realisation* have all been regarded as varieties of grounding by at least some philosophers. It is controversial whether there is one grounding relation (sometimes called 'big "G" Grounding') or many different grounding relations (sometimes called 'little "g" grounding'). Some philosophers do not believe in grounding at all.

Hope To a first approximation, to hope that something is true is to wish that it is true while holding that there is some probability greater than zero that it is true. How to make this account more accurate is currently philosophically controversial.

Horrendous Evil *see* Evil, Horrendous

Hume's Principle Hume's Principles says that the number of Fs is equal to the number of Gs if and only if there is a one-to-one correspondence between the Fs and the Gs.

Ideal Agnostic According to Peter van Inwagen's (2006, 44–47) definition, an ideal agnostic with respect to some claim has (1) no initial opinion about whether the claim is true; (2) no predilection, emotional or otherwise, to accept or reject the claim; (3) a strong desire to know whether the claim is true; and (4) unlimited leisure, superhuman patience, and the highest possible intelligence and degree of logical and philosophical acumen. *See also* Agnostic.

Ideological Commitment *see* Commitment, Ideological

Ideological Simplicity *see* Simplicity, Ideological

Immutability To be immutable is to be not subject or susceptible to change or variation in form or quality or nature. Some classical theists* take immutability to be one of the divine* attributes.

Impassibility To be impassible is to be unable to suffer or experience emotions. Some classical theists* take impassibility to be one of the divine* attributes.

Indeterminism A system is indeterministic just in case it is not deterministic*. If a process is indeterministic, then, prior to the completion of the process, there are at least two different ways in which it is possible for the process to terminate. *See also* Objective Chance.

Infinite Cardinality The cardinality* of a set is infinite if it is greater than or equal to the cardinality of the set of natural numbers, that is, the set {1, 2, 3, . . . }.

Innocent To be innocent with respect to a claim is to have never so much as entertained the claim. Innocence is different from all of belief, disbelief, and suspension of judgment*. It is often forgotten that, at least historically, there were lots of innocents with respect to the claim that God* exists.

Instantiation In metaphysics, those who commit themselves to the existence of properties* often claim that there is a relation of instantiation that holds between objects* and properties. If 'a is F' is true, where 'a' denotes an object, and '. . . is F' expresses a property, then, on this line of thought, the object instantiates the property in question.

Intentionality Roughly, intentionality is the ability of mental states and linguistic expressions to be about, to represent, or to stand for, things (objects, events*, states of affairs, etc.).

Intrinsic Property Roughly, a thing has a certain property* intrinsically just in case whether the thing has the property is just a matter of how that thing is in itself, and not even partly a matter of how other things are related to it. For example, that a thing has certain parts is an intrinsic property of that thing.

Invalidity *see* Argument, Invalid

Irreflexivity A relation is irreflexive just in case it does not relate any element to itself. Familiar examples of relations that are irreflexive include being taller than and being older than. Quite generally, any relation of the form *being F'er than* is irreflexive.

Judgment, Suspension of *see* Suspension of Judgment

Law of Excluded Middle *see* Excluded Middle

Logic Logic is the study of the logical consequence* relation. Different logics study the logical behaviour of different groups of logical terms. For example, propositional logics study logical terms like: *not, and, or,* and *if . . . then*; predicate logics study, in addition, logical terms like *all* and *some* (*see* Quantifier); and modal logics study, in addition, logical terms like *must, might, should*, and *can* (*see* Modal Operator).

Logical Consequence A is a logical consequence of B just in case there is a logically correct derivation* of A from B.

Logical Necessity *see* Necessity, Logical

Logical Possibility *see* Possibility, Logical

Maxim In general, a maxim is a concise expression of a fundamental moral rule or principle. In Kant's philosophy, when I act for a reason, the maxim of my action is the practical judgment* that drives it. According to Kant, we act wrongly when our maxim is inconsistent, that is, when we do not think that our maxim expresses what it would be right for everyone to do in the kinds of circumstances that we are in.

Mereology is the general (formal, abstract) theory of part/whole relations. Mereological relations are part/whole relations.

Metaphor A metaphor is a particular kind of figurative use of words in which we speak of one thing as and in terms of a second thing. Examples: 'Steve is a rock'; 'Love is a rose'; 'Golden retrievers are vacuum cleaners'.

Metaphysical Necessity *see* Necessity, Metaphysical

Metaphysical Possibility *see* Possibility, Metaphysical

Metaphysics Any definition of 'metaphysics' is controversial. Very roughly, metaphysics seeks a certain kind of very general account of what there is and what it is like. Categories for discussion in metaphysics include objects*, properties*, states, laws, propositions, necessities*, causes, space, values, and meanings.

Minded entities are entities possessing mindedness.

Mindedness To be minded is to have certain kinds of dispositions, abilities, states, and so forth. Minded things typically have a range of the following attributes: consciousness, agency, perception, belief, desire, intention, memory, empathy, and so forth.

Miracle Very roughly, miracles are events in the natural world that have some special connection to God* that most events in the natural world do not have. Different philosophers give different spellings out of the nature of this special connection. *See also* Special Divine Action.

Modalised Claim A modalised expression is one in which all other parts of the expression—except, perhaps, for sentential logical connectives—fall within the scope of modal operators. 'It must be that $2 + 2 = 4$' is modalised. 'It must be that $2 + 2 = 4$ and it is possible that cows eat grass' is modalised. 'Cows eat grass and it must be that $2 + 2 = 4$' is not modalised.

Modality Metaphysical modalities categorise different ways or modes of being. Very roughly: some things must be (i.e. they are of necessity*); some things are but need not be (i.e. they are contingently*); some things are not but could be (i.e. they contingently are not); and some things cannot be (i.e. they necessarily are not). Things that contingently are not could be (i.e. it is possible* for them to be). Things that contingently are could fail to be (i.e. it is possible for them not to be). See also Necessity.

Modal Ontological Argument An argument that is suitably similar to the following argument: *(1) It is possible that God exists. (2) Necessarily, if God exists, then it is necessary that God exists. (3) (Therefore) God exists.* In general, modal ontological arguments move from a premise concerning the possibility* of God's existence to the conclusion that God* does exist.

Modal Operator Modal operators are expressions like 'it must be that', 'it could be that', 'it should be that', 'it might be that', and so on. Modal logic is the study of the logical behaviour of modal operators.

Moderately Successful An argument is moderately successful if and only if, upon considering the argument, some members of the audience are rationally obligated to endorse the conclusion. See also Argument, Successful.

Monism *see* Priority Monism

Monotheism Monotheism is the claim that there is exactly one god*: God*.

Monotheistic Religion *see* Religion, Monotheistic

Monotheistic Religious Belief *see* Monotheism; Religion, Monotheistic; Religious Belief; Religious Experience, Monotheistic (MRE).

Monotheistic Religious Experience *see* Religious Experience, Monotheistic (MRE)

MRE *see* Religious Experience, Monotheistic (MRE)

Naturalism Very roughly, naturalism is the claim that natural reality exhausts causal reality: among the causal beings, there are none but natural beings; and among the causal properties of the causal beings, there are none but natural properties; and there is nothing beyond natural reality upon which natural reality in any way depends.

Natural Reality According to naturalists, natural reality is the entirety of causal reality; according to classical theists*, natural reality is, roughly, God's* creation. Either way, near enough, natural reality is our universe, or, if there are many universes, the ensemble of universes.

Necessary A Posteriori A claim is necessary* *a posteriori** if it is both necessary and knowable only *a posteriori*. An example of a claim that is both necessary and knowable only *a posteriori* is that water is two parts hydrogen to one part oxygen. An example of a claim that is contingent* and knowable only *a posteriori* is that there is a major pandemic that is raging as I draft these words.

Necessary A Priori A claim is necessary* *a priori** if it is both necessary and knowable *a priori*. An example of a claim that is both necessary and knowable *a priori* is that 2 + 2 = 4. An example of a claim that is contingent* and knowable *a priori* by me is that I exist.

Necessary Being In the language of possible worlds*, a necessary being is a being that exists in every possible world. That is, a necessary being is a being for which the following is true: it must be that it did exist, or that it does exist, or that it will exist. Some philosophers restrict the notion of a necessary being to beings for which something more like the following is true: it must be that it has always existed, and that it exists, and that it will always exist.

Necessitating Explanation *see* Explanation, Necessitating

Necessity In general, a necessary claim is a claim that could not have been otherwise. According to context, a claim that something is necessary may be a claim that it is logically necessary, or that it is metaphysically necessary, or that it is physically necessary, or that it is epistemically necessary, or that it is doxastically necessary, or perhaps that it has some other kind of necessity. It is not always clear from context that these different kinds of necessities are being distinguished.

Necessity, Logical A logical necessity is something whose truth is guaranteed by logic alone. Examples of (classical) logical necessities include *All cats are cats. Everything is self-identical. Something is self-identical. Nothing is both bigger than a breadbasket and not bigger than a breadbasket.*

Necessity, Metaphysical A claim is metaphysically necessary if it holds in all metaphysically possible worlds*; a claim is metaphysically possible if it holds in at least one metaphysically possible world. What you take to be metaphysically necessary and metaphysically possible depends upon what you take to be the modal status of the laws and boundary conditions of the actual world.

Necessity, Physical A claim is physically necessary if it holds in all physically possible worlds*; a claim is physically possible if it holds in at least one physically possible world. A physically possible world is a world that has the same laws of nature as ours and where those laws are never violated. What you take to be physically necessary and physically possible depends upon your views about what are the laws of physics and what you take to be the modal status of the boundary conditions of the actual world.

Nominal Definition *see* Definition, Nominal

Nominalisation A nominalisation is a noun phrase generated from a verb or adjective. Examples: 'judgment' is a nominalisation of 'judge'; 'departure' is a nominalisation of 'depart'; 'ownership' is a nominalisation of 'own'.

Nominalism 'Nominalism' is sometimes used to refer to the rejection of universals* and sometimes to refer to the rejection of abstract objects*. Some metaphysicians are nominalists in both of these senses; some metaphysicians are only nominalists in the first of these senses.

Non-cognitivism According to a non-cognitivist account of a domain of discourse, the sentences in that domain of discourse are not truth-apt (i.e. not candidates for assessment in terms of truth and falsity).

Non-contradiction The classical logical principle of non-contradiction claims that it is a law of logic* that no claim is both true and false (or more precisely: for any proposition that p, not both p and not-p.). For example, it is an instance of this principle that *nothing is both taller than Donald Trump and not taller than Donald Trump.*

Non-modal A non-modal claim is a claim whose expression does not require the use of any modal auxiliary verbs: 'must', 'might', 'should', 'can', and so on. Often, the focus of talk about non-modal claims is on claims whose expression does not involve any use of the words 'necessary', 'possible', 'actual', and their cognates.

Nowism The claim that everything that there is now exists now. Note that this claim is subtly different from presentism*; it is consistent with the claim that there are things that exist but that do not exist now. So, unlike presentism, it is consistent with four-dimensionalism.

Object In ordinary language, there are a number of terms for the most general metaphysical category: *thing, being, entity, item, existent,* and *object*. Philosophers regularly make stipulative definitions about the use of these terms. For example, we might use 'thing' for the most general metaphysical category, and 'object' for the category of things that belong to the domains of first-order quantifiers (perhaps, roughly, things that occupy regions of spacetime and are somehow involved in causal relations, though not necessarily as the direct relata of causal relations).

Objective Chance Objective chances are probabilities* associated with the possible outcomes of causally indeterministic* processes. If, for example, radioactive decay is an indeterministic process, then, for a given radioactive particle, the probability that it will decay within some fixed time period is an objective chance. Some philosophers use the term 'objective chance' to apply to deterministic processes where there is a clearly correct answer about the probability that one should have about the outcome of that process (e.g. the rolling of a fair die).

Omnipotence Omnipotence is the property of being all-powerful, and is one of the attributes of God* in both classical theism* and traditional theism*. Omnipotence is sometimes said to be the power to do anything, but this definition faces serious problems, such as the Stone Paradox*. No attempt to define omnipotence in terms of, for example, the range of God's abilities, or the range of God's powers, or the range of the outcomes that God can bring about has won the approval of all interested philosophers.

Omniscience Omniscience is the property of being all-knowing, and is one of the attributes of God in both classical theism* and traditional theism*. Omniscience is sometimes defined as knowledge of all truths, but there are philosophical objections that have been raised against this definition.

Ontological Arguments At least roughly, ontological arguments are arguments from what are typically alleged to be none but analytic*, *a priori** and necessary* premises* to the conclusion* that God* exists. Perhaps the best known ontological arguments—at least in Western philosophy—are due to

Anselm, Descartes, Leibniz, Hegel, Godel, and Plantinga. *See also* Modal Ontological Argument.

Ontological Commitment *see* Commitment, Ontological

Ontological Simplicity *see* Simplicity, Ontological

Ontology Ontology is the study of what there is, the general features of what there is, the range of opinion about what there is (and how that range of opinion is ascertained), and what is involved in settling questions about what there is.

Optimism In ordinary language, 'optimism' means expecting things to turn out for the best. In philosophical theology, optimism is the view that, because the world is created by God*, everything *is* the best. That is, according to optimism, God has created the best of all possible worlds. Optimism was famously defended by Leibniz, but Kenny rejects it.

Parsimony Very roughly, parsimony is a preference for lesser complexity* over greater complexity. When it comes to theories, most people suppose that, *all else being equal*, we should prefer theories that have fewer ontological*, ideological*, and theoretical commitments* to theories that have more ontological, ideological, and theoretical commitments. We can think of this view as justified by the more fundamental claim that theoretical beliefs require reasons: we should not hold theoretical beliefs where we have no reason to do so. *See also* Simplicity.

Pascal's Wager A practical argument* for belief in God*, attributed to Blaise Pascal. The argument suggests, roughly, that we should expect better outcomes if we believe in God, and so should set out to try to become believers in God.

Perception *see* Sensory Perception

Perfection Many classical theists* suppose that God* is a supremely perfect being. Many classical theists also suppose that God's possession of many of the other traditional divine* attributes is a logical consequence* of God's possession of supreme perfection.

Physical Necessity *see* Necessity, Physical

Physical Possibility *see* Possibility, Physical

Possibility In general, a possibility is a way things could be. According to context, a claim that something is a possibility may be a claim that it is a logical possibility*, or that it is a metaphysical possibility*, or that it is a physical possibility*, or that it is an epistemic possibility*, or that it is a doxastic possibility*, or perhaps that it is some other kind of possibility.

It is not always clear from context that these different kinds of possibilities are being distinguished. *See also* Necessity.

Possibility, Doxastic To say that it is doxastically possible that p is to say that a rational person could believe that p. Doxastic possibilities include impossibilities whose impossibility is recognisable only *a posteriori**. It was not irrational for people in earlier times to believe that water is something other than two parts hydrogen to one part oxygen.

Possibility, Epistemic To say that it is epistemically possible that p is to say that, for all one knows, it is true that p. For example, it is typically supposed that it is epistemically possible that Goldbach's conjecture* is false.

Possibility, Logical A claim is logically possible if and only if it does not have a contradiction* among its logical consequences*.

Possibility, Metaphysical A claim is metaphysically possible if and only if it is true in some metaphysically possible world*. Metaphysical possibility is usually understood to be broader than physical possibility* but narrower than logical possibility*. Graham rejects the category of metaphysical possibility understood in this sense.

Possibility, Physical A claim is physically possible if and only if it is true in some physically possible world*. A world is physically possible if and only if it has the same natural laws as our world and those laws are never violated.

Possible World A possible world is a complete way that reality could be. Some philosophers think that talk about possible worlds is metaphysically serious: we should think that there are possible worlds. Other philosophers think that talk about possible worlds is just a useful aid to understanding more basic talk about what is possible* and what is necessary*. There is a contested question about whether talk of possible worlds has more expressive power* than talk about what is possible and what is necessary.

Power Set The power set of a given set S is the set of all of the subsets of S. Cantor proved that the cardinality of the power set of a set is greater than the cardinality of the set itself. It is a logical consequence of this result that there are infinitely many distinct infinite cardinals.

Practical Judgment A practical judgment is a judgment that issues in action. It contrasts with a theoretical judgment, which is a judgment that issues in belief. Practical judgments typically draw on beliefs, desires, intentions, and perhaps other kinds of inputs as well. One way to think of practical judgment is as a weighing of reasons for action.

Predicate Roughly, a predicate is what you get when you delete one or more noun phrases from a sentence. For example, in the sentence 'John is bald', '. . . is bald' is a predicate. It is possible to take predicates to express properties: the predicate '. . . is bald' expresses the property of baldness, and the sentence 'John is bald' attributes the property of baldness to John.

Predication Roughly, predication is the act of using predicates. We engage in predication every time we make a sincere declarative utterance. Some philosophers have a more metaphysical understanding: predication is a link that connects a property to one or more things in a way that gives rise to a proposition.

Premise Premises are the parts of an argument* that are distinct from the conclusion*. Premises typically form the starting point of a derivation* of the conclusion. There are, however, zero-premise arguments: arguments whose derivations begin from assumptions made merely for the sake of derivation, and that are discharged in the subsequent course of the derivation.

Presentism Presentism is the claim that only presently existing things exist: there are no merely past things and there are no merely future things. Perhaps the strongest objection to presentism comes from general relativity*: it seems that there is no objective fact about what is happening *now* in distant parts of the universe. Presentism is rejected by four-dimensionalists*.

Primitive Commitment *see* Commitment, Primitive

Principle of Sufficient Reason A principle of sufficient reason is a principle of something like the following form: *nothing happens without a sufficient reason*. A sufficient reason is a full explanation* of why the thing happens. The broader family of these principles also includes casual principles such as the following: *nothing begins to exist without a cause of its beginning to exist*.

Priority Monism The view that, although there are many things, they are all ultimately grounded* in one fundamental* thing. Kenny's version of classical theism* is a kind of priority monism.

Probability Probabilities are mathematical representations of uncertainty or chance. Probabilities are real numbers between 0 and 1.

Property First-order properties are features possessed by objects*. For instance, redness is a property of ripe tomatoes. Higher-order properties are properties of properties. For instance, according to classical theists, perfection is a property of divine goodness.

Property, Essential *see* Essential Property

Property, Intrinsic *see* Intrinsic Property

Quantifier Terms such as 'there is', 'some', 'many', or 'all' that are used to say something about the objects* in a given domain*. In ordinary language, the domain is usually inferred from context. For instance, if you say 'there are no cookies', you are more likely to mean 'there are no cookies in this cookie jar' than 'there are no cookies in the universe'. The sentence is said to quantify over only the objects in the cookie jar. Similarly, if you say 'everyone passed the exam', you are probably quantifying over the students in the class and not all the people in the universe.

Rationality Rationality is the property of believing and acting according to reason.

Rational Obligation People are rationally obligated to believe a claim if and only if they would be irrational if they did not believe that claim. A person may also be rationally obligated to disbelieve, or to suspend judgment*, about a particular claim.

Real Definition *see* Definition, Real

Realisation It is often thought that certain higher level states could be realised by many different lower level states. This has been much discussed in the philosophy of mind. For instance, it is often thought that pain (a higher level state) is realised by one neurological state in humans, but the very same state (pain) has a totally different neurological realisation in octopuses. Realisation is sometimes thought to be a kind of grounding* relation.

Realism Roughly, in philosophy, realism about X or Ys is understood in terms of ontological commitment* to X or Ys. A realist about X says that X exists; a realist about Ys says that there are Ys. Some philosophers impose stronger conditions on realism. For example, some philosophers suppose that realism about X or Ys requires in addition that the existence of X or Ys is not dependent upon beliefs, linguistic practices, conceptual schemes, and so forth.

Reductio A reductio is an argument* whose conclusion* is an absurdity. In classical logic*, explicit contradictions* are absurdities. In debating contexts, a reductio starts from premises* an opponent accepts and ends with a conclusion the opponent finds absurd. A successful reductio shows that the opponent must reject one of the premises.

Reduction A reduction of one domain of discourse to a second domain of discourse is a translation of all of the claims that belong to the former domain into claims that belong to the second domain. Some philosophers think that biology can be reduced to chemistry, chemistry can be reduced to physics, and so on. According to this view, biology is just a kind of shorthand for dealing with certain complicated physical facts. Kenny and Graham both reject this view.

Reidian Epistemology Approaches to epistemology* influenced by the work of Thomas Reid. On these approaches, we must begin with an appropriate attitude of trust* towards our cognitive faculties*. Reidian epistemologists disagree about how wide the scope of this attitude of trust should be. *See also* Religious Epistemology, Reidian.

Reincarnation The view that, following death, people may be reborn to live new lives.

Relativity *see* General Relativity

Reliable Religious Experience *see* Religious Experience, Reliable

Religion The embedding of religious experience* within a form of life*. [K.P.]

Very, very roughly, theistic religions are shared, costly, hard-to-fake commitments to non-natural agents that enable mastery of people's existential anxieties about death, deception, and the like; non-theistic religions differ from theistic religions in being committed to the overcoming of supernatural causal regulative structures such as cycles of reincarnation*, reward, and punishment. [G.O.]

Religion, Monotheistic A religion based on belief in one God*. *See also* Abrahamic Religious Traditions.

Religious Belief Belief based on (the interpretation of) religious experience* or testimony* of religious experience. [K.P.]

Very roughly, the religious beliefs of a given person are the beliefs that they hold only because of their participation in, or belonging to, a particular religion. [G.O.]

Religious Belief, Monotheistic *see* Monotheism

Religious Epistemology The part of philosophy concerned with the nature of faith* and religious belief* and the question of whether faith or religious belief could be rational*.

Religious Epistemology, Reidian An application of Reidian epistemology to the interpretation of religious belief*. On Kenny's version of Reidian religious epistemology, the demand for a general attitude of trust* towards human cognitive faculties justifies the claim that many people are justified in taking themselves and/or others in their community to have reliable religious experiences*. *See also* Reidian Epistemology.

Religious Experience Experience that is taken to have special religious significance. There is enormous variation in religious experience across time, place, and culture. Religious experience may include dreams, visions, a sense of oneness with the universe, emotional responses to religious rituals or texts, and so on.

Religious Experience, Authentic An authentic experience is one that is appropriately anchored to external reality. Authentic experiences contrast with illusions and hallucinations, where there need not be anything in external reality that causes the experience. Authentic religious experiences—if there are such—are anchored in religious entities such as gods* or God*.

Religious Experience, Monotheistic (MRE) Experience that is interpreted as experience of God.

Religious Experience, Reliable Religious experience that results in mostly true beliefs.

Reproducibility In science, the ability of a different research group to repeat the same experiment and get the same results.

Revelation Information (allegedly) conveyed to a religious community by God* (or a god*, or the gods). The Abrahamic religious traditions (and some other world religions) believe that their sacred texts contain revelation.

Salvation Many religions have some concept of salvation, that is, of being saved. There are widely different concepts of salvation because there are widely different concepts of what we need to be saved *from*. For instance, Christians hold that we need to be saved from sin and guilt while Buddhists hold that we need to be saved from suffering caused by unfulfilled desire. Many religious concepts of salvation involve claims about what happens to a person after death.

Sceptical Theism The view that we humans should not expect to be able to understand God's reasons for creating the kind of world God* created and, in particular, should not expect to be able to understand God's reasons for permitting evil*.

Scepticism In the strictest sense, scepticism is the view that it is impossible for humans to know anything. In a looser sense, scepticism may be the view that it is impossible for humans to know anything within some particular domain, or it may simply be the view that humans have much less knowledge than we normally think we do.

Scepticism, External World The view that it is impossible for human beings to know whether external objects exist and, if so, what they are like.

Scope The scope of an operator (such as a modal operator* or a quantifier*) is the domain within which it has the ability to affect the interpretation of other expressions. Consider the following expression, which involves a scope ambiguity: 'Everyone loves someone'. If 'everyone' takes wider scope, then it means 'For each person, there is some person or other that they love'. If 'someone' takes narrower scope, then it means 'There is someone such that everyone loves them'.

Self-Evidence A self-evident claim is one that can be recognized as true as soon as it is understood. For instance, it is self-evident that 2 = 2. *See also* Analytic; Conceptual Truth.

Sensory Perception Experience of the world by means of the senses (vision, touch, smell, etc.).

Set Theory A mathematically rigorous system for dealing with arbitrary collections of objects. Set theory is the basis of most modern mathematics.

Simplicity A theory* or worldview* is simpler to the extent that it has fewer and simpler primitive commitments. Other things being equal, it is rational to prefer simpler theories and worldviews over more complex ones. *See also* Parsimony.

Simplicity, Ideological Having fewer and simpler primitive* ideological commitments*.

Simplicity, Ontological Having fewer and simpler primitive* ontological commitments*.

Simplicity, Theoretical Having fewer and simpler primitive* theoretical commitments*.

Soul Making According to soul-making theodicies*, no one can have genuine virtues, such as courage or compassion, without going through adversity. According to proponents of this view, God* is justified in permitting evil* in order to bring about these valuable traits of character in humans.

Soundness *see* Argument, Sound.

Special Divine Action Events in which God* (or a god*) is involved in a way that goes beyond creating and sustaining the universe. *See also* Miracle.

Split the Horns To respond to a (supposed) dilemma* by arguing that there is in fact a third option.

Stone Paradox The following question, which causes problems for many theories of omnipotence*: could God* make a stone too heavy for God to lift?

Strongly Successful An argument is strongly successful if and only if, upon considering the argument, all members of the audience are rationally obligated to endorse the conclusion. *See also* Argument, Successful.

Supervenience Necessarily, the As supervene on the Bs if and only if (1) it is impossible for there to be change in the As without change in the Bs; (2) it is possible for there to be change in the Bs without change in the As; and (3) it is possible for there to be change in the As. For instance, a digital image supervenes on its pixels. There cannot be change in the image without change in the pixels; there can be change in a single pixel without change in the image; and there can be change in the image. Many philosophers think that the mental facts supervene on the physical facts, and many philosophers think that the moral facts supervene on the non-moral facts.

Suspension of Judgment A person suspends judgment with respect to a claim if, after considering the claim, they neither believe it nor disbelieve it. A person who suspends judgment about a claim does not believe it, does not disbelieve it, and is not innocent* in relation to it.

Symmetry A relation is symmetrical if and only if, necessarily, if A stands in the relation to B, then B stands in the relation to A. Examples of symmetric relations: *being the same height as*, *being a member of the same family as*, and *being of the same gender as*.

Teleological Arguments Arguments that attempt to derive the existence of God* from the appearance of design in nature. Arguments based on fine-tuning* are among the most widely discussed varieties of teleological arguments in recent philosophy, but there are also many other kinds of teleological arguments.

Tension An instance in which a believer is pulled both ways regarding a certain claim. That is, a case where someone finds within her own worldview* good reasons for accepting the claim and also good reasons for rejecting it. The most severe kind of tension is contradiction*. The more tension there is in a worldview, the less coherent* it is. [K.P.]

Testimony In epistemology, testimony is understood very broadly as any case where a person makes a claim with the expectation that the claim will be accepted on her say-so.

Theism Belief in God* or gods*.

Theism, Classical A tradition of metaphysical theorising about God* developed by Jewish, Christian, and Muslim philosophers drawing on Greek philosophy to try to make rational sense of traditional theism*. Important proponents include Avicenna, Maimonides, Aquinas, and Lebiniz. In addition to the attributes included in traditional theism, classical theists usually regard God as a necessary being* who possesses all the attributes essentially* and is atemporal*, immutable*, and impassible*. Kenny defends a version of classical theism.

Theism, Traditional The view of God held by most ordinary believers in the Abrahamic religious traditions*. This includes the belief that God is omnipotent*, omniscient*, and morally perfect.

Theodicy An attempt to explain why God allows evil* in the world. Leibniz coined this term from the Greek words for 'God' and 'justice'.

Theological Compatibilism *see* Compatibilism, Theological

Theological Determinism *see* Determinism, Theological

Theoretical Commitment *see* Commitment, Theoretical

Theoretical Simplicity *see* Simplicity, Theoretical

Theory In one sense, a theory is a set of claims that is closed under logical consequence*. In this sense, any claim that is a logical consequence of claims in the theory is itself in the theory. What Graham calls 'ideal worldviews' are theories in this sense. In another sense, a theory is a proposed explanation of some evidence. In this work, Kenny and Graham mostly use the term 'theory' in this latter sense.

Theory-Ladenness of Experiment In philosophy of science, the observation that scientists use theories to interpret the results of their experiments. There are no completely uninterpreted results totally separate from all theories.

Theory-Theory Theory-theory is the view that we use a folk-psychological theory—couched in terms of beliefs, desires, intentions, and the like—in order to predict and explain the behaviour of others. By way of contrast, for example, simulation-theory says that we predict and explain the behaviour of others by running our own interpretative and decision-making processes 'off-line' on our best guesses about others' input data.

Traditional Theism *see* Theism, Traditional

Transitivity A transitive relation is one where it must be that, if A bears that relation to B, and B bears that relation to C, then A also bears that relation to C. For instance, in math the '=' sign designates a transitive relation: it must be that, if $x = y$ and $y = z$, then $x = z$. Also, the relation 'taller than' is a transitive relation: it must be that, if Mary is taller than Anne and Anne is taller than Bob, then Mary is taller than Bob.

Trust Trust is an attitude we have towards those we hope will be trustworthy. Trust requires at least making oneself vulnerable to others, thinking well of others (at least in relevant respects), and being optimistic that others will prove competent (at least in relevant respects). In epistemology*, to trust something or someone is to regard that person or thing as a reliable source of information. Thus, we trust our sense of vision, we trust our parents, and so on.

Universal According to a fairly standard metaphysical distinction, universals are things that are capable of instantiation*. The contrast is with individuals, which are not capable of instantiation. While there are many candidates to be individuals—objects*, events*—the standard candidates to be universals are properties and relations. Some metaphysicians use the word 'universal' for particular sub-classes of properties and relations.

Univocity The use of a word in its ordinary everyday sense, without changing its meaning. *See also* Use of Language, Univocal.

Use of Language, Analogical Language is said to be used analogically when it is applied to a new context in a way that alters its meaning. This is often based on some kind of comparison or similarity with the original use, as when light waves are called 'waves' because they can be described with the same math used for water waves. Classical theists* have historically held that most or all of our use of language for talking about God* is analogical. Analogical use of language was traditionally thought of as a kind of middle ground between equivocal and univocal uses.

Use of Language, Equivocal Language is used (purely) equivocally when two or more unrelated meanings happen to be associated with the same word. For instance, 'bat' (flying mammal) and 'bat' (sporting equipment) or 'bank' (financial institution) and 'bank' (the side of a river).

Use of Language, Univocal Language is said to be used univocally when it is used in the ordinary everyday sense, without analogy* or equivocation*.

Valid Argument see Argument, Valid.

Validity *see* Argument, Valid.

Virtue A virtue is an excellence of character: a deeply entrenched disposition to act, value, desire, and choose excellently in some particular respect.

Virtue Ethics is an approach to normative ethics that emphasises moral character and virtue*. It contrasts with deontologism*, which emphasises moral rules and norms, and consequentialism*, which emphasises goodness and badness of consequences of actions.

Worldview In principle, a worldview is a total theory of everything. In practice, a worldview is our best approximation to a total theory of everything. That is, in practice, a worldview is a total system of belief.

Worldview Comparison A philosophical methodology that proceeds by outlining different worldviews and comparing their relative merits. The two authors endorse different versions of this methodology.

Zombie In philosophy, a zombie is an imaginary being that is indistinguishable from an ordinary human in its anatomy, physiology, and behavior but nevertheless has no conscious experience There is extensive philosophical debate about whether zombies are metaphysically possible*, and this question is often thought to have implications for the relationship between mind and body. See Chalmers (1996).

Bibliography

Adams, Douglas. (1979) 1996. *The Hitchhiker's Guide to the Galaxy.* In *The Ultimate Hitchhiker's Guide: Complete and Unabridged,* 1–143. New York: Wing Books.

Adams, Robert Merrihew. (1972) "Must God Create the Best?" *Philosophical Review* 81 (3): 317–332. www.jstor.org/stable/2184329.

Aizama, Kenneth, and Gillett, Carl, eds. (2016) *Scientific Composition and Metaphysical Ground.* Basingstoke: Palgrave Macmillan.

al-Ghazali, Abu Hamid Muhammad. *Freedom and Fulfillment.* Translated in McCarthy 1980.

al-Ghazali, Abu Hamid Muhammad. *The Incoherence of the Philosophers.* Translated in Marmura 2000.

Allen, Ira, and Allen, Saul. (2016) "God Terms and Activity Systems: A Definition of Religion for Political Science." *Political Research Quarterly* 69 (3): 557–570. www.jstor.org/stable/44018555.

Alston, William P. (1986) "Epistemic Circularity." *Philosophy and Phenomenological Research* 47 (1): 1–30. www.jstor.org/stable/2107722.

Alston, William P. (1989) *Divine Nature and Human Language.* Ithaca: Cornell University Press.

Alston, William P. (1991) *Perceiving God: The Epistemology of Religious Experience.* Ithaca, NY: Cornell University Press.

Anderson, Ronald. (2014) *Human Suffering and Quality of Life.* Dordrecht: Springer.

Annas, Julia. (1993) *The Morality of Happiness.* Oxford: Oxford University Press.

Anselm of Canterbury. *Proslogion.* Translated in Williams 2007.

Aquinas, Thomas. *Summa Contra Gentiles.* Translated by Laurence Shapcote. Vols. 11–12 of *Latin-English Opera Omnia.* Steubenville, OH: Emmaus Academic, 2019. https://aquinas.cc/la/en/~SCG1.

Aquinas, Thomas. *Summa Theologiae.* Abridged translation: Davies and Leftow 2006. Complete translation: Fathers of the English Dominican Province 1920.

Ariew, Roger, and Garber, Daniel, eds. and trans. (1989) *Philosophical Essays. By G. W. Leibniz.* Indianapolis: Hackett.

Aristophanes. *The Clouds.* Translated by Peter Meineck. Indianapolis: Hackett, 2000.

Aristotle. *Nicomachean Ethics.* 3rd ed. Translated by Terence Irwin. Indianapolis: Hackett, 2019.

Armstrong, David. (1968) *A Materialist Theory of Mind.* London: Routledge.

Armstrong, David. (1978) *A Theory of Universals.* Cambridge: Cambridge University Press.

Arntzenius, Frank, and Maudlin, Tim. (2013) "Time Travel and Modern Physics." In *The Stanford Encyclopedia of Philosophy.* Winter 2013 ed., edited by Edward N. Zalta. https://plato.stanford.edu/archives/win2013/entries/time-travel-phys/.

Atran, Scott. (2002) *In Gods We Trust.* Oxford: Oxford University Press.

Atran, Scott, and Norenzayan, Ara. (2004) "Religion's Evolutionary Landscape: Counterintuition, Commitment, Compassion, Communion." *Behavioural and Brain Sciences* 27: 713–770.

Avicenna. *Metaphysica.* Translated in Morewedge 1973.

Axelrod, Robert. (1984) *The Evolution of Cooperation.* New York: Basic Books.

Azzouni, Jody. (2004) *Deflating Existential Consequence.* Oxford: Oxford University Press.

Baars, Bernard. (1988) *A Cognitive Theory of Consciousness.* Cambridge: Cambridge University Press.

Baker, Lynne Rudder. (2007) *The Metaphysics of Everyday Life: An Essay in Practical Realism.* Cambridge Studies in Philosophy. Cambridge: Cambridge University Press.

Barrett, Justin L. (2000) "Exploring the Natural Foundations of Religion." *Trends in Cognitive Sciences* 4 (1): 29–34. https://doi.org/10.1016/S1364-6613(99)01419-9.

Barrow, John. (2005) *The Infinite Book.* New York: Vintage.

Batterman, Robert W. (2010) "Reduction and Renormalization." In *Time, Chance and Reduction: Philosophical Aspects of Statistical Mechanics,* edited by Gerhard Ernst and Andreas Hüttemann, 159–179. Cambridge: Cambridge University Press.

Bealer, George. (1982) *Quality and Concept.* Oxford: Oxford University Press.

Bentley, Michael, ed. (1997) *Companion to Historiography.* London: Routledge.

Berkeley, George. (1710) 2002. *A Treatise Concerning the Principles of Human Knowledge: Wherein the Chief Causes of Error and Difficulty in the Sciences, with the Grounds of Scepticism, Atheism, and Irreligion, are Inquired Into.* Edited by Col Choat and Al Haines. Salt Lake City: Project Gutenberg. www.gutenberg.org/ebooks/4723.

Bigelow, John. (1988) *The Reality of Numbers.* Oxford: Clarendon.
Blackburn, Simon. (2001) *Being Good.* New York: Oxford University Press.
Blackford, Russell, and Broderick, Damien, eds. (2017). *Philosophy's Future.* Malden: Wiley-Blackwell.
Blackmore, Susan. (1993) *Dying to Live.* Amherst: Prometheus.
Bliss, Ricki, and Priest, Graham, eds. (2018) *Reality and Its Structure.* New York: Oxford University Press.
Bliss, Ricki, and Trogdon, Kelly. (2016) "Metaphysical Grounding." In *The Stanford Encyclopedia of Philosophy.* Winter 2016 ed., edited by Edward N. Zalta. Metaphysics Research Lab, Stanford University. https://plato.stanford.edu/archives/win2016/entries/grounding/.
Block, Ned. (1978) "Troubles With Functionalism." *Minnesota Studies in the Philosophy of Science* 9: 261–325.
Block, Ned. (1981) "Psychologism and Behaviourism." *The Philosophical Review* 90: 5–43.
Bokulich, Alisa. (2014) "Metaphysical Indeterminacy, Properties, and Quantum Theory." *Res Philosophica* 91 (3): 449–475. https://doi.org/10.11612/resphil.2014.91.3.11.
Boyer, Pascal. (2001) *Religion Explained.* New York: Basics Books.
Braddock, Matthew. (2018) "An Evidential Argument for Theism from the Cognitive Science of Religion." In *New Developments in the Cognitive Science of Religion: The Rationality of Religious Belief,* edited by Hans van Eyghen, Rik Peels, and Gijsbert van den Brink, 171–198. New Approaches to the Scientific Study of Religion. Cham, Switzerland: Springer.
Bradley, Ben. (2009) *Well-Being and Death.* Oxford: Oxford University Press.
Brower, Jeffrey E. (2009) "Simplicity and Aseity." In *The Oxford Handbook of Philosophical Theology,* edited by Thomas P. Flint and Michael C. Rea. Oxford: Oxford University Press. https://doi.org/10.1093/oxfordhb/9780199596539.013.0006.
Budd, Malcolm. (2008) *Music and the Emotions.* London: Routledge.
Byrne, Richard. (1995) *The Thinking Ape.* Oxford: Oxford University Press.
Cahn, Steven M. (1969) "The Irrelevance to Religion of Philosophic Proofs for the Existence of God." *American Philosophical Quarterly* 6 (2): 170–172. www.jstor.org/stable/20009304.
Calvin, John. (1536) 1845. *Institutes of the Christian Religion.* Translated by Henry Beveridge. Edinburgh: Calvin Translation Society. www.ccel.org/ccel/calvin/institutes.
Camp, Elisabeth. (2006) "Metaphor in the Mind: The Cognition of Metaphor." *Philosophy Compass* 1 (2): 154–170. https://doi.org/10.1111/j.1747-9991.2006.00013.x.

Campbell, Keith. (1990) *Abstract Particulars*. Oxford: Blackwell.
Carroll, Noel. (1999) *Philosophy of Art*. New York: Routledge.
Carroll, Noel. (2007) *Comedy Incarnate*. Malden: Blackwell.
Carroll, Sean. (2012) "Does the Universe Need God?" In *The Blackwell Companion to Science and Christianity*, edited by J. B. Stump and Alan G. Padgett, 185–197. Chichester: Wiley-Blackwell. https://doi.org/10.1002/9781118241455.ch17.
Cartwright, Nancy. (1980) "The Truth Doesn't Explain Much." *American Philosophical Quarterly* 17 (2): 159–163. www.jstor.org/stable/20013859.
Cartwright, Nancy. (1999) *The Dappled World*. Cambridge: Cambridge University Press.
Castañeda, Hector-Neri. (1984) "Causes, Causity, and Energy." *Midwest Studies in Philosophy* 9 (1): 17–27. https://doi.org/10.1111/j.1475-4975.1984.tb00050.x.
Chafe, Wallace. (2007) *The Importance of Not Being Earnest*. Amsterdam: John Benjamins.
Chalmers, Alan. (1982) *What Is This Thing Called Science?* Brisbane: University of Queensland Press.
Chalmers, David J. (1995) "Facing Up to the Problem of Consciousness." *Journal of Consciousness Studies* 2 (3): 200–219. www.ingentaconnect.com/contentone/imp/jcs/1995/00000002/00000003/653.
Chalmers, David J. (1996) *The Conscious Mind*. New York: Oxford University Press.
Chalmers, David J. (2012) *Constructing the World*. Oxford: Oxford University Press.
Chalmers, David J., Manley, David, and Wasserman, Ryan, eds. (2009) *Metametaphysics: New Essays on the Foundations of Ontology*. Oxford: Clarendon Press.
Chang, R. (2000) "Understanding *Di* and *Tian*: Deity and Heaven from Shang to Tang Dynasties." *Sino-Platonic Papers* 108.
Charlesworth, Brian, and Charlesworth, Deborah. (2003) *Evolution*. Oxford: Oxford University Press.
Chihara, Charles. (2004) *A Structuralist Account of Mathematics*. Oxford: Oxford University Press.
Churchland, Patricia S. (1980) "Language, Thought, and Information Processing." *Noûs* 14 (2): 147–170. www.jstor.org/stable/2214858.
Churchland, Patricia S. (1996) "The Hornswoggle Problem." *Journal of Consciousness Studies* 3 (5–6): 402–408. www.ingentaconnect.com/contentone/imp/jcs/1996/00000003/f0020005/726.
Churchland, Paul M. (1981) "Eliminative Materialism and the Propositional Attitudes." *Journal of Philosophy* 78: 67–90. www.jstor.org/stable/2025900.
Churchland, Paul M. (1985) "Reduction, Qualia and the Direct Introspection of Brain States." *Journal of Philosophy* 82 (1): 8–28. www.jstor.org/stable/2026509.

Churchland, Paul M. (1996) "The Rediscovery of Light." *Journal of Philosophy* 93 (5): 211–228. www.jstor.org/stable/2940998.

Clark, Stephen R. L. (1987) "How to Believe in Fairies." *Inquiry* 30: 337–355. https://doi.org/10.1080/00201748708602128.

Clarke, Randolph. (1996) "Contrastive Rational Explanation of Free Choice." *Philosophical Quarterly* 46 (183): 185–201. https://doi.org/10.2307/2956386.

Coady, C. A. J. (1992) *Testimony: A Philosophical Study*. Oxford: Oxford University Press. https://doi.org/10.1093/0198235518.001.0001.

Cohen, Ted. (1999) *Jokes*. Chicago: University of Chicago Press.

Colson, F. H., and Whitaker, G. H., trans. (1929a) *On the Creation. Allegorical Interpretation of Genesis 2 and 3*. By Philo of Alexandria. Loeb Classical Library 226. Cambridge, MA: Harvard University Press. www.loebclassics.com/view/LCL226/1929/volume.xml.

Colson, F. H., and Whitaker, G. H., trans. (1929b) *On the Unchangeableness of God: On Husbandry. Concerning Noah's Work as a Planter. On Drunkenness. On Sobriety*. By Philo of Alexandria. Loeb Classical Library 247. Cambridge, MA: Harvard University Press. www.loebclassics.com/view/LCL247/1930/volume.xml.

Colyvan, Mark. (2001) *The Indispensability of Mathematics*. New York: Oxford University Press.

Correia, Fabrice. (2008) "Ontological Dependence." *Philosophy Compass* 3 (5): 1013–1032. https://doi.org/10.1111/j.1747-9991.2008.00170.x.

Correia, Fabrice, and Schnieder, Benjamin, eds. (2012) *Metaphysical Grounding: Understanding the Structure of Reality*. Cambridge: Cambridge University Press.

Craig, William Lane. (1979) *The Kalām Cosmological Argument*. New York: Barnes & Noble.

Craig, William Lane. (2003) "Design and the Anthropic Fine-Tuning of the Universe." In *God and Design*, edited by N. Manson, 155–177. London: Routledge.

Crick, Francis, and Koch, Christof. (2003) "A Framework for Consciousness." *Nature Neuroscience* 6: 119–126. www.nature.com/articles/nn0203-119.

Cuneo, Terence. (2014) "Ritual Knowledge." *Faith and Philosophy* 31 (4): 365–385. https://place.asburyseminary.edu/faithandphilosophy/vol31/iss4/1.

D'Alessandro, William. (2019) "Explanation in Mathematics: Proofs and Practice." *Philosophy Compass* 14 (11). https://doi.org/10.1111/phc3.12629.

Daly, Chris. (2012) "Scepticism about Grounding." In Correia and Schnieder 2012, 81–100.

Danto, Arthur. (2013) *The Transfiguration of the Commonplace*. Cambridge, MA: Harvard University Press.

Dasgupta, Shamik. (2016) "Metaphysical Rationalism." *Noûs* 50 (2): 379–418. https://doi.org/10.1111/nous.12082.

Davidson, Donald. (1978) "What Metaphors Mean." *Critical Inquiry* 5 (1): 31–47. www.journals.uchicago.edu/doi/10.1086/447971.

Davies, Brian, and Leftow, Brian, eds. and trans. (2006) *Summa Theologiae: Questions on God*. By Thomas Aquinas. Cambridge Texts in the History of Philosophy. Cambridge: Cambridge University Press.

Davies, James. (2012) *The Importance of Suffering*. New York: Routledge.

De Cruz, Helen, and De Smedt, Johan. (2015) *A Natural History of Natural Theology: The Cognitive Science of Theology and Philosophy of Religion*. Cambridge, MA: The MIT Press.

Del Rey, Lester. (1951) "...and It Comes Out Here." *Galaxy Science Fiction*, February, 62–74. https://archive.org/details/galaxymagazine-1951-02/page/n63.

De Morgan, Augustus. (1915) *A Budget of Paradoxes*. 2nd ed. Edited by David Eugene Smith. 2 vols. Chicago and London: Open Court. https://www.google.com/books/edition/A_Budget_of_Paradoxes/qTYEAAAAYAAJ.

Deng, Natalja. (2019) *God and Time*. Elements in the Philosophy of Religion. Cambridge: Cambridge University Press. https://doi.org/10.1017/9781108653176.

Dennett, Daniel C. (1984) *Elbow Room*. Cambridge, MA: MIT Press.

Dennett, Daniel C. (1991) *Consciousness Explained*. Boston: Little and Brown.

Dennett, Daniel C. (2006) *Breaking the Spell: Religion as a Natural Phenomenon*. New York: Viking.

Descartes, René. (1637) 1998. *Discourse on the Method for Conducting One's Reason Well and for Seeking Truth in the Sciences*. 3rd ed. Translated by Donald A. Cress. Indianapolis: Hackett.

Descartes, René. (1641) 1993. *Meditations on First Philosophy: In Which the Existence of God and the Distinction of the Soul from the Body are Demonstrated*. 3rd ed. Translated by Donald A. Cress. Indianapolis: Hackett.

Diller, Jeanine. (2016) "Global and Local Atheisms." *International Journal for Philosophy of Religion* 79 (1): 7–18. https://link.springer.com/article/10.1007/s11153-015-9550-1.

Dretske, F. (1988) *Explaining Behaviour*. Cambridge, MA: MIT Press.

Dummett, Michael. (2010) *The Nature and Future of Philosophy*. New York: Columbia University.

Dworkin, Ronald. (2000) *Sovereign Virtue*. Cambridge, MA: Harvard University Press.

Dworkin, Ronald. (2013) *Religion Without God*. Cambridge, MA: Harvard University Press.

Earman, John. (1986) *A Primer on Determinism*. Dordrecht: Riedel.

Earman, John. (1995) *Bangs, Crunches, Whimpers, and Shrieks: Singularities and Acausalities in Relativistic Spacetimes*. New York: Oxford University Press.

Earman, John. (2000) *Hume's Abject Failure*. Oxford: Oxford University Press.
Edwards, Jonathan. (1765) "Concerning the End for which God Created the World." In *Two Dissertations: I. Concerning the End for Which God Created the World. II. The Nature of True Virtue*, 1–115. Boston: S. Kneeland. https://archive.org/details/twodissertations00edwa/.
Eells, Ellery. (1991) *Probabilistic Causality*. Cambridge: Cambridge University Press.
Efird, David, and Stoneham, Tom. (2013) "Methodological Separatism, Modal Pluralism, and Metaphysical Nihilism." In Goldschmidt 2013, 144–166.
Egan, Andy, and Weatherson, Brian, eds. (2011) *Epistemic Modality*. Oxford: Oxford University Press.
Enderton, Herbert B. (2002) *A Mathematical Introduction to Logic*. 2nd ed. San Diego: Harcourt Academic Press.
Enoch, David. (2011) *Taking Morality Seriously*. Oxford: Oxford University Press.
Fales, Evan. (1990) *Causation and Universals*. London: Routledge.
Fathers of the English Dominican Province. (1920) *The Summa Theologica of St. Thomas Aquinas*. 2nd ed. London: Burns Oates & Washbourne. www.newadvent.org/summa/.
Feldman, Fred. (1994) *Confrontations with the Reaper*. Oxford: Oxford University Press.
Fernandes, Alison. (Forthcoming) "Time Travel and Counterfactual Asymmetry." *Synthese*. https://link.springer.com/article/10.1007%2Fs11229-019-02186-w.
Fine, Kit. (2001) "The Question of Realism." *Philosophers' Imprint* 1 (2): 1–30. http://hdl.handle.net/2027/spo.3521354.0001.002.
Fodor, J. A. (1974) "Special Sciences (Or: The Disunity of Science as a Working Hypothesis)." *Synthese* 28 (2): 97–115. www.jstor.org/stable/20114958.
Fogelin, Robert. (2003) *A Defence of Hume on Miracles*. Princeton: Princeton University Press.
Foot, Philippa. (2001) *Natural Goodness*. Oxford: Clarendon.
Frankfurt, Harry. (2004) *The Reasons of Love*. Princeton: Princeton University Press.
Frans, Joachim, and Weber, Erik. (2014) "Mechanistic Explanation and Explanatory Proofs in Mathematics." *Philosophia Mathematica* 22 (2): 231–248. https://doi.org/10.1093/philmat/nku003.
French, Steven. (2019) "Identity and Individuality in Quantum Theory." In *The Stanford Encyclopedia of Philosophy*. Winter 2019 ed., edited by Edward N. Zalta. Metaphysics Research Lab, Stanford University. https://plato.stanford.edu/archives/win2019/entries/qt-idind/.
French, Steven, and Krause, Décio. (2003) "Quantum Vagueness." *Erkenntnis* 59 (1): 97–124. www.jstor.org/stable/20013213.

Fricker, Miranda. (2007) *Epistemic Injustice*. Oxford: Oxford University Press.
Friend, Stacie. (2007) "Fictional Characters." *Philosophy Compass* 2 (2): 141–156. https://doi.org/10.1111/j.1747-9991.2007.00059.x.
Garson, James. (2018) "Modal Logic." In *The Stanford Encyclopedia of Philosophy*. Fall 2018 ed., edited by Edward N. Zalta. https://plato.stanford.edu/archives/fall2018/entries/logic-modal/.
Gaunilo of Marmoutiers. *Reply on Behalf of the Fool*. Translated in Williams 2007.
Geach, P. T. (1973) "Omnipotence." *Philosophy* 48 (183): 7–20. www.jstor.org/stable/3749704.
Gendler, Tamar, and Hawthorne, John, eds. (2002) *Conceivability and Possibility*. Oxford: Clarendon.
Gigerenzer, Gerd. (2007) *Gut Feelings*. London: Allen Lane.
Glick, David. (2017) "Against Quantum Indeterminacy." *Thought: A Journal of Philosophy* 6 (3): 204–213. https://doi.org/10.1002/tht3.250.
Godfrey-Smith, Peter. (2003) *Theory and Reality*. Chicago: Chicago University Press.
Goldman, Alvin. (1999) *Knowledge in a Social World*. Oxford: Oxford University Press.
Goldschmidt, Tyron, ed. (2013) *The Puzzle of Existence: Why Is There Something Rather Than Nothing?* New York and London: Routledge.
Greene, Brian. (2005) *The Fabric of the Cosmos: Space, Time, and the Texture of Reality*. New York: Vintage Books.
Greene, Brian. (2011) *The Hidden Reality: Parallel Universes and the Deep Laws of the Cosmos*. New York: Alfred A. Knopf.
Grünbaum, Adolf. (1989) "The Pseudo-Problem of Creation in Physical Cosmology." *Philosophy of Science* 56 (3): 373–394. www.jstor.org/stable/187991.
Guthrie, Stewart. (1995) *Faces in the Clouds*. New York: Oxford University Press.
Hale, Bob. (1987) *Abstract Objects*. Oxford: Blackwell.
Halpern, Cynthia. (2002) *Suffering, Politics, Power*. Albany: State University of New York Press.
Hanrahan, Rebecca. (2009) "Getting God Out of Our (Modal) Business." *Sophia* 48 (4): 379–391. https://doi.org/10.1007/s11841-009-0138-z.
Harrison, Gerald K. (2017) "A Radical Solution to the Problem of Evil." *Sophia* 56 (2): 279–287. https://doi.org/10.1007/s11841-016-0526-0.
Hartshorne, Charles. (1984) *Omnipotence and Other Theological Mistakes*. Albany: State University of New York Press.
Heil, John. (2003) *From an Ontological Point of View*. Oxford: Oxford University Press.
Hewitson, Mark. (2014) *History and Causality*. New York: Palgrave Macmillan.

Hewitt, Simon. (Forthcoming) "Grammatical Thomism." *Religious Studies*. https://doi.org/10.1017/S0034412518000896.
Hill, Daniel. (2005) *Divinity and Maximal Greatness*. Abingdon: Routledge.
Hill, Scott. (2014) "Giving Up Omnipotence." *Canadian Journal of Philosophy* 44 (1): 97–117. https://doi.org/10.1080/00455091.2014.914289.
Hitchcock, Christopher. (1999) "Contrastive Explanation and the Demons of Determinism." *British Journal for the Philosophy of Science* 50 (4): 585–612. www.jstor.org/stable/40072258.
Hofweber, Thomas. (2009) "Ambitious, Yet Modest, Metaphysics." In Chalmers, Manley, and Wasserman 2009, 260–289.
Hohwy, Jakob. (2013) *The Predictive Mind*. Oxford: Oxford University Press.
Holton, Richard. (2009) *Willing, Wanting, Waiting*. New York: Oxford University Press.
Hornsby, Jennifer. (1997) *Simple-Mindedness*. Cambridge, MA: Harvard University Press.
Horty, John. (2007) *Frege on Definitions*. New York: Oxford University Press.
Howard-Snyder, Daniel, ed. (1996) *The Evidential Argument from Evil*. Bloomington: Indiana University Press.
Howard-Snyder, Daniel, and Howard-Snyder, Frances. (1994) "How an Unsurpassable Being can Create a Surpassable World." *Faith and Philosophy* 11 (2): 260–268. https://place.asburyseminary.edu/faithandphilosophy/vol11/iss2/7/.
Huemer, Michael. (2016) *Approaching Infinity*. London: Palgrave Macmillan.
Hughes, Christopher. (1989) *On a Complex Theory of a Simple God: An Investigation of Aquinas' Philosophical Theology*. Cornell Studies in Philosophy of Religion. Ithaca, NY: Cornell University Press.
Hume, David. (1739–40) 2010. *A Treatise of Human Nature*. Edited by Col Choat and David Widget. Salt Lake City: Project Gutenberg. www.gutenberg.org/ebooks/4705.
Hume, David. (1748) 2003. *An Enquiry Concerning Human Understanding*. Edited by L. A. Selby-Bigge and Jonathan Ingram. Salt Lake City: Project Gutenberg. www.gutenberg.org/ebooks/9662.
Hume, David. (1757) 2007. "The Natural History of Religion." In *A Dissertation on the Passions and the Natural History of Religion: A Critical Edition*, edited by Thomas L. Beauchamp. The Clarendon Edition of the Works of David Hume. Oxford: Clarendon Press.
Hume, David. (1779) 2002. *Dialogues Concerning Natural Religion*. Edited by Col Choat and Al Haines. Salt Lake City: Project Gutenberg. www.gutenberg.org/ebooks/4583.
Hursthouse, Rosalind. (1999) *On Virtue Ethics*. Oxford: Oxford University Press.

Jackson, Frank. (1982) "Epiphenomenal Qualia." *Philosophical Quarterly* 32: 127–136. https://www.jstor.org/stable/2960077.
Jackson, Frank. (1998) *From Metaphysics to Ethics*. Oxford: Oxford University Press.
James, William. (1902/2012) *The Varieties of Religious Experience*. Oxford: Oxford University Press.
Johnson, Elizabeth A. (1992) *She Who Is: The Mystery of God in Feminist Theological Discourse*. New York: Crossroad.
Kagan, Shelley. (2012) *Death*. New Haven: Yale University Press.
Kahane, Guy. (2011) "Should We Want God To Exist?" *Philosophy And Phenomenological Research* 82, 774–796. https://dx.doi.org/10.1111/j.1933-1592.2010.00426.x.
Kahneman, Daniel. (2011) *Thinking Fast and Slow*. London: Penguin.
Kahneman, Daniel, et al. (1982) *Judgment Under Uncertainty*. Cambridge: Cambridge University Press.
Kant, Immanuel. (1781) 1998. *The Critique of Pure Reason*. Edited and translated by Paul Guyer and Allen W. Wood. The Cambridge Edition of the Works of Immanuel Kant. New York: Cambridge University Press.
Kant, Immanuel. (1785) 2012. *Groundwork of the Metaphysics of Morals*. Revised ed. Edited by Mary Gregor and Jens Timmerman. Cambridge Texts in the History of Philosophy. Cambridge: Cambridge University Press.
Kant, Immanuel. (1797) 2017. *The Metaphysics of Morals*. Revised ed. Edited by Lara Denis. Translated by Mary Gregor. Cambridge Texts in the History of Philosophy. Cambridge: Cambridge University Press.
Katz, Jerrold. (1988) *Realistic Rationalism*. Cambridge, MA: MIT Press.
Kaufmann, Stuart. (1993) *The Origins of Order*. New York: Oxford University Press.
Kim, Jaegwon. (1998) *Mind in a Physical World*. Cambridge, MA: MIT Press.
Kitcher, Patricia. (1984a) "In Defense of Intentional Psychology." *Journal of Philosophy* 81 (2): 89–106. www.jstor.org/stable/2026024.
Kitcher, Philip. (1984b) "1953 and All That: A Tale of Two Sciences." *Philosophical Review* 93 (3): 335–373. www.jstor.org/stable/2184541.
Kivy, Peter. (1980) *The Corded Shell*. Princeton: Princeton University Press.
Kment, Boris. (2014) *Modality and Explanatory Reasoning*. Oxford: Oxford University Press.
Koch, Christof, and Tsuchiya, Naotsugu. (2007) "Attention and Consciousness: Two Distinct Brain Processes." *Trends in Cognitive Sciences* 11 (1): 16–22. https://doi.org/10.1016/j.tics.2006.10.012.
Kolb, Bryan, and Ian Q. Whishaw. (2014) *An Introduction to Brain and Behavior*. 4th ed. New York: Worth.
Koons, Robert, and Pickavance, Timothy. (2017) *The Atlas of Reality*. Malden: Wiley-Blackwell.

Kornblith, Hilary. (2002) *Knowledge and Its Place in Nature*. Oxford: Oxford University Press.
Korsgaard, Christine M. (1996a) *Creating the Kingdom of Ends*. Cambridge: Cambridge University Press.
Korsgaard, Christine M. (1996b) *The Sources of Normativity*. Cambridge: Cambridge University Press.
Korsgaard, Christine M. (2009) *Self-Constitution: Agency, Identity, and Integrity*. Oxford: Oxford University Press.
Koslicki, Kathrin. (2012) "Varieties of Ontological Dependence." In Correia and Schnieder 2012, 186–213.
Kotzen, Matthew. (2013) "The Probabilistic Explanation of Why There Is Something Rather Than Nothing." In Goldschmidt 2013, 215–234.
Kripke, Saul A. (1972) *Naming and Necessity*. Cambridge, MA: Harvard University Press.
LaFollette, Hugh. (1996) *Personal Relationships*. Cambridge: Blackwell.
Lakoff, George, and Johnson, Mark. (1980) "Conceptual Metaphor in Everyday Language." *Journal of Philosophy* 77 (8): 453–486. www.jstor.org/stable/2025464.
Lange, Marc. (2010) "What Are Mathematical Coincidences (and Why Does It Matter)?" *Mind* 119 (474): 307–340. www.jstor.org/stable/40865281.
Larmer, Robert A. (1985) "Miracles and the Laws of Nature." *Dialogue* 24 (2): 227–235. https://doi.org/10.1017/s0012217300043067.
Lebens, Samuel. (2019) "A Commentary on a Midrash: Metaphors about Metaphor." In *Jewish Philosophy in an Analytic Age*, edited by Samuel Lebens, Dani Rabinowitz, and Aaron Segal. Oxford: Oxford University Press. https://doi.org/10.1093/oso/9780198811374.003.0005.
Leftow, B. (2012) *God and Necessity*. Oxford: Oxford University Press.
Leibniz, G. W. (1684) 1989. "Meditations on Knowledge, Truth, and Ideas." In Ariew and Garber 1989, 23–27.
Leibniz, G. W. (1697) 1989. "On the Ultimate Origination of Things." In Ariew and Garber 1989, 149–155.
Leibniz, G. W. (1710) 2005. *Theodicy: Essays on the Goodness of God, the Freedom of Man, and the Origin of Evil*. Edited by Austin Farrer. Translated by E. M. Huggard. La Salle, IL: Open Court. Reprint, Salt Lake City: Project Gutenberg. www.gutenberg.org/ebooks/17147.
Leibniz, G. W. (1714) 1989a. "Principles of Nature and Grace, Based on Reason." In Ariew and Garber 1989, 206–213.
Leibniz, G. W. (1714) 1989b. "The Principles of Philosophy, or, the Monadology." In Ariew and Garber 1989, 213–224.
Leslie, John. (1979) *Value and Existence*. Totowa: Rowman and Littlefield.
Leuenberger, Stephan. (2014) "Grounding and Necessity." *Inquiry: An Interdisciplinary Journal of Philosophy* 57 (2): 151–174. https://doi.org/10.1080/0020174X.2013.855654.

Levine, Joseph. (1983) "Materialism and Qualia: The Explanatory Gap." *Pacific Philosophical Quarterly* 64 (4): 354–361. https://doi.org/10.1111/j.1468-0114.1983.tb00207.x.
Levine, Joseph. (2001) *Purple Haze*. Cambridge, MA: MIT Press.
Levine, Michael. (1989) *Hume and the Problem of Miracles*. Dordrecht: Kluwer.
Levy, Neil. (2011) *Hard Luck*. New York: Oxford University Press.
Lewis, David. (1969) *Convention*. Cambridge, MA: Harvard University Press.
Lewis, David. (1976) "The Paradoxes of Time Travel." *American Philosophical Quarterly* 13 (2): 145–152. www.jstor.org/stable/20009616.
Lewis, David. (1986) *On the Plurality of Worlds*. Malden, MA: Blackwell.
Loar, Brian. (1990) "Phenomenal States." *Philosophical Perspectives* 4: 81–108. www.jstor.org/stable/2214188.
Lowe, E. J. (2013) "Metaphysical Nihilism Revisited." In Goldschmidt 2013, 167–181.
Luper, Steven. (2012) *The Philosophy of Death*. Cambridge: Cambridge University Press.
Luther, Martin. (1520) 2018. *The Babylonian Captivity of the Church*. Abridged. In *The Essential Luther*, edited and translated by Tryntje Helfferich. Indianapolis and Cambridge: Hackett.
Mackie, J. L. (1955) "Evil and Omnipotence." *Mind* 64 (254): 200–212. www.jstor.org/stable/2251467.
Mackie, J. L. (1974) *The Cement of the Universe*. Oxford: Oxford University Press.
Mackie, J. L. (1982) *The Miracle of Theism*. Oxford: Clarendon.
Maddy, Penelope. (1990) *Realism in Mathematics*. Oxford: Clarendon.
Maddy, Penelope. (1997) *Naturalism in Mathematics*. Oxford: Clarendon Press.
Maimonides, Moses. *The Guide of the Perplexed*. Abridged translation: Rabin 1995.
Maitzen, Stephen. (2013) "Questioning the Question." In Goldschmidt 2013, 252–271.
Malament, David B. (1984) "'Time Travel' in the Gödel Universe." *PSA: Proceedings of the Biennial Meeting of the Philosophy of Science Association*, 91–100. www.jstor.org/stable/192497.
Mancosu, Paolo. (2018) "Explanation in Mathematics." In *The Stanford Encyclopedia of Philosophy*. Summer 2018 ed., edited by Edward N. Zalta. https://plato.stanford.edu/archives/sum2018/entries/mathematics-explanation/.
Manson, Neil, ed. (2003) *God and Design*. London: Routledge.
Marmura, Michael E., trans. (2000) *The Incoherence of the Philosophers*. 2nd ed. By Abu Hamid Muhammad al-Ghazali. Islamic Translations Series. Provo, UT: Brigham Young University Press.

Martin, Michael, and Augustine, Keith, eds. (2015) *The Myth of an Afterlife*. Lanham: Rowman & Littlefield.

Maudlin, Tim. (1993) "Buckets of Water and Waves of Space: Why Spacetime is Probably a Substance." *Philosophy of Science* 60 (2): 183–203. www.jstor.org/stable/188350.

Maudlin, Tim. (2007) *The Metaphysics Within Physics*. New York: Oxford University Press.

Maudlin, Tim. (2012) *Philosophy of Physics: Space and Time*. Princeton Foundations of Contemporary Philosophy. Princeton and Oxford: Princeton University Press.

Mayerfield, Jamie. (2002) *Suffering and Moral Responsibility*. Oxford: Oxford University Press.

Mayr, Ernst. (2001) *What Evolution Is*. New York: Basic Books.

McCann, Hugh J. (2012) *Creation and the Sovereignty of God*. Bloomington: Indiana University Press.

McCarthy, Richard Joseph, trans. (1980) *Freedom and Fulfillment: An Annotated Translation of Al-Ghazālī's al-Munqidh min al-ḍalāl and Other Relevant Works of Al-Ghazālī*. Library of Classical Arabic Literature. Boston: Twayne.

McCauley, Robert. (2011) *Why Religion Is Natural and Science Is Not*. Oxford: Oxford University Press.

McDermid, Kirk. (2008) "Miracles: Metaphysics, Physics, and Physicalism." *Religious Studies* 44 (2): 125–147. www.jstor.org/stable/27749944.

McFague, Sally. (1983) *Metaphorical Theology*. London: SCM Press.

Mele, Alfred. (2017) *Aspects of Agency*. New York: Oxford University Press.

Mellor, Hugh. (1995) *The Facts of Causation*. London: Routledge.

Mellor, Hugh, and Oliver, Alex, eds. (1997) *Properties*. Oxford: Oxford University Press.

Menzel, Christopher. (1987) "Theism, Platonism, and the Metaphysics of Mathematics." *Faith and Philosophy* 4 (4): 365–382. https://place.asburyseminary.edu/faithandphilosophy/vol4/iss4/1.

Metzinger, Thomas. (2009) *The Ego Tunnel*. New York: Basic Books.

Millikan, Ruth. (1984) *Language, Thought, and Other Biological Categories*. Cambridge, MA: MIT Press.

Molnar, George. (2005) *Powers*. Oxford: Oxford University Press.

Morewedge, Parviz, trans. (1973) *The Metaphysica of Avicenna (ibn Sīnā): A Critical Translation-Commentary and Analysis of the Fundamental Arguments in Avicenna's Metaphysica in the Dānish Nāma-i ʿalāʾī (The Book of Scientific Knowledge)*. Persian Heritage Series 13. London: Routledge.

Morreall, John. (2009) *Comic Relief*. Malden: Wiley-Blackwell.

Morris, Thomas V., and Menzel, Christopher. (1986) "Absolute Creation." *American Philosophical Quarterly* 23 (4): 353–362. www.jstor.com/stable/20014160.

Nagel, Thomas. (1997) *The Last Word*. Oxford: Oxford University Press.
Norenzayan, Ara. (2013) *Big Gods*. Princeton: Princeton University Press.
Nussbaum, Martha. (1996) *Love's Knowledge*. Oxford: Oxford University Press.
O'Connor, Timothy. (2008) *Theism and Ultimate Explanation: The Necessary Shape of Contingency*. London: Wiley-Blackwell.
O'Neill, Onora. (2013) *Acting on Principle: An Essay on Kantian Ethics*. 2nd ed. Cambridge: Cambridge University Press.
Oppy, Graham. (1995) *Ontological Arguments and Belief in God*. New York: Cambridge University Press.
Oppy, Graham. (2005) "Omnipotence." *Philosophy and Phenomenological Research* 71: 56–84. https://doi.org/10.1111/j.1933-1592.2005.tb00430.x.
Oppy, Graham. (2006a) *Arguing about Gods*. New York: Cambridge University Press.
Oppy, Graham. (2006b) *Philosophical Perspectives on Infinity*. Cambridge: Cambridge University Press.
Oppy, Graham. (2011) "Über Die Aussichten Erfolgreicher Beweise Für Theismus Oder Atheismus." In *Gottesbeweise*, edited by J. Bromand and G. Kreis, 599–644. Berlin: Suhrkamp Verlag.
Oppy, Graham. (2013a) *The Best Argument against God*. London: Palgrave MacMillan.
Oppy, Graham. (2013b) "Ultimate Naturalistic Causal Explanations." In Goldschmidt 2013, 46–63.
Oppy, Graham. (2014) *Describing Gods*. Cambridge: Cambridge University Press.
Oppy, Graham. (2015) "What Derivations Cannot Do." *Religious Studies* 51 (3): 323–333. https://doi.org/10.1017/S0034412515000256.
Oppy, Graham. (2018a) *Atheism and Agnosticism*. Elements in the Philosophy of Religion. Cambridge: Cambridge University Press. https://doi.org/10.1017/9781108555340.
Oppy, Graham. (2018b) *Naturalism and Religion*. New York: Routledge.
Oppy, Graham. (2019) *Atheism: The Basics*. New York: Routledge.
Overall, Christine. (1985) "Miracles as Evidence Against the Existence of God." *Southern Journal of Philosophy* 23 (3): 347–353. https://doi.org/10.1111/j.2041-6962.1985.tb00404.x.
Pallen, Mark. (2009) *Evolution*. London: Rough Guide.
Panchuk, Michelle. (2016) "Created and Uncreated Things." *International Philosophical Quarterly* 56 (1): 99–112. https://doi.org/10.5840/ipq201612855.
Parfit, Derek. (2011) *On What Matters*. Oxford: Oxford University Press.
Parsons, Terence. (1980) *Non-Existent Objects*. New Haven: Yale University Press.

Paul, Laurie, and Hall, Ned. (2013) *Causation*. Oxford: Oxford University Press.

Pearce, Kenneth L. (2011) "Omnipotence." In *The Internet Encyclopedia of Philosophy*, edited by James Fieser and Bradley Dowden. November 8, 2011. www.iep.utm.edu/omnipote/.

Pearce, Kenneth L. (2017a) "Counterpossible Dependence and the Efficacy of the Divine Will." *Faith and Philosophy* 34 (1): 3–16. https://place.asburyseminary.edu/faithandphilosophy/vol34/iss1/1.

Pearce, Kenneth L. (2017b) "Foundational Grounding and the Argument from Contingency." *Oxford Studies in Philosophy of Religion* 8: 245–268. www.oxfordscholarship.com/view/10.1093/oso/9780198806967.001.0001/oso-9780198806967-chapter-11.

Pearce, Kenneth L. (2019) "Infinite Power and Finite Powers." In *The Infinity of God: New Perspectives in Theology and Philosophy*, edited by Benedikt Paul Göcke and Christian Tapp, 233–257. Notre Dame, IN: Notre Dame University Press.

Pearce, Kenneth L. (2020) "Are We Free to Break the Laws of Providence?" *Faith and Philosophy* 37 (2): 1–23. https://doi.org/10.37977/faithphil.2020.37.2.2.

Pearce, Kenneth L., and Pruss, Alexander R. (2012) "Understanding Omnipotence." *Religious Studies* 48 (3): 403–414. www.jstor.org/stable/23260033.

Pearl, Judea. (2000) *Causality*. Cambridge: Cambridge University Press.

Pereboom, Derk. (2017) "Theological Determinism and the Relationship with God." In *Free Will and Classical Theism: The Significance of Freedom in Perfect Being Theology*, edited by Hugh J. McCann, 201–220. New York: Oxford University Press. www.oxfordscholarship.com/view/10.1093/acprof:oso/9780190611200.001.0001/acprof-9780190611200-chapter-11.

Phillips, D. Z. (1986) *Belief, Change, and Forms of Life*. Hampshire: Macmillan.

Philo of Alexandria. *On the Account of the World's Creation Given by Moses*. Translated in Colson and Whitaker 1929a.

Philo of Alexandria. *On the Unchangeableness of God*. Translated in Colson and Whitaker 1929b.

Pincock, Christopher. (2015) "The Unsolvability of The Quintic: A Case Study in Abstract Mathematical Explanation." *Philosophers' Imprint* 15 (3): 1–19. http://hdl.handle.net/2027/spo.3521354.0015.003.

Pinnock, Clark, Rice, Richard, Sanders, John, Hasker, William, and Basinger, David. 1994. *The Openness of God: A Biblical Challenge to the Traditional Understanding of God*. Downers Grove, IL: InterVarsity Press.

Plantinga, Alvin. (1977) *God, Freedom and Evil*. Grand Rapids: Wm. B. Eerdmans.

Plantinga, Alvin. (1981) "Is Belief in God Properly Basic?" *Noûs* 15 (1): 41–51. www.jstor.org/stable/2215239.

Plantinga, Alvin. (2000) *Warranted Christian Belief*. New York: Oxford University Press.

Plato. "Euthyphro." In *Five Dialogues: Euthyphro, Apology, Crito, Meno, Phaedo*. 2nd ed., translated by G.M.A. Grube, revised by John M. Cooper. Indianapolis and Cambridge: Hackett, 2002.

Platvoet, Jan. (1990) "The Definers Defined: Traditions in the Definition of Religion." *Method & Theory in the Study of Religion* 2 (2): 180–212. www.jstor.org/stable/23549483.

Popper, Karl R. (1963) 1972. "Science: Conjectures and Refutations." In *Conjectures and Refutations: The Growth of Scientific Knowledge*. 4th ed., 33–65. London and Henley: Routledge.

Price, Huw. (2011) *Naturalism Without Mirrors*. Oxford: Oxford University Press.

Prinz, Jesse. (2012) *The Conscious Brain*. Oxford: Oxford University Press.

Prior, Arthur. (1957) *Time and Modality*. Oxford: Clarendon.

Provine, Robert. (2000) *Laughter*. Harmondsworth: Penguin.

Pruss, Alexander R. (2006) *The Principle of Sufficient Reason: A Reassessment*. Cambridge Studies in Philosophy. Cambridge: Cambridge University Press.

Pruss, Alexander R. (2016) "Divine Creative Freedom." *Oxford Studies in Philosophy of Religion* 7. www.oxfordscholarship.com/view/10.1093/acprof:oso/9780198757702.001.0001/acprof-9780198757702-chapter-9.

Pruss, Alexander R., and Rasmussen, Joshua L. (2018) *Necessary Existence*. New York: Oxford University Press.

Quine, Willard. (1953) *From a Logical Point of View*. Cambridge, MA: Harvard University Press.

Rabin, Chaim, trans. (1995) *The Guide of the Perplexed*. Abridged. By Moses Maimonides. Edited by Julius Guttman. Indianapolis: Hackett.

Radhakrishnan, Sarvepalli, and Moore, Charles A., eds. (1957) *A Source Book in Indian Philosophy*. Princeton: Princeton University Press.

Randall, Lisa. (2005) *Warped Passages: Unraveling the Mysteries of the Universe's Hidden Dimensions*. New York: Harper Perennial.

Rasmussen, Joshua. (2019) *How Reason Can Lead to God*. Downers Grove: Intervarsity Press.

Raz, Joseph. (2001) *Value, Respect and Attachment*. Cambridge: Cambridge University Press.

Reid, Thomas. (1764) 1997. *An Inquiry into the Human Mind: On the Principles of Common Sense*. Edited by Derek R. Brookes. The Edinburgh Edition of the Works of Thomas Reid. University Park, PA: The Pennsylvania State University Press.

Reimer, Marga. (2001) "Davidson on Metaphor." *Midwest Studies in Philosophy* 25 (1): 142–155. https://doi.org/10.1111/1475-4975.00043.

Resnick, Michael. (1997) *Mathematics as a Science of Patterns*. New York: Oxford University Press.
Rickles, Dean. (2014) *A Brief History of String Theory*. Berlin: Springer.
Rodriguez-Pereyra, Gonzalo. (2013) "The Subtraction Arguments for Metaphysical Nihilism: Compared and Defended." In Goldschmidt 2013, 197–214.
Rolls, Edmund, and Deco, Gustavo. (2010) *The Noisy Brain*. Oxford: Oxford University Press.
Rosenberg, Jay. (1998) *Thinking Clearly about Death*. Indianapolis: Hackett.
Routley, Richard. (1980) *Exploring Meinong's Jungle*. Canberra: Research School of the Social Sciences.
Rowe, William. (1975) *The Cosmological Argument*. New York: Fordham University Press.
Rowe, William. (1979) "The Problem of Evil and Some Varieties of Atheism." *American Philosophical Quarterly* 16: 335–341. https://www.jstor.org/stable/20009775.
Rowe, William. (1993) *Philosophy of Religion*. Belmont: Wadsworth.
Rowe, William. (2004) *Can God Be Free?* Oxford and New York: Clarendon Press.
Rucker, Rudy. (2004) *Infinity and the Mind*. Princeton: Princeton University Press.
Rundle, Bede. (2004) *Why Is There Something Rather Than Nothing?* Oxford: Oxford University Press.
Russell, Bertrand. (1952) 1997. "Is There a God?" In *Last Philosophical Testament, 1943–68*, vol. 11 of The Collected Papers of Bertrand Russell, edited by John G. Slater, 542–548. London and New York: Routledge. https://russell.humanities.mcmaster.ca/cpbr11p69.pdf.
Sachsenmaier, Dominic. (2011) *Global Perspectives on Global History*. Cambridge: Cambridge University Press.
Salmon, Nathan. (1981) *Reference and Essence*. Oxford: Blackwell.
Salmon, Wesley. (1998) *Causality and Explanation*. Oxford: Oxford University Press.
Savellos, Elias, and Yalcin, Ümit, eds. (1995) *Supervenience*. Cambridge: Cambridge University Press.
Scanlon, Thomas. (1998) *On What We Owe to Each Other*. Cambridge, MA: Harvard University Press.
Scarry, Elaine. (1988) *The Body in Pain*. Oxford: Oxford University Press.
Schaffer, Jonathan. (2009a) "On What Grounds What." In Chalmers, Manley, and Wasserman 2009, 347–383.
Schaffer, Jonathan. (2009b) "Spacetime the One Substance." *Philosophical Studies* 145 (1): 131–148. www.jstor.org/stable/27734469.
Schaffer, Jonathan. (2010) "Monism: The Priority of the Whole." *Philosophical Review* 119 (1): 31–76. www.jstor.org/stable/41684359.

Scheffler, Samuel. (2016) *Death and the Afterlife*. Oxford: Oxford University Press.
Schilbrack, Kevin. (2013) "What Isn't Religion?" *Journal of Religion* 93 (3): 291–318. www.jstor.org/stable/10.1086/670276.
Schroeder, Mark. (2005) "Cudworth and Normative Explanations." *Journal of Ethics and Social Philosophy* 1 (3): 1–28. https://doi.org/10.26556/jesp.v1i3.15.
Schwitzgebel, Eric. (2011) *Perplexities of Consciousness*. Cambridge, MA: MIT Press.
Scott, Michael. (2013) *Religious Language*. London: Palgrave Macmillan.
Searle, John. (1980) "Minds, Brains, and Programs." *Brain And Behavioural Sciences* 3: 417–424.
Segal, Aaron. (Forthcoming) "Dependence, Transcendence, and Creaturely Freedom: On the Incompatibility of Three Theistic Doctrines." *Mind*. https://doi.org/10.1093/mind/fzz082.
Sidelle, Alan. (1989) *Necessity, Essence and Individuation*. Ithaca: Cornell University Press.
Sider, T. (2011) *Writing the Book of the World*. Oxford: Oxford University Press.
Singh, Simon. (2004) *Big Bang: The Origin of the Universe*. New York: Fourth Estate.
Skiles, Alexander. (2015) "Against Grounding Necessitarianism." *Erkenntnis* 80 (4): 717–751. https://link.springer.com/article/10.1007%2Fs10670-014-9669-y.
Skyrms, Brian. (1980) *Causal Necessity*. New Haven: Yale University Press.
Slote, Michael. (2011) *The Impossibility of Perfection*. Oxford: Oxford University Press.
Smith, Tiddy. (2019) *The Methods of Science and Religion*. New York: Lexington Books.
Smith, Tiddy. (2020) "The Common Consent Argument for the Existence of Nature Spirits." *Australasian Journal of Philosophy* 98 (2): 334–348. https://doi.org/10.1080/00048402.2019.1621912.
Snow, Nancy. (2010) *Virtue as Social Intelligence*. New York: Routledge.
Sobel, Jordan Howard. (2004) *Logic and Theism: Arguments for and Against Beliefs in God*. Cambridge: Cambridge University Press.
Sober, Elliott. (2015) *Ockham's Razor*. Cambridge: Cambridge University Press.
Soble, Alan. (1990) *The Structure of Love*. New Haven: Yale University Press.
Solomon, Robert. (1988) *About Love*. New York: Simon & Schuster.
Soskice, Janet. (1985) *Metaphor and Religious Language*. Oxford: Clarendon.
Spinoza, Benedictus de. (1670) 2007. *Theological-Political Treatise*. Edited by Jonathan Israel. Cambridge Texts in the History of Philosophy. Cambridge: Cambridge University Press.

Stich, Stephen. (1983) *From Folk Psychology to Cognitive Science*. Cambridge, MA: MIT Press.
Stoljar, Daniel. (2017) *Philosophical Progress*. New York: Oxford University Press.
Stump, Eleonore. (2016) *The God of the Bible and the God of the Philosophers*. Milwaukee: Marquette University Press.
Suppes, Patrick. (1970) *A Probabilistic Theory of Causation*. Amsterdam: North-Holland.
Surowiecki, James. (2004) *The Wisdom of the Crowds*. New York: Anchor.
Swanton, Christine. (2013) *The Virtue Ethics of Hume and Nietzsche*. Oxford: Wiley-Blackwell.
Swinburne, Richard. (1994) *The Christian God*. Oxford: Oxford University Press.
Talmont-Kaminski, Konrad. (2013) *Religion as Magical Ideology*. Durham: Acumen.
Taves, Ann. (2000) *Fits, Trances and Visions*. Princeton: Princeton University Press.
Thalos, Mariam. (2013) *Without Hierarchies*. New York: Oxford University Press.
Thomasson, Amie. (1999) *Fiction and Metaphysics*. Cambridge: Cambridge University Press.
Tooley, Michael. (1987) *Causation*. Oxford: Clarendon.
Tremlin, Todd. (2006) *Minds and Gods*. Oxford: Oxford University Press.
Tucker, Aviezer, ed. (2009) *Companion to the Philosophy of History and Historiography*. Cambridge: Cambridge University Press.
Tuomela, Raimo. (1995) *The Importance of Us*. Stanford: Stanford University Press.
Tweedt, Chris. (2013) "Splitting the Horns of Euthyphro's Modal Relative." *Faith and Philosophy* 30 (2): 205–212. https://place.asburyseminary.edu/faithandphilosophy/vol30/iss2/7.
Twelftree, Graham, ed. (2009) *Companion to Miracles*. Cambridge: Cambridge University Press.
Unger, Peter K. (1979) "I Do Not Exist." In *Perception and Identity: Essays Presented to A. J. Ayer with His Replies to Them*, edited by G. F. Macdonald. London: Palgrave. https://link.springer.com/chapter/10.1007/978-1-349-04862-5_10.
Van Cleve, James. (1999) *Problems from Kant*. New York and Oxford: Oxford University Press.
Van Cleve, James. (2003) "Is Knowledge Easy—Or Impossible? Externalism as the Only Alternative to Skepticism." In *The Skeptics: Contemporary Essays*, edited by Stephen Luper. Farnham: Ashgate.
van Fraassen, Bas. (1989) *Laws and Symmetry*. Oxford: Clarendon.
Van Gulick, Robert. (2018) "Consciousness." In *The Stanford Encyclopedia of Philosophy*. Spring 2018 ed., edited by Edward N. Zalta.

Metaphysics Research Lab. Stanford University. https://plato.stanford.edu/archives/spr2018/entries/consciousness/.

van Inwagen, Peter. (1996) "Why is There Anything at All?" *Aristotelian Society Supplementary Volume* 70 (1): 95–110. www.jstor.org/stable/4107004.

van Inwagen, Peter. (2006) *The Problem of Evil: The Gifford Lectures Delivered in the University of St Andrews in 2003*. Oxford: Clarendon Press. https://doi.org/10.1093/acprof:oso/9780199245604.001.0001.

Vicens, Leigh, and Simon Kittle. (2019) *God and Human Freedom*. Elements in the Philosophy of Religion. Cambridge: Cambridge University Press. www.cambridge.org/core/elements/god-and-human-freedom/D0EE63BB14A6F9C4F85DB3CFE347E891.

Voltaire. (1759) 2016. *Candide: Or, Optimism*. 3rd ed. Edited by Nicholas Cronk. Translated by Robert M. Adams. Norton Critical Editions. New York and London: W. W. Norton.

Walton, Kendall L. (1990) *Mimesis as Make-Believe*. Cambridge, MA: Harvard University Press.

Walton, Kendall L. (1993) "Metaphor and Prop Oriented Make-Believe." *European Journal of Philosophy* 1 (1): 39–57. https://doi.org/10.1111/j.1468-0378.1993.tb00023.x.

Wetzel, Linda. (2009) *Types and Tokens*. Cambridge, MA: MIT Press.

White, Roger. (2010) *Talking about God*. Aldershot: Ashgate.

Willette, Damian A., Simmonds, Sara E., Cheng, Samantha H., Esteves, Sofia, Kane, Tonya L., Neutzel, Hayley, Pilaud, Nicholas, Rachmawati, Rita, and Barber, Paul H. (2017) "Using DNA Barcoding to Track Seafood Mislabeling in Los Angeles." *Conservation Biology* 31 (5): 1076–1085. https://doi.org/10.1111/cobi.12888.

Williams, Thomas, ed. and trans. (2007) *Basic Writings*. By Anselm of Canterbury. Indianapolis and Cambridge: Hackett.

Williamson, Timothy. (2008) *The Philosophy of Philosophy*. Malden: Blackwell.

Wilson, Jessica M. (2014) "No Work for a Theory of Grounding." *Inquiry: An Interdisciplinary Journal of Philosophy* 57 (5/6): 535–579. https://doi.org/10.1080/0020174X.2014.907542.

Wittgenstein, Ludwig. (1953) 2009. *Philosophical Investigations*. 4th ed. Translated by G.E.M. Anscombe, P.M.S. Hacker, and Joachim Schulte. Malden, MA: Wiley-Blackwell.

Wittgenstein, Ludwig. (1972) *On Certainty*. Edited by G.E.M. Anscombe and G. H. von Wright. Translated by Denis Paul and G.E.M. Anscombe. New York: Harper Torchbooks.

Wolf, Susan. (1990) *Freedom Within Limits*. New York: Oxford University Press.

Wolf, Susan. (2010) *Meaning in Life and Why It Matters*. Princeton: Princeton University Press.

Wolff, Johanna. (2015) "Spin as a Determinable." *Topoi* 34 (2): 379–386. https://doi.org/10.1007/s11245-015-9319-2.

Wong, David. (2006) *Natural Moralities*. Oxford: Oxford University Press.

Wood, Allen W. (1999) *Kant's Ethical Thought*. Cambridge: Cambridge University Press.

Wu, Wayne. (2018) "The Neuroscience of Consciousness." In *The Stanford Encyclopedia of Philosophy*. Winter 2018 ed., edited by Edward N. Zalta. Metaphysics Research Lab. Stanford University. https://plato.stanford.edu/archives/win2018/entries/consciousness-neuroscience/.

Yablo, Stephen. (2001) "Go Figure: A Path Through Fictionalism." In P. French and H. Wettstein (eds.). *Midwest Studies in Philosophy* XXV: 72–102.

Yablo, Stephen. (2005) "The Myth of the Seven." In *Fictionalism in Metaphysics*, edited by M. Kalderon. Oxford: Clarendon.

Yourgrau, Palle. (2019) *Death and Non-Existence*. Oxford: Oxford University Press.

Zagzebski, Linda Trinkaus. (2012) *Epistemic Authority: A Theory of Trust, Authority, and Autonomy in Belief*. New York: Oxford University Press. https://doi.org/10.1093/acprof:oso/9780199936472.001.0001.

Ziman, John. (2000) *Real Science*. Cambridge: Cambridge University Press.

Index

Abrahamic Religious Traditions 3–4, 17–22, 28–9, 235, 252–4; *see also* Christianity, Islam, Judaism
abstract object 108, 122–124
actual 56–7, 61, 104–106, 143, 168, 229
actualism 107
Adams, Douglas 152, 253
afterlife 148, 157, 159
agnostic 87, 93, 126, 179–180, 256
agnosticism 93
Aguirre, Anthony 160
alethic modalities 160
al-Ghazali 4, 20–2
Alston, William 2–3, 75–7, 250
Amis, Kingsley 152
analogy *see* use of language: analogical
analysis 125
analytic 120, 162
Anselm of Canterbury 25, 29, 51–7,
antelope *see* pronghorn
a posteriori 160, 275
a priori 141, 159, 197–8, 275
Aquinas, Thomas 3, 17–20, 55n34, 195, 203–4, 209–10, 212–14
argument 13, 93–95, 177–83, 219–220, 256, 261–265, 298–301, 304; good 177–83, 261–265, 283, 301; invalid 168; sound 95, 220, 291; successful 94–95, 177–180, 219, 262, 299; valid 13, 32–3, 55–7, 70, 168, 178–9
Aristophanes 44

Aristotle 146, 195, 224
art 151–153
aseity 272
atemporality 3, 18, 23–4, 213, 228, 249
atheism 4, 13–17, 25, 51–3, 77–8, 93, 104, 168
atheist 6, 93–95, 98–101, 150, 172, 287–288
atonement 228
authentic religious experience *see* religious experience: authentic.
autonomy 197, 289
autonomous fact 36, 51, 57–8, 191–2, 202, 268, 277, 282–283
Avicenna 3, 17, 19, 20, 209–10
axiom 57, 105, 116, 192–3, 201, 221, 269
axiomatisation 116–117, 192–3, 267–269, 278

background theory 76, 80–1, 86
Baha'i 235
Baker, Lynne Rudder 43n22
Baldwin, James 152
Bayesianism 160
Bible 18, 21–2, 67–8, 78, 84–5
big bang 4, 38–9, 62–3
black and white room 139
Blockhead 138
brain in a vat 205
Brecht, Bertolt 152
brute fact 35–6, 51, 58–9, 64, 105, 181–5, 202, 263, 279–283

brute contingency 111, 164–165, 231, 281
brute necessity 105, 164–165, 183–202, 269, 275–279
Buddhism 1, 3, 71, 235

Calvin John 4, 21–2
Calvino, Italo 152
Camp, Elizabeth 214
cannonball 40
canonical notation 122
car *see* dented car
Carnap, Rudolph 6
Castañeda, Hector-Neri 41–2
causal compatibilism *see* compatibilism, causal
causal determinism *see* determinism, causal
causal explanation *see* explanation, causal
causal reality 16–17, 23, 31–2, 65, 102–106, 127, 164, 168, 204, 242
causation 31–2, 37–42, 103, 109–112, 142–143, 164, 176, 184, 247–8
cephalonomancy 233
chance: objective *see* objective chance
Chekhov, Anton 152
chocolate cake 196–7
China brain 138
Chinese room 138
Christianity 1, 6, 19–21, 25, 28, 65, 67–8, 78, 84–5
Churchland, Patricia and Paul 243–4
classical foundationalism 2–3, 70–4
classical theism *see* theism: classical.
clay *see* statue
cognitive science of religion 4, 79–80, 83
coherence 3, 14–15, 220, 235–6, 250
commitment of a worldview 115–117, 121, 165, 170, 228–9, 266; ideological 2, 115–117, 119, 121, 158, 164–5, 170, 191, 211–16, 221, 228, 272–4; ontological 2, 106, 115–118, 120–1, 158, 164–5, 170, 191, 209–11, 220, 228, 269–72; primitive 114, 117–118, 191–4, 209–16, 278; theoretical 2, 95, 105, 108, 115–17, 119, 121–3, 140, 158, 164–5, 170, 191–4, 220–1, 228, 255, 267–9
compatibilism 28, 143
composition 44, 114–116
concept 21, 211–16
conceptual truth 99–100
conclusion 13, 32–3, 93–5, 102, 168, 177–81
Confucianism 235
Conrad, Joseph 152
consciousness 96, 103, 137–40, 211–12, 243–5
consequence *see* logical consequence.
consequentialism 145
consistency 14–15, 143–4, 149, 169, 221
constitution 43, 114, 116, 224–5, 248–9
consubstantiality 272
contingency. 106n15, 110–11, 164–5, 183–5, 201, 229; *see also* necessity.
contradiction 3, 14–15, 24–5, 181–2, 200, 249–50
contrastive explanation *see* explanation, contrastive
Correia, Fabrice 44n23, 46n26
cosmological arguments 4, 29–65, 113, 163n55, 177, 181–2, 263; Kalam 97
Cowper, William 150
credence 130, 159–60, 166–7

Daoism 235
Dasgupta, Shamik 36, 191
data 221, 266; *see also* evidence.
death 130, 135, 137, 157–159, 168
debt 44–5
definition 66, 93, 99, 101, 103, 116, 119–21, 134, 168, 202; nominal 36, 53–4, 276; real 36–7, 54–9, 192, 195–6, 275, 282–3, 289; stipulative 120
Deng, Natalja 24
dented car 31
deontologism 145; *see also* consequentialism; ethics: Kantian; virtue ethics
dependence 104, 114, 131, 275–9, 284; *see also* grounding

derivation 94, 219, 262
Descartes, René 2, 71–3
determinable / determinate 114
determination 114–115
determinism: causal 143; theological 27–8, 143, 298–9
disagreement 78–84, 87–9, 117, 167–72
divination 233–234
divine 103–104,106–107, 164
divine simplicity 209–10, 228
domain of quantification 221, 269–72
doxastic possibility *see* possibility: doxastic
doxastic practice 76–82
Dreaming, The 236

Edwards, Jonathan 21
Egan, Greg 152
Einstein, Albert 89
Einstein's Field Equations 62–3, 222–3, 246
elephant *see* pink elephant
Eliot, George 152
embrace one horn 194
epistemic possibility *see* possibility: epistemic
epistemology 70–90, 249–252
equivocation *see* use of language, equivocal.
essential property 119
ethics 186–7; Kantian 196–200, 289; theistic 288–90; *see also* Euthyphro Dilemma
Euclid 39–40
Euthyphro Dilemma 189–90, 194–6, 199, 285–8, 290
events 103, 111–12, 128–9, 131–3, 270
evidence 98, 132–3, 150, 160, 171–2
evil 14–15, 28, 49, 96, 148, 156, 287; horrendous 98–100, 171
evolution 124, 126–8, 133–4, 136–7, 140–1, 151, 154–6, 163, 243–4
excluded middle 101
existence 93, 105, 107, 111–13, 128, 157, 162
existentialism 108
explanation 100, 104–5, 110–13, 117, 124, 127, 129, 133, 137, 142, 145, 153, 155–6, 160, 162, 165, 171, 183–202, 222, 224–5, 275–9, 283–4; causal 31, 41–2, 156, 224–5; contrastive 111–12, 127, 183–5, 230, 279–81; necessitating 47, 60
explanatory comprehensiveness 15–16, 31–2, 59, 63–5, 90–1, 177,193–4, 201–2, 278
expressive power 122–3, 265
external world scepticism *see* scepticism: external world

facts 111–12, 139, 145, 165n56, 270
faculties (of the mind) 72–4, 78–82, 84, 87, 90–1, 177, 205, 207, 232, 234, 249–52, 293
faith 95, 166–7
fairies 12
falsifiability 69–70, 89
family resemblance 273
Fielding, Sarah 150
Fine, Kit 42
figuralism 122
fine-tuning 97–8, 127–8
flourishing 146–7
form of life 69–70, 256
foundationalism *see* classical foundationalism
four-dimensionalism 108
freedom 26–8, 48–51, 100, 105, 110, 142–5, 165n56, 199–200, 274
Friend, Stacie 52
functionalism 138
fundamentality 42–3, 60n36, 64, 113–15, 191–4, 209–11, 216, 270

Gaunilo of Marmoutiers 53–4
general relativity 61–3, 88, 108, 127, 223, 243–7
generalized continuum hypothesis 285
geometry 39–40, 197–8
Ghazali *see* Al-Ghazali
Gibbs, Phebe 150
God 4–5, 12–29, 93, 96–102, 104, 107, 109, 112–13, 124, 127–8, 132–4, 136, 139, 141–2, 145, 155–7, 163, 167, 171, 201–16, 222,

232, 235, 282–3, 285–8, 298–301, 304 see also Theism
Gödel, Kurt 62
gods 4–5, 13–14, 33–4, 78, 85, 93–6, 102–4, 129, 132–4, 149, 168, 171, 189, 205
Godzilla 166–167
Goldbach's Conjecture 161
good 4–5, 105, 118, 120, 145, 147–8, 153, 190
Gorky, Maxim 152
Graves, Robert 152
Greene, Brian 23, 38–9
greatness 163
groundhogs 85
grounding 4, 41–7, 59, 60, 64, 113–15, 188–9, 224–9, 247–9, 275–9

halibut sushi 206–8, 251–2
hallucination 4, 76, 78–87, 207–8, 251–2
Higgs Boson 75–6
Hinduism 1, 235
history 4, 32–65, 128–129, 130–131, 136, 172, 181–2, 215–16, 248–9, 258
Holbach, Baron 172
Holocaust 100
Holmes, Sherlock 53
hope 166–7
horrendous evil see evil, horrendous
Housman, A. E. 152
Hughes, Christopher 210
Hume, David 14, 37, 41, 79–80, 172, 203–4
Hume's Principle 284
humour 154
hypostatic union 272

Ibn Sina See Avicenna
Ibsen, Henrik 152
ice cream cone 52
ideal agnostic 179–80; see also agnostic.
ideological commitment see commitment, ideological.
ideological simplicity see simplicity, ideological.
ideology 117
immutability 3, 18, 22, 228

impassibility 3, 18, 228
indeterminism 60–1, 143, 183–5, 230–1, 281
indigenous religions 235
infinity 161–2, 167
informational content 275
innocent 93
instantiation 162
intentionality 138–40
intrinsic property 119, 156
invalidity see argument, invalid.
irreflexivity 109
Islam 1, 17, 19–21, 28, 78

Jainism 235
John, Elton 215
Johnson, Elizabeth 22n7
Judaism 1, 17, 19, 21, 85
judgment: suspension of see suspension of judgment.

Kafka, Franz 152
Kant, Immanuel 29n13, 54n33, 194–200
killing 144
Korsgaard, Christine 198, 199n6
Koslicki, Katherin 42–3

Lange, Marc 185
Laplace, Pierre-Simon 175–6
Larkin, Philip 152
law of excluded middle see excluded middle.
Leibniz, Gottfried Wilhelm 3, 4, 18, 20, 27–9, 33, 39–40, 47, 49–51, 55, 200–1
Lem, Stanislaw 152
Levi, Primo 152
Lewis, Sinclair 152
Locke, John 2
logic 48, 56–7, 105, 130, 141, 178, 187, 192, 199 see also argument: valid
logical closure 169
logical consequence 105, 265, 269
logical necessity see necessity: logical
logical possibility see possibility: logical
London, Jack 152

Lost Island 53–4
love 149–150
Luther, Martin 4, 21–2

Maddy, Penelope 186
Maimonides, Moses 3, 17, 19, 209–10
Maitzen, Stephen 30–1
mathematics 30, 31, 60, 123–4, 130, 145, 185–6, 192–4, 199–202, 275–9, 284–6
Maudlin, Tim 23, 41, 61, 62
Maugham, Somerset 152
maxim 197, 289–290
McCann, Hugh 28
meaningfulness 147–149
Meslier, Jean 172
metaphor 119, 212–15, 274
metaphysical necessity *see* necessity, metaphysical
metaphysical possibility *see* possibility, metaphysical
metaphysics 17–18, 30–1, 44–5, 48, 63, 65–6, 88–9, 104–6 *see also* necessity: metaphysical
mindedness 102–3, 107, 136–9, 157, 211–12, 243–4
miracle 67, 96, 131–4, 136, 202–4, 296–7 *see also* special divine action.
modal ontological argument 55–8, 282–3
modal operator 55–7, 187
modalised claim 104
modality 63, 104, 106n15; *see also* necessity.
monism *see* priority monism
monotheism 66–70, 78, 83–4, 93, 136
monotheist 93, 296
monotheistic religion *see* religion, monotheistic
monotheistic religious experience *see* religious experience: monotheistic
morality 48–9, 96, 99, 141,144–5, 147–9, 152–3, 155, 186–7, 189–90, 194–9, 275–9, 287
Mozart, Wolfgang Amadeus 153
MRE *see* religious experience: monotheistic
multiverse 38–9, 103
Murdoch, Iris 152

Napoleon 175
natural reality 31–2, 98, 102–103, 106–109, 112–113, 128, 162, 165
naturalism 2–5, 16–17, 31–2, 34–5, 41, 44–9, 58–65, 71, 73–5, 77, 79–83, 88, 90–1, 102–4, 106–7, 127, 132–4, 136, 142–3, 147–60, 164–5, 168–72, 176–7, 181–2, 185, 186, 188, 200–2, 209–10, 241–7, 255–8, 260–1, 295, 303
necessary a posteriori 160, 275
necessary a priori 198, 275
necessary being 3, 18, 23–7, 41, 51–8, 200–2, 231, 258, 291
necessitating explanation *see* explanation: necessitating
necessity 24–6, 55–7, 97–8, 104–7, 111, 113, 144, 152, 157, 183–202, 284; logical 24–6; metaphysical 24–6, 48, 275–9; physical 24–6
Newton, Isaac 20, 88
Nietzsche, Friederich 148
nominal definition *see* definition: ominal
nominalisation 120
nominalism 122–3
non-cognitivism 130
non-modal 104
nowism 107
numbers 30, 124, 200, 285–6

object 103, 108–9, 120, 122–4, 270, 279
objective chance 61, 97–8, 105–6, 109–12, 127, 143, 183–4
objectivity 197, 279
omnipotence 3, 17, 27, 100–1, 105, 163, 179, 210, 228, 272
omniscience 3, 17, 27, 105, 163, 210, 228, 272
ontological arguments 25, 29, 51–8, 282–3
ontological commitment *see* commitment, ontological
ontological simplicity *see* simplicity, ontological
ontology 117
optimism 27–8, 49–50, 298–9
Overall, Christine 203

parsimony 125 see also simplicity.
parthood 44, 97, 103, 109, 114, 116, 119, 165, 225–6
Pascal, Blaise 296
Pascal's Wager 160, 167
penguins 30–1
perception see sensory perception
Pereboom, Derk 28
perfection 13–14, 48–51, 105, 162–4, 176, 210, 298–9
perichoresis 272
physical necessity see necessity: physical
physical possibility see possibility: physical
philosophy 13–17, 71–2, 84, 87–8, 120, 125–126, 141, 147, 172, 177–83, 218, 233, 235, 255–7, 295, 304
Philo of Alexandria 3, 17, 19
pink elephant 80–3 see also Hallucination
Plantinga, Alvin 2–3, 14n2, 29n12, 55n35, 75
Plato 189
Platvoet, Jan 65, 69–70
play 153–155
Pope, Alexander 150
Popper, Karl 89
possibility 27, 47, 50, 54–7, 61, 104, 187–8, 192; doxastic 106n15, 160; epistemic 106n15; metaphysical 106n15, 223; physical 61–3, 222–223, 246; see also necessity
possible world 27–8, 50, 56–7, 61, 153, 161, 229
Potter, Harry 52
powers 270
practical judgment 197–8, 289
predicate 118–22, 221
predication 118, 122
premise 13, 32–4, 94–5, 97–102, 113, 168–9, 178–80, 182
presentism 108
primitive commitment see commitment: primitive.
Principle of Sufficient Reason 33, 35, 51, 112
priority monism 209
probability 60, 61, 159, 281

pronghorn 86–7
property 114, 119–22; see also essential property, intrinsic property
prototypes 273
Proust, Marcel 152
Pruss, Alexander 25n10, 29n12, 33n17, 40, 47n29, 50, 57, 179, 184, 200, 210, 216

quantifier 120
quantum mechanics 60–1, 210–11, 223, 245–7
Quine, Willard 121–122
Quran 18, 20–1, 78, 85

rainbow 251–2
Rainbow Serpent 236
Rasmussen, Joshua 25n10, 57, 165n56
rational obligation 179–80
rationality 13, 26, 48–51, 59, 70, 74–7, 88–9, 94, 119, 132, 141, 170, 179–83, 196–200, 210, 251–2; see also reason
real definition see definition: eal
realisation 114–15
realism 108, 122–123
reason 12, 20–2, 26–7, 32, 34–5, 48–51, 71–4, 84, 94, 98n5, 103, 118, 137, 140–142, 168, 170–1, 196–9, 215, 250, 274, 284–6; see also Rationality
reductio 288
reduction 45
Reid, Thomas 71–2; see also Reidian epistemology
Reidian epistemology 70–5, 86, 88, 205, 207, 218, 251, 292–301, 304
reincarnation 157
relativity see general relativity
reliable religious experience see religious experience: reliable
religion 17–18, 21–2, 65–70, 79–84, 87–9, 129, 134–6, 141, 149, 152, 159, 205, 208; monotheistic 66–70, 83–4; see also Abrahamic Religious Traditions.

religious belief 12–13, 68–9, 74–5, 133, 136, 141; monotheistic *see* monotheism.
religious epistemology 70–8
religious experience 4, 65–90, 96, 133–4, 136, 168, 176–7, 202–8, 232–7, 249–54, 292–7, 304; authentic 4, 84–7, 206–8, 235, 251–2, 295–7; monotheistic (MRE) 66–70, 77, 78, 81, 85–6, 90, 203, 252–4, 294–7; reliable 79–90, 202, 206–8, 295–297
reproducibility 125
revelation 21–2
rocks 30–1
Rowe, William 49n30
Russell, Bertrand 12, 65
Russell's Teapot 12, 65, 81, 83, 260

sandwich 43–4, 64
salvation 96, 159–60, 166–7
sceptical theism 100
scepticism 73–4, 202–8, 250, 292–3; external world 171, 205, 292
Schaffer, Jonathan 42, 52, 209
science 16–17, 30–1, 36, 44–6, 60–3, 68–77, 87–9, 103, 117, 125–6, 141, 164, 186, 204, 206–7, 222, 241–7
self-evidence 2, 70–1, 73–4; *see also* analytic; conceptual truth.
self-explanation 37–8, 226
sensory perception 2, 71–7, 82, 84–7, 137, 141, 202–3, 205, 207, 250–2
Shaw, George Bernard 152
Shintoism 235
Sikhism 235
simplicity 15, 63–4, 83, 84, 90, 115, 117, 164–5, 170, 208–17, 251, 275–6; ideological 115, 164, 211–16, 275; ontological 115, 118, 164, 209–11, 270, 275; theoretical 115, 164, 191–4, 275, 295; *see also* parsimony
Slartibartfast 253–4
Socrates 189
soul making 100
soundness *see* argument: sound.
special divine action 203–4, 297; *see also* Miracle.

split the horns 194–200
states 270
statue 43, 46, 60
Stone Paradox 14, 179
Stump, Eleonore 22n6,
substitutionary atonement 272
suffering 100n8, 155–8
supervenience 114–116, 226–7
suspension of judgment 93, 267, 298
Swift, Jonathan 150
Swinburne, Richard 24
symmetry 151

teapot *See* Russell's Teapot
teleological arguments 30, 113, 128
tension 3, 6, 15, 74, 77–80, 90, 180–3, 191, 242, 249–51, 267, 300
testimony 68, 77, 84, 129–32, 136, 141, 206
theism 12–17, 38, 41–2, 47, 54–5, 78, 83, 93, 107, 165, 167, 171–2, 176–9, 182, 200, 203–4, 242; classical 2–4, 17–65, 88–9, 189–90, 194–202, 209–16, 236–7; traditional 17–18, 26–9, 48–9, 65–6, 252–3
theist 14, 16, 18–22, 24, 25, 28–30, 32–3, 41–2, 47–51, 54–5, 65, 93, 113, 123, 153, 155, 176–7, 194–5, 200, 203–4, 209–10, 212–13, 255, 287–8
theodicy 100
theological compatibilism *see* compatibilism, theological
theological determinism *see* determinism, theological
theoretical commitment *see* commitment, theoretical
theoretical simplicity *see* simplicity, theoretical
theory 17–18, 32, 80–1, 89, 95, 117, 119, 140, 186–7, 219, 304
theory-ladenness of experiment 75–6
theory-theory 273–4
thermometer 76
Thomism 123
time travel 37–8, 62
traditional theism *see* theism: traditional
transitivity 109

Trump, Donald 271
trust 72–7, 130, 132, 205, 207–8, 242–3, 251–2
truth 94, 99–100, 106, 108, 121–123, 126, 136, 141, 144–5, 153, 171, 200–2

Unger, Peter 71
universal 122
univocity *see* use of language: univocal.
use of language: analogical 18, 117–19, 212–16, 249, 257, 273–4; equivocal 117; univocal 117, 212–16, 273

validity *see* argument: valid.
van Inwagen, Peter 60, 179–80,
Vidal, Gore 152
virtue 140, 145, 148–149, 195
virtue Ethics 145, 194–6
Vonnegut, Kurt 152

water 25–6, 36, 47, 203
waves 215

Wikipedia 86
Wilson, Jessica 42–3
Wittgenstein, Ludwig 68–9, 71, 72, 255–6
Wolfe, Tom 152
Wolfe, Virginia 152
Women's World Cup 56
Woodin, Hugh 123
worldview 1–3, 5–6, 14, 82–3, 94–6, 102, 104, 106–7, 109–10, 115–19, 143–5, 149, 152, 159–60, 164, 169–71, 176–7, 180–3, 233, 260, 265–7, 298–301, 303
worldview articulation 220, 266
worldview comparison 2–3, 5–6, 13–17, 31–2, 35, 51, 59–60, 63–4, 73–4, 77–8, 84–5, 88–9, 115–17, 164, 169–71, 190–4, 205, 208–16, 220–21, 237, 249–51, 255–8, 262, 266, 275–6, 298–301

Zagzebski, Linda 75, 76n41
zombie 139
Zoroastrianism 235